RED NOTICE

A True Story of High Finance, Murder,
and One Man's Fight for Justice

Bill Browder

Simon & Schuster
New York London Toronto Sydney New Delhi

Simon & Schuster
1230 Avenue of the Americas
New York, NY 10020

First Simon & Schuster hardcover edition February 2015

SIMON & SCHUSTER and colophon are registered trademarks of Simon & Schuster, Inc.

For information about special discounts for bulk purchases, please contact Simon & Schuster Special Sales at 1-866-506-1949 or business@simonandschuster.com.

The Simon & Schuster Speakers Bureau can bring authors to your live event. For more information or to book an event contact the Simon & Schuster Speakers Bureau at 1-866-248-3049 or visit our website at www.simonspeakers.com.

Manufactured in the United States of America

10 9 8 7 6

Library of Congress Cataloging-in-Publication Data

Browder, Bill, 1964-
  Red notice : a true story of high finance, murder, and one man's fight for justice / Bill Browder.
    pages cm
  Includes index.
  1. Browder, Bill, 1964- 2. Capitalists and financiers—United States—Biography. 3. Investments, Foreign—Russia (Federation) 4. Finance—Russia (Federation) 5. Political corruption—Russia (Federation) I. Title.
  HG172.B77A3 2015
  332.6092—dc23
  [B]
                          2014027558

ISBN 978-1-4767-5571-7
ISBN 978-1-4767-5575-5 (ebook)

To Sergei Magnitsky,
the bravest man I've ever known.

Author's Note

Everything in this book is true and will surely offend some very powerful and dangerous people. In order to protect the innocent, some names and locations have been changed.

Red Notice *n.* A communication issued by Interpol requesting the arrest of wanted persons, with a view to extradition. An Interpol Red Notice is the closest instrument to an international arrest warrant in use today.

Contents

1	Persona Non Grata	1
2	How Do You Rebel Against a Family of Communists?	12
3	Chip and Winthrop	18
4	"We Can Get You a Woman to Keep You Warm at Night"	26
5	The Bouncing Czech	40
6	The Murmansk Trawler Fleet	52
7	La Leopolda	64
8	Greenacres	77
9	Sleeping on the Floor in Davos	87
10	Preferred Shares	94
11	Sidanco	104
12	The Magic Fish	114
13	Lawyers, Guns, and Money	122
14	Leaving Villa d'Este	131
15	And We All Fall Down	138
16	*Tuesdays with Morrie*	143
17	Stealing Analysis	154
18	Fifty Percent	163
19	A Threat to National Security	170

Contents

20	Vogue Café	174
21	The G8	183
22	The Raids	190
23	Department K	201
24	"But Russian Stories Never Have Happy Endings"	206
25	High-Pitched Jamming Equipment	216
26	The Riddle	228
27	DHL	236
28	Khabarovsk	246
29	The Ninth Commandment	254
30	November 16, 2009	269
31	The Katyn Principle	279
32	Kyle Parker's War	289
33	Russell 241	298
34	Russian Untouchables	310
35	The Swiss Accounts	316
36	The Tax Princess	324
37	Sausage Making	327
38	The Malkin Delegation	340
39	Justice for Sergei	349
40	Humiliator, Humiliatee	356
41	Red Notice	363
42	Feelings	371
	Acknowledgments	381
	Index	383

RED
NOTICE

1

Persona Non Grata

November 13, 2005

I'm a numbers guy, so I'll start with some important ones: 260; 1; and 4,500,000,000.

Here's what they mean: every other weekend I traveled from Moscow, the city where I lived, to London, the city I called home. I had made the trip 260 times over the last ten years. The "1" purpose of this trip was to visit my son, David, then eight, who lived with my ex-wife in Hampstead. When we divorced, I made a commitment to visit him every other weekend no matter what. I had never broken it.

There were 4,500,000,000 reasons to return to Moscow so regularly. This was the total dollar value of assets under management by my firm, Hermitage Capital. I was the founder and CEO, and over the previous decade I had made many people a lot of money. In 2000, the Hermitage Fund had been ranked as the best performing emerging-markets fund in the world. We had generated returns of 1,500 percent for investors who had been with us since we launched the fund in 1996. The success of my business was far beyond my most optimistic aspirations. Post-Soviet Russia had seen some of the most spectacular investment opportunities in the history of financial markets, and working there had been as adventurous—and occasionally, dangerous—as it was profitable. It was never boring.

I had made the trip from London to Moscow so many times I knew it backward and forward: how long it took to get through security at Heathrow; how long it took to board the Aeroflot plane; how long it took to take off and fly east into the darkening country that, by mid-November, was moving fast into another cold winter. The flight time was 270 minutes. This was enough to skim the *Financial Times*, the *Sunday Telegraph*, *Forbes*, and the *Wall Street Journal*, along with any important emails and documents.

As the plane climbed, I opened my briefcase to get out the day's reading. Along with the files and newspapers and glossy magazines was a small leather folder. In this folder was $7,500 in $100 bills. With it, I would have a better chance of being on that proverbial last flight out of Moscow—like those who had narrowly escaped Phnom Penh or Saigon before their countries fell into chaos and ruin.

But I was not escaping from Moscow, I was returning to it. I was returning to work. And, therefore, I wanted to catch up on the week-end's news.

One *Forbes* article I read near the end of the flight caught my eye. It was about a man named Jude Shao, a Chinese American who, like me, had an MBA from Stanford. He had been a few years behind me at business school. I didn't know him, but also like me, he was a suc-cessful businessman in a foreign land. In his case, China.

He'd gotten into a conflict with some corrupt Chinese officials, and in April 1998, Shao was arrested after refusing to pay a $60,000 bribe to a tax collector in Shanghai. Shao was eventually convicted on trumped-up charges and sentenced to sixteen years in prison. Some Stanford alumni had organized a lobbying campaign to get him out, but it didn't work. As I read, Shao was rotting away in some nasty Chinese prison.

The article gave me the chills. China was ten times safer than Russia when it came to doing business. For a few minutes, as the plane descended through ten thousand feet over Moscow's Sheremet-yevo Airport, I wondered if perhaps I was being stupid. For years, my main approach to investing had been shareholder activism. In Russia that meant challenging the corruption of the oligarchs, the twenty-some-odd men who were reported to have stolen 39 percent of the country after the fall of communism and who became billionaires almost overnight. The oligarchs owned the majority of the companies trading on the Russian stock market and they were often robbing those companies blind. For the most part, I had been successful in my battles with them, and while this strategy made my fund successful, it also made me a lot of enemies.

As I finished the story about Shao, I thought, *Maybe I should cool it. I have a lot to live for.* Along with David, I also had a new wife in London. Elena was Russian, beautiful, incredibly smart, and very pregnant with our first child. *Maybe I should give it a rest.*

But then the wheels touched down and I put the magazines away, powered up my BlackBerry, and closed my briefcase. I started checking emails. My focus turned from Jude Shao and the oligarchs to what I had missed while in the air. I had to get through customs, to my car, and back to my apartment.

Sheremetyevo Airport is a strange place. The terminal that I was most familiar with, Sheremetyevo-2, was built for the 1980 Summer Olympics. It must have looked impressive when it opened, but by 2005 it was far worse for the wear. It smelled of sweat and cheap tobacco. The ceiling was decorated with row upon row of metal cylinders that looked like rusty cans of Folgers coffee. There was no formal line at passport control, so you had to take your place in a mass of people and stay on guard so that no one jumped ahead of you. And God forbid you checked a bag. Even after your passport was stamped you'd have to wait another hour to claim your luggage. After a four-hour-plus flight, it was not a fun way to gain entry into Russia, particularly if you were doing the trip every other weekend as I was.

I had done it this way since 1996, but around 2000 a friend of mine told me about the so-called VIP service. For a small fee it saved about an hour, sometimes two. It was by no means luxurious, but it was worth every penny.

I went directly from the plane to the VIP lounge. The walls and ceiling were painted pea-soup green. The floor was tan linoleum. The lounge chairs, upholstered with reddish brown leather, were just comfortable enough. The attendants there served weak coffee or overbrewed tea while you waited. I opted for the tea with a slice of lemon and gave the immigration officer my passport. Within seconds, I was engrossed in my BlackBerry's email dump.

I barely noticed when my driver, Alexei, who was authorized to enter the suite, came in and started chatting with the immigration officer. Alexei was forty-one like me, but unlike me was six feet five inches, 240 pounds, blond, and hard-featured. He was a former colonel with the Moscow Traffic Police and didn't speak a word of English. He was always on time—and always able to talk his way out of minor jams with traffic cops.

I ignored their conversation, answered emails, and drank my lukewarm tea. After a while, an announcement came over the public address system that the baggage from my flight was ready for retrieval.

That's when I looked up and thought, *Have I been in here for an hour?*

I looked at my watch. I *had* been there for an hour. My flight landed around 7:30 p.m. and now it was 8:32. The other two passengers from my flight in the VIP lounge were long gone. I shot Alexei a look. He gave me one back that said, *Let me check.*

While he spoke with the agent, I called Elena. It was only 5:32 p.m. in London so I knew she would be home. While we talked, I kept an eye on Alexei and the immigration officer. Their conversation quickly turned into an argument. Alexei tapped the desk as the agent glared at him. "Something's wrong," I told Elena. I stood and approached the desk, more irritated than worried, and asked what was going on.

As I got closer, I realized something was seriously wrong. I put Elena on speakerphone and she translated for me. Languages are not my thing—even after ten years, I still spoke only taxi Russian.

The conversation went around and around. I watched like a spectator at a tennis match, my head bouncing back and forth. Elena said at one point, "I think it's a visa issue, but the agent isn't saying." Just then two uniformed immigration officers entered the room. One pointed at my phone and the other at my bags.

I said to Elena, "There're two officers here telling me to hang up and go with them. I'll call back as soon as I can."

I hung up. One officer picked up my bags. The other collected my immigration papers. Before I left with them, I looked to Alexei. His shoulders and eyes drooped, his mouth slightly agape. He was at a loss. He knew that when things go bad in Russia, they usually go bad in a big way.

I went with the officers and we snaked through the back hallways of Sheremetyevo-2 toward the larger, regular immigration hall. I asked them questions in my bad Russian, but they said nothing as they escorted me to a general detention room. The lights there were harsh. The molded-plastic chairs were bolted to the ground in rows. The beige paint on the walls peeled here and there. A few other angry-looking detainees lolled around. None talked. All smoked.

The officers left. Sealed off behind a counter-and-glass partition on the far side of the room was a collection of uniformed agents. I chose a seat near them and tried to make sense of what was happening.

For some reason I was allowed to keep all my things, including my mobile phone, which had a workable signal. I took this as a good sign. I tried to settle in, but as I did, the story of Jude Shao reregistered in my mind.

I checked my watch: 8:45 p.m.

I called Elena back. She wasn't worried. She told me she was preparing a briefing fax for the British embassy officials in Moscow and would fax it to them as soon as it was ready.

I called Ariel, an Israeli ex-Mossad agent who worked as my company's security adviser in Moscow. He was widely considered to be one of the best in the country, and I was confident that he could sort out this problem.

Ariel was surprised to hear what was happening. He said he'd make some calls and get back to me.

At around 10:30 I called the British embassy and spoke to a man named Chris Bowers, in the consular section. He had received the fax from Elena and already knew my situation, or at least knew as much as I did. He double-checked all my information—date of birth, passport number, date my visa was issued, everything. He said because it was Sunday night, he probably wouldn't be able to do much, but he would try.

Before hanging up, he asked, "Mr. Browder, have they given you anything to eat or drink?"

"No," I answered. He made a little humming noise, and I thanked him before saying good-bye.

I tried to make myself comfortable on the plastic chair but couldn't. Time crawled by. I got up. I paced through a curtain wall of cigarette smoke. I tried not to look at the vacant stares of the other men who were also being detained. I checked my email. I called Ariel, but he didn't answer. I walked to the glass and started talking to the officers in my poor Russian. They ignored me. I was nobody to them. Worse, I was already a prisoner.

It bears mentioning that in Russia there is no respect for the individual and his or her rights. People can be sacrificed for the needs of the state, used as shields, trading chips, or even simple fodder. If necessary, anyone can disappear. A famous expression of Stalin's drives right to the point: "If there is no man, there is no problem."

That's when Jude Shao from the *Forbes* article wedged back into my consciousness. Should I have been more cautious in the past? I'd gotten so used to fighting oligarchs and corrupt Russian officials that I had become inured to the possibility that, if someone wanted it badly enough, I could disappear too.

I shook my head, forcing Jude out of my mind. I went back to the guards to try to get something—anything—out of them, but it was useless. I went back to my seat. I called Ariel again. This time, he answered.

"What's going on, Ariel?"

"I've spoken to several people, and none of them are talking."

"What do you mean none of them are talking?"

"I mean none of them are talking. I'm sorry, Bill, but I need more time. It's Sunday night. No one's available."

"Okay. Let me know as soon as you hear anything."

"I will."

We hung up. I called the embassy again. They hadn't made any progress either. They were getting stonewalled or I wasn't in the system yet or both. Before hanging up, the consul asked again, "Have they given you anything to eat or something to drink?"

"No," I repeated. It seemed like such a meaningless question, but Chris Bowers clearly thought otherwise. He must have had experience with this type of situation before, and it struck me as a very Russian tactic not to offer either food or water.

The room filled with more detainees as the clock passed midnight. All were men, all looked as if they had come from former Soviet republics. Georgians, Azerbaijanis, Kazakhs, Armenians. Their luggage, if they even had any, was simple duffel bags or strange, oversize nylon shopping bags that were all taped up. Each man smoked incessantly. Some spoke in low whispers. None showed any kind of emotion or concern. They made as much effort to notice me as the guards did, even though I was clearly a fish out of water: nervous, blue blazer, BlackBerry, black rolling suitcase.

I called Elena again. "Anything on your end?"

She sighed. "No. And yours?"

"Nothing."

She must have heard the concern in my voice. "It'll be fine, Bill. If this really is just a visa issue, you'll be back here tomorrow. I'm sure of it."

Her calmness helped. "I know." I looked at my watch. It was 10:30 p.m. in England. "Go to sleep, honey. You and the baby need the rest."

"Okay. I'll call you straightaway if I get any information."

"Me too."

"Good night."

"Good night. I love you," I added, but she'd already hung up.

A flicker of doubt crossed my mind: *What if this wasn't simply a visa issue? Would I ever see Elena again? Would I ever meet our unborn child? Would I ever see my son, David?*

As I fought these dire feelings, I tried to arrange myself across the hard chairs, using my jacket as a pillow, but the chairs were made for preventing sleep. Not to mention I was surrounded by a bunch of menacing-looking people. How was I going to drift off around these characters?

I wasn't.

I sat up and started typing on my BlackBerry, making lists of people I had met over the years in Russia, Britain, and America who might be able to help me: politicians, businesspeople, reporters.

Chris Bowers called one last time before his shift ended at the embassy. He assured me that the person taking over for him would be fully briefed. He still wanted to know whether I had been offered food or water. I hadn't. He apologized, even though there was nothing he could do. He was clearly keeping a record of mistreatment should the need for one ever arise. After we hung up, I thought, *Shit*.

By then it was two or three in the morning. I turned off my Black-Berry to conserve its battery and tried again to sleep. I threw a shirt from my bag over my eyes. I dry-swallowed two Advil for a headache that had started. I tried to forget about it all. I tried to convince myself that I'd be leaving tomorrow. This was just a problem with my visa. One way or another, I'd be leaving Russia.

After a while, I drifted off.

I woke at around 6:30 a.m., when there was a crush of new detainees. More of the same. No one like me. More cigarettes, more whispering. The smell of sweat increased by several orders of magnitude. My mouth tasted foul, and for the first time I realized how thirsty I was. Chris Bowers had been right to ask if they'd offered me anything to eat or drink. We had access to a rank toilet, but these bastards should have given us food and water.

All the same, I'd awakened feeling positive that this was just a bureaucratic misunderstanding. I called Ariel. He still hadn't been able to figure out what was going on, but he did say that the next flight to

London left at 11:15 a.m. I had only two alternatives: I would either be arrested or deported, so I tried to convince myself I'd be on that flight.

I busied myself as best I could. I answered some emails as if it were a normal workday. I checked with the embassy. The new consul on duty assured me that once things started opening for the day, they'd take care of me. I got my stuff together and tried once more to talk to the guards. I asked them for my passport, but they continued to ignore me. It was as if that were their only job: to sit behind the glass and ignore all the detainees.

I paced: 9:00; 9:15; 9:24; 9:37. I grew more and more nervous. I wanted to call Elena, but it was too early in London. I called Ariel and he still had nothing for me. I stopped calling people.

By 10:30 a.m. I was banging on the glass, and the officers still ignored me with the utmost professionalism.

Elena called. This time she couldn't soothe me. She promised we'd figure out my situation, but I was beginning to feel that it didn't matter. Jude Shao was looming large in my mind now.

10:45. I really began to panic.

10:51. *How could I have been so stupid? Why would an average guy from the South Side of Chicago think he could get away with taking down one Russian oligarch after another?*

10:58. *Stupid, stupid, stupid! ARROGANT AND STUPID, BILL! ARROGANT AND JUST PLAIN STUPID!*

11:02. *I'm going to a Russian prison. I'm going to a Russian prison. I'm going to a Russian prison.*

11:05. Two jackbooted officers stormed into the room and made a beeline for me. They grabbed my arms and gathered my stuff and pulled me from the detention room. They took me out, through the halls, up a flight of stairs. This was it. I was going to be thrown into a paddy wagon and taken away.

But then they kicked open a door and we were in the departures terminal and moving fast. My heart lifted as we passed gates and gawking passengers. Then we were at the gate for the 11:15 London flight, and I was being ushered down the Jetway and onto the plane and hustled through business class and deposited in a middle seat in coach. The officers didn't say a word. They put my bag in the overhead compartment. They didn't give me my passport. They left.

People on the plane tried hard not to stare, but how could they not? I ignored them. I was *not* going to a Russian prison.

I texted Elena that I was on my way home and that I would see her soon enough. I texted her that I loved her.

We took off. As the wheels thumped into the fuselage, I experienced the biggest sense of relief I have ever felt in my life. Making and losing money by the hundreds of millions of dollars didn't compare.

We reached cruising altitude and the meal service came around. I hadn't eaten for more than twenty-four hours. Lunch that day was some kind of awful beef Stroganoff, but it was the best thing I had ever eaten. I took three extra rolls. I drank four bottles of water. And then I passed out.

I didn't wake until the plane hit the runway in England. As we taxied, I made a mental catalog of all the things I was going to have to deal with. First and foremost was working my way through British customs without a passport. But that would be easy enough. England was my home and, ever since I had taken British citizenship in 1998, my adopted country. The bigger picture had to do with Russia. How was I going to get out of this mess? Who was responsible for it? Whom could I call in Russia? Whom in the West?

The plane stopped, the public address system chimed, and the seat belts all came off. When it was my turn, I walked down the aisle to the exit. I was totally preoccupied. I got closer to the exit and didn't notice the pilot at the front watching the passengers deplane. When I reached him, he interrupted my thoughts by holding out a hand. I looked at it. In it was my British passport. I took it without saying a word.

Customs took five minutes. I got in a cab and went to my apartment in London. When I arrived, I gave Elena a long hug. I'd never felt so thankful for the embrace of another person.

I told her how much I loved her. She gave me a big, doe-eyed smile. We spoke about my predicament as we made our way, hand in hand, to our shared home office. We sat at our desks. We turned on the computers and picked up the phones and got to work.

I had to figure out how I was going to return to Russia.

2

How Do You Rebel Against a Family of Communists?

If you heard me speaking right now, you would probably ask, "How did this guy with an American accent and a British passport become the largest foreign investor in Russia only to get kicked out?"

It's a long story, and one that indeed started in America, in an unusual American family. My grandfather, Earl Browder, was a labor union organizer from Wichita, Kansas. He was so good at his job that he was spotted by the Communists and invited to come to the Soviet Union in 1926. Not long after he got there, he did what most red-blooded American men do in Moscow: he met a good-looking Russian girl. Her name was Raisa Berkman. They fell in love and got married. They would have three boys; the first was my father, Felix, who was born in the Russian capital in July 1927.

In 1932, Earl returned to the United States, moving his family to Yonkers, New York, to head the American Communist Party. He ran for president twice on the Communist ticket, in 1936 and 1940. Even though he'd garnered only about eighty thousand votes in each race, Earl's candidacy focused Depression-era America on the failings of mainstream capitalism and caused all the political players to revise their policies leftward. He was so effective that he even appeared on the cover of *Time* magazine in 1938, with the caption "Comrade Earl Browder."

This same effectiveness also drew the ire of President Roosevelt. In 1941, after my grandfather was arrested and convicted for "passport violations," he began serving four years in the Atlanta Federal Penitentiary in Georgia. Fortunately, due to the Second World War alliance between the United States and the Soviet Union, Earl was pardoned one year later.

After the war ended, Earl spent the next few years in the political wilderness—until Senator Joseph McCarthy started his infamous witch-hunt, trying to rid the country of every last communist. The 1950s were a paranoid time in America, and it didn't matter if you were a good communist or a bad communist, you were still a communist. Earl was subpoenaed and interrogated for months by the House Un-American Activities Committee.

My grandfather's political persecution and beliefs weighed heavily on the rest of the family. My grandmother was a Russian Jewish intellectual and had no desire for any of her sons to go into the dirty business of politics. For her, the highest calling was academia, specifically in science or mathematics. Felix, my father, dutifully lived up to and exceeded her expectations, attending MIT at the age of sixteen. Remarkably, he received his bachelor's degree in only two years, enrolled in Princeton's math program, and had his PhD by the age of twenty.

Even though my father was one of America's brightest young mathematicians, he was still the son of Earl Browder. When President Truman instituted the peacetime draft after the Second World War, Felix asked for a deferment, but his employer, the Institute for Advanced Study in Princeton, refused to write a letter for him. None of his superiors wanted to be on record defending the son of a famous communist. With no deferment on file, Felix was promptly drafted and started serving in the army in 1953.

After basic training, my father was assigned to an army intelligence unit at Fort Monmouth, New Jersey, where he worked for several weeks before his commanding officer noticed his last name. The wheels turned quickly then. Late one night, Felix was yanked from his bunk, thrown into a military transport, and taken to Fort Bragg, North Carolina, where he was assigned to pump gas at a service station on the edge of the base for the next two years.

When he was discharged in 1955, he applied for the first academic job opening he found: a junior-professor position at Brandeis University. The Brandeis faculty couldn't believe their luck at having a top Princeton mathematician applying for the job. But when they presented their recommendation, the board of trustees balked at the idea of supporting the son of the ex-leader of the American Communist Party.

At the time, Eleanor Roosevelt was chair of the board, and even though her husband was the one responsible for imprisoning my grandfather, she said that it would be the most "un-American thing we could do to deny a great scientist his profession because of who his father was." Felix ultimately got the job, which led to positions at Yale, Princeton, and the University of Chicago, where he eventually became chairman of the math department. He had a long and successful career, and in 1999 President Clinton awarded him the National Medal of Science, the top mathematics honor in the country.

My mother's story was no less remarkable. Eva was born to a Jewish single mother in Vienna in 1929. By 1938 it was obvious that the Nazis were targeting Jews, and any Jew who had the opportunity got as far away from Europe as possible. Because so many people were fleeing, getting a US visa was almost impossible, and my grandmother made the heartbreaking decision to put my mother up for adoption just so she could have the chance of a better life in America.

The Applebaums, a nice Jewish family from Belmont, Massachusetts, agreed to take in Eva. At the age of nine, she traveled alone across Europe by train, got on a steamship, and sailed to America to meet her new family. When she got there, she was amazed at the sanctuary into which she'd stumbled. For the next few years my mother lived in a comfortable house with her own room, a cocker spaniel, a mowed lawn, and no genocidal war raging around her.

As Eva was adjusting to her new life, my grandmother Erna managed to escape Austria, getting as far as the United Kingdom. The separation from her daughter was unbearable, and she spent every day trying to get a US visa so she could reunite with Eva. After three years, the visa finally came. She traveled from England to Boston and showed up on the Applebaums' doorstep in Belmont, expecting a joyful reunion. However, my grandmother was greeted by a child she barely knew, an American girl who had become so comfortable with the Applebaums that she didn't want to leave. After a traumatizing struggle, my grandmother prevailed, and the two of them moved into a one-room tenement in Brookline, Massachusetts. My grandmother worked eighty hours a week as a seamstress to support them, but they were so poor that their main luxury was sharing a tray of roast beef and mashed potatoes once a week at a local cafeteria. Going from poverty to comfort and then back to poverty was so traumatic that, to this day, my mother collects sugar packets and sneaks rolls from restaurant breadbaskets into her handbag. In spite of her meager teenage life, my mother excelled academically and was offered a full scholarship to MIT. She met Felix there in 1948, and within a few months they were married.

I was born in 1964 into this strange, academic, left-wing family. The main topics of conversation at the dinner table were mathematical theorems and how the world was going to hell because of crooked businessmen. My older brother, Thomas, followed in my father's footsteps and attended the University of Chicago—*at the age of fifteen.* He graduated (Phi Beta Kappa, of course) with a degree in physics. He went straight into a PhD program at the age of nineteen, and is now one of the world's top particle physicists.

I, on the other hand, lived on the opposite end of the academic spectrum. When I was twelve, my parents announced that they were taking a yearlong sabbatical and gave me the option of joining them or going to boarding school. I chose the latter.

Feeling guilty, my mother allowed me to choose whichever school I wanted. Since I wasn't interested in academics but was interested in skiing, I looked up schools that were close to ski areas and found a tiny one called the Whiteman School, located in Steamboat Springs, Colorado.

My parents were so involved in their own academic world that they hadn't bothered to conduct any due diligence on this school. Had they done so, they would have discovered that at the time Whiteman was a less-than-selective school that attracted a number of problem students: kids who had been kicked out of other schools or had problems with the law.

In order to attend this boarding school I had to skip eighth grade, and so I arrived at the Whiteman School as a small thirteen-year-old, the youngest and smallest student there. When the other kids saw this scrawny boy dressed in a blue blazer, they immediately saw a victim. On my first night, a band of students came to my room and started rummaging through my drawers, taking whatever they wanted. When I objected, they jumped me, held me down, and chanted over and over, "Time for the titty-twisters, Billy Browder! Time for the titty-twisters!"

This scene played out night after night for the first few weeks. I was bruised and humiliated, and every night when the lights went out, I was terrified of the horrors these kids had in store for me.

My mother came for a visit at the beginning of October. Out of pride, I hadn't told her anything about what was going on. I hated all of it, but I thought I could take it.

As soon as I got in my mother's car to go to dinner, though, I broke down.

Alarmed, she asked what was going on.

"I hate it here!" I yelled through tears. "It's terrible!"

I decided not to tell her about getting beat up every night or the titty-twisters, and I didn't know whether she suspected any of it, but she said, "Billy, if you don't want to stay here, just say so. I'll take you back to Europe with me."

I thought about it and didn't give her an answer right away. As we got closer to the restaurant, I decided that while returning to the warm bosom of my mother sounded like the most appealing thing in the world at that moment, I didn't want to walk away from Whiteman a defeated loser.

We got a table at the restaurant and ordered our food. I calmed down as we ate, and halfway through the meal I looked at her and said, "You know, I think I'll stay. I'll make it work."

We spent the weekend together away from school, and she dropped me off on Sunday night. After saying good-bye, I returned to my room, and as I passed the sophomore bunk area, I could hear a pair of boys hissing, "TTs for BB, TTs for BB."

I started walking faster, but the two boys got up and followed me. I was so full of anger and humiliation that, just before turning the corner into my room, I spun and lunged at the smaller boy. I hit him square in the nose. He fell down and I got right on top of him and kept punching him and punching him, blood spattering on his face, until his friend grabbed me by the shoulders and threw me aside. The two of them then gave me a good beating before the housemaster showed up to stop the fight.

But from that moment on, nobody ever touched me again at the Whiteman School.

I spent the whole year there and learned about all sorts of things I'd never known. I started smoking cigarettes, sneaking out at night, and bringing hard alcohol back to the dorms. I got into so much trouble that I was expelled at the end of the year. I returned to my family in Chicago, but I was not the same Billy Browder.

In my family, if you weren't a prodigy, then you had no place on earth. I was so far off the rails that my parents didn't know what to do with me. They sent me to a string of psychiatrists, counselors, and doctors to try to determine how I could be "fixed." The more this went on, the more forcefully I rebelled. Rejecting school was a good start, but if I really wanted to upset my parents, then I would have to come up with something else.

Then, toward the end of high school, it hit me. I would put on a suit and tie and become a capitalist. Nothing would piss my family off more than that.

3

Chip and Winthrop

The only problem was that since I was such a poor student, every university I applied to rejected me. Only after the intervention of my high school's guidance counselor did I get a place at the University of Colorado in Boulder on appeal. While barely getting into Boulder was humiliating, I recovered pretty quickly when I realized the school had been ranked as the number one party school in the country by *Playboy* magazine.

Based on countless viewings of the movie *Animal House*, I decided that if I was going to go to a party school, I might as well do it right and join a fraternity. I pledged the Delta Upsilon fraternity and, after the requisite hazing, was accepted as a member. Everyone had a nickname there—Sparky, Whiff, Doorstop, Slim—and mine, on account of my curly, black hair, was Brillo.

Being Brillo *was* fun, but after a few months of too much beer, chasing girls, ridiculous pranks, and watching countless hours of sports on TV, I started to think that if I kept it up, then the only kind of capitalist I was going to be was the kind who collected tips as a parking lot attendant. It all came to a head when one of my fraternity brothers, and someone I idolized, was caught robbing the United Bank of Boulder to fund an out-of-control coke habit. After he was sentenced to a long stretch in federal prison, I had something of a wake-up call. I realized that if I kept it up, then the only person who would suffer from this particular form of rebellion would be me.

From that moment forward I stopped partying, spent every night in the library, and began to get straight As. At the end of my sophomore year, I applied to top universities around the country and was accepted to the University of Chicago.

I worked even harder at Chicago, and my ambition grew. But as I approached graduation, I felt an overriding need to figure out what I was going to do with my life. How was I going to go about being a capitalist? As I mulled this over, I came across an announcement for a lecture by the dean of the graduate business school. Since my plan was to go into the business world in some capacity, I decided to attend. The speech he gave was about the career paths of Chicago MBA graduates, all of whom seemed to be doing important things and getting paid well to do them. Business school, it seemed, was the obvious next step for me.

According to the dean, the best way to get accepted at one of the top business schools was to get into one of the two-year pre-MBA programs at McKinsey or Goldman Sachs, or at one of the twenty-five other firms with similar programs. I bombarded all of them with letters and phone calls asking for a job. But of course it wasn't as simple as that, because every other college senior with similar ambitions was doing the exact same thing. In the end, I received twenty-four rejection letters, along with a single offer from Bain & Company in Boston, one of the top management-consulting firms in the country. It wasn't clear how I'd slipped through their filter, but somehow I had, and I grabbed their offer with both hands.

Bain chose students with top grades from good schools who were ready to work sixteen hours a day, seven days a week, for two years. In return, they promised you would get into one of the top business schools in the country. There was a rub that year, though. Bain's business was growing so quickly that they needed to hire 120 smart "student slaves" instead of just twenty, like all the other firms running two-year pre-MBA programs. Unfortunately, this ruined the implicit deal Bain had with the business schools. These schools did indeed like to admit young consultants from Bain, but they also liked McKinsey, Boston Consulting Group, Morgan Stanley, Goldman Sachs, and dozens of other sweatshops for ambitious young capitalists. So in the best case, these schools could accept only twenty people from Bain, not the full 120. In essence, Bain was offering the opportunity to work your fingers to the bone for $28,000 a year, and your reward was a 16 percent chance, at best, of getting into Harvard or Stanford.

The resulting business school application process created a crisis for all of us at Bain. We eyed each other suspiciously for weeks, trying to figure out how we were going to differentiate ourselves from one another. I certainly wasn't better than my classmates. Many had gone to Harvard, Princeton, or Yale, and many had better performance reviews than me at Bain.

But then it dawned on me. My colleagues may all have had better résumés, but who else was the grandson of the leader of the Communist Party of the United States? No one else, that's who.

I applied to two schools, Harvard and Stanford, and told them my grandfather's story. Harvard was quick to reject me, but amazingly, Stanford said yes. I was one of only three Bain employees accepted to Stanford that year.

In late August 1987, I packed up my Toyota Tercel and drove across the country to California. When I got to Palo Alto, I turned right off El Camino Real onto Palm Drive, which led up to Stanford's main campus. The road was lined with twin rows of palm trees ending at Spanish-style buildings with terra-cotta roofs. The sun was shining, and the sky was blue. This was California, and I felt as if I were arriving in heaven.

I soon learned that it *was* heaven. The air was clean, the sky was blue, and every day felt as if I were living in some kind of paradise. Everyone at Stanford had killed himself to get there, working eighty-hour weeks at places like Bain, poring over spreadsheets, falling asleep at their desks, sacrificing fun at the altar of success. We were all strivers who had competed against one another for the right to be there, but once we got there, the whole paradigm shifted. Stanford didn't allow you to show your grades to potential employers. All hiring decisions were made on the basis of interviews and past experience. The upshot of this was that the normal academic competition was replaced with something that none of us expected: an air of cooperation, camaraderie, and friendship. I quickly realized that success at Stanford wasn't in doing well there, but rather just *being* there. Everything else was gravy. It was for me, and for every one of my classmates, the best two years of our lives.

Aside from just enjoying the experience, the other purpose of Stanford was to figure out what to do after business school. From the moment we arrived, my classmates and I spent nearly every day going to corporate information sessions, brown-bag lunches, evening receptions, dinners, and interviews trying to choose which job, among thousands available, was the right job.

I went to a standing-room-only Procter & Gamble brown-bag lunch and watched three female junior marketing executives in pleated blue skirts, white shirts, and floppy ties talk in excited corporate jargon about all the fantastic ways they sold soap.

I went to a Trammell Crow cocktail reception. I felt so out of place that I curled my toes in my shoes as smooth-talking, good-looking Texans slapped each other on the back and shot the shit about baseball, big money, and real estate development (which was Trammell Crow's business).

Then there was the Drexel Burnham Lambert reception where I tried to stay awake as a team of balding bond salesmen with fancy suits droned on about the thrilling world of high-yield bond trading in their Beverly Hills office.

I thought, *No, no, and no thank you.*

The more I went to these things, the more out of place I felt, and one interview in particular drove it home for me. It was for a summer-associate job at JP Morgan. I didn't particularly want to work there, but how could I not interview for a job at JP Morgan, one of the top firms on Wall Street?

I went into a small room at the career-management center and was greeted by two tall, square-jawed, broad-shouldered men in their early thirties. One was blond, the other brown-haired, and both wore monogrammed, button-down shirts, dark Brooks Brothers suits, and red suspenders. As the blond one thrust his hand forward, I noticed an expensive-looking Rolex. They each handed me their business card from a small stack on the desk. Their names were something like Jake Chip Brant III and Winthrop Higgins IV.

The interview began with the most standard question: "Why do you want to work at JP Morgan?" I considered answering, *Because you invited me and I need a summer job*, but I knew that's not what I was supposed to say. Instead I said, "Because JP Morgan has the best attributes of an investment and commercial bank, and I think that combination is the most compelling formula for success on Wall Street."

I thought, *Did I really just say that? What the hell does that even mean?*

Chip and Winthrop didn't like my answer either. They carried on with some more standard questions and I batted them back with some more similarly insipid answers. Winthrop finished with a soft-ball question, offering me a way to find some common ground. "Bill, can you tell me what sports you played in college?"

This was an easy one—I hadn't played any sports in college. I was such a nerd that I barely had time to eat and go to the bathroom, let alone play a sport. I said flatly, "Well, none, really . . . but I like skiing and hiking," hoping that those sports were cool enough for these two guys.

They weren't. Neither Chip nor Winthrop said another word or bothered to look up from the stack of résumés. The interview was over.

As I walked out of the building, I realized that these guys didn't care what I said. All they wanted to determine was whether I "fit" the JP Morgan culture. I clearly didn't.

I made my way to the cafeteria, feeling awkward and dejected. I stood in line, got some food, wandered to a table, and ate distractedly. As I finished my sandwich, my best friend, Ken Hersh, walked in wearing his suit, which was a sign that he too had just gone to some job interview.

"Hey, Ken. Where've you been?" I asked.

He pulled out a chair. "Just interviewed with JP Morgan."

"Really? You must have met Chip and Winthrop too. How'd it go?"

Ken laughed at my nicknames and shrugged. "Not sure. It wasn't going very well until I told 'Chip' that he could use my polo ponies at the club in the Hamptons this summer. Things turned around very nicely from there." Ken smiled.

He was a short, middle-class Jewish guy from Dallas, Texas. The closest he'd ever been to polo ponies was seeing them on the Ralph Lauren logo at the Galleria mall in Dallas. "How 'bout you?"[1]

"You and I will be working together, then! I know I'll get the job for sure since I told 'Winthrop' I'd take him sailing on my skiff at the Kennebunkport yacht club."

Neither Ken nor I got an offer, but from that day forward, Ken called me Chip and I called him Winthrop.

After the JP Morgan experience I couldn't stop wondering why I subjected myself to being rejected by the Chips and Winthrops of the world. I wasn't like them and I didn't want to work for them. I had chosen this direction in life in reaction to my parents and my upbringing, but I couldn't escape the fact that I was still a Browder.

I then started looking for jobs with some type of personal relevance. I went to a lecture by the head of the United Steelworkers union and loved it. As I listened to him talk, I heard the voice of my grandfather, a man with white hair and a mustache whom I fondly remembered sitting in his study, surrounded by books, the sweet smell of pipe tobacco infusing everything. I was so inspired that after the speech I approached the man and asked if he would hire me to help the union negotiate with its exploitative corporate employers. He thanked me for my interest, but said that they only employed steelworkers in the union's head office.

Undeterred, I looked at other aspects of my grandfather's life that

---

1   This is the same Ken Hersh who went on to run Natural Gas Partners, one of the most successful energy private-equity firms in the world.

I might emulate and came up with the idea of Eastern Europe. He had spent an important part of his life in the Soviet Bloc, and his experience there had catapulted him into global significance. If that's where my grandfather had carved out his niche, then maybe I could too.

In the midst of this soul-searching, I had also started lining up real job offers in the event that my search for utopia didn't bear fruit. One was with the Boston Consulting Group in its Midwest headquarters in Chicago. I was from Chicago and had worked in consulting at Bain, which meant that I checked all the right boxes for its new recruits.

Only I didn't want to go back to Chicago, I wanted to get out and see the world—more than that, I wanted to *work* in the world (what I really wanted was to be Mel Gibson in *The Year of Living Dangerously*, my favorite movie). In an effort to get me to accept its offer, BCG flew me to Chicago for a "selling day," where I was joined by other recruits. We were subjected to meeting after meeting with bright-eyed first- and second-year consultants who regaled us with tales of their exciting lives at BCG. It was nice, but I wasn't buying it.

My last meeting was with the head of the office, Carl Stern. This was meant to be the end of the process, where I would shake the big man's hand, thank him profusely, and say, "Yes."

When I entered his office, he said warmly, "So, Bill, what do you think? Will you join us? Everyone here likes you a lot."

I was flattered, but there was no way I could accept. "I'm really sorry. Your people have made me feel very welcome, but the fact is I can't see myself living and working in Chicago."

He was a bit confused, since I hadn't voiced any objections to Chicago during the interview process. "It's not BCG, then?"

"No, not exactly."

He leaned forward. "In that case, please tell me—where *would* you like to work?"

This was it. If I really could go anywhere, I might as well tell him. "Eastern Europe."

"Oh," he said, clearly caught off guard. Nobody had told him that before. He leaned back in his chair and looked at the ceiling. "Let me think. . . . Yes . . . As I'm sure you know, we don't have any offices in Eastern Europe, but there's someone in our London office who specializes in that area named John Lindquist. We can arrange for you to meet him if you think that might change your mind."

"It might."

"Great. I'll figure out when he's available and we'll arrange it for you."

Two weeks later, I was on my way to London.

4

"We Can Get You a Woman to Keep You Warm at Night"

The London offices of BCG were right above the Green Park Tube stop on the Piccadilly Line in the heart of Mayfair. I presented myself at reception and was shown into John Lindquist's corner office, which resembled that of an absentminded professor, with books and papers stacked everywhere.

When I laid eyes on him, I could immediately see that John was something of an anomaly. An American, he looked like a more refined version of Chip or Winthrop in his Savile Row suit, Hermès tie, and horn-rimmed glasses. But he also had a bookish awkwardness about him. Unlike his blue-blooded juniors at JP Morgan, John had a soft, almost whisperlike voice and never made direct eye contact.

After getting settled in his office he said, "The people in Chicago tell me you want to work in Eastern Europe, right? You're the first person I've ever met at BCG who wants to work there."

"Yes—believe it or not, that's what I want to do."

"Why?"

I told him the story of my grandfather, how he'd lived in Moscow and then returned to the United States and ran for president and became the face of American communism. "I want to do something interesting like him. Something that's relevant to me and who I am."

"Well, we've never had a *communist* working at BCG before," he said with a wink. He straightened. "At the moment, we don't have anything happening in Eastern Europe, but I'll tell you what. If you come work here, I promise that the first piece of Eastern European business that comes our way will be yours, right?" I quickly guessed that he said *right?* at the end of almost every sentence, as if it were a tic.

I couldn't pinpoint why, but I liked John. I accepted his offer on the spot and became the first employee in BCG's East European practice group.

I moved to London in August 1989 and rented a small house in Chelsea with two of my Stanford classmates who were also starting new jobs in London. On the first Monday in September, I hopped on the Piccadilly Line with butterflies in my stomach, ready to take on Eastern Europe at BCG.

Only, as John had explained, there wasn't any work in Eastern Europe—not yet, anyway.

But then, in November of that year, as I sat in my tiny living room watching television with my Stanford buddies, the world shifted beneath my feet. The Berlin Wall had just come down. East and West Germans emerged with sledgehammers and chisels and began breaking it down chunk by chunk. We watched as history unfolded before our eyes. Within weeks, the Velvet Revolution took hold of Czechoslovakia, and the communist government there fell as well.

The dominoes were falling; soon all of Eastern Europe would be free. My grandfather had been the biggest communist in America, and as I watched these events unfold, I decided that I wanted to become the biggest capitalist in Eastern Europe.

My first break came in June 1990 when John popped his head in my office and said, "Hey, Bill, you're the one who wanted to go to Eastern Europe, right?" I nodded. "Excellent. The World Bank is looking for restructuring advisers to go to Poland—I need you to put together a proposal for turning around a failing Polish bus company, right?"

"Okay, but I've never done a proposal before. What should I do?"

"Go to Wolfgang. He'll tell you."

Wolfgang. Wolfgang Schmidt. Just hearing his name made my skin crawl.

Wolfgang was a BCG manager who led some of the case teams day to day. He was widely considered one of the most difficult managers to work for in the London office. A thirtysomething Austrian, he enjoyed shouting, forced all-nighters, and chewing up and spitting out young consultants. Nobody wanted to work for him.

But if I really wanted to go to Poland, then I would *have* to work for Wolfgang. I had never been to his office, but I knew where it was. Everyone did, if for no other reason than to avoid it.

I walked there and found a complete mess—his room was strewn with empty pizza boxes, crunched-up papers, and piles of reports. Wolfgang was hunched over a three-ring binder, running his finger along the page. His sweaty brow glowed in the fluorescent light, and his unkempt hair shot out at different angles. His expensive English shirt was untucked, his bare and round stomach peeking out on one side.

I cleared my throat.

He cocked his head in my direction. "Who're you?"

"Bill Browder."

"What do you want? Can't you see I'm busy?"

I thought that he should have been busy cleaning the sty that passed for his office, but didn't say as much. "I need to prepare a proposal for a Polish bus company restructuring. John Lindquist told me to talk to you."

"Christ," he grumbled. "Listen, Browner, start by finding résumés of BCG consultants who have experience in trucks, buses, cars— whatever you think could be related. Get as many as you can."

"Okay, should I bring them back to you—"

"Just do it!" He returned to his binder and resumed reading.

I left his office and went to the library. Flipping through the résumé book, I saw why BCG had such an amazing international reputation. There were people with experience in every field and in every corner of the globe. A team of consultants in the Cleveland office were experts in automobile manufacturing; a group from Tokyo had worked on just-in-time inventory implementation for Japanese car companies; and some consultants in Los Angeles were specialists on operations research. I photocopied these and quickly returned to Wolfgang's office.

"Back so soon, Brower?"

"It's Browder, actua—"

"Yeah, yeah. Listen, there's a couple other Polish assignments coming up as well—the guys doing those proposals will tell you what to do from here. I don't have time for this. Now if you don't mind . . ." Wolfgang flicked an open hand at the doorway, indicating I should leave.

I found the other consultants, and thankfully, they were more than happy to lend a hand. Over the next few weeks we made timetables, work plans, and compiled more information about what a great firm BCG was. When we were done, the presentations were so polished and slick that I didn't see how we could possibly lose. We handed them over to John, who submitted them to the World Bank, and we all waited.

Two months later, Wolfgang came by my office looking uncharacteristically cheerful and put together. "Bill, pack your bags. You're going to Poland."

"We won?"

"We did indeed. Now the real work begins."

I was elated. "Should I start calling the experts we put in the proposal to make sure they can come to Poland as well?"

Wolfgang furrowed his eyebrows. "What are you talking about? Of course not. You're the only one who's going to be working on this case." He clapped his hand on the doorframe, turned, and stomped off.

I couldn't believe it. I had put all those impressive people in the proposal, and the Poles were getting only *me*? A first-year associate who knew absolutely nothing about buses, or business for that matter? I was appalled, but I kept my misgivings to myself. This was my dream assignment. I was just going to have to bite my tongue and make it work.

In late October 1990, nearly a year after the Berlin Wall came down, John, Wolfgang, two other first-year associates, and I boarded a LOT[1] Airlines flight bound for Warsaw. There, we were met by four men from the World Bank and two employees from Autosan, the troubled bus company we were supposed to help save from bankruptcy. After retrieving our luggage, we boarded one of Autosan's buses and made our way to its headquarters in Sanok.

It was a long ride. Warsaw quickly gave way to the Polish countryside, which was in the throes of autumn; it was picturesque but also a little depressing. Poland's communist regime had recently collapsed, and conditions on the ground were harsher than I expected. It was like stepping into a time machine set to 1958. The cars were ancient. Horses pulled carriages on the roadside. Farms were dilapidated, and the housing in towns—those ubiquitous concrete blocks in the Soviet style—were crumbling. The Poles suffered from food shortages, hyperinflation, electricity blackouts, and all sorts of other dysfunctions.

Yet, as I sat in the rumbling bus with my forehead pressed against the glass, I thought, *This is exactly where I want to be.* The road ahead was open and full of possibility.

Six hours later, we arrived in Sanok, a town of less than fifty thousand in the wooded and hilly southeastern corner of Poland, ten miles from the Ukrainian border. We arrived at Autosan's company restaurant and made our way inside for a banquet with Autosan's management team and the executives from the World Bank. None of the guests wanted to touch the meal—greasy pork chops, overboiled potatoes, and some kind of savory gelatin containing bits of pork. In addition to the unappetizing food, an underlying odor of industrial solvent from the nearby factory wafted through the air. I got the feeling that everyone who was not from Sanok wanted to get out of there as quickly as possible. The bus company management wasn't going to let us go, however, and continued with toasts well into the evening. Finally, at 11:15 p.m., as coffee was being served, the World Bank team awkwardly rose, made their excuses, climbed

---

1   The Polish national airline.

back on the bus, and took it to Rzeszow, the closest town with a decent hotel.

My BCG colleagues waited until the World Bank team was safely out of sight before they also rose and made their excuses. They went outside and Wolfgang negotiated with two taxi drivers to take them the whole six hours back to Warsaw that night.

I was the only one left—a twenty-six-year-old MBA with one year of consulting experience—to save this company from disaster.

After coffee I said my good-byes to the management, who didn't seem to understand that I was a nobody compared to everyone who had just left. I was then escorted to the Hotel Turysta, which would be my home for the next few months.

The Turysta was a musty, four-story concrete building a couple of blocks from the San River. It had no elevator so I had to take the stairs. The passageway was narrow and dimly lit, and my room was tiny. More hall than room, it had two twin beds that were pushed against opposite walls, and the only floor space was the gap between them. Bolted to the wall over one of the beds was a thirteen-inch, black-and-white television. A plain, chintzy end table was pushed between the beds. On top of this was a single lamp. Above the lamp was a small window that overlooked a vacant lot.

It wasn't the Four Seasons, but I was so excited to be in Poland that I didn't care.

I tried the plastic rotary phone to see if it worked, but the line only connected to the matronly woman at the front desk, who didn't speak a word of English. I unpacked, stuffing my clothes into the wardrobe. The room was cold and the radiator wasn't working, so I put on the parka I'd brought for the upcoming winter. I turned on the TV—there were only three stations, all in Polish. One channel was news, one was soccer, and one was some show about sheep. I turned off the TV. I fiddled fruitlessly with the dial of a shortwave radio I'd brought, but found nothing and gave up.

I got into bed and tried to sleep, but it was simply too cold. I tapped the radiator and turned the valve near the floor, but no heat came. Normally I would have called the front desk, but given the language barrier, that wouldn't have helped. I got some more clothing out of my wardrobe and pulled the blankets off the other bed and buried myself under all of it. Even though I was still wearing my parka, this didn't work either. I tossed and turned all night and barely slept. When the sun began to rise, I turned on the shower, hoping that at least would warm me. I waited and waited for the stream of hot water, but it never got better than lukewarm.

I skipped the shower, got dressed, and went down to the Turysta's small restaurant to meet my translator for the first time. A trim man in an ill-fitting, gray polyester suit stood bolt upright as soon as I appeared. He tucked a rolled-up newspaper under an arm and extended a hand. "Mr. William?"

I took his hand. "Yes. That's me."

"Hello. My name is Leschek Sikorski!" he said enthusiastically.

Leschek, a few years older and a little taller than me, had light brown hair, bright green eyes, and a neatly trimmed beard. In different circumstances he might have been good-looking, but the bad suit—and his crooked teeth—dashed that possibility.

"Please, sit." Leschek motioned toward a chair. "How was your sleep?" he asked, nearly shouting at the end of the sentence.

"Cold, actually. There was no heat in the room."

"Yes. They don't turn it on until winter officially starts!" He again shouted the last word. He spoke English so unnaturally that I was certain he'd learned it from a set of Berlitz tapes.

The waitress showed up and poured me a cup of tea while Leschek told her something in Polish. When she disappeared, I asked, "What did you say to her?"

"To bring you the breakfast."

"Is there a menu?"

"No, no. Only one breakfast!"

A few minutes later breakfast arrived: overcooked sausages and some strange Polish processed cheese. I was so hungry that I choked it all down.

Leschek ate his meal dutifully, neither disgusted nor excited. Midway through the meal, his mouth full of food, he asked, "You are from London, yes?"

"That's right."

A smile spread across his face. "Then I have favor to ask." He lowered his voice and whispered, "Can you introduce me to Samantha Fox?" Samantha Fox was a busty English pop singer who'd gotten her start by modeling topless on Page 3 of the British tabloid the *Sun*.

I gave Leschek a funny look. "I'm afraid not. I don't know her."

He leaned back in his chair with a doubtful look and insisted, "But you must. You're from London."

"Leschek, I wish I could help, but there are seven million people in London." I didn't want to be rude, but this was ridiculous. How was I going turn around a failing bus company if my main connection to the outside world was this strange guy obsessing about a topless model from England?

After breakfast, Leschek and I left the hotel and folded ourselves into the tiny, red Polski Fiat that the bus company had provided for me during my stay. After several attempts, I got the engine to sputter to life. Leschek smiled as he directed me to Autosan's headquarters, a seven-story, white concrete building near the river. We parked, and as I passed into the lobby, I detected the same unpleasant smell of industrial solvents from dinner the night before. Leschek and I took the elevator to the top floor and found our way to the general manager's office. The general manager stood in the doorway like a barricade—his broad shoulders taking up nearly the whole space—his thick mustache perched over a beaming smile. He appeared to be twice my age and had worked at Autosan for his entire career. As I drew near, he stuck out the thick-fingered hand of a laborer, and when I took it, he squeezed so hard it felt as if my small hand had been trapped in a wringer.

He ushered Leschek and me into his office and began speaking quickly in Polish. "Welcome to Sanok," Leschek translated, talking over him. "He wants to know if you would like some brandy to toast your arrival?"

"No thank you," I said awkwardly, wondering if I was making some cultural faux pas by rejecting his offer of hard alcohol at 10:00 a.m.

The general manager then launched into a speech that once again expressed his excitement that I was there. He explained that Autosan was Sanok's main employer. If the company failed, then the town would also fail. He and everyone else at Autosan thought that BCG—and by default me—was going to save the whole lot from financial ruin. I tried to look serious and nodded at all of this, attempting to convey some semblance of confidence, but inwardly I was completely mortified by the scope of my responsibility.

When he finished his little speech, he said, "Mr. Browder, before you get to work, I must ask—is there anything we can do to make your stay in Sanok more pleasant?"

From the moment I'd walked into his office I had realized how warm it was, especially after my fitful night in my freezing room. I noticed a quietly buzzing space heater in the corner that emitted a comforting orange glow. Eyeing it, I nervously asked, "Do you think I could get a heater like that one for my room, sir?"

There was a moment of silence as Leschek translated. Then the general manager's face lit up. With rosy cheeks, he winked and said, "Mr. Browder, we can do much better than that. We can get you a woman to keep you warm at night!"

I looked sheepishly at my shoes and stammered, "N-no thank you. A space heater will be just fine."

I promptly got to work, and my first week in Poland was the biggest culture shock I had experienced in my life. Everything in Sanok—the smells, the language, the customs—was different. But what made it particularly hard for me was the food. The only available meat was pork, and it was ubiquitous. Sausage for breakfast, ham sandwiches for lunch, pork chops for dinner—every single day. There were no fruits or vegetables. Chicken was a delicacy. Worst of all, every single meal was drenched in heavy grease, as if this were some kind of magical condiment that made everything more palatable, which it didn't.

By day five I was starving. I had to do something and decided to go to Warsaw and check into the Marriott to get some decent food. As soon as I arrived, I dropped my bag in the room and headed for the restaurant. I had never been so happy to be at a hotel buffet in my life. I scooped piles of salad, fried chicken, roast beef, cheese, and French bread onto my plate and ate like a man possessed. I went back for seconds—and then thirds. By the time I was ready for dessert, my stomach started to rumble and I knew that if I didn't hurry to a bathroom, I would be in trouble.

I made my way to the men's room as fast as I could, but just as I was crossing the lobby, there was Wolfgang Schmidt standing right in front of me.

"Browner! What the hell are you doing in Warsaw?" he demanded.

I was so surprised to see him that I didn't know what to say. "I-I just figured that since it was Friday night—"

"Friday night?" he barked. "Are you kidding? You need to get your ass back to Sanook—"

"Sanok," I corrected, shifting uncomfortably from foot to foot.

"Whatever the fuck. You need to get back there and integrate yourself with the client on the weekend. That's how this business works."

The gas in my stomach was so intense, I barely heard Wolfgang. "Okay. I'll go back. Sorry. Really, I am." The bathroom was *right there* and time was wasting.

"All right, Browner." When he finally stepped aside, I hurried toward the toilet at full speed.

After the Wolfgang run-in I was so intimidated that I didn't dare set foot in Warsaw again. Instead, on weekends I drove my little Polski Fiat around the countryside, foraging for food. I would stop at small restaurants and, since I didn't speak a word of Polish, point at three or four random entrées on the menu hoping that one would be edible. I prayed for chicken and occasionally got it. I could afford to do this because the Polish zloty was so depressed that each dish cost the equivalent of forty-five US cents. It was fun to get out of Sanok, but no matter how far I went, the food was still generally awful. Eight weeks into the assignment, I had lost almost fifteen pounds.

The food situation was one of many signs of how dire everything was in Poland. Autosan was a total mess and faced imminent disaster. Following the economic "shock therapy" implemented after the fall of communism, the Polish government canceled all of its orders for Autosan buses. As a result, the company had lost 90 percent of its sales and would either have to find an entirely new customer base or drastically cut costs.

Finding new customers would be next to impossible because, at the time, Autosan made some of the worst buses in the world. The only plausible option for them to avoid bankruptcy was to fire a lot of people. Given that the whole town depended on this company for its livelihood, this was the last thing they needed—and the last thing I wanted to tell them. The whole thing left me feeling sick, and my romantic notions of doing business in Eastern Europe were quickly starting to disappear. I didn't want to hurt these people.

Three weeks before the Christmas holidays, with my dread growing ever greater, I met Leschek for our ritual breakfast. I'd learned not to wander into ridiculous Samantha Fox–like conversations by simply being quiet, which he respected. In spite of our awkward start, I'd learned that Leschek was genuine and helpful, and after spending every day together for two months, I'd warmed to him. I felt sorry that he would be the one who had to translate my dire recommendations to the Autosan management team, and even more, I knew that when I finally left Sanok, I would actually miss him.

That morning, as I picked at slices of pork sausage, I glanced across the table at Leschek's newspaper. He seemed to be perusing the personals, but then I looked closer. In little boxes were numbers— financial figures—surrounded by words I couldn't read.

I leaned over and asked, "Leschek, what are those?"

"These are the very first Polish privatizations!" he announced proudly.

I'd heard that Poland was privatizing its formerly state-owned companies, but I was so wrapped up in Autosan that I hadn't been following this at all. "That's interesting. . . . What's that number?" I pointed to a figure near the top of the page.

"That's the share price."

"And this one?"

"The profit from last year."

"How about that one?"

"The number of shares being offered."

I did some quick math. The share price valued this company at $80 million, while the company's profits for the previous year were $160 million, which meant that the Polish government was selling this company for one-half of the previous year's earnings! I was stunned. In simple terms, this meant that if you invested in this company and it stayed in business for six months, you would effectively make your money back.

I asked my questions again just to make sure that I wasn't missing anything—and I wasn't. This was *extremely* interesting. We went through the same exercise for some of the other companies in the newspaper, and the results were roughly the same.

I'd never bought a single share in my life, but as I lay in bed that night, I couldn't stop thinking about the Polish privatizations. I thought, *I need to do this. Isn't this exactly what I went to business school for?*

My net worth at the time was a total of $2,000. After confirming with John Lindquist that there were no rules against my buying the shares, I decided to invest all my money in these privatizations. I had the cash wired to me in Poland, then asked Leschek if he could help me. During our lunch break, we went to the local savings bank and stood in line to convert my money to Polish zloty, then walked to the post office to fill out the subscription forms for the privatizations. The process was complicated and required Leschek to make four trips to the teller window to ask questions about how to fill out the detailed forms. But in the end, I successfully subscribed to the very first privatizations in Eastern Europe.

In mid-December, I returned to London to prepare BCG's final presentation to Autosan and the World Bank, which we would make after the holidays. I was completely conflicted. My analysis showed that the company should fire a good part of the workforce if it wanted to stay in business. But after spending so much time with these people, I knew that mass layoffs would decimate them. I didn't know how some would survive. I thought about Leschek and his extended family, and I pictured the hardships they were already forced to endure. I had to recommend layoffs, but I wanted to soften the blow. I decided to couch the whole idea of firings as just one of the possible "strategic options" in our report, hoping the government would ultimately consider the other option: continuing to subsidize Autosan.

But when I showed this "softened" presentation to Wolfgang in London, he was furious.

"What is this shit?"

"These are their options."

"What are you, stupid? They don't have any fucking options. They have to fire everybody, Browder." He was being a complete bastard, but at least he got my name right.

Wolfgang forced me to delete all the other strategic options, then had me pass the presentation off to another consultant to fix the analysis. BCG wound up recommending that Autosan fire the vast majority of its employees.

We returned to Sanok, and Wolfgang insisted I take the lead in presenting our findings. BCG, the World Bank, and Autosan's entire senior management gathered in the company's largest conference hall. The lights were dimmed and I started up the projector, my transparencies ready to go. First, I put out the summary slide about the overall level of firings. The gasps were audible. I then described the layoff recommendations department by department. Leschek nervously translated all of it. With every new slide the shock diminished and the anger increased, and people started challenging me at every turn. The World Bank representatives looked at John and Wolfgang, hoping that they would intervene, but both avoided our clients' gazes and didn't say a word. When I was done, every person in the room glared at me. The general manager was notably quiet, eyeing me with a look of profound disappointment.

I was supposed to have been Autosan's knight in shining armor, but instead I was a traitor. I was filled with a mixture of anger, self-doubt, and humiliation. Maybe Eastern Europe wasn't the place for me after all.

I left Poland knowing one thing for certain, though: I hated consulting.

Over the following months I thought a lot about Autosan, wondering what had happened and if I could have done anything differently. Communication with them was almost impossible, but later I got word that the Polish government had completely ignored BCG's recommendations and continued to subsidize Autosan. Normally consultants hope that their advice is followed, but in this case I was thrilled that it hadn't been.

My only remaining connection to Poland was my little stock portfolio, which I regularly checked. After leaving Sanok, they rose steadily. With every percentage point increase I became more and more convinced that I had found my calling.

What I really wanted to do was become an investor in the privatizations of Eastern Europe.

As it turned out, I couldn't have been more right. Over the course of the following year my investments would double, and then double again. Ultimately, they went up almost ten times. For those who don't know, the sensation of finding a "ten bagger" is the financial equivalent of smoking crack cocaine. Once you've done it, you want to repeat it over and over and over as many times as you can.

5

The Bouncing Czech

I now knew exactly what I wanted to do with my life—only it was in a field that barely existed. Although the Iron Curtain had been lifted, nobody was investing any money in Eastern Europe. I knew that would eventually change, but in the meantime my best option was to simply stay at BCG—assuming they would let me.

After returning from the fiasco in Sanok, I kept my head down, praying that Wolfgang hadn't submitted a recommendation to fire me. To my great relief, he was either too distracted or had forgotten, because nobody came to my office with a pink slip. I finally knew I was in the clear in late January 1991 when John Lindquist suggested that he and I write an article together. If I were going to be fired, why would one of the top partners in the firm want to write an article with me?

The piece he had in mind was about investing in Eastern Europe, which we would submit to a trade magazine called *Mergers & Acquisitions Europe*. I looked into *M&A Europe* and it appeared to have an almost nonexistent circulation, but I didn't care. I was ready to exploit any avenue that would help me establish myself as an expert on investing in the region.

To write the article, I studied everything I could get my hands on. I read a stack of more than two hundred news stories and quickly learned that fewer than twenty deals had ever been done in the former Soviet Bloc in the previous decade. The most prolific investor was Robert Maxwell, a maverick 350-pound British billionaire who was originally from Czechoslovakia, and who had done three of the twenty deals.

I figured I would impress John if I could get an interview with someone in Maxwell's organization, so I called Maxwell's press office, mentioning the article. They must not have done any homework on *M&A Europe*, because amazingly I was offered a meeting with the deputy chairman of Maxwell Communications Corporation (MCC), Jean-Pierre Anselmini.

The following week I showed up at Maxwell House, a modern building halfway between Mayfair and the neighborhood known as the City of London. I met Anselmini, a suave, English-speaking Frenchman in his late fifties, and he welcomed me into his plush office.

As we made small talk, I arranged my paperwork neatly between us. But just as I started to ask my first question, Anselmini pointed at one of my spreadsheets and asked, "What's that?"

"That's my Eastern European deal list," I said, happy that I had come so well prepared.

"May I have a look at it?"

"Of course." I pushed the spreadsheet across the table.

He examined it and tensed up. "Mr. Browder, what kind of journalist makes an M-and-A deal list?" It had never occurred to me that I might be *too* well prepared for this meeting. "Could you tell me a bit more about this magazine you work for?"

"Well, I—I don't exactly work for a magazine. I'm actually with the Boston Consulting Group. I'm doing this article freelance because I'm fascinated by investing in Eastern Europe."

He leaned back and gave me a thoughtful frown. "Why are you so interested in Eastern Europe?"

I then told him the story of how excited I was to be an investor in the very first privatizations in Poland, and about Autosan, and my career ambition of investing in the Eastern Bloc.

When it became clear to him that I wasn't there to spy on Maxwell or his company, Anselmini started to relax. "You know, your coming here today might actually be very fortuitous." He stroked his chin. "We're in the process of setting up an investment fund called the Maxwell Central and East European Partnership. You strike me as just the type of person we'd like to hire. Would you be interested?"

Of course I would. I tried to conceal my eagerness, but I couldn't, and by the time I left, I had a job interview scheduled in my calendar.

To prepare for it I spent the next two weeks tracking down anyone who knew what it was like to work for Robert Maxwell. He owned the *Daily Mirror* in London, a local tabloid, and was regarded as not merely eccentric but imperious, testy, and impossible to deal with— so I had my concerns.

I found an ex-BCG consultant named Sylvia Greene who had once worked for him. I got her on the phone and asked for her advice.

After a long silence, she said, "Listen, Bill, forgive me if I'm being blunt—but in my opinion you'd be totally out of your mind going to work for Maxwell."

"Why's that?"

"Robert Maxwell is a monster. He fires everybody all the time," Sylvia said with feeling, making me wonder if she'd been one of the people he'd fired.

"That's not very comforting."

She paused again. "No, it isn't. There are lots of stories I could tell you, but there's a dramatic one that's been making the rounds. About six months ago, Maxwell was on his private jet in Tampa, Florida. The plane was taxiing toward the runway and he asked his assistant for a pen to sign some documents. When she handed him a Biro ballpoint instead of his usual Montblanc, he became furious. He demanded to know how she could be so stupid not to have the right pen. She didn't have a good answer and he fired her on the spot. She was literally deposited right onto the tarmac. This poor little twenty-six-year-old secretary from Essex had to find her way back to London all on her own."

I found three more ex-Maxwell employees and got three equally outrageous and colorful anecdotes, all with one common denominator: everyone was getting fired. One banker, a friend at Goldman Sachs, said to me, "The probability of you lasting a year there is zero, Bill."

I considered these stories carefully as the interview drew nearer, but they never succeeded in scaring me off. So what if I got fired? I had a Stanford MBA and BCG on my résumé. Surely I could find another job if I needed to.

I did the interview, then two more. Within days of the last one I was offered the position.

Against all the warnings, I accepted it.

I started my new job in March 1991. With my higher salary, I moved into my own place, a nice little cottage in Hampstead, North West London. From there I walked down a narrow road and got on the Northern Line to Chancery Lane, where I made my way to Maxwell House. Robert Maxwell had purchased this building in part because it was one of only two in all of London that allowed helicopters to land on the roof. This enabled Maxwell to commute from his home at Headington Hill Hall in Oxford to his office by helicopter, avoiding the traffic.

The idea of the boss arriving in such style sounded impressive until I experienced it for the first time. With windows open on a warm spring day, I heard the staccato whirl of a helicopter approaching. As it got closer, the sound became more intense. By the time it was directly overhead, papers in the office started to fly everywhere. All telephone conversations had to stop because of the noise. Things returned to normal only when the helicopter had safely landed and the rotors were switched off. The whole ordeal lasted four minutes.

On my first day of work I was told that I could pick up a copy of my employment contract from Maxwell's secretary. I headed up to the tenth floor and waited in the reception area for his secretary to get around to dealing with me. As I flipped through an annual report, Maxwell himself burst out of his office. His face was red and the underarms of his shirt were soaked through with dark circles of sweat.

"Why have you not yet got me Sir John Morgan on the telephone!" he shouted at his assistant, an unflappable blond woman in a dark skirt who was neither surprised nor offended by this outburst.

"You didn't tell me that you wanted to speak to him, sir," she said calmly over the top of her glasses.

Maxwell barked, "Look, missus, I haven't got time to tell you everything. If you do not learn to take the initiative, you and I are going to fall out."

I slunk into my chair and tried not to be noticed, and as quickly as Maxwell appeared, he lumbered back into his office. The assistant finished what she was doing and then handed me an envelope with a knowing look. I grabbed it and made my way back to the eighth floor.

Later that day, I mentioned the incident to one of the secretaries near my desk. "That's nothing," she huffed. "A few weeks ago he shouted so loudly at someone from his Hungarian newspaper, the poor man had a heart attack."

I went back to my desk, my contract suddenly heavy in my hands. That evening, as if to confirm what everyone really thought of Maxwell, as soon as the *whomp-whomp* of his helicopter could be heard, indicating that he was leaving, loud cheers rose across the office floor. I couldn't help but wonder, *Have I made a big mistake by coming here?*

On the Monday of my second week, I arrived in my office and found a new addition, a fair-haired Englishman a few years older than me, sitting at the spare desk. He stood and offered his hand. "Hello, I'm George. George Ireland. I'm going to be sharing this office with you." His English accent was so upper-crust and pronounced that at first I thought he was faking it. George wore a dark, three-piece suit and had a copy of the *Daily Telegraph* on his desk. A tightly furled, black umbrella leaned against his filing cabinet. He struck me as a caricature of the perfect English gentleman.

I found out later that George had previously worked as Maxwell's private secretary, but unlike the others in that position, he had quit before he was fired. As he was a close childhood friend and Oxford roommate of Maxwell's son Kevin, another place was found for George. Whatever humiliations Maxwell inflicted on his staff, he had a strange and well-developed sense of family loyalty, which he had extended to George.

But as soon as I met George, I was suspicious. Was he going to report back to the boss everything I said?

After our introduction, George and I settled at our desks, and a few minutes later he asked, "Bill, have you seen Eugene anywhere?" Eugene Katz was one of Maxwell's financial-bag carriers who sat nearby.

"No," I said offhandedly. "I heard that Maxwell sent him to do some due diligence on a company in the US."

George sneered incredulously. "Due diligence on a company! That's the most ridiculous thing I've ever heard. Eugene knows nothing about companies. You might as well send your local publican[1] to do this *due diligence*," he said, inflecting the last two words for effect.

Over the course of our first day together, George proceeded to destroy the possibility of my feeling deferential toward anyone in the organization. He had such a keen eye for absurdity and hypocrisy— and such a razor-sharp wit—that I had a hard time not laughing anytime one of Maxwell's top lieutenants was mentioned in conversation.

That was how I learned that George was not spying on me.

From George's running commentary, it became obvious that Maxwell managed his company more like a corner shop than a major multinational corporation. Everything about it reeked of nepotism, dysfunction, and bad decision making. Yet, I still felt that I'd landed the best job in the world. I'd achieved my goal of being an investor in Eastern Europe. Maxwell was the only person making investments in the region, and if anyone in Eastern Europe wanted to raise capital, they had to come to us. Since I was the one who vetted all the deals, I was effectively the gatekeeper for every Western financial transaction in that part of the world—all at the tender age of twenty-seven.

By the fall of 1991 I had reviewed more than three hundred deals, I had traveled to nearly every country of the former Soviet Bloc, and I was responsible for making three significant investments for our fund. I was exactly where I wanted to be.

But then, after returning from lunch on November 5, I switched on my computer and was greeted with a red Reuters headline: "Maxwell

---

1 Pub manager.

Missing at Sea." I chuckled and swiveled in my chair. "Hey, George—how did you do that?" George was always organizing pranks, and I figured this was one of them.

Without looking up from his work he said, "What on earth are you talking about, Bill?"

"This thing on my Reuters screen. It's really convincing."

"What's on your Reuters screen?" He rolled his chair to my desk and we stared at it together. "I . . ." he said slowly. That's when I realized that it wasn't a joke at all.

Our small office had glass interior walls and I could see Eugene, white as a ghost, running toward the elevators. Then a few senior executives rushed past, struck with similar looks of panic. Robert Maxwell *was* indeed missing at sea. This was horrible news. Maxwell may have been a bastard, but he was also the undisputed patriarch of the organization, and now, for better or worse, he was gone.

Nobody in the office knew anything about what had happened, so George and I stayed glued to Reuters (this was before the Internet, and Reuters was all we had for breaking news). Six hours after the first headline appeared, we learned that Maxwell's enormous body had been lifted out of the Atlantic Ocean off the Canary Islands by a Spanish naval search-and-rescue helicopter. He was sixty-eight years old. To this day, nobody knows whether it was an accident, suicide, or murder.

The day after Maxwell died, the share price of MCC plummeted. This was to be expected, but it was made worse because Maxwell had used shares of his companies as collateral to borrow money to support the share price of MCC. These loans were now being called in by the banks, and nobody knew what could be repaid and what couldn't. The most visible effect of this uncertainty was the endless procession of well-dressed, nervous bankers who lined up to meet with Eugene, desperate to get their loans repaid.

While we were all shocked by Maxwell's death, we couldn't help worrying about our own futures. Would our jobs be safe? Would we get our year-end bonuses? Would the company even survive?

A little more than a week after Maxwell's death, my boss called me into his office and said, "Bill, we're going to pay bonuses a little early this year. You've done a fine job and we're going to give you fifty thousand pounds."

I was stunned. This was more money than I had seen in my entire life, and twice what I was expecting. "Wow. Thank you."

He then handed me a check—not a machine-typed check issued by the payroll department, but a handwritten one. "It's very important that you go down to the bank and ask for express clearing of this to your account straightaway. As soon as you're done, I'd like you to come back here and let me know how it went."

I left the office, walked quickly to Barclays on High Holborn, and nervously presented the check to the teller, requesting that it be cleared to my account immediately.

"Please take a seat, sir," the teller said before disappearing. I turned and sat on an old brown sofa. I tapped my feet nervously, reading a savings-account brochure. Five minutes passed. I picked up another leaflet on mutual funds, but couldn't focus. I started thinking about the Thai vacation I was going to book for the Christmas holidays when this was all over. Thirty minutes passed. Something wasn't right. Why was it taking so long? Finally, after an hour, the teller returned with a bald, middle-aged man in a brown suit.

"Mr. Browder, I'm the manager." He shuffled slightly and looked at his toes before eyeing me warily. "I'm sorry, but there aren't sufficient funds in the account to clear this check."

I couldn't believe it. How could MCC—a multibillion-pound company—not have enough money to cover a £50,000 check? I grabbed the uncashed check and quickly made my way back to the office to tell my boss the news. His bonus was going to be orders of magnitude larger than mine, and to say that he was unhappy is putting it mildly.

I went home that evening crestfallen. In spite of the dramatic developments at work, it was my turn to host a weekly expat poker game. My nerves were so frayed that I could easily have done without it, but by the time the day was over, six of my friends were already on their way to my cottage. In the age before cell phones, it would have been impossible to track each of them down to cancel.

I went home and one by one my friends showed up—mostly bankers and consultants, plus a new guy, a reporter from the *Wall Street Journal*. When they were all there, we opened some beers and started to play dealer's choice. After a few rounds, my friend Dan, an Australian at Merrill Lynch, was already down £500, which was a big loss in our game. Several of us thought he would give up and go home, but he put on a brave face. "No worries, mates," he said cockily. "I'm going to make a comeback. Besides, bonus time is coming up, so who cares about losing five hundred quid."

The combination of a few beers, the boastful talk, and Dan's impending payday made it impossible for me to keep my mouth shut. I looked around and said, "Guys—you wouldn't believe what happened to me today."

I started to tell the story, but before continuing, I said, "You guys have got to promise to keep this to yourselves." Heads nodded around the table, and I went through the day's drama. My banking friends were transfixed. Bonuses are the only thing that investment bankers care about, and the idea of getting a check and then not being able to cash it is an investment banker's worst nightmare.

The game finished shortly after midnight—Dan never did make his money back—and everyone went home. Even though I had finished the game £250 down, I was satisfied, knowing that I had told the best story of the night.

I went to work the next day as if everything were fine, but when I got to the office, there was a strange group of men assembling in the reception area. They were so out of place that I pointed them out to George. He rolled his chair over to my desk and we watched them together.

Unlike the parade of dark-suited bankers from before, these men wore ill-fitting blazers and raincoats and looked completely uncomfortable. They huddled briefly before fanning out across our floor.

A young man, not more than twenty-five years old, walked into our room. "'Morning, gents," he said in a thick cockney accent. "You probably don't know why we're here. My name is PC[2] Jones. And this"—he waved his arm in a grand gesture—"is now a crime scene."

PC Jones took our details and, as George and I watched, started placing white evidence tape over our desks, computer screens, and briefcases. He then asked us to leave.

"When can we come back?" I asked nervously.

"I'm afraid I don't know that, sir. All I know is you have to go. Now."

"Can I take my briefcase?"

"No. That's part of the investigation."

George and I looked at each other, grabbed our coats, and quickly left the building. As soon as we got outside, we were met by a swarm of reporters at the building's entrance.

"Were you part of the fraud?" one shouted, thrusting his microphone into my face.

"Where's the pensioners' money?" another demanded, a camera rolling over his shoulder.

"What did you do for Maxwell?" a third one yelled.

I could barely think as we pushed our way free of the reporters. Several of them trailed us for a half a block before giving up. We didn't know what to do, so we walked briskly toward Lincoln's Inn Fields and ducked into Sir John Soane's Museum. As soon as we were safe, George started to laugh. He thought that the whole thing was a big joke. I, on the other hand, was in shock. How could I have been so stupid not to listen to everyone's advice about Maxwell?

When I got home that afternoon, I turned on the news and the lead story on every channel was the £460 million hole that had been discovered in MCC's pension fund. Maxwell had looted the firm's pension fund in an attempt to prop up the company's sagging share price, and now thirty-two thousand pensioners had lost their life sav-

---

2   Police constable.

ings. On the BBC I saw the melee at the entrance of our building and even caught a glimpse of myself fighting through the crowd. Later that night, the BBC reported that Maxwell's was the biggest fraud in British history.

As I was trying to calm down, my phone rang. It was the *Wall Street Journal* reporter who had been at my poker game. He was working on a story about the Maxwell fraud and was keen to include the anecdote I told on poker night about the bounced check. I was very skittish. My colleagues would be furious if they knew I had been blabbing to reporters, but he persevered and reassured me that his story wouldn't identify me. I grudgingly agreed, but felt mortified as soon as I had hung up.

On Monday morning I left my peaceful cottage and walked to the Hampstead Tube stop. I picked up the *Wall Street Journal*, and there was his article. Toward the end, after referring to Maxwell as "The Bouncing Czech," he wrote, "A senior Maxwell employee says his paycheck didn't clear when he tried to bank it this week. Then, on Friday, he arrived at his office to find Fraud Office investigators clearing out his files."

I got on the Tube and reread the piece. He didn't use my name, but I was sure that everyone I worked with would know it was me. I felt like I had made a monumental fuckup. Why couldn't I have just kept my mouth shut?

When I got to work I fought my way through the scrum of reporters and made my way to the eighth floor. As I crossed the office I stared straight ahead, avoiding the eyes of my co-workers, and went right to my desk. George arrived a few minutes later, completely oblivious to my indiscretion. But just as I was bracing myself to tell George about my stupidity, a new group of strangers showed up in reception. This time, they were the bankruptcy administrators. One walked over to our office, popped his head in, and said, "Go to the auditorium. There's about to be an important announcement."

George and I followed his instructions and found two empty seats together. About half an hour later, a middle-aged man carrying a clipboard appeared. His sleeves were rolled up, he had no tie, and his hair was mussed, as if he had nervously been running his fingers through it over and over. He took the podium and started reading from a prepared statement.

"Good morning, everyone. I'm David Solent from Arthur Andersen. Last night, Maxwell Communications Corporation and all of its subsidiaries were put into administration. The court has appointed Arthur Andersen as bankruptcy administrators to wind up the company. Following standard procedures, our first course of action is to announce redundancies." He then began to read names, in alphabetical order, of all the people who were being fired. Here and there, secretaries started weeping. One man stood and shouted obscenities. This man tried to get close to the stage, but was stopped by a pair of security guards and escorted away. Then George's name was called, along with that of Robert Maxwell's son Kevin, and just about everybody else I knew at the company.

Amazingly, my name *wasn't* called. Of all the things I had been warned about before taking the job, the one thing that was sure to happen—my being fired—didn't happen. I soon learned that the administrators had kept me on because they had no idea what to do with the investments in Eastern Europe. They needed someone around to help them sort it out.

I grabbed onto this little victory, thinking that it would make it easier for me to find a new job when everything was over. Unfortunately, I could not have been more wrong. I was no golden boy anymore. Having Maxwell on my résumé was as toxic as it could get, and I soon discovered that nobody in London would touch me.

6

The Murmansk Trawler Fleet

Nobody, except for one firm: Salomon Brothers.

In 1991, just as Maxwell had generated a huge scandal in Britain, Salomon Bothers had done the same in the United States. In the previous autumn, the Securities and Exchange Commission (SEC) caught some top Salomon traders trying to manipulate the US Treasury bond market. It was unclear how hard the SEC would pursue its case or even whether Salomon would survive. A similar thing happened a year before at another firm, Drexel Burnham Lambert, and it went bankrupt, leaving many people unemployed. Fearing a similar fate at Salomon, many of the good employees had jumped ship and found new work elsewhere.

This left gaping holes at Salomon that needed to be filled, and I was desperate for a job. In better times, Salomon might have shunned me, but they were as desperate as I was, and after an intense round of interviews, they offered me a position as an associate on the East European investment-banking team in London. It wasn't exactly what I wanted. My dream was to be an investor—the person deciding what shares to buy—not an investment banker, the guy organizing the sale of shares. Moreover, the title wasn't as good as my title at Maxwell, and it came with a significant pay cut. But beggars can't be choosers, so I gratefully took the offer. I was determined to put my head down and do whatever was necessary to get my career back on track.

Unfortunately, Salomon was probably the most unnatural place to do that. If you've ever read *Liar's Poker*, then you know that Salomon Brothers was one of the most dog-eat-dog firms on Wall Street. To say that I was nervous on my first day would be a gross understatement.

I arrived at Salomon's offices above Victoria Station on Buckingham Palace Road in June 1992. It was an unusually warm and sunny day, and I walked through a large set of wrought-iron gates and took the long escalator up three flights to the main reception area. I was met by a well-dressed vice president a few years older than me. He was curt and impatient and seemed annoyed at having been tasked with greeting me. We walked across the atrium and through some glass doors to the investment bank. He showed me to my desk and pointed to a box of business cards. "Listen, things are pretty simple around here. You generate five times your salary in the next twelve months and things will be fine. Otherwise, you're sacked. Clear?"

I nodded and he left. That was it. No training program, no mentors, no orientation. Just do it or get fired.

I tried to settle into my chair in the bullpen, the open area where all junior employees sat, unsure of what to do next. As I leafed through the Salomon Brothers employee handbook, I noticed a secretary sitting nearby speaking loudly into the phone about flights to Hungary. When she put down the receiver, I walked over. "Sorry to eavesdrop, but I'm a new associate and couldn't help hearing you talking about Hungary. Do you know what the firm's doing over there?"

"Oh, that's okay," she said reassuringly. "We all listen to each other's conversations. I was making reservations for the Malev privatization team to go to Budapest next week."

"Who's working on that?"

"You can see for yourself." She pointed toward a group of men sitting in one of the glass-windowed conference rooms just off the bullpen. While I'd been there for only a few hours, I knew that if I was going to succeed, I needed to take some initiative. I thanked the secretary and marched over to the conference room. As I opened the door, the six people on the Malev team stopped talking, turned toward me, and stared.

"Hi, I'm Bill Browder," I said, trying to mask my awkwardness.

"I'm new on the East European team. I was hoping you guys could use some help on your deal." The uncomfortable silence was broken by two younger team members, who giggled under their breath. The team leader then politely said, "Thanks for stopping by, Bill, but I'm afraid we're fully staffed."

That was a little embarrassing, but I didn't let it affect me. I kept my eyes open and asked around and found another opportunity several days later. The Polish telecom privatization team was having a meeting to discuss the next phase of their project. I knew they were getting a much bigger fee than the Malev team, so I figured they might not be so resistant to having another person around.

When I showed up to their meeting, the man in charge was much less polite than the Malev team leader. "Who told you to come here?" he demanded. "We don't need you on this or any other deal we're doing in Poland!"

Nobody wanted to share their revenue with me because they were all struggling with the same "five times" formula that I was; everybody was simply fighting to protect their turf in Eastern Europe. For several weeks I racked my brain trying to figure out how I was going to survive at Salomon. But then I noticed something interesting. Nobody was doing anything in Russia, meaning there was no one to fight me over it. I decided to take a chance. I declared myself the investment banker in charge of Russia, held my breath, and waited to see if anyone would object. Nobody did.

From that moment on, Russia was my territory.

But there was a good reason why no one cared about Russia: there was no paid investment-banking work to do there. While Russia may have been politically free, it was still Soviet in every respect, including their use of investment bankers. I stubbornly ignored this fact and set out to find whatever business I could. I tirelessly went to conferences, meetings, luncheons, and networking events all around London, hoping some business would fall into my lap.

Three months in, I still hadn't made a single penny for Salomon and my prospects were not looking good. But then, a lawyer whom

I'd met at a networking event told me about an advisory assignment for the Murmansk Trawler Fleet, a Russian fishing operation two hundred miles north of the Arctic Circle. The fleet had put out a tender for a privatization adviser. I didn't know the first thing about fishing, but I'd learned how to make an excellent proposal at BCG, and I set to work.

I searched Salomon's deal database, looking for anything to do with trawlers or fishing. Remarkably, fifteen years earlier the Tokyo office had been involved in several transactions involving Japanese fishing companies. Fifteen years seemed like a long time, and these were debt deals, not privatizations, but what the hell? I stuck all the Japanese experience in the proposal, tidied it up, and sent it off to Murmansk.

A few weeks later, the phone rang. A woman named Irina was calling on behalf of the Murmansk Trawler Fleet's president.

"Mr. Browder," she said in a thick Russian accent, "we would like to inform you that we have accepted your proposal." I briefly wondered if they had even received any others. "When can you come to Murmansk to begin the assignment?" she asked awkwardly. It sounded as if this was the first time she had ever spoken to a Western investment banker.

I was elated—I had brought in my first piece of real business—but the tender didn't say how much they would pay. Since I hadn't made any progress toward the goal of making five times my salary, I was hoping for something significant. In a deliberate and formal voice that I thought would make me sound older and more credible, I said, "I'm very honored you've chosen our firm. Could I inquire how much you intend to pay for this assignment?"

Irina spoke in Russian with someone in the background, then said, "Mr. Browder, we have budget of fifty thousand dollars for two months for this assignment. This is acceptable for you?"

My heart sank. It's hard to describe how small $50,000 is to an investment banker. Linda Evangelista, a supermodel from the 1980s and 1990s, once famously declared, "I don't get out of bed for less than ten thousand dollars a day." For an investment banker, that number is more like $1 million. But here I was having earned nothing for Salomon, and $50,000 was that much more than zero, so I agreed.

A week later, I set off for Murmansk. The first leg of the trip was a 9:30 a.m. British Airways flight to Saint Petersburg. It took four and a half hours, and with the three-hour time difference, I arrived in the late afternoon at Saint Petersburg's Pulkovo Airport. I stared out of my window as the plane taxied to the terminal and was astonished to see the burned-out carcass of an Aeroflot passenger plane lying on the side of the runway. I had no idea how it had gotten there. Apparently it was too much of a bother for the airport authorities to have it moved.

Welcome to Russia.

Since Aeroflot scheduled lots of its regional flights in the middle of the night, I had to sit in the airport for another ten hours until 3:30 a.m. to make the connection to Murmansk. Waiting all that time would have been painful in any airport, but it was particularly so at Pulkovo. There was no air-conditioning, and even though it was so far north, the air was hot and stuffy. Everyone was smoking and sweating. I tried to get away from the bodies and cigarettes, but even after I'd found a row of empty seats, a large stranger plopped down next to me. He didn't say a word, but he pushed my arm off the armrest between our seats and promptly lit a cigarette, taking pains to blow the smoke in my direction.

I got up and moved.

I finally boarded an old Aeroflot Tupolev 134 just before 3:30 a.m. Its seats were threadbare and sunken. The cabin smelled of tobacco and old age. I settled into a window seat, but it wouldn't lock into position and every time I leaned back, it would fall into the person's lap behind me, so I didn't lean back.

The cabin door closed and we moved out to the runway without the slightest hint of a safety announcement. We took off and were treated to a short but exceedingly bumpy flight. When the plane neared Murmansk, the pilot announced something in Russian. Another passenger who spoke English explained that we had been diverted to a military airport an hour-and-a-half drive from Murmansk because of a problem at the municipal airport.

I was relieved when the plane finally came in to land, but my relief was short-lived. The runway was so potholed and crooked, and the landing so violent, that I thought the wheels were going to be torn off the plane.

When I finally disembarked at 5:30 a.m., I was completely exhausted. Because I was so far north, the late-summer sun was low in the sky and had barely set. There was no terminal at the military airport—just a small warehouse-like building and a parking lot—but I was happy to see that the trawler fleet's president, Yuri Prutkov, had made the trip to greet me. Irina, an unsmiling and leggy blonde with too much makeup, was there too. Prutkov was almost a carbon copy of the general manager of Autosan—late fifties, large, and with a handshake like a vise. He and I sat in the back of the company car while Irina sat in the passenger seat, twisting around to translate. The driver took off across a desolate tundra landscape that looked like the moon. Ninety minutes later, we arrived in Murmansk.

I was dropped off at Murmansk's best hotel, the Arctic. I checked in and went to my room. The bathroom smelled like urine, there was no toilet seat, and large chunks of porcelain were missing from the sink. The room's window screen was broken, allowing mosquitoes the size of golf balls to fly in and out freely. There were no curtains to blot out the barely setting sun and the mattress was lumpy and sunken in the middle, as if it hadn't been changed in twenty-five years. I didn't even unpack. My only thought was *How soon can I get the hell out of here?*

A few hours later, Prutkov returned and drove me to the docks for a tour of the fleet. We walked up a rusting gangplank to one of the trawlers. It was a huge oceangoing factory that stretched hundreds of feet long, boasted a crew of more than a hundred men, and was capable of holding thousands of tons of fish and ice. As we descended into one of the subdecks, I was hit by the overpowering odor of rancid, spoiled fish that hung in the air. I felt like throwing up the whole time Prutkov spoke. Remarkably, he was unfazed by the smell. I pitied the poor guys who worked on these ships for six months at a stretch without any reprieve.

We toured the vessel for twenty minutes, then made our way to the fleet's offices at 12 Tralovaya Street. These were just as decrepit and tumbledown as the boats, but thankfully they didn't smell. The lighting in the hall was weak and green, and the walls of the reception area looked as if they hadn't been painted in decades. I couldn't help but think that everything about this operation was an insult to the senses, but then, as we settled down to a cup of lukewarm tea, we started to discuss the financial situation of the company and my perceptions started to shift.

"Tell me, Mr. Prutkov—how much does one of those boats cost?" I asked, Irina still translating.

"We got them for twenty million dollars new out of a shipyard in East Germany," he answered.

"How many do you have?"

"About a hundred."

"And how old are they?"

"Seven years on average."

I did the math. A hundred trawlers at $20 million each meant that they had $2 billion worth of ships. I figured that if the fleet was seven years old, then it was about half-depreciated, meaning that they had $1 billion of ships at the current market value.

I was amazed. These people had hired me to advise them on whether they should exercise their right under the Russian privatization program to purchase 51 percent of the fleet for $2.5 million. *Two and a half million dollars! For a half stake in over a billion dollars' worth of ships!* Of course they should! It was a no-brainer. I couldn't understand why they needed anyone to tell them this. More than anything, I wished I could have joined them in buying the 51 percent.

As I went over all this with Prutkov, I felt the release of that familiar chemical in my stomach—the one I'd felt after my ten bagger in Poland. I wondered, *Is this deal unique to the Murmansk Trawler Fleet, or is the same thing happening all over Russia? And if it is, how can I get involved?*

I was scheduled to return to London the following day, but I was so excited and agitated that I bought a one-way ticket to Moscow instead. I had to find out if the shares of every other Russian company were just as cheap as this one. Nobody would miss me in London, anyway—they barely knew I existed.

After arriving in Moscow and collecting my bags, I went to an airport kiosk and bought a small, English-language business-phone directory. I'd never been to Moscow, didn't speak a word of Russian, and hardly knew a soul. I got in an airport taxi and told the driver that I wanted to go to the Metropol Hotel on Red Square (he must have known that I was easy pickings because I later learned that he charged me four times the normal rate). We sat in snarled traffic on Leningradsky Prospekt, a boulevard that was wider than a football field, slowly passing hundreds of identical Soviet-era apartment blocks and billboards advertising strange-sounding companies.

The cab pulled up to the Metropol two hours later, across from the Bolshoi Theatre. When I got to my room, I called a friend in London who had worked in Moscow and he gave me the numbers of a driver and a translator, each of whom charged $50 a day. The next morning I went through the phone directory and started cold-calling anyone who seemed relevant to see if they would be willing to discuss the Russian privatization program with me. I ended up seeing officials from the US embassy, some people at Ernst & Young, a junior Russian official at the privatization ministry, and a Stanford alum who worked at American Express, among others. Over four days, I arranged a total of thirty meetings, and from them I pieced together the full story of what was going on with the Russian privatization program.

I found that to transition from communism to capitalism, the Russian government had decided to give away most of the state's property to the people. The government was going about this in a number of ways, but the most interesting was something called voucher privatization. In this part of the program, the government granted one privatization certificate to every Russian citizen—roughly 150 million people in total—and taken together these were exchangeable for 30 percent of nearly all Russian companies.

One hundred and fifty million vouchers multiplied by $20—the market price of the vouchers—equaled $3 billion. Since these vouchers were exchangeable for roughly 30 percent of the shares of all Russian companies, this meant that the valuation of the entire Russian economy was only *$10 billion*! That was *one-sixth* the value of Wal-Mart!

To put this in perspective, Russia had 24 percent of the world's natural gas, 9 percent of the world's oil, and produced 6.6 percent of the world's steel, among many other things. Yet this incredible trove of resources was trading for a mere $10 billion!

Even more astonishing was that *there were no restrictions* on who could purchase these vouchers. I could buy them, Salomon could buy them, anyone could buy them. If what had happened in Poland was profitable, then this was off the charts.

I returned to London a man possessed. I wanted to tell everyone at Salomon that they were giving money away for free in Russia. I started by going to one of the guys on the East European investment banking desk with my discovery. But instead of congratulating me, he frowned and asked, "Where are the advisory fees on this?" How could he not understand that this could easily go up a hundred times? Advisory fees? Was he serious? Who gave a shit about advisory fees?

I then went to someone in the investment-management division, expecting him to hug me since I was sharing the most jaw-dropping investment opportunity he would ever see in his life. Instead he looked at me as if I were suggesting that the firm invest in Mars.

After that, I went to one of the traders on the emerging-markets desk, but he looked at me quizzically and asked, "What're the spreads and trading volumes on these vouchers?" *What? Who cares whether they're 1 percent or 10 percent? I'm talking about making 10,000 percent!*

Nobody at Salomon could divorce themselves from their own narrow mind-set. Perhaps if I had been more subtle and clever I could have found a way to pierce their myopia, but I wasn't. I had no political skills, and for weeks I just kept presenting my idea over and over, hoping that by repetition I would eventually get through to someone.

Instead, I completely ruined my reputation inside Salomon Brothers. No one wanted anything to do with me because I was that "crazy fuck who wouldn't shut up about Russia." The other associates I used to hang out with stopped inviting me for lunch and after-work drinks.

It was now October 1993, and I'd been at Salomon Brothers for just over a year. I was an object of ridicule throughout Salomon, and worst of all I'd made the firm only $50,000 in total, meaning I was sure to be fired at any moment. As I despaired over my impending dismissal, my phone rang. I didn't recognize the New York extension: 2723. I answered. The man on the other end had a deep Southern drawl, like a Georgia lawman. "Hey, there. This Bill Browder?"

"Yes. Who's calling?"

"Name's Bobby Ludwig. I heard you got something going on in Russia."

I'd never heard of this guy before and wondered who he was. "Yeah, I do. Do you work for the firm?"

"Yep. In New York. I was wondering if you might do me a favor and come tell me about what you're up to?"

"Uh, sure. Can I check my schedule and get back to you?"

"'Course."

We hung up. I immediately called someone I knew on the emerging-markets desk who had worked in New York and asked him about this Ludwig person.

"*Bobby* Ludwig?" he asked, as if I were stupid *not* to know who he was. "He's one of the top producers at the firm. Weird guy, though. Some people think he's crazy. But he makes money year after year, so he kind of does whatever he wants. Why do you want to know?"

"No reason. Thanks."

Bobby was exactly the person I needed to get me out of my rut.

I phoned him back immediately. "Hi, this is Bill again. I'd love to come to New York and give you a presentation on Russia."

"Friday work for you?"

"Sure. I'll be there. See you then."

I stayed up two nights in a row, putting together a PowerPoint presentation on Russian equities. That Thursday, I took a 6:00 p.m. British Airways flight to New York, skipping the on-board movies and reviewing the presentation over and over. I couldn't blow this opportunity.

I arrived at Salomon Brothers headquarters at 7 World Trade Center on Friday morning. The Twin Towers glistened in the bright morning sun just to the southwest. I was sent up to the thirty-sixth floor and met by Bobby's secretary. She greeted me and swiped us through the door to the trading floor. It was huge—desks went as far as the eye could see—and the energy was palpable. This was raw, aggressive capitalism to the core.

We walked along the side of the floor, passing a dozen rows of desks, and then through a short hallway that led to Bobby's office. Bobby's secretary announced me and left. Bobby was behind his desk staring out the window toward New York Harbor. He was around fifty but looked much older with his unkempt red hair and a stringy mustache that fell over the corners of his mouth. Except for a bunch of messy stacks of reports, his office was spartan, and aside from his desk and chair, the only furniture was a small, round table and two other seats. As Bobby asked me to sit, I noticed that he wore a pair of beat-up leather slippers and that his red tie was stained. I later learned that this was his lucky tie, which he'd worn nearly every day since he'd made $50 million on a single trade. Bobby settled behind his desk and I got out my presentation, put a copy in front of him, and started to talk.

Normally when one gives presentations, audiences indicate that they're interested or bored or curious, but Bobby didn't do any of that. He just stared vacantly at the charts and graphs as I flipped through them. There were no *Uh-huh*s or nods or anything else to give me an indication that I was getting through—just a blank stare. It was unsettling. Then, when I was about halfway through the slides, Bobby abruptly stood and, without saying a word, walked out of his office.

I didn't know what to think. This was my final chance to save my career at Salomon and I was blowing it. *What have I done wrong? How am I going to salvage this meeting? Should I speed up the presentation? Slow it down? What the hell should I do?*

For nearly forty minutes I stewed in panic and uncertainty, but then I saw Bobby returning. He stopped to say something to his secretary and then, slowly, came back in. I stood, ready to beg if that's what it was going to take.

But before I could even get a word out, Bobby said, "Browder, that story's the most amazing thing I've ever heard. I just went down to the risk committee and got twenty-five million for us to invest in Russia. Don't waste time doing anything else. You get back to Moscow and let's put this money to work before we miss out, you hear?"

Yes. I did. I heard loud and clear.

7

La Leopolda

Those words changed everything for me. I did as I was told, returned to London, and got right to work on investing Salomon Brothers' $25 million. Unfortunately, since this was Russia, I couldn't just call my broker. There wasn't even a stock market in Russia yet. If I wanted to invest, then I was going to have to make it up as I went along.

On the Monday after I returned from New York, I sat at my desk in the bullpen and began cold-calling contacts to try to figure out how I was going to move forward. When I was on my fifth call, I noticed a serious-looking middle-aged man walking briskly toward me, two armed security guards flanking him. When he got closer, he barked accusatorily, "Mr. Browder, I'm head of compliance. Can you tell me what you're doing?"

"Excuse me. Have I done something wrong?"

He nodded. "We've heard that you're conducting securities trading from inside the investment bank. As I'm sure you know, that would be a violation of the employee code of conduct."

For those who may be unfamiliar, investment banks are divided into two halves: the sales and trading division, which buys and sells stocks, and the investment banking division, which advises companies on such things as mergers and new-share issues. These halves are separated by what they call a Chinese wall so that the stock traders can't trade on confidential information that the investment bankers have acquired from their clients. I worked in the investment bank and was, therefore, not allowed to trade stocks. In practical terms, this meant that when we finally figured out how to buy Russian stocks, I would have to move onto the trading floor. But that was still a long way off.

"I'm not buying any securities," I explained timidly. "I'm just trying to figure out how it's done."

"I don't care what you call it, Mr. Browder. You have to cease what you're doing immediately," the head of compliance commanded.

"But I'm not investing, I'm coming up with a *plan* to invest. It's all been agreed to by senior management in New York. I'm not doing anything wrong," I pleaded.

After the Treasury bond scandal that had nearly destroyed its business, Salomon wasn't taking any chances. "Sorry. Pack your desk," he said gruffly, nodding to the security guards. "You can no longer stay in the investment bank."

As I packed up, the guards stepped forward and crossed their arms, enjoying a rare opportunity to be tough. They then escorted me through the door that separated the investment bank from the trading floor. On the way we passed one of the young guys from the Hungarian team. He winked at me before silently mouthing, *Fuck you*. No mystery about who turned me in.

Once we were on the trading floor, the security guards asked me to hand over my investment-banking entry pass and left me with my boxes on the floor. Traders walked by, staring at me. I was totally humiliated and felt like I did on my first day at boarding school. I had no idea what to do, so I pushed my boxes under a nearby desk, found a phone, and called Bobby.

"Bobby," I said breathlessly. "Compliance just kicked me out of the investment bank! I'm on the trading floor with no place to sit. What should I do?"

He didn't seem at all concerned by my dilemma, exhibiting the same total lack of empathy that he'd demonstrated when I'd presented the Russian idea the week before. "I don't know. Find another place to sit, I guess. I've got another call." He cut me off and hung up.

I gazed across the vast trading floor. It was as big as a football field. Hundreds of people sat at row upon row of desks, shouting into phones, waving their arms, and pointing at computer screens, all trying to eke out small discrepancies in the prices of every kind of financial instrument imaginable. Amid this beehive of activity were occasional empty desks, but you couldn't just pick one and sit. You had to have permission from someone.

I tried to hide my discomfort and walked to the emerging-markets bond desk because I knew the head of that desk. I described my problem and he was sympathetic, but he simply didn't have any room, so he referred me to the European equities desk. Same story.

I then tried the derivatives desk, since it had a few empty seats. I walked up to the head of the team as confidently as I could and introduced myself, dropping Bobby Ludwig's name. The man didn't even turn as I spoke. I had to address the back of his bald head.

When I was done, he swiveled around and leaned back. "What the fuck?" he blurted. "You can't just walk over here and ask me for a desk. That's fucking ridiculous. If you need a place to sit, go to management and sort something out." He snorted as he turned his chair back to his screens and grabbed a call on his blinking phone.

I walked away in a daze. Traders aren't known for their manners, but still. I called Bobby back. "Bobby, I've tried. Nobody will give me a desk. Can you please do something?"

This time, Bobby was annoyed. "Bill, why are you bothering me with this? If they won't give you a desk, then just work from home. I don't care where you work. This is about investing in Russia, not desks."

"Okay, okay," I said, not wanting to mess things up with Bobby. "But how can I get my travel authorized and expenses reimbursed and that kind of stuff?"

"I'll sort that out," he said gruffly, and hung up.

The next day an overnight package arrived at my home containing twenty presigned travel authorization forms. I filled in the details on one of them, faxed it to the Salomon travel department, and got a ticket to Moscow for two days later.

Once I arrived in Moscow, I set up a makeshift office in a room at the Baltschug Kempinski Hotel on the south bank of the Moscow River, across from Saint Basil's Cathedral. The first step was to get the money to Russia, which meant we needed somebody who could receive the cash and help us buy the vouchers. Fortunately, we found a Russian bank that was owned by a relative of an employee at Salomon. Bobby thought that would be better than wiring our money into an unknown Russian bank, so he had someone from the back office organize the paperwork, and authorized the transfer of $1 million for a trial run.

Ten days later we began purchasing vouchers. The first step was to collect the cash at the bank. I watched as the clerks withdrew the cash from the vault in crisp $100 bills and loaded it into a canvas sack the size of a gym bag. This was the first time I had ever seen a million dollars in cash, and it was strangely unimpressive. From there, a team of security guards took it by armored car to the voucher exchange.

The Moscow voucher exchange was in a dusty, old Soviet convention hall across from the GUM department store[1] several blocks from Red Square. It was organized in a series of concentric rings of picnic tables under an electronic trading board hanging from the ceiling. All transactions were done in cash, and, since it was completely open to the public, anyone could walk in with vouchers or cash and transact business. There was no security, so the bank kept its guards around at all times.

The way these vouchers found their way to Moscow was a story in itself. The Russian people had no idea what to do with the vouchers when they received them for free from the state and, in most cases, were happy to trade them for a $7 bottle of vodka or a few slabs of pork. A few enterprising individuals would buy up blocks of vouchers in small villages and sell them for $12 each to a consolidator in larger towns. The consolidator might then travel to Moscow and sell a package of a thousand or two thousand vouchers at one of the picnic tables on the periphery of the exchange for $18 each. Finally, an even

---

1   GUM was a major department store like Macy's.

bigger dealer would consolidate them into bundles of twenty-five thousand vouchers or more and sell them for $20 each at the center tables. Sometimes individuals would bypass the whole process and lurk around the outskirts of the exchange, trying to find good prices on small lots. In this profusion of cash and paper, there were hustlers, businessmen, bankers, crooks, armed guards, brokers, Muscovites, buyers and sellers from the provinces—all of them cowboys on a new frontier.

Our first bid was $19.85 per voucher for ten thousand. After we announced our bid, there was a commotion on the floor and a man raised a card with the number 12 printed on it. I followed the bank employees and guards to a picnic table with 12 displayed on it, where our team presented the cash and the people at the table presented the vouchers. The sellers took our $10,000 bricks of hundreds and put them one by one into the dollar counter. The machine whirred until it stopped at $198,500. At the same time, two people from our side inspected the vouchers, looking for forgeries. After about thirty minutes, the deal was concluded. We took the vouchers to our armored car and dealer number 12 took the cash to his.

This exercise was repeated over and over for a number of weeks until Salomon had bought $25 million worth of vouchers—but this was only half the battle. After that, we needed to get the vouchers invested in shares of Russian companies, which was done at so-called voucher auctions. These auctions were unlike any other, since the buyers didn't know the price they were paying until the auction concluded. If only one person showed up with a single voucher, then the entire block of shares being auctioned would be exchanged for that one voucher. On the other hand, if the whole population of Moscow showed up with all of their vouchers, then that block of shares would be evenly divided among every single voucher that was submitted at that auction.

The scenario was ripe for abuse, and many companies whose shares were being sold would do things to prevent people from attending the voucher auctions so that insiders could buy the shares cheaply.

Surgutneftegaz, a large oil company in Siberia, was rumored to have been behind the closure of the airport the night before its voucher auction. Another oil company supposedly put up a roadblock of burning tires on the day of its auction to prevent people from participating.

Because these auctions were so bizarre and hard to analyze, few people participated—least of all Westerners. This resulted in an acute lack of demand, which meant that the prices were remarkably low, even by Russian standards. Although Salomon was effectively bidding blind at each auction, I'd carefully analyzed every major voucher auction in the past, and in each case the price of the shares started trading at a significant premium to the price paid in the auction—sometimes double or triple. Unless something changed, the firm was essentially guaranteed to make a sizable return just for participating in the auctions.

Once we started accumulating vouchers, I watched the government's announcements of auctions like a hawk. In the end, I recommended to Bobby that we participate in a half dozen auctions, including the sale of Lukoil, a Russian oil company; Unified Energy System (UES), the national electricity company; and Rostelecom, the national phone company.

By the time we were done, Salomon Brothers had used these auctions to become the owner of $25 million worth of the most undervalued shares that had ever been offered anywhere in history. Bobby and I were convinced that Salomon would make a fortune. We just needed to wait.

And we didn't have to wait long. In May 1994, the *Economist* published an article entitled "Time to Bet on Russia?" This laid out in simple terms the same math regarding the valuation of Russian companies that I had learned on my first trip to Moscow. In the following days billionaires, hedge fund managers, and other speculators started calling their brokers asking them to look into Russian stocks. This caused the nascent Russian market to move, and move dramatically.

In a short time our $25 million portfolio was transformed into $125 million. We had made $100 million!

With this success I became a local hero on the Salomon Brothers' London trading floor, where I had finally found a desk. The same "buddies" who had stopped inviting me for lunch and drinks were now lining up at my desk each morning before I arrived, hoping I might throw them a bone to help them make five times their money in the Russian stock market.

In the weeks that followed, Salomon's top institutional salespeople started coming around too, asking if I would be willing to meet their most important clients. "Bill, it would be a great favor to me if you could come and brief George Soros." "Bill, Julian Robertson[2] would really love to hear about Russia from you." "Bill, can you spare some time for Sir John Templeton?[3]"

Of course I could! It was ridiculous—here I was, a twenty-nine-year-old vice president,[4] and the most important global investors wanted to hear what I had to say. I flew all over the world first-class on the Salomon Brothers expense account. I went to San Francisco, Paris, Los Angeles, Geneva, Chicago, Toronto, New York, the Bahamas, Zurich, Boston. After nearly every meeting I was asked, "Bill, can you manage some money for us in Russia?"

I didn't have a ready answer. Our desk was set up to manage only the firm's money at that point and couldn't take outside capital. "I don't know," I said to them. "Let me go back to the bosses and see whether they'll let us."

This type of decision wasn't in Bobby's domain. He may have been the firm's best investor, but he had no authority to decide these types of organizational issues. So once I was back in London, I went to the corner office of the head of sales and trading, and pitched him the idea. Unlike my previous experience when nobody wanted to

---

2 The founder of Tiger Management Corp., one of the industry's most successful hedge funds.

3 The founder of Templeton Asset Management, one of the largest mutual fund companies in the world.

4 If this sounds notable, there were probably more vice presidents than secretaries at Salomon.

know anything about Russia, he gave me a much warmer reception. "That's a great idea, Bill. I like it a lot. I'll tell you what. We're going to form a task force to study it."

A task force! I thought. *What the hell?* Nothing was ever simple with these people. Here was a golden opportunity staring them right in the face and they had to bring their organizational nonsense into the picture.

I went back to my desk, and ten minutes after I sat down my phone rang with an unidentified outside caller. I picked it up. It was Beny Steinmetz, a charismatic Israeli billionaire whom I'd met on my Salomon world tour. Beny was in his late thirties with intense gray eyes and close-cropped, wiry brown hair. He had inherited the reins of his family's rough-cut-diamond business, and he was one of Salomon's biggest private clients.

"Bill, I've been thinking a lot about the presentation you made in New York a few weeks ago. I'm in London and I'd like you to come over to the Four Seasons and meet some of my colleagues."

"When?"

"Now."

Beny didn't ask questions, he made demands.

I had some meetings scheduled that afternoon, but they weren't as important as a billionaire who wanted to invest in Russia, so I canceled them and hopped in a black cab up to Hyde Park Corner. I went into the hotel lounge and found Beny sitting with a group of people who worked for him in his diamond business. He made the introductions. There was Nir from South Africa, Dave from Antwerp, and Moishe from Tel Aviv.

We sat. Beny didn't waste any time with pleasantries. "Bill, I think we should go into business together."

I was flattered that someone as wealthy as Beny would react so strongly to my idea, but I looked at him and his diamond-dealer colleagues and thought there was no way I could be business partners with such a motley crew. Before I could say anything, Beny continued, "I'll put up the first twenty-five million. What do you think?"

That gave me pause. "That sounds interesting. How do you see this business being set up?"

He and his people then launched into a rambling discourse that showed that they knew next to nothing about the asset management business. All they knew was that they had money and wanted more of it. At the end of the meeting, I was simultaneously excited and disappointed.

I walked out of the hotel thinking that this was exactly what I wanted to do, but exactly the type of people that I didn't want to do it with. I spent the rest of that day and the whole night turning over this dilemma in my head. If I went out on my own, then I would need seed money, but there was no way a partnership with Beny and his guys would get off the ground because they had no asset management experience, and neither did I. Ultimately, I was going to have to turn Beny down.

I called him the next morning and braced myself for the difficult prospect of saying no to a billionaire. "Beny, I'm really tempted by your offer, but unfortunately I can't accept. I'm sorry, but I need a partner who knows the asset management business. As accomplished as you are, this isn't your field either. I hope you understand."

People don't turn down Beny Steinmetz, and without a trace of disappointment he said, "Sure I do, Bill. If you need someone with asset management experience, then I'll bring in someone with asset management experience."

I winced as he said this. I imagined him coming back to me with a cousin from some small brokerage firm and putting me in an even more awkward position as I turned him down a second time.

But twenty minutes later he called back. "How would you feel if Edmond Safra did the deal with us, Bill?"

Edmond Safra! Safra was the owner of Republic National Bank of New York, and his name was like gold in the world of private banking. If Edmond Safra was willing to join this venture, it would be like winning the lottery.

"Yeah, that would address the issue. I'm *very* interested, Beny."

"Good. I'll set up a meeting."

The same afternoon he phoned back. "It's all set. Fly to Nice and be on the Carlton pier in Cannes tomorrow at noon."

But I have to work tomorrow, I thought. "Beny, can we do this next week sometime so I can—"

"Safra is ready to see you tomorrow, Bill," Beny interrupted, irritated. "Do you think it's easy to get a meeting with him?"

"Uh, of course not. Okay, I'll be there."

I bought a ticket, and when I woke up the next morning, I put on my suit, went straight to Heathrow, and checked in for the 7:45 a.m. flight to Nice. Before boarding I called the trading desk, faked a raspy cough, and said I needed the day off.

I arrived in Nice, and, following Beny's instructions, I took a taxi to the Carlton Hotel in Cannes. The bellman thought I was checking in, but instead I asked how to get to the pier. He pointed across the Boulevard de la Croisette at a long gray pier that extended past the beach and into the blue Mediterranean. I crossed the street squinting against the sun (I'd forgotten my sunglasses in cloud-covered London) and stepped onto the pier. I walked over the planks passing beautiful, tanned people in their tiny swimsuits. I was completely out of place with my dark wool suit and my pasty-white skin. By the time I reached the end, I was sweating. I checked my watch. Five minutes to noon.

A couple minutes later, I noticed a bright speedboat approaching from the west. As it got closer, I realized that it was Beny. He pulled his boat—a forty-five-foot, white-and-blue Sunseeker—to a chortling stop at the edge of the pier and yelled, "Bill, get on!"

Beny was dressed like a Côte d'Azur playboy in a light apricot shirt and white linen pants. The contrast between us couldn't have been starker. I unsteadily hopped aboard. "Take your shoes off!" he ordered. I did, revealing black socks pulled above my ankles.

Beny maneuvered the boat away, and as soon as we were free of the no-wake zone, he punched it. I tried to talk about the meeting and

Safra, but the engine and the wind were so loud it was impossible. We rode east back toward Nice hard and fast for half an hour, rounding the Antibes peninsula and crossing the Baie des Anges before arriving at the port of Villefranche-sur-Mer.

Beny pulled into an empty slip, tied off the boat, and had a rapid-fire exchange with the harbormaster in French about mooring for the afternoon. When Beny was done, we made our way to the parking lot, where a pair of armed security guards ushered us to a waiting black Mercedes. The car climbed up through winding roads to one of the highest points above Villefranche. We eventually entered the grounds of a sprawling private residence, which I later learned was the most expensive house in the world. This was La Leopolda. It looked a lot like the Palais de Versailles, the difference being that here dozens of ex-Mossad bodyguards in black tactical gear patrolled the grounds with Uzis and SIG Sauer pistols.

We got out of the car and were escorted through a colorful garden with a splashing fountain surrounded by pointed cypress trees. We were shown into a vast and ornate living room overlooking the sea. The walls were covered with eighteenth-century oil paintings in gilt wooden frames, and a huge crystal chandelier hung high overhead. Safra wasn't there, which was not surprising. I'd learned by then that standard billionaire etiquette was for guests to arrive, get settled, and be ready to start the meeting before the billionaire arrived so as not to waste his time. Since Beny was lower in the billionaire pecking order, he was subjected to this treatment as well.

Fifteen minutes later Safra entered. We stood to greet him.

Safra was a short, bald man with a pudgy face, rosy cheeks, and a warm smile. "Hello, Mr. Browder," he said, speaking with a thick Middle Eastern accent. "Please, sit."

I had never seen Safra before, even in pictures, and he looked nothing like the square-jawed, archetypal Master of the Universe that most people might have imagined. He was dressed casually in a pair of tan trousers and an elegant, handmade Italian shirt with no tie.

The Chips and Winthrops of the world were playing dress-up in their pressed suits, red suspenders, and Rolexes. None of that stuff mattered to a man like Safra. He was the real deal.

Beny gave a short preamble and then I took Safra through my standard presentation. He had a short attention span, and every five minutes or so he would either take a call or make one that was completely unrelated to the topic at hand. By the end of our meeting, I had been interrupted so many times that I wasn't sure if he had taken in any information.

When I was done, Safra rose, indicating that the meeting was over. He thanked me for my time and bid me farewell. That was it.

One of Safra's assistants called a taxi to take me back to the airport, and as I waited in the gravel driveway, Beny said, "I thought that went well."

"Really? I didn't."

"I know Edmond. That went well," Beny said reassuringly.

The taxi pulled up; I got in and went home.

The following Friday was the day of the Salomon task force meeting. I went to work and made my way directly to the boardroom. I was surprised that they had booked such a large space. As 10:00 a.m. approached, the room began to fill and within a quarter of an hour forty-five people had arrived. Most I had never seen before. There were senior managing directors, managing directors, directors, senior vice presidents—and me. As the discussion got under way, a big argument broke out about who was going to get the economic credit for this new Russian business. It was like watching a cage fight, and it was impressive to see how people with absolutely nothing to do with this new business in Russia could make such persuasive arguments for why they were entitled to a share of any future earnings. I had no idea who would win this fight, but I was absolutely sure who would lose it, and that was me.

The meeting was so upsetting that I couldn't sleep properly for several nights. I hadn't made five times my salary for the firm, I had made *five hundred times* my salary, and I wasn't going to let some empty-suited corporate hacks steal this business away from me.

I made my decision. The Monday after the meeting took place I went to work, sucked up my gut, walked into the head of sales and trading's corner office, and quit. I told him I was going to Moscow to start my own investment firm.

I would call it Hermitage Capital.

8

Greenacres

While I was certain that leaving Salomon was the right thing to do, I couldn't help but worry that life on the outside would be much tougher. Would doors open for me without my Salomon Brothers' business card? Would people take me seriously? What was I taking for granted by going out on my own?

These questions swirled in my head as I burrowed away in my Hampstead cottage, typing up a prospectus and a presentation for my new fund. When these documents were in good shape I bought a super-saver ticket to New York and started calling investors to set up meetings.

The first one was with a jovial Frenchman named Jean Karoubi. Jean was a fifty-year-old financier who ran an asset management firm specializing in hedge-funds. We had met on a flight to Moscow the previous spring and he told me to look him up if I ever set up my own fund.

I went to his office in the Crown Building on Fifth Avenue and Fifty-seventh Street, just down the block from Bergdorf Goodman. When I arrived, he greeted me like an old friend. I pulled out my presentation and placed it on the table in front of him. He put on his reading glasses and carefully followed along as I went through it page by page. When I was done, he lowered his glasses to the tip of his nose and gave me a satisfied look. "This is very impressive, Bill, and I'm interested. Tell me, how much money have you raised so far?"

"Well, none, actually. This is my first meeting."

He rubbed his chin pensively. "I'll tell you what. If you can raise at least twenty-five million, I'm in for three. Okay?"

His offer was entirely sensible. He didn't want to invest in a fund that wasn't going to get off the ground, no matter how promising the underlying investments might be. All of my meetings in New York went almost exactly the same way. Most people liked the idea and some were interested, but no one wanted to commit unless I could guarantee that I had raised a critical mass of capital.

Basically, I needed someone to write me a giant check to get my start-up off the ground. In a perfect world, that someone would have been Edmond Safra, but Beny had gone completely silent since the meeting at La Leopolda. This meant I needed to find another anchor investor, so I cast my net wide.

A few weeks later I got my first solid lead from a British investment bank called Robert Fleming. Flemings, as it was known, had been successful in emerging markets and was toying with the idea of investing in Russia, so they invited me to meet several members of the senior management team in London.

The meeting went well and I was invited back to make a similar presentation to one of its directors. I returned the following week and was met at the entrance by a security guard, who escorted me to the boardroom. The room looked exactly the way an interior decorator might have thought an old-world, blue-blooded British merchant bank should look. There were dark Oriental carpets, an antique mahogany conference table, and oil paintings of different members of the Fleming family adorning the walls. A butler in a white coat offered me tea in a china cup. I couldn't help but feel that this whole display of upper-class Englishness was designed to make people like me feel like unsophisticated outsiders.

A man in his early fifties appeared a few minutes later, offering me a limp handshake. He had gray hair and dandruff on the shoulders of his slightly creased, handmade suit. We sat and he pulled a memo out of a transparent folder and placed it carefully in front of him. I read the title upside down: "Browder Fund Proposal."

"Mr. Browder, thank you very much for coming in," he said in an English accent that was an exact replica to that of George Ireland, my former officemate at Maxwell. "My colleagues and I are quite impressed by the Russian opportunity you presented last week. To move forward, we'd like discuss your salary and bonus expectations."

Salary and bonus expectations? Where in the world did he get the idea that I was here for a job interview? After subjecting myself to the vicious snake pit of Salomon Brothers, the last thing I wanted was to be a servant for a bunch of upper-class amateurs pretending to be businessmen and whose main expletive was the word *quite.*

"I'm afraid there must be some misunderstanding," I said, keeping my voice steady. "I'm not here for a job interview. I'm here to discuss the possibility of Flemings becoming an anchor investor in my new fund."

"Oh." He looked confused and fumbled with his briefing paper. This was not part of his script. "Well, what kind of deal were you hoping to do with us?"

I looked directly into his eyes. "I'm looking for a twenty-five-million-dollar investment in exchange for fifty percent of the business."

He glanced around the room, avoiding my gaze. "Hmm. But if we get fifty percent of the business, who gets the other fifty percent?"

I wasn't sure whether he was serious. "I do."

His face tightened up. "But if the Russian market goes up as much as you say, you would make millions."

"Yes, that's the point—and so would you."

"I'm terribly sorry, Mr. Browder. That type of arrangement definitely wouldn't fly around here," he uttered, without a flicker of recognition about how ridiculous this sounded. In his eyes, it seemed that enriching an upstart outsider was so far beyond the rules of the antiquated English class system that he would rather pass on the opportunity than make his bank a fortune.

We ended the meeting on a polite note, but as I left I vowed never to return to one of these stuck-up banks again.

I had a number of other false starts and dead ends over the following weeks before finally coming across a promising prospect: American billionaire Ron Burkle. A former Salomon broker, Ken Abdallah, had introduced me to Burkle, hoping to get a cut of the deal for making the introduction.

Burkle was a forty-three-year-old California bachelor with sandy brown hair and a nice tan. He was one of the most prominent figures in private equity on the West Coast. He had done a series of successful leveraged buyouts on supermarkets and had gone from a checkout bagboy to one of the top Americans on the *Forbes* list. In addition to his business success, he was regularly pictured in the society pages with Hollywood celebrities and political heavyweights such as President Clinton.

I arrived in Los Angeles on a bright sunny day in September 1995. After getting my rental car and checking in at the hotel, I looked at Burkle's address: 1740 Green Acres Drive, Beverly Hills. I got back in the car and cruised into the hills above Los Angeles, passing gated houses and front gardens overflowing with flowers. Trees were everywhere: palms and maples and oaks and the odd sycamore. Green Acres Drive was about a mile from Sunset, and 1740 was at the end of a cul-de-sac. I pulled my car up to the black iron gates, buzzed the intercom, and was told to come in and park. "I'll see you at the front door, Bill," a man's voice said.

The gates swung open and I looped the car up a driveway guarded by lines of pointed cypress trees on either side. When I turned into the main lot, I was confronted by the most ostentatious mansion I had ever seen. La Leopolda may have been the most expensive house in the world, but Greenacres, which had been built by the silent-film star Harold Lloyd in the late 1920s, was the one of the biggest. The main house was a forty-four-room, forty-five-thousand-square-foot Italian palazzo, surrounded by manicured lawns, a tennis court, a pool, fountains, and every accoutrement of wealth imaginable. I've never been particularly awed by people's possessions, but it was hard not to be impressed by Greenacres. Burkle was a regular guy from Pomona, California, who had gone from nothing to living like a Saudi prince.

I rang the doorbell. Burkle answered it in person, and standing right behind him was Ken Abdallah. Burkle welcomed me in and gave me the short tour, then the three of us went to his study to discuss the terms of a deal. Burkle was surprisingly relaxed and basically accepted my terms: a $25 million investment for a 50 percent stake in the fund. On the less important terms such as start date, control of hiring decisions, and working capital for the office, he didn't have much to say. For a guy with a reputation as one of the fiercest guys on Wall Street, he seemed downright laid-back.

After wrapping up, he took me and Ken to dinner and then to his favorite nightclub. I was struck by what a pleasant guy Burkle was. He had none of that Wall Street bravado that I had been expecting. As I was getting into my car at the end of the evening, he promised that his lawyers would draft the contract and send it to me in London a few days later. As I flew home the following day, I felt that I'd cleared the main hurdle to starting my business. I drank a glass of red wine on the plane, silently toasting my good fortune, watched part of the movie, and drifted off to sleep.

As promised, four days later, the fax machine in my Hampstead cottage spat out a long document from Burkle's lawyers. I grabbed it nervously and started reading to make sure everything was in order. The first page looked fine. So did the second page, the third, and so on. But then I got to the seventh page. In the section entitled "Fund capital," where it should have read, "Yucaipa[1] commits $25 million to the fund," it read, "Yucaipa will use its best efforts to raise $25 million for the fund." What did "best efforts" mean? This wasn't what I had agreed to. I reread the contract to make sure I wasn't making a mistake. I wasn't. Burkle wasn't committing any of his own money, just a promise to raise the money if he could. In exchange for using his *best efforts*, he wanted 50 percent of my business.

---

1 The name of Burkle's investment company.

No wonder he was so relaxed in the negotiations. He wasn't risking anything!

I called his office immediately. His secretary politely told me that he was unavailable. I called three more times, and he continued to be unavailable. I decided to try Ken Abdallah.

"I know you've been trying to reach Ron," Ken said in a breezy California accent, as if he had just wandered in from the beach. "How can I help?"

"Listen, Ken. I've just got the contract and it says that Ron's not actually committing any money to the fund, but just offering to help raise it. That's not what we agreed to," I said tersely.

"Bill, I was there and that's *exactly* what Ron agreed to," he said in a much sharper tone, replacing that of the California cool guy.

"But what happens if he can't raise the money?"

"That's simple. His fifty percent reverts back to you."

What did these guys think they were playing at? Burkle would effectively get a free option on 50 percent of my business for making a few successful fund-raising calls. If he was too busy to make the calls or his friends didn't want to invest, I would be sitting in an empty office in Moscow.

Ken could hear that I was upset, but he didn't want the deal to crater and risk losing his cut. "Listen, Bill, don't worry. Ron is one of the most successful financiers in the country. If he says he'll raise twenty-five million dollars, he'll raise twenty-five million dollars. He puts together deals twenty times that size with his eyes closed. Just relax. This'll all work out fine. I'm sure of it."

I wasn't sure of it at all. But I agreed to think it over. Perhaps I had been so eager to hear what I wanted to hear that I had imagined that Burkle said he would commit the $25 million. Whatever the case, the way this was playing out felt unpleasant. I would have rejected the deal right away, but I didn't have any other options and the clock was ticking. The opportunity in Russia was perishable. Once the Russian market started to rise, I would miss what appeared to be a once-in-a-lifetime chance to make a fortune.

Edmond Safra was the one I *really* wanted to work with, not Burkle, so I decided to give Safra one last try. I couldn't call him directly, so I tracked down Beny in Antwerp. He picked up on the first ring.

"Hi, Beny, it's Bill. Sorry I haven't been in touch for a while, but out of courtesy I wanted to let you know that I'm planning to do a deal with Ron Burkle to set up the Russian fund."

He was silent for a moment. We both knew this wasn't a courtesy call.

"What's that you said? Who's Burkle?"

"An American billionaire in the supermarket business."

"But I thought you wanted someone who knew asset management. What does this Burkle guy know about that?"

"I don't know, but you and Safra seem to have lost interest."

After another silence, Beny said, "Hold on, Bill. We haven't lost interest. Don't do anything until you hear from me. I'm calling Edmond right now."

I hung up and paced my Hampstead cottage, nervously waiting.

An hour later Beny called back. "Bill, I just spoke to Edmond. He's ready to do this with you."

"He is? Are you sure? Just like that?"

"Yes, Bill. He's offered to send his top guy, Sandy Koifman, to London from Geneva the day after tomorrow. I'll fly over as well. We'll sit down and get this done right then and there."

This was typical billionaire psychology. If I hadn't had a competing offer, Safra wouldn't have done anything. But since another deal *was* on the table, Safra couldn't resist.

Two days later at 11:00 a.m. I met Beny and Sandy at Edmond Safra's elaborate six-story town house on Berkeley Square. Sandy was about forty years old, six feet tall, and had swarthy, Mediterranean features. A former Israeli fighter pilot, he had a reputation for taking bold bets in the financial markets, driving Ferraris, and vigilantly keeping Safra out of trouble. As we settled into the library, I could feel Sandy sizing me up. He liked to put everybody through the wringer before doing any business, but Safra had told him to cut a deal and that's what he did.

The offer was straightforward and fair: Edmond Safra and Beny Steinmetz would put $25 million in the fund and provide some seed money for the company's operations. Safra's bank would settle trades, value the fund, and do all the paperwork. Most importantly, if I did a good job, Safra would introduce me to all of his clients, who were among the richest and most important families in the world. In return, Safra would get half the business and give some of his share to Beny for bringing us together. The offer was a no-brainer and I accepted it on the spot.

What made this deal particularly sweet was that Safra had a reputation for doing business only with people whom he and his family had known for generations. It was unprecedented for him to do business with a stranger like me. It wasn't clear why he had made this exception, but I wasn't going to question my good fortune. As if Sandy could read my thoughts, after I accepted he said, "Congratulations, Bill. I know Edmond is excited about this, but I'll be watching you very closely."

In contrast to Burkle's contract, the one I received from Safra's lawyers a week later said exactly what I thought it would say and we signed it shortly thereafter. When I told Burkle I wasn't doing the deal with him, he lost his temper, swore at me, and threatened to sue. Nothing came of it, but at least I'd finally gotten to see the sharp-elbowed tough guy he was famous for being.

I was now ready to go. I spent the months leading up to Christmas tying up loose ends as I prepared to move to Moscow. Only it wouldn't just be me moving to Moscow—because I'd met a girl.

Her name was Sabrina and we'd met six months earlier at a loud party in Camden Town. She was a beautiful, dark-haired Jewish girl from North West London, and unlike anyone I'd ever known. Underneath her pleasant appearance was a combination of fiery determination and delicate fragility that I found overpowering. She'd been orphaned at birth and adopted by a poor family from East London, but somehow she'd managed to leave the East End, lose the cockney accent, and become an actress in British soap operas. On the night we met, we left the party together, went straight to her house, and were inseparable from that moment forward. Two weeks later, I gave her the keys to my cottage, and the following day when I returned from a jog, I found two large suitcases in the hallway. Without ever talking about it, we were living together. Under normal circumstances I would have slowed things down, but I was so charmed by her that she could have done anything and I wouldn't have minded.

After signing the deal with Safra, I called her from the law firm's office and asked her to meet me that evening at Ken Lo's, our favorite Chinese restaurant, near Victoria Station, to celebrate. She was strangely sad at the meal and I didn't understand what was going on. But then, over dessert, she leaned forward and said, "Bill, I'm really happy for you, but I don't want to lose you."

"You're not losing me. You're coming with me!" I said passionately.

"Bill, if you're asking me to give up everything and move to Moscow, you have to commit and marry me. I'm thirty-five years old and I want to have kids before it's too late. I can't just go gallivanting around the world with you for fun." Underneath that happy-go-lucky, sexy, crazy woman was a regular Jewish girl who just wanted to start a family, and it all came out that night at Ken Lo's. I didn't want to break up, but marrying her after having known her less than a year seemed rash. I didn't respond, and when we went home she started packing her suitcases.

Her taxi arrived, and without saying a word, she opened the door and awkwardly dragged her suitcases down the gravel path toward the street.

I was so overcome with the thought of her leaving me that I decided, *What the hell, in for a penny, in for a pound*, and chased after her. I swung around in front of her, blocking her way. "Sabrina, I don't want to lose you, either. Let's get married, move to Moscow, and start a life together." Tears welled in her eyes. She let go of her suitcases, fell into my arms, and kissed me.

"Yes, Bill. I want to go everywhere and do everything with you. I love you. Yes. Yes. Yes."

9

Sleeping on the Floor in Davos

Everything was falling into place. I had a $25 million commitment from Safra, I had great investment ideas, and I was about to start an amazing adventure in Moscow with the girl I loved. But one big fly in the ointment had the potential to ruin everything: the upcoming Russian presidential elections in June 1996.

Boris Yeltsin, Russia's first democratically elected president, was running for reelection, but things did not look good for him. His plan to take the country from communism to capitalism had failed spectacularly. Instead of 150 million Russians sharing the spoils of mass privatization, Russia wound up with twenty-two oligarchs owning 39 percent of the economy and everyone else living in poverty. To make ends meet, professors had to become taxi drivers, nurses became prostitutes, and art museums sold paintings right off their walls. Nearly every Russian was cowed and humiliated, and they hated Yeltsin for it. When I was getting ready to move to Moscow in December 1995, Yeltsin had an approval rating of only 5.6 percent. At the same time, Gennady Zyuganov, his communist opponent, had been rising in the polls and enjoyed the highest approval rating of any of the candidates.

If Zyuganov became president, many people feared that he would expropriate everything that had been privatized. I could stomach a lot of bad things in Russia such as hyperinflation, strikes, food shortages, even street crime. But it would be an entirely different story if the government just seized everything and declared capitalism over.

What was I supposed to do? There was still a chance Yeltsin

would win, so I wasn't going to back out of Safra's deal. But I also couldn't pour Safra's money into a country that could literally take it away overnight. I decided that the best course of action was to go through with the move to Moscow and wait. The fund could keep all the money in cash until it became clear who would win the election. In the worst case, I could pack it all in, the fund could return the money to Safra, and I could return to London and start over.

Whatever my plans were, Sandy Koifman had his own ideas about how to protect Safra's interests. In January 1996 he called to tell me that I needed to produce something called an operating procedures manual before they would release any money. *What the hell is an operating procedures manual?* I thought. This wasn't in the contract. Safra was obviously getting cold feet, and this request seemed like an elegant way for him to buy some time as he decided whether to move forward or renege on his commitment to the fund.

I could have fought Sandy on this, but I didn't want to force the issue. I started working on Sandy's project while watching the Russian opinion polls to see if things were going to break in my favor.

A week into writing the operating procedures manual, I got a call from my friend Marc Holtzman. Marc and I had met in Budapest five years earlier when I was working for Maxwell. He ran a boutique investment bank that focused on Eastern Europe and Russia and was the most capable networker I had ever met. He could parachute into any developing country and within twenty-four hours secure meetings with the president, the foreign minister, and the head of the central bank. Although he was roughly my age, I felt like an amateur around him whenever he turned on his finely tuned political skills.

"Hey, Bill," Marc said as soon as I picked up the phone. "I'm going to go to Davos—you want to come with me?"

Marc was referring to the World Economic Forum in Davos, Switzerland, an annual event that was attended by CEOs, billionaires, and heads of state. It was the ultimate A-list party of the business world, and the terms of admission—running a country or a globally important corporation, along with a $50,000 registration fee—were intended to make sure that rabble such as Marc and I could not just "go to Davos."

"I'd love to, Marc, but I haven't been invited," I said, pointing out the obvious.

"So what? Neither have I!"

I shook my head at Marc's unique combination of chutzpah, obliviousness, and sense of adventure. "Okay, but where would we stay?" This was another obstacle since it was well known that every hotel for miles around was booked a year in advance.

"Oh, that's not a problem. I found a single room at the Beau-Séjour Hotel, right in the center of town. It's basic, but it'll be fun. C'mon."

I didn't know. I had a lot of work to do. But then Marc said excitedly, "Bill, you have to come. I've organized a big dinner for Gennady Zyuganov."

Gennady Zyuganov? How the hell had Marc pulled that off?

Apparently, Marc had had the foresight to cultivate Zyuganov long before he'd registered on anyone's political radar. When it was announced that Zyuganov would attend Davos, Marc called him up and said, "A number of billionaires and Fortune Five Hundred CEOs I know are very eager to meet you. Would you be interested in having a small private dinner with us in Davos?" Of course Zyuganov was interested. Marc then turned around and wrote letters to every billionaire and CEO attending Davos, saying, "Gennady Zyuganov, the possible next president of Russia, would like to meet you personally. Are you free for dinner on January twenty-sixth?" Of course they were. That's how Marc got things done. The strategy was crude but amazingly effective.

After hearing about Zyuganov, I jumped at the opportunity. The following Tuesday we flew to Zurich and took the train up to Davos. Although Davos has a reputation as an exclusive resort, I was surprised to discover that it wasn't fancy at all. The town has an almost industrial and utilitarian feel. It's one of the most populated towns in the Swiss Alps and is lined with large, functional apartment blocks that look more like public housing than something you'd expect in a quaint Swiss ski resort.

Marc and I arrived at the Beau-Séjour. The clerk behind the desk gave us a funny look as we checked in—we were two grown men bunking in a room with a single twin-size bed—but we didn't let that bother us. We went upstairs and unpacked our bags. He got the bed and I got the floor.

It felt ridiculous. We were total interlopers. We hadn't been invited, we hadn't paid the registration fee, and we lacked any credentials to get into the actual conference center. But none of that mattered because the action we were interested in took place at the Sunstar Parkhotel, where all the Russians convened for meetings in the lobby.

As soon as we were settled, we went to the Sunstar and made a circuit through the lobby. Russians of all shapes and sizes were there. I quickly spotted a businessman I knew named Boris Fyodorov, the chairman of a small Moscow brokerage firm who'd been Russia's finance minister from 1993 to 1994. He was chubby and had short brown hair, round cheeks, and beady eyes that were framed by a pair of square glasses. Fyodorov carried himself with an absurd air of arrogance considering he wasn't even forty. As Marc and I approached the table where he was having coffee, he shot us a condescending look and said in English, "What are *you* doing here?"

It reminded me of high school. Fyodorov may once have been the finance minister of Russia, but he was now just a small-time Moscow stockbroker.

"I've got twenty-five million dollars to invest in Russia," I said matter-of-factly. "But before investing I have a lot of questions about how things are going to play out for Yeltsin in the election. *That's* what I'm doing here."

The moment I said "twenty-five million dollars," Fyodorov's manner changed completely. "Please, please join me, Bill. What's your friend's name?" I introduced Marc and we sat. Almost immediately, Fyodorov said, "Don't worry about the election, Bill. Yeltsin is going to win for sure."

"How can you say that?" Marc asked. "His approval rating is barely six percent."

Fyodorov stuck out his hand and swept his finger over the lobby. "These guys will fix that."

I followed his hand and recognized three men: Boris Berezovsky, Vladimir Gusinsky, and Anatoly Chubais. This trio was engaged in an intense huddle in a corner. Berezovsky and Gusinsky were two of the most famous Russian oligarchs. Each had clawed his way up from nowhere, knocking over anyone in his way, to become billionaire owners of banks, television stations, and other major industrial assets. Chubais was one of Russia's shrewdest political operators. He had been the architect of Yeltsin's economic reforms, including the disastrous mass privatization program. By January 1996, he had resigned from the government to focus full-time on turning around Yeltsin's failing campaign.

I didn't know it at the time, but this scene in the lobby of the Sunstar Parkhotel was the infamous "Deal with the Devil," where the oligarchs decided to throw all their media and financial resources behind Yeltsin's reelection. In exchange, they would get whatever was left of the unprivatized Russian companies for next to nothing.

As Marc and I made our way around the room, various other oligarchs and minigarchs we spoke with each repeated Fyodorov's sentiment that Yeltsin would be reelected. They might have been right, but these men might just have been predicting what they wanted to be true. Russian oligarchs are hardly the most credible people at the best of times, and Yeltsin had a long way to go to get the 51 percent needed to win the presidency.

I thought it was far better to assess the intentions of the candidate who was the front-runner than to listen to the pipe dreams of some people who stood to lose everything if Yeltsin was defeated. This whole trip was about assessing Zyuganov, which I would have the opportunity to do at Marc's dinner.

The evening of the dinner arrived and I went to a packed private dining room in the Bridge Room at the Flüela Hotel. The Flüela was one of only two five-star hotels in Davos, and Marc had scored a major coup by hosting the dinner there. That night, Marc's dinner was the hottest ticket in town.

The table was arranged in a large square, the chairs around the outside. I scanned the faces of the guests as they arrived and took their seats. I'd never before seen such an impressive collection of people: George Soros; Heinrich von Pierer, CEO of Siemens; Jack Welch, CEO of GE; and Percy Barnevik, CEO of Asea Brown Boveri, among others. In total there were a couple of dozen billionaires and CEOs—plus Marc and me. I wore my best suit in an attempt to look the part, but I knew I was the only person in that room who would be sleeping on the floor that night.

A few minutes after everyone was settled, Zyuganov made a grand entrance with a translator and a pair of bodyguards and took his seat. Marc clinked his glass and stood.

"Thank you all so much for joining us this evening. I'm very honored to be hosting this dinner for Gennady Zyuganov, the leader of the Communist Party of Russia and candidate for president." Zyuganov was about to take his cue and stand as well, but then Marc added spontaneously, "And I'd like to also thank my cohost, Bill Browder, who helped to make all this possible." Marc held out his hand, palm up, in my direction. "Bill?"

I rose halfway out of my seat, gave a perfunctory wave, and quickly sat back down. I was completely mortified. It was a nice gesture for Marc to recognize me, but all I wanted to do at that moment was blend into the woodwork.

When the main course was over, Zyuganov stood and gave his speech through his translator. Zyuganov rambled on, covering all sorts of unmemorable talking points, until he said, "For those of you who are afraid that I'm going to renationalize assets, you shouldn't be."

I perked up.

He carried on. "These days *communist* is just a label. A process of private property has started in Russia that cannot be reversed. If we were to renationalize assets, there would be civil unrest from Kaliningrad to Khabarovsk." He gave a curt nod. "I hope to meet all of you again when I'm president of Russia."

In the stunned silence, Zyuganov sat, took up his silverware, and tucked into his dessert.

Had he really just ruled out renationalization? That's what it sounded like.

The dinner finished shortly afterward, and Marc and I eventually ended up back in our room. As I lay on the floor, my mind raced. If what Zyuganov was saying was true, then regardless of who won the election, I was back in business. I had to share this news with Sandy Koifman as soon as possible.

I called him in Geneva early the next morning and told him the story, but he wasn't impressed. "You don't honestly believe him, do you, Bill? These guys will say anything."

"But Sandy, Zyuganov said it in front of the most important businessmen in the world! That has to count for something."

"That means nothing. People lie, politicians lie, everybody lies. Christ, you're talking about a *Russian politician*. If I believed everything politicians said to me, Safra would be broke by now."

I didn't know what to think, but everything I'd heard in Davos made me feel that things had at least a small chance of working out, and I intended to do everything I could to see that they would.

10

Preferred Shares

I finally finished writing Sandy's operating procedures manual six weeks after Davos. Now Sandy either would have to send the money that Safra had committed to the fund or renege on the deal.

If Yeltsin's approval rating had stayed at 5.6 percent, Sandy would surely have reneged. But the oligarchs' plan appeared to be working. By early March, Yeltsin's approval rating had risen to 14 percent and this put Sandy in a quandary. A clause in the contract said that if Safra pulled out, then he would have to pay a multimillion-dollar penalty. However, if Sandy released the money and Yeltsin wasn't reelected, Safra stood to lose even more than that. To buy a little more time, Sandy released $100,000 of working capital, which allowed me at least to set up the office in Moscow.

I was in a quandary too. I didn't like the idea of moving to Moscow without any real business, but it didn't make sense for me to force the issue. If Safra decided to pull out now, I wouldn't be able to find another $25 million investor in the three months before the Russian elections.

I went about my work and continued to prepare for the move to Moscow with Sabrina, but things had become more complicated between us. She had become pregnant almost the moment I proposed and was hit with severe morning sickness. She was in such bad shape that several times I had to take her to the hospital to be rehydrated.

As we were packing our bags in our bedroom on the eve of our trip to Moscow, she finally said what I was dreading she might say.

"Bill, I've been up all night thinking, and I'm . . ."

"What is it?"

"I'm sorry, but I just can't go to Russia."

"Because of the morning sickness?"

"Yes, and . . ."

"What? You're going to come when the morning sickness passes, right?"

She turned away, looking confused. "Yes. I mean, I think so. I don't know, Bill. I just don't know."

While I wanted her to be with me in Moscow, I couldn't fault her. She was going to be my wife and she was carrying our child. Whatever our previous arrangements were, she had to be comfortable and happy. That was what mattered most.

I accepted that she would stay in London, and the next morning Sabrina drove me to Heathrow. We said our good-byes on the curb and I promised to call her twice a day, every day. I kissed her and went through the airport, hoping that she would be able to join me soon.

I thought about all of this as I flew east. But then I landed at Sheremetyevo and was confronted with the crowds and the chaos, and I didn't have the capacity to think about anything other than dealing with real life on the ground in Moscow.

I had a two-page-long to-do list, and the first item was to find an office. After checking into the National Hotel, I called Marc Holtzman, who had recently set up his own office in Moscow. He told me about an empty room just down the hall from his and I made an appointment to see it right away.

The next morning, I left the hotel to hail a cab. As soon as I stuck out my hand, an ambulance swerved dangerously from the middle lane and came to an abrupt stop in front of me. The driver leaned across, rolled down the window, and said, *"Kuda vy edete?"* He wanted to know where I was headed.

"Parus Business Center," I told him without a hint of a Russian accent. *"Tverskaya Yamskaya dvacet tre"*—the street address in Russian. That was about the extent of my fluency. Unlike many other

Westerners in Moscow, I had never studied Russian literature, trained as a spy, or done anything useful to prepare for life in Russia.

"Piat teesich rublei," he said. Five thousand rubles—roughly one dollar—to go about two miles. As he spoke, four other random cars also stopped, queuing in case I decided to reject the ambulance. I was in a hurry so I jumped in. I looked over my shoulder as I slid into the passenger seat, praying that no bodies or injured people were in the back. Thankfully there weren't. I shut the door and we pulled into traffic, heading up Tverskaya.

I soon learned that an ambulance stopping to pick up a fare in Moscow wasn't unusual. Every vehicle was a potential taxi. Private cars, dump trucks, police cruisers—everyone was so desperate for money that any and all would take fares.

Ten minutes later we stopped in front of the Parus Business Center. I gave the driver his money, got out, and walked through the underpass to the other side of the street. I entered the building, passing a Chevy dealership on the ground floor, and met the building's manager, a fast-talking Austrian.

He took me up to the empty office on the fourth floor. It was only two hundred square feet, about the size of an average master bedroom. The plate-glass windows, which opened only a few inches, looked over the parking lot to the west and a decrepit set of Soviet apartment blocks beyond that. The space wasn't pretty but it was functional, had multiple phone jacks, and was just down the hall from Marc. The Austrian wanted $4,000 a month, making this one of the most expensive office spaces in Moscow per square foot. I tried to negotiate, but the Austrian just laughed at me. After a bit more bickering, I gave in and signed the lease.

Once I had the office, I needed people to help me run it. While tens of millions of Russians were desperate to make a living, hiring a good English-speaking employee in Moscow was almost impossible. Seventy years of communism had destroyed the work ethic of an entire nation. Millions of Russians had been sent to the gulags for showing the slightest hint of personal initiative. The Soviets severely penalized independent thinkers, so the natural self-preservation reaction was to do as little as possible and hope that nobody would notice you. This had been fed into the psyches of ordinary Russians from the moment they were on their mothers' breasts. To run a Western-style business, therefore, you either had to completely brainwash a fresh young Russian about the virtues of efficiency and clear thinking or find some miraculous person whose natural psychology had somehow defied the pressures of communism.

Fortunately, I got lucky. A local brokerage firm with a number of Western-trained employees had recently gone bankrupt, and less than a week after arriving in Moscow I was able to hire three good people: Clive, a British junior trader and researcher; Svetlana, a secretary who spoke perfect English; and Alexei, an experienced driver who spoke only Russian.

After getting them in the office, I sent Svetlana to find some furniture. She was a short, pretty, twenty-two-year-old Lithuanian with dark hair and a sunny disposition, who enthusiastically went about her mission. When she got to the furniture store, she called to tell me about some nice Italian chairs and desks she thought would be perfect for the office.

"How much?" I asked.

"Around fifteen thousand dollars."

"Fifteen thousand bucks? You've got to be kidding. What else have they got?"

"Not much. Just some ugly picnic tables and folding chairs."

"How much for those?"

"About six hundred dollars."

"We'll take them."

By the end of that day we had four picnic tables and eight folding chairs—plus a houseplant Svetlana bought on her own initiative. We then purchased some computers and set them up, and by the end of the week my fledgling operation was ready to go.

As I got set up, Yeltsin's poll numbers continued to move in the right direction, but the election was still more than ten weeks away and Sandy was still not releasing any more of the funds. In the interim, I started researching companies for the fund on the assumption that eventually Safra was going to honor his $25 million commitment.

The first company I targeted was the Moscow Oil Refinery, known as MNPZ. At Salomon we had made a lot of money on oil-related companies in Russia, so a big Moscow refinery seemed like a promising place to start looking.

Svetlana made an appointment with MNPZ's chief accountant and in early April we went to meet her at the company's headquarters. Plump, blond, and in her fifties, she wore an unfashionable maroon pantsuit. She met us at the entrance of an ugly, old building and led us inside. The place had clearly seen better days. Lights flickered on and off, tiles were missing from the floor, and the walls were filthy.

In her office I asked a series of basic questions: "What were your revenues last year?" "What were your profits?" "Can you tell me how many shares are outstanding?" These questions may sound mundane, but in Russia there was no public information on companies and the only way of getting any was by going to the company and asking.

Svetlana translated as the accountant answered the revenue and profits questions, but when we got to the question about shares outstanding, she asked, "Do you mean common shares or preferred shares?"

I'd heard the term *preferred shares* before, but I didn't know what she was talking about. "What are those?"

"Preferred shares were given to the workers during the privatization process."

"How are they different from the ordinary shares?"

"They pay out forty percent of profits in dividends."

"How much do the ordinary shares pay out?"

"Let me see." The accountant grabbed a large binder off her desk, inspected several stained sheets of paper, and said, "It says here that they paid nothing last year."

"So the preferred shares paid out dividends equal to forty percent of the profits and the ordinary shares paid out nothing," I offered, not quite understanding this discrepancy.

"Yes, exactly."

As soon as I was done with the meeting, Svetlana and I jumped into Alexei's beat-up Zhiguli—a type of small, boxy Soviet car that was ubiquitous in Moscow—and puttered back to the office. As we inched through the midday traffic, I called Yuri Lopatinski, one of my favorite local brokers. Yuri was a Russian émigré from New York who'd recently moved back to Moscow to work for the brokerage firm Creditanstalt-Grant. He was not like the other brokers who trafficked in what I called tourist stocks, the banking equivalent of hawking $10 coconuts on a beach in Fiji when the locals bought them in town for twenty cents.

Yuri was in his early twenties and had a hushed way of speaking, as if he were always telling secrets. It was often difficult to understand anything he said, but when I did understand him, his information was usually interesting.

"Hey, Yuri, do you have a price on preferred shares of MNPZ?" I asked.

"Dunno. Probably. Let me see." He cupped the receiver and mumbled to his trader. I heard some garbled shouting in the background and Yuri came back on the line. "Yeah, I can get you a hundred thousand at fifty cents." He said this so inaudibly that I had to ask him to repeat it.

"How much for the ordinary shares?"

He mumbled something again and got another response. "A hundred thousand at seven bucks."

"You sure about that?"

"Yep. Those are the prices."

I didn't want to tip my hand, but my heart started beating fast. "Let me get back to you on this."

I hung up and wondered: *These preferred shares seem much more attractive than the ordinary shares. Is there something wrong with them? Why are they trading at a 95 percent discount to the ordinary shares?*

When we finally made it back to the office, I sent Svetlana back to MNPZ to get a copy of the corporate charter, which would contain the details of the rights of different classes of shares. She came back two hours later and we pored over it. The only substantive difference between preferred shares and ordinary shares was that preferred shares didn't have voting rights. That didn't seem to be a problem because foreign investors such as ourselves never voted our shares at annual general meetings in Russia, anyway.

I was convinced that there must be some other explanation for the deep discount and spent the next several days searching for it. Did the preferred shares have different par values? No. Was the ownership restricted to workers? No. Could the higher dividends be arbitrarily changed or canceled by the company? No. Did they represent only some minuscule part of the share capital? No. *There was no explanation.* The only reason I could fathom for why they were so cheap was that no one had showed up to ask about them—until I had.

Amazingly, I found that this anomaly wasn't restricted to MNPZ. Nearly every company in Russia had preferred shares and most of them traded at a huge discount to the ordinary shares. These things were a potential gold mine.

I intended to leave Sandy alone until after the election, but this situation was too compelling. These preferred shares were trading at a 95 percent discount to the ordinary shares, and the ordinary shares were trading between a 90 and 99 percent discount to the shares of comparable Western companies. Whatever Sandy's concerns about Zyuganov, valuation anomalies like these were too rare to ignore. You're lucky if you find something at a 30 percent discount, maybe even a 50 percent discount, but to find something this cheap was unheard of. I had to tell Sandy about them right away.

When I told him the numbers, he immediately perked up and started grilling me for more information. We finished the conversation and I could practically hear the wheels turning in his head about how he was going to justify this investment to Safra.

Two days later, the Levada polling agency[1] published Yeltsin's latest approval ratings. They had jumped from 14 to 22 percent. About three minutes after this announcement hit the wires, my phone rang. "Bill," Sandy said excitedly, "have you seen the polls?"

"Yes. Amazing, isn't it?"

"Listen, Bill, I think we should start buying some of those preferred shares. I'm wiring two million for tomorrow."

I told Clive and Svetlana the good news and we high-fived each other. I even walked over to Alexei, who hadn't learned about high-fiving in his previous job in the Moscow Traffic Police. I awkwardly grabbed his arm, raised it in the air, and slapped his hand. He gave me a polite, toothy smile. Clearly he enjoyed being a part of this strange American ritual.

We were now in business, and by the end of the next day the fund had invested all of this new money in Russian preferred shares.

Over the next three weeks Yeltsin's approval ratings jumped from 22 to 28 percent. For the first time since his campaign began, people started to factor in a real possibility that Yeltsin would win. New buyers entered the stock market, pushing my fund up 15 percent.

Unlike other decisions in life, with investing you know if you're right or wrong, based on the market price. There is no ambiguity. That Sandy could see a $300,000 profit on his first $2 million gave him more confidence than any words or analysis. He called me that Saturday afternoon on my mobile phone to let me know he was wiring an additional $3 million into the fund for Monday morning.

With the probability of an apocalypse now fading, and the market starting to rise in reaction, other investors didn't want to miss out, and more and more started to enter this small, illiquid stock market at once. Panic buying ensued. The week after Safra put in his additional $3 million, the fund was up a further 21 percent. Since we'd

---

1 The Russian equivalent to Gallup in the United States.

started investing a few weeks before, the fund was up a total of 40 percent, which in the world of hedge fund investing would have been an amazing year—only we had made it in three weeks!

The following Monday, Sandy wired an additional $5 million without even telling me.

In the midst of this excitement, I had a wedding to attend—my own. Sabrina and I were going to be married on May 26, 1996, only three weeks before the Russian presidential election. I rushed back to London on the Wednesday before the ceremony to prepare.

We'd invited 250 guests from all over the world, and when Sabrina and I stood on the bimah of the Marble Arch Synagogue and she vowed to love and cherish me as long as we might live, I was moved. The words felt as real as any I'd ever heard. As I made my vows, I stared through tears at my beautiful, vulnerable wife. After the ceremony we had a raucous party with an Israeli band, which started off by playing "Hava Nagila." We were lifted into the air on chairs and then danced all night. It was an amazing wedding with friends and family, and it felt as if all the planets had lined up for both of us.

I'd promised Sabrina a honeymoon, but I could do it only after the election, and I flew back to Moscow the following Monday exhausted but happy. When I got to the office, Clive told me that we had another $5 million in the account from Safra. Over the next two weeks, two more tranches of $5 million arrived. By the second week of June, only a week before the presidential election, Safra had invested the entire $25 million he had committed, and the Hermitage Fund was up 65 percent from inception.

The first round of the Russian presidential elections took place on June 16. Clive, Svetlana, Alexei, and I got to the office at 6:00 a.m. to track the results from Russia's Far East, which was seven hours ahead of Moscow. The results were good for Yeltsin. In Sakhalin, he had 29.9 percent versus 26.9 percent for Zyuganov. The results moved west, and in Krasnoyarsk, Yeltsin got 34 percent. Finally, results came in from Moscow, where he won 61.7 percent of the votes.

In all, Yeltsin had beaten Zyuganov 35.3 percent to 32 percent, the rest of the votes going to other marginal candidates. He had won, but since the Russian constitution requires a candidate to get 51 percent of the vote, there would be a second round on July 3.

Over the next two weeks, anyone with a vested interest in getting Yeltsin reelected went all in. I was a bit worried that the race would be too close to call, but I needn't have been. By midday on July 3 it was clear that Yeltsin would retain the presidency. When the final votes were tallied, he had beaten Zyuganov by nearly 14 percentage points.

The markets went wild, and the fund was up 125 percent since we launched. That was it. I was well and truly in business.

11

Sidanco

Late on a Friday afternoon in August 1996, I learned of another intriguing investment idea. It was a sizzling-hot day. The only sounds in our office were the gentle whir of the computers, the hum of our air conditioner, and the intermittent buzzing of a large horsefly. The city outside lay unnaturally still. On summer Fridays, all of Moscow's citizens poured into their countryside cabins, called dachas. That afternoon, it felt as if we were the only people left in the city.

As my small team was about to leave for the weekend, the phone rang. "Hermitage, *zdravstvuite*," Svetlana said, sounding bored. She swiveled in her chair and cupped her hand over the receiver. "Bill, it's Yuri."

"Yuri? Put him through."

I picked up the phone and he whispered, "Hey, Bill. I've got a four percent block of Sidanco. You interested?"

"What's that?"

"It's a big oil company in western Siberia that no one's heard of."

"Who controls it?"

"A group headed by Potanin." Everyone knew who Vladimir Potanin was: a tough-looking Russian billionaire oligarch with a pockmarked face, who was also a deputy prime minister of Russia.

"How much do they want for the four percent?"

"Thirty-six point six million." Although my fund was growing, it couldn't buy a block that big no matter how attractive it was. However, if the stock was interesting, the fund could buy *part* of the block. I remained silent as I thought about it.

"If it's not interesting, don't worry," Yuri said.

"No, no, Yuri, it may very well be. I'd like to do some homework."

"No problem."

"How long do I have?"

"I don't know. I can probably keep it quiet for a week before the seller starts pressing, but it's not as if there are many people out there looking for second-tier stocks."

I hung up with Yuri and my little team and I left the office for the weekend. But as I went home that day I had that tingling, greedy tension in my gut, similar to when I saw my $2,000 Polish investment multiply by nearly ten times, or when I'd first unearthed the Russian voucher scheme. I knew Yuri wouldn't shop the deal to someone behind my back, but I also knew that a truly good opportunity wouldn't last very long.

I came back to the office early on Saturday morning and started to leaf through analyst reports and articles to see if I could learn anything about Sidanco, but there wasn't anything in our files. As soon as my team arrived on Monday morning, I called Clive over to my desk. "I've been looking for information on Sidanco, but couldn't find anything. Can you call around and see if any of our brokers have something?"

He said he'd get right on it.

I left for a series of meetings and when I returned around noon I asked Clive if he'd learned anything—but he hadn't. There were no research reports, articles, data, or even reliable gossip. There was nothing on Sidanco.

This was frustrating, but it made sense. A company like Lukoil, which had 67 percent of its shares trading in the market, was a liquid stock and generated lots of commissions for brokers. These commissions paid for research analysts to write reports for investors looking at the shares. Conversely, in the case of Sidanco, which had only 4 percent of its shares trading in the market, there weren't going to be enough commissions to compel any analyst to waste time writing research reports.

"Well, I guess we'll just have to go and get the information our-selves, then," I said.

Going after information in Russia was like hurtling down the rab-bit hole. Ask a question, get a riddle. Track a lead, hit a wall. Nothing was self-evident or clear. After seventy years of KGB-instilled para-noia, Russians were careful to guard their information. Even inquir-ing after a person's health could feel like asking someone to reveal a state secret, and I knew that asking about the condition of a company would prove exponentially more difficult.

I was undaunted, though. As I got started, I remembered that one of my classmates at Stanford ran a monthly trade magazine about oil and gas. Maybe he would have some information on Sidanco. I called him up, but instead of talking about Sidanco, he tried to get me to sign up for a subscription. "It's only ten thousand dollars!" he said cheerfully.

I had no interest in subscribing. "That's a little out of my price range."

He laughed. "Tell you what, Bill. Since we were at Stanford to-gether, I'll send you some back issues for free."

"Great. Thanks."

Next, I turned to the pile of business cards on my desk. If I'd been a London investment banker, my Rolodex would have been bursting with embossed cards on thick stock. In Russia, my collection was humbler. Some were printed on cardboard. Others were orange or green or light blue. Some looked as if they'd been printed on a home computer. Two cards were stuck together because of cheap ink. Still, I went through them.

I peeled a couple of cards apart and discovered someone I'd for-gotten: Dmitry Severov, a consultant at a Russian finance company. I'd met Dmitry while still at Salomon Brothers and remembered that he was in the business of advising Russian oil companies on how to get bank loans. I figured he would know something about Sidanco. I picked up the phone, called his office, and asked for a meeting. He didn't seem to be a man in demand and readily agreed.

Dmitry's office was in a residential apartment building on a quiet side street north of the Kremlin, which was one of the most desirable neighborhoods in Moscow. A single guard was sitting in a security booth at the entrance, smoking a cigarette, dressed in an all-black uniform. He could have passed for a Special Forces soldier were it not for his rubber sandals. Without even looking up, he waved me through to the elevator.

I pulled out the address Svetlana had written down and frowned. Dmitry's office was located on the fifth-and-a-half floor. I had no idea what that meant. Did I take the elevator to the fifth floor and walk up, or the sixth and walk down?

A man brushed past me and hit the call button. The elevator was slow to arrive and was as narrow as a telephone booth. I had to squeeze in next to the man or risk waiting another ten minutes. He hit 5 and eyed me suspiciously. I looked at the floor and said nothing.

We exited the elevator and went our separate ways. I followed a trail of cigarette butts up a half flight of stairs. There, a round, elderly woman let me into the apartment and I wondered if she was Dmitry's mother or his secretary. She told me he was having lunch and directed me to the kitchen.

"Sit! Sit!" he said when I entered, pushing aside a basket of gray bread and a glass jar full of sugar. I sat in a vinyl chair opposite him and tried not to watch as he sopped up his cabbage soup with the bread. "What can I do for you?" he asked between mouthfuls.

"I'm researching oil companies."

"Good! You came to the right place."

"Can you tell me anything about Sidanco?"

"Of course. I know everything about Sidanco." He got up and left the kitchen, and in a moment he was back with a large spreadsheet. "What do you want to know?"

"How about their reserves, for a start."

We looked through the spreadsheet together and he pointed to a column. According to his data, Sidanco had six billion barrels of oil reserves. By multiplying the price of the 4 percent block by twenty-five I got the price of the whole company: $915 million. I divided that by the number of barrels of oil in the ground, which told me that Sidanco was trading at $0.15 per barrel of oil reserves in the ground, which was crazy because at the time the market price for a barrel of oil was $20.

I frowned. Something wasn't right. If these numbers were even close to correct, Sidanco was cheap beyond belief.

"Unbelievable," I said under my breath.

I thanked Dmitry and left. When I got back to the office, I had Clive figure out the valuation for Lukoil, the most widely followed Russian oil company. After hanging up with a broker, Clive passed me his calculation.

I stared at the figures for several seconds. "These can't be right."

"These are the numbers the broker gave me," he said defensively.

What didn't seem right was that Lukoil was trading at a price six times higher than that of Sidanco per barrel of oil reserves, yet they appeared to be comparable companies.

"Why would Lukoil's valuation be so much higher?"

Clive narrowed his eyes. "Maybe there's something wrong with Sidanco?"

"Maybe. But what if there isn't? It really could just be cheaper."

"That would be brilliant. But how can we know for sure?"

"We're going to ask them. And if they won't tell us, we'll ask someone else until we figure it out."

The following day, we began our investigation.

We started with Sidanco. Its offices were located in a former czar's mansion on the western embankment of the Moscow River, not far from the British ambassador's residence. Svetlana came with me. A pretty secretary with long blond hair and pencil-thin heels met us in reception and ushered us into a seventies-era conference room with wood-veneer sideboards and a faded velveteen sofa. She told us that a manager would be with us shortly.

We were made to wait for half an hour before an executive in the strategic development department entered the room. He carried himself with the air of a board chairman who'd been shuttling between meetings all morning. He was tall and thin, in his early thirties, and already balding. He mumbled something in Russian, which I did not understand.

"He is sorry to keep you waiting," Svetlana translated. "He asks what can he help you with?"

"*Pozhalujsta,*" the man said. "*Chai?*"

"He wants to know if you would like tea," Svetlana said, awkwardly sitting on a leather chair between the two of us.

The man checked his watch. The clock was ticking. I turned down his offer of tea.

"Tell him I would like to know how large their oil reserves are," I said. I already had a number, but I wanted to know if it was right.

He squirmed in his seat, as if he understood me, but waited for Svetlana to translate. He drew his lips in a tight smile, crossed one leg over his opposite knee, and launched into an explanation.

After a few minutes, he paused so Svetlana could speak. "He says the most important thing about oil reserves is a company's drilling technique. He says Sidanco has the finest equipment and best engineers in the country."

Before I could jump in, he held up his hand to shush me. He droned on, telling me about drilling, pipeline bottlenecks, and marketing subsidiaries, as Svetlana dutifully translated.

"He asks if that is all?" she said suddenly.

"Can you ask him about the oil reserves?"

"I already did," she said, confused.

"But he didn't answer. Ask him again."

Svetlana turned back to him, her cheeks flushed. He leaned back and waited for her to finish. Then he nodded, as if he'd finally understood my question and was about to reveal everything.

He talked for a while longer. When I realized he wouldn't pause for Svetlana to translate, I handed her a scrap of paper and a pen. She quickly started scribbling everything down. After five minutes, she glanced at me nervously to see if she should keep going. After ten minutes, she stopped writing.

Finally, he wrapped up his lecture and sat forward. He nodded for Svetlana to translate.

She looked at her notes. "He says the best oil in Russia comes from western Siberia—it is much better than the heavy oil coming from the central provinces of Tatarstan and Bashkortostan. He says—"

"Did he say how large the reserves are?" I asked, cutting her off.

"No."

"Are you sure?"

"Yes."

"Ask him again."

Svetlana froze.

"Go ahead," I nudged. "It's okay."

Slowly, she turned to face him. He was no longer smiling. Annoyed, he pulled a mobile phone from his pocket and began to flip through its menus. She meekly asked him the question a third time.

He stood and brusquely said something to Svetlana.

"He says he is very late for another meeting," she translated quietly. Clearly, he had no intention of answering my question. I didn't understand why he was afraid to tell us his reserve numbers. Perhaps he didn't know himself, but in Russia the conventional wisdom was that only bad things could come from passing real information to anyone. The best way for Russians to deal with direct questions was to talk pointlessly for hours and essentially filibuster the issue. Most people are too polite to keep pushing in this kind of situation and they often forget the question they asked in the first place. With a good Russian dissembler, you have to be incredibly focused to have even a chance of finding out what you need.

"He says he hopes he has told you everything you need to know."

The man reached out to shake my hand. "Please, come again soon," he said in perfect English. "We are always happy to meet with Western investors."

Clearly, the people at Sidanco weren't going to reveal any information about the company. So I started meeting with other oil companies to see if they knew anything about their competitor.

At Lukoil, I was patted down, my possessions x-rayed, my mobile phone and passport held aside until I left. Then I was handed over to a former KGB officer who'd been hired by the investor relations department to deal with foreigners. He took me through an hour-long PowerPoint presentation showing oil rigs complete with beaming company managers posing in hard hats.

At the oil company Yuganskneftegaz, the CFO tried to get me to lend the company $1.5 billion to pay for its new refinery.

At the Moscow office of Tatneft, a smaller but still large oil company headquartered in Tatarstan, I was invited to help build a highway. Each meeting went the same way. I started out hopeful and optimistic, then I was bombarded with irrelevant information, and I left without anything useful.

By then, my hunch about Sidanco had developed into something that was taking up way too much time and energy. What did I hope to find out when every analyst at every investment bank had written off Sidanco? Maybe there was a good reason why no one was interested in the 4 percent block.

When I returned to the office after my last meeting, ready to give up, Svetlana handed me a brown envelope.

"This just arrived from the US," she said excitedly. "From that trade-magazine guy you spoke to."

"You can toss it," I said without looking at the envelope. I figured it was probably more marketing material promoting the benefits of investing in oil rigs. But then I thought better of it. Maybe there was something in there.

"Hang on," I called. "Bring it back."

As I leafed through the magazine, I realized that my Stanford classmate had sent me a treasure trove, the golden ticket to this whole puzzle. This obscure glossy oil magazine had an appendix with all the relevant data on Russian oil companies, including the elusive

Sidanco. Everything I could have wanted to know was there: oil reserves, production, refining, everything. I didn't have to visit all these companies. It was all here—in one place, looking authoritative and accurate.

I pulled out a piece of paper and drew two columns. I titled the first Sidanco, and the second Lukoil, and wrote down every fact about each company that I could find in the magazine. When I was done, I looked over the accumulated information. There was practically no difference between the two companies. Little infrastructure had been developed since the fall of the Soviet Union, and they both had the same rusting oil derricks and used the same leaky pipelines, and they both had the same unproductive workers who were paid the same measly salaries.

The only obvious difference between them was that Lukoil was well-known and had lots of brokerage reports written about it, whereas Sidanco had none. When we compiled the information from these reports and compared them to the information on Lukoil from the magazine, they matched up perfectly. This led me to believe that the information on Sidanco was reliable too.

This was a remarkable discovery. Everyone knew that Lukoil was a steal, since it controlled the same amount of oil and gas as British Petroleum but was ten times cheaper. Now here was Sidanco, sitting on a bit less oil than Lukoil, but not much, only it was *six times* cheaper than Lukoil. In other words, Sidanco was *sixty* times cheaper than BP!

This was one of the most obvious investment ideas I had ever seen. My fund bought 1.2 percent of the company starting at $4 per share, spending roughly $11 million. It was the largest single investment decision I had ever been involved with in my life. When Edmond Safra heard about what was happening he wanted to get involved as well, and he promptly bought the same amount for himself.

Typically, when a company's shares are publicly traded, the market sets the price for them. But in the case of Sidanco—where 96 percent was held by one investment group and 4 percent by minority shareholders, including us—hardly any stock was trading. Therefore we had no idea if we had done a good deal or not. For a while I was comfortable with this, but as the months started to pass I became increasingly worried. Good legwork and a bit of self-confidence is one thing, but if I'd screwed up I would lose a large portion of the fund. As time passed, I began to wonder if maybe I should have stuck with the crowd and not gotten involved in something so adventurous. I fought this trepidation and forced myself to stay hopeful that something good would eventually happen. Finally, a little more than a year later, something *did*.

On October 14, 1997, BP announced it was buying 10 percent out of Vladimir Potanin's 96 percent block of Sidanco for a 600 percent premium to the price we had paid a year earlier.

It was a home run.

12

The Magic Fish

It had been an eventful year. Not only had my business finally taken off, but more importantly, my son, David, was born in November 1996. As Sabrina had promised, she brought him to Moscow after his birth and we'd lived there as a family ever since. She decorated the nursery, even making the curtains and cushions herself, and found a few other expat mothers to be friends with.

Even though she made these efforts, Moscow didn't gel for her. During 1997 she made more and more frequent trips to London and by Thanksgiving she and David were barely in Moscow at all. I wasn't happy about it, but I couldn't force her to stay if she was miserable. So I went back to London every other weekend to see her and David.

That Christmas, Sabrina insisted on taking a vacation to Cape Town, South Africa. I'd grown up associating South Africa with apartheid and racism, so I had no desire to visit. Sabrina's persistence was more powerful than my prejudices, though, and in the end I agreed. I didn't care that much, anyway, since I had to keep working—as long as my cell phone had a signal and I had access to a fax machine, I'd be fine.

We flew to Cape Town on December 19, 1997, and checked in to the Mount Nelson Hotel—and my low expectations vanished. I'd never seen such an amazing place in my life.

The Mount Nelson was a grand British colonial building under the fortresslike shadow of Table Mountain. The Cape Town sun shone every day and the green lawns, guarded by dark, swaying palms, went on forever. The pool was full of frolicking children as parents lounged nearby. A continual warm breeze fluttered through the white tablecloths of the outdoor dining area and waiters with perfect manners stood by attentively, ready to bring drinks, food, or anything else we desired. The Mount Nelson was like heaven. It was the polar opposite of Moscow in December.

We settled in and I started to relax for the first time in years. As I lounged on a sun bed next to the pool, watching David play with his toys on a towel, I became aware of just how tired I was. I drifted into a state of complete relaxation. Sabrina was right to have chosen this place. I closed my eyes. I could have sat in that chair and basked in the sun for days.

But a few days after we arrived, just as I'd started to truly decompress, my mobile phone rang. It was Vadim, my new head of research. Vadim was a twenty-seven-year-old financial analyst with a PhD in economics from the top university in Moscow whom I'd hired five months earlier to professionalize my fledgling operation. He had thick glasses, a mop of curly dark hair, and the ability to figure out the most complex economic puzzles in minutes. "Bill," he said gravely, "some really disturbing news just came across the Reuters wire."

"What is it?"

"Sidanco is doing a share issue. They're going to nearly triple the total number of shares, and they're selling them cheap—almost ninety-five percent lower than the market price."

I didn't get it. "Is that good or bad?" If everyone was allowed to buy the new shares, it might have been neutral or even marginally good for us.

"Very, very bad. They're allowing every shareholder *other than us* to buy these new securities!"

This was absurd. If Sidanco was able to increase the total number of shares by nearly a factor of three without letting us in on the action, then Safra and the fund would essentially go from owning 2.4 percent of the company to owning 0.9 percent of the company and get nothing in return. In broad daylight Potanin and the people around him were going to get $87 million of value from Safra and my clients with the simple stroke of a pen.

I sat upright. "This is unbelievable! Are you sure, Vadim? Maybe Reuters got the announcement wrong or something."

"I don't think so, Bill. It looks real to me."

"Go and get the original documents and translate them for yourself. This *can't* be right."

I was shocked. If this dilutive share issue ended up having a bad ending, the credibility I'd built by finding Sidanco would evaporate and bring my investors enormous losses.

I was also confused. I couldn't fathom why Potanin would do something like this. What was his purpose? Why dilute the value of our shares and create a scandal when he had just had a spectacular windfall himself? After his big sale to BP, he still owned 86 percent of the company, and with this dilution he was only getting the benefit of 1.5 percent from us. It didn't make any financial sense.

Then I remembered why he would do this: because it is the Russian thing to do.

There's a famous Russian proverb about this type of behavior. One day, a poor villager happens upon a magic talking fish that is ready to grant him a single wish. Overjoyed, the villager weighs his options: "Maybe a castle? Or even better—a thousand bars of gold? Why not a ship to sail the world?" As the villager is about to make his decision, the fish interrupts him to say that there is one important caveat: whatever the villager gets, his neighbor will receive two of the same. Without skipping a beat, the villager says, "In that case, please poke one of my eyes out."

The moral is simple: when it comes to money, Russians will gladly—gleefully, even—sacrifice their own success to screw their neighbor.

This was the exact principle on which Potanin and his control group seemed to be operating. Never mind that they'd made forty times more money than us: that a group of unconnected *foreigners* also had a big financial success was unbearable to them. This was simply not supposed to happen. It was not . . . *Russian.*

What *was* Russian was to have your business ruined—which was exactly what would happen to me if I didn't get back to Moscow and fix this situation. I spent the next few nights in Cape Town trying to forget about my problems, but I simply couldn't.

Our vacation ended several days later, and Sabrina, who wanted nothing to do with winter in Russia, took David back to London. I arrived in Moscow on January 12, 1998, the day before Russian New Year's Eve (Russia celebrates the Gregorian calendar's New Year on January 1, and then twelve days later celebrates again for the Julian calendar's New Year's Eve on January 13). As soon as I got there, I spoke with Vadim, who had confirmed everything. The share dilution would take about six weeks to worm its way through the regulatory apparatus, but the deal was going to happen.

I needed to do something to stop it.

A day later, on January 13, I saw an opportunity. I received a call from a friend who told me about a Russian New Year's party at the home of Nick Jordan, a wealthy Russian American banker at JP Morgan. Nick had a brother, Boris, who was Potanin's financial adviser and the head of a new investment bank called Renaissance Capital. I knew them both as acquaintances, and I convinced my friend to bring me along to the party.

The party was in an enormous luxury Brezhnev-era apartment several blocks from the Kremlin—the type that investment banks paid $15,000 a month for so that their expat employees could "endure the hardships of Moscow." It didn't take long to pick out Boris from the crowd of caviar-eating, champagne-swilling Russian American expats. In many ways Boris Jordan was what Russians considered a classic American: a loud, chubby glad-hander cut from the same cloth as your stereotypical Wall Street broker.

I went straight for him. When he caught sight of me, he was

clearly surprised, but he didn't overreact. Instead he met me head-on with a meaty handshake. "Bill, how are ya?"

I cut right to the chase. "Not great, Boris. What's going on with Sidanco? If this dilutive share issue goes through, it's going to be a real problem for me."

Boris was taken aback. He didn't want a confrontation at his brother's New Year's party. He looked at the other guests, a toothy smile plastered to his face. "Bill, it's all a big misunderstanding. Don't worry about a thing."

He turned his attention to a silver tray of hors d'oeuvres and carefully picked one. Avoiding my gaze, he said, "Tell you what. Come over to Renaissance tomorrow at four-thirty and we'll sort it out." He popped the morsel into his mouth and spoke freely, food clinging to his gums and teeth. "Seriously, Bill. Everything's going to be fine. Have a drink. It's a New Year's party!"

And that was that. He was so convincing—and I so wanted to believe him—that I stayed at the party for a while and left with some measure of calm.

I woke the next morning in the darkness (in January, the sun in Moscow doesn't rise until around 10:00 a.m.) and went to work. By the time I headed to Boris's office the sky was dark again. At 4:30 p.m. sharp I walked into Renaissance Capital, which was located in a modern glass office building close to Russia's White House, the big white building where the government sits. I was unceremoniously shown to a windowless conference room. I was not offered anything to eat or drink, so I sat there and waited.

And waited.

And waited.

After an hour my paranoia began to get the better of me. I felt like a fish in a tank and I started to peer around for hidden cameras, though I couldn't see any. Regardless, I was starting to think that Boris had lied. Everything was *not* going to be fine.

I was ready to leave when the door finally opened—only it wasn't Boris. It was Leonid Rozhetskin, a thirty-one-year-old Russian-born,

Ivy League–educated lawyer whom I'd met on a few occasions (and who would, a decade later, be murdered in Jurmula, Latvia, after a spectacular falling-out with various people he did business with).

Leonid, who'd clearly watched the film *Wall Street* one too many times, had slicked-back, Gordon Gekko–styled hair and sported red suspenders over a custom, monogrammed, button-down shirt. He took the chair at the head of the table and laced his fingers over one knee. "I'm sorry Boris couldn't make it," he said in lightly accented English. "He's busy."

"I am too."

"I'm sure you are. What brings you here today?"

"You know what, Leonid. I'm here to talk about Sidanco."

"Yes. What about it?"

"If this dilution goes forward, it's going to cost me and my investors—including *Edmond Safra*—eighty-seven million dollars."

"Yes, we know. That's the intention, Bill."

"What?"

"That's the intention," he repeated matter-of-factly.

"You're *deliberately* trying to screw us?"

He blinked. "Yes."

"But how can you do this? It's illegal!"

He recoiled slightly. "This is Russia. Do you think we worry about these types of things?"

I thought of all my clients. I thought of Edmond. I couldn't believe this. I shifted in my seat. "Leonid, you may be fucking me over, but some of the biggest names on Wall Street are invested with me. The pebble may drop here, but the ripples go everywhere!"

"Bill, we're not worried about that."

We sat in silence as I processed this.

He looked at his watch and got up. "If that's all, I have to go."

Shocked, I tried to think of something else to say and blurted, "Leonid, if you do this, I'm going to be forced to go to war with you."

He froze, and I did too. After a few seconds he began to laugh. What I'd said was preposterous and we both knew it. Still, while I didn't exactly want to take the words back, I wondered what exactly I'd meant. Go to war? Against an oligarch? In Russia? Only a fool would do that.

My nerves shuddered but I remained stock-still. When Leonid was finally able to contain himself, he said, "Is that so? Good luck with that, Bill." Then he turned and left.

I was so upset that for several seconds I couldn't move, and when I finally could, I shook with humiliation, shock, and a ton of trepidation. I marched out of the Renaissance offices in a daze into the minus-fifteen-degree Moscow night. I climbed into my car, a second-hand Chevy Blazer that I'd recently bought, and Alexei put it in gear and started for my apartment.

After a few minutes of silence I opened my cell phone and tried to reach Edmond in New York. My first few attempts failed, but eventually I got through. His secretary told me he was busy, but I insisted that we needed to speak. I was afraid to talk to him, but now that it was clear that we were about to get screwed out of $87 million, I had to explain the situation. He was calm, but clearly upset. Nobody likes to lose money—and Edmond was a notoriously bad loser. When I had finished, he asked, "What are we going to do, Bill?"

"We're going to fight these bastards, that's what. We're going to go to war."

The words were mine but they still felt foreign.

There was a silence. The line crackled. "What are you talking about, Bill?" Edmond asked seriously. "You're in Russia. You'll be killed."

I gathered my wits. "Maybe I will, maybe I won't. But I'm not going to let them get away with it." I didn't care if I was being brave or stupid, or if there was even a difference. I'd been backed into a corner and I meant what I said.

"I can't be part of this, Bill," he said slowly, safe in New York, 4,650 miles away.

I was not safe, though, and it filled me with adrenaline. I ran with it. "Edmond," I said as Alexei pulled the car around onto Bolshaya

Ordynka, the street I lived on, "you're my partner, not my boss. I'm going to fight these guys whether you're with me or not."

He didn't have anything else to say and we hung up. Alexei parked in front of my building, the engine idling and the heat blasting. I got out and went upstairs. I did not sleep at all that night.

The next morning I walked into my new office, a bigger space that we'd moved into a few months earlier, with my head down. Regret, along with a lot of uncertainty, had crept into me overnight. But when I reached the reception area, a commotion shook me from my thoughts. Packed into the room were more than a dozen heavily armed bodyguards. The one in charge came up to me, his hand outstretched, and in an Israeli accent pronounced, "I'm Ariel Bouzada, Mr. Browder. Mr. Safra sent us. We have four armored cars and fifteen men. We'll be with you for as long as this situation lasts."

I shook Ariel's hand. He was roughly my age and shorter than me, but everything about him was tougher, stronger, and more menacing than I could ever be. He walked with an air of authority coupled with the imminent threat of violence. Apparently, Edmond was going to join my fight after all.

After meeting each of the senior bodyguards I retreated to my office and sat down at my desk. I put my head in my hands. *How am I going to take on an oligarch? How am I going to take on an oligarch? How am I going to take on a goddamn oligarch?*

By meeting him head-on, that's how.

I gathered my team in our small conference room. I then went to the stationery cabinet and got a ream of white paper and some tape. I dropped the paper on the table and held out the tape, telling everyone to cover the walls and make the whole room into a whiteboard. "Get out your markers," I announced. "We need to come up with ideas that will cause Vladimir Potanin economic pain that is greater than the benefit he'll get from screwing us. All ideas are good ideas. Let's get to work."

13

Lawyers, Guns, and Money

We hatched a three-part plan that would sequentially ratchet up the pressure on Potanin.

The first part was to expose the dilutive share issue to Potanin's Western business contacts. As a billionaire oligarch, he had a lot of business interests that weren't directly related to Sidanco. These included joint investments with men such as George Soros, and entities such as the Harvard University endowment and the Weyerhaeuser pension fund.

Edmond and I split up the list and called each personally. After our discussions, we sent them a PowerPoint presentation detailing the dilutive share issue. Our message was simple: this is how Potanin is screwing us. If you don't stop him, you could be next.

Most of these people then contacted Potanin and complained. I wasn't privy to their conversations, but I imagined them saying that this dilutive share issue would compromise the value of the investments they had together and that he should stop what he was doing to us out of self-interest.

We waited for Potanin's response, thinking he might back off. But unfortunately, he didn't. All he did was escalate. He probably thought, *Who is this little shit from Chicago? I've spent a lot of time and effort cultivating these relationships, and now this guy wants to ruin my good name! How can this be happening?*

It was a good question. Every other time a foreigner got ripped off in Russia, they would engage in heated brainstorming sessions behind closed doors, attempting to figure out how to resist (just as we had done). But then their lawyers and advisers would point out that retaliation was infeasible and dangerous (just as Edmond had done initially), and after all the tough talk, they would slink away like wounded animals.

But this wasn't every other time. I wasn't an employee of a big investment bank or Fortune 500 company. I was a principal in my own hedge fund business. What Potanin didn't understand was that I was never going to let him get away with this without a fight.

Another person who didn't understand this was Sabrina. She was fully aware of my intentions, and from the outset she was not happy about them. I'd spoken to her the same night that I told Edmond, and she was hysterical. "Bill, how can you do this to us?" she shouted over the phone.

"Sweetheart, I have to do this. I can't let these guys get away with it."

"How can you say that? How can you be so selfish? You're a father and a husband. These people will kill you!"

"I hope not, but I have a responsibility to the people who trusted me with their money. I got them into this mess, I have to get them out."

"But who cares about them? *You have a family.* I don't understand why you can't just have a normal job in London like everyone else we know!"

She was right about having a family, but I was so angry and indignant with Potanin that I couldn't hear her.

We hung up at a complete impasse, but for better or worse I couldn't dwell on Sabrina. I was just starting this fight and had to carry on.

Unfortunately, stage one failed. Still, it had caught Potanin's attention. I'd sliced open a vein and let the blood drain into the water, and by the end of the week Potanin's shark, Boris Jordan, showed up.

Potanin must have given him a real earful, because when Boris called he was irate and rattled. "B-Bill," he spluttered, "what the hell are you doing calling our investors?"

I tried to sound as calm as possible as I said, "Didn't Leonid tell you about our meeting?"

"Yes, but I thought you understood the score."

I continued to play along, praying that my voice wouldn't crack. "What score?"

"Bill, you don't seem to understand—you're not playing by the rules!"

I eyed one of my burly Russian guards standing just by the entry to the office. Scared or not, I'd thrown caution to the wind when I decided to go to war with these people.

With a steadiness that surprised even me, I said, "Boris, if you think I'm not playing by the rules now, wait until you see what I'm about to do to you next." I didn't wait for his response and hung up. I felt as high as a kite.

We then forged ahead to stage two, which was to make the whole story public.

Foreign reporters were a staple of Moscow's expat community and I had come to know a number of them, a few quite well. One of these was Chrystia Freeland, the Moscow bureau chief of the *Financial Times*. An attractive brunette a few years younger than me, she stood at barely five feet tall. Not that you ever thought of her as short, though; she had a zealous fire in her belly, and what she lacked in physical stature she made up for in her approach to life. In various social interactions, Chrystia had made it clear how hungry she was for an oligarch story, but couldn't find anyone brave enough (or stupid enough, depending on your perspective) to speak on the record—until now.

I called her up and we agreed to meet at my favorite Moscow restaurant, a Middle Eastern place called Semiramis. As we ordered, she produced a small black tape recorder and placed it in the middle of the table. I'd never worked with the press before. I was new to the whole process, so I launched into the story from the very beginning. The waiters brought hummus and baba ghanoush, and Chrystia scribbled a few notes as I spoke between bites. Then came the lamb kebabs. I kept talking, and she kept listening. Finally, I was finished. Her reticence had been a little off-putting and a small voice inside my head wondered if my tale was as good as I thought it was. As the mint tea and baklava arrived, I asked, "So—what do you think?"

I tried not to fidget as she calmly wrapped her hands around her gilt tea glass and looked up. "Bill, this is huge. I've been waiting for something like this for a long time."

The following day Chrystia called Potanin to get his side of the story and he reacted in typical—and perfect—Russian fashion.

Under normal conditions, this would have been the obvious point for him to back down. Potanin was making billions of dollars on the recent success of the BP deal. Why risk that so he could grab a couple of percent from us? But these were not normal conditions. This was Russia, and the far more important consideration was to not show any weakness.

This whole exercise was teaching me that Russian business culture is closer to that of a prison yard than anything else. In prison, all you have is your reputation. Your position is hard-earned and it is not relinquished easily. When someone is crossing the yard coming for you, you cannot stand idly by. You have to kill him before he kills you. If you don't, and if you manage to survive the attack, you'll be deemed weak and before you know it, you will have lost your respect and become someone's bitch. This is the calculus that every oligarch and every Russian politician goes through every day.

Potanin's logical response to Chrystia's questions should have been, "Ms. Freeland, this is all a big mistake. Mr. Browder saw some early drafts of the share issue that should never have gone to the financial regulators. The secretary who released it has been fired. Of course, every Sidanco shareholder will be treated fairly in the issue, including Mr. Browder's investors and Mr. Safra."

However, because we were in Russia, Potanin couldn't afford to be disrespected by some weak foreign investor, so he had no choice but to escalate. Therefore, his response was along the lines of "Bill

Browder is a terrible and irresponsible fund manager. If he had done his job properly, he would have known I was going to do this. His clients should sue him for every penny he's worth."

It was tantamount to an admission of his intent to screw us, and it was on the record.

Chrystia filed a long story that same week. It was immediately picked up by Reuters, Bloomberg, the *Wall Street Journal*, and the local English-language daily, the *Moscow Times*. Over the next few weeks, Sidanco's dilutive share issue became the cause célèbre that everyone who was interested in Russian financial markets talked about. The same people also talked about how long I was going to survive.

It seemed to me that Potanin would now either have to retreat and cancel the issue or include us in it. Instead of folding, though, Potanin contrived to escalate. He and Boris Jordan held a series of press conferences and briefings in an attempt to justify their actions. But rather than convince people that he was right and I was wrong, all he did was keep the story alive.

The major downside to what I was doing was that I was seriously disrespecting a Russian oligarch in public, and in Russia that had often led to lethal results in the past. The imagination is a horrible thing when it's preoccupied with exactly how someone might try to kill you. Car bomb? Sniper? Poison? The only time I felt truly safe was when I got off the plane at Heathrow during my visits to London.

It also didn't help that there'd been a recent case just like mine. An American named Paul Tatum, who'd been in Moscow since 1985, ended up in a big fight over his ownership of Moscow's Radisson Slavyanskaya Hotel. During the dispute he published a full-page ad in a local paper accusing his partner of blackmail—not unlike what I had done in accusing Potanin of attempting to steal from me. Shortly after the ad came out, on November 3, 1996, and despite wearing a bulletproof vest, Tatum was shot dead in an underpass near the hotel. To this day, nobody has been prosecuted for his murder.

It wasn't a stretch for me to think that I could be the next Paul Tatum.

Naturally, I took precautions, and I trusted the fifteen bodyguards Edmond had assigned to me. Throughout the conflict, whenever I moved around Moscow I'd travel in a convoy made up of a lead car, two side cars, and a trail car. Near my home, the lead car would peel off so that two of the guards could arrive a few minutes before the rest and check for bombs or snipers. Then the other cars would pull up and more guards would jump out, create a protective cordon, and take me safely into the building. Once I was upstairs, two men sat on my sofa with loaded submachine guns as I tried to sleep. Some of my American friends thought this arrangement was pretty cool, but I can definitively say that there's nothing cool about having giant bodyguards armed to the teeth in your home at all times, even if they are there for your safety.

With stage two also having failed, we enacted stage three of our plan to stop Potanin. It was a desperate play, and if I didn't succeed I wasn't sure what I would do or how my business would survive.

This last effort started with a meeting with Dmitry Vasiliev, chairman of the Russian Federal Securities and Exchange Commission (FSEC).

I met Vasiliev, a small, wiry man with steel-rimmed glasses and an intense stare, at his office in a block of Soviet-era government buildings and told him the story. He listened carefully, and when I was finished I asked if he could help.

His answer was a simple question: "Have they broken the law?"

"Of course they have."

He removed his glasses to clean one of the lenses with a neatly folded handkerchief. "Here's how it works. If you believe you have a bona fide complaint, write up a detailed description of Mr. Potanin's transgressions and file it with us. Then we'll consider it and respond in due course."

I wasn't sure if he was encouraging me or brushing me off, but I chose to take him at his word. I rushed back to the office, called in a team of lawyers, and had them draw up a detailed complaint. When we were finished, we had a two-hundred-page document in Russian reciting all the laws we thought the dilutive share issue would have broken. I submitted it the day it was completed, eager and nervous with anticipation.

To my surprise, two days later an article in red appeared across the Reuters screen: "FSEC to Investigate Cases of Violating Investors' Rights." We were shocked. It looked as if Vasiliev was actually going to take on Potanin.

All the same, I was uncertain about what would happen during this investigation. It wasn't just the foreigner versus the oligarch anymore. Vasiliev was in the game too, and because he was Russian he was probably more vulnerable. It didn't matter that he was the head of the FSEC. Anything could happen.

Throughout the following weeks as Vasiliev did his job, I held daily telephone briefings with Edmond's deputies in New York regarding Sidanco, and I was forced to give them increasingly lukewarm reports. I learned that Edmond had begun to lose confidence in my ability to sort out this situation.

I wasn't sure what Edmond was up to, but the trepidation in his voice and the frequency of calls from Sandy and his legal team in New York suggested something wasn't right.

It became clear when one of my brokers called to say that he had spotted Sandy in the lobby of the Kempinski Hotel. There was only one reason why he would be in Moscow without my knowledge—to negotiate with Potanin behind my back.

I couldn't believe it. If I was right, this would have projected total weakness on our side. Potanin and Boris Jordan were probably chuckling at our internal disarray.

I called Safra's general counsel in New York and asked, "Have you sent Sandy to Moscow to negotiate with Potanin?" There was a stunned silence. I wasn't supposed to know, and he was embarrassed. He collected himself before saying, "Bill, I'm sorry, but you're way out of your league here. This is serious business involving a lot of money. I think it's best if you let us take over from here."

He may have been right if this were New York, where the courts worked and a sixty-two-year-old Wall Street lawyer was more capable than a thirty-three-year-old hedge fund manager—but this was Russia and the rules were different. I replied, "With respect, you have no idea what you're doing here. If you show even the smallest sign of weakness to these guys, our investors will lose everything and that will be on you." I was emphatic and asked him at least to give me some time to see my approach through to the end. He was resistant, but said he would check with Edmond. He called me back late that evening and grudgingly said, "Edmond will give you ten more days. After that, if nothing's happened, we're taking over."

I called Vasiliev's office the next day to try to find out where he stood on his investigation, but his secretary told me he was unavailable. I called our lawyers and asked if they could estimate how long the FSEC might take to make a decision. They had no idea.

As the days ticked by, I had daily calls with Safra's general counsel. Things didn't look good. By day six, he said, "Look, Bill, we promised you ten days, but nothing seems to be happening. Sandy's going to come back to Moscow on Monday to see Potanin. We appreciate all that you've done, but it's not working."

I went home that night feeling as bad as I'd ever felt. Not only was I being screwed by the Russians, but my business partner had lost confidence in me. We would probably get 10 or 20 percent of what was being taken by Potanin if we were lucky, and this was probably the end of my partnership with Safra. For all intents and purposes, this was the end of Hermitage Capital.

The next morning I dragged myself into the office with the intention of controlling the damage any way I could. But I didn't have to. Without any warning, a fax arrived with a printout of the front page of the *Financial Times*. The headline read, "Watchdog Annuls Sidanco Bond Issue." Vasiliev had shut the whole dilutive share issue down.

That was it.

I had won. This nobody from the South Side of Chicago had beaten the Russian oligarch on his own turf. Edmond Safra called to congratulate me. Even his general counsel grudgingly admitted that I had been right.

With the deal officially dead, Potanin backed off. This reaction was every bit as Russian as his desire to go after me in the first place: once the money was off the table, there was no reason to struggle.

I'd met the oligarch in the prison yard and earned some respect. More than that, I'd learned how to fight the Russians, who weren't as invincible as they wanted to appear.

14

Leaving Villa d'Este

Along with my win over Potanin, everything else seemed to be going my way in Russia. In 1997 the Hermitage Fund was ranked the best-performing fund in the world, up 235 percent for the year and 718 percent from inception. Our assets under management had grown from the original $25 million to more than *$1 billion*. The *New York Times*, *BusinessWeek*, the *Financial Times*, and *Time* magazine all profiled me as a wunderkind of modern-day finance. My clients competed with each other to invite me to their yachts in the south of France, and I was being wined and dined in every city in which I set foot. All of this was hugely exhilarating, and it was happening to me, a thirty-three-year-old who had started his business only two years earlier.

In hindsight, I should probably have been a little more circumspect. Any one of these developments was cause to celebrate, but taken collectively they constituted, in the parlance of Wall Street, one big "sell signal." I understood this intellectually, but viscerally I just wanted my blessed life to carry on forever. Therefore, I stayed fully invested, thinking that everything would continue the way that it had.

Others did not share my optimism, principally Edmond Safra.

He gave me a call in early April 1998 and said, "Bill, I'm concerned about all the stuff going on with Asia. Shouldn't we be liquidating our positions?" He was referring to the Asian economic crisis that had started in the summer of 1997, in which Thailand, Indonesia, Malaysia, and South Korea suffered major currency devaluations, bond defaults, and severe recessions.

"I think we should hold tight and wait until this storm passes, Edmond. Russia will be okay."

"How can you say that, Bill? We've taken a huge hit already."

He was justified in his concern. In January 1998 the fund lost 25 percent of its value, but by April it had recovered about half of its losses, and I was convinced that things were on the way back up.

"The market is bouncing now. When things calm down, we'll make everything back."

"Tell me why you think that's the case," he said, sounding unconvinced.

"Because the fear that Russia is on the brink is just that—fear. It's based on sentiment, not fundamentals."

"What do you mean?"

"Well, first, Russia doesn't do much trade with Asia. Second, Russia doesn't compete with Asia. And third, the Asians don't invest in Russia. I just don't see how the Asian problems will jump over here."

Edmond took a second or two before he said, "I really hope you're right, Bill."

I hoped I was right too.

Unfortunately, I was dead wrong.

What I'd completely missed was that the world is one big sea of liquidity. If the tide goes out in one place, then it goes out everywhere. When big investors started to lose money in Asia, they began unloading risky securities from their portfolios everywhere else in the world and anything Russian was at the top of that list.

This created a pernicious situation for the Russian government. Over the previous few years Russia, running a huge budget deficit to pay for public services, had borrowed $40 billion by issuing three-month ruble Treasury bills. That meant, just to keep its head above water, every three months the government had to sell $40 billion of new bonds to pay back the $40 billion of previous ones that were due. On top of that, Russia had to pay interest rates in excess of 30 percent to attract buyers, so the debt bills kept getting bigger and bigger.

This wouldn't be a prudent financing strategy in the best of times, but it became downright suicidal in the worst of times.

The only thing that could now save Russia was the International Monetary Fund (IMF). As spring arrived in Moscow in 1998, IMF intervention was all that brokers and investors could talk about.

Interestingly, the Russian government didn't share our obsession. I wasn't sure whether it was arrogance or stupidity, but the Kremlin was playing hardball with the IMF when it should have been on its knees begging. In mid-May, Larry Summers, then the US deputy secretary of the Treasury, traveled to Russia to decide how the United States should deal with what appeared to be an impending meltdown. Since the United States was the biggest member of the IMF, Summers's view would effectively determine the outcome. Although every Western politician understood that he was one of the world's most influential financial power players, when the Russian prime minister, Sergei Kiriyenko, saw that Summers was merely a "deputy secretary," he was insulted and refused to take the meeting. A few days later, on May 23, 1998, the IMF mission that had traveled to Russia to negotiate a $20 billion bailout package ran into similar obstinacy and gave up on its talks. Both Summers and the IMF left the country without an agreement on the table.

With no IMF money to prop up the Russian bond market, the Russian government had to raise the interest rate it paid on its domestic bonds from 30 percent to 44 percent to entice buyers. However, instead of attracting investors, this had the opposite effect. Wall Street smelled blood. "If Russia needs to raise rates from thirty to forty-four percent," the thinking went, "then there must be something seriously wrong and I don't want anything to do with it."

This lack of confidence caused the Russian stock market to crash, and my fund fell a jaw-dropping 33 percent in May, leaving us down 50 percent for the year.

Edmond had been right.

Losing so much money threw me into a quandary. *Should we sell when we're already down 50 percent? Or should we stand firm and wait for a recovery?* The thought of locking in a 50 percent loss forever was mortifying. I thought the market had bottomed, so I recommended holding our positions and waiting for an IMF bailout.

In early June, rumors started to circulate that the IMF was back at the negotiating table. The markets jumped and the fund went up 9 percent in a single week. But then the following week the rumors turned negative and the fund dropped by 8 percent.

By July, interest rates on Russian bonds had reached a staggering 120 percent. Russia would certainly default if the IMF didn't step in. People such as Larry Summers and the technocrats at the IMF may have been furious at the Russian government for being so arrogant, but they knew a disorderly sovereign default in Russia would be catastrophic, and at the last minute the United States threw its weight behind a huge bailout package. On July 20 the IMF and World Bank stepped in with $22.6 billion, immediately releasing the first tranche of $4.8 billion.

When I saw the headlines, I felt an overpowering sense of relief. My nerves had been completely fried by the drumbeat of bad news, but now a backstop was in place. It looked as if this bailout would save Russia—as well as my investors' money. The following week, the fund recovered 22 percent of its losses. The phone started ringing as I took calls from relieved clients, and we started to discuss how the recovery might play out.

But I was too quick to declare victory. The bailout package may have been big, but it was viewed by the Russian oligarchs not as a backstop but as a massive piggy bank that they could use to convert their rubles into dollars in order to get that money as far away from Russia as possible. Over the next four weeks, $6.5 billion worth of rubles were converted to dollars by Russian oligarchs. Just like that, the country was right back where it had started before the IMF stepped in.

As if these financial gyrations weren't enough, my marriage was also slowly deteriorating. Ever since the Sidanco incident, Sabrina had grown more and more angry with me. She saw my decision to fight Potanin as a betrayal and she wanted me to move back to London. I reminded her that in spite of all the scary stuff, moving to Moscow was what she had agreed to, but she didn't see it that way. She was also completely unsympathetic to my arguments about my duty to my investors.

We were having a difficult time finding any meaningful way to connect. Aside from taking care of David, which she did beautifully, the only part of our marriage that she was engaged with was planning our family holidays. These were the only times that Sabrina and I spent more than a weekend in each other's company, so I gave her full rein to organize whatever she wanted in the hope that these trips would draw us closer together.

Earlier in the summer, before everything was falling apart in the Russian financial markets, Sabrina had booked a suite at the Villa d'Este Hotel on Lake Como in Italy. A suite at this five-star hotel cost $1,200 per night, which was more money than I'd spent on my entire postcollege summer vacation. I was always uncomfortable with these extravagant holidays, whether I could afford them or not. My mother, who had fled the Holocaust, had instilled in me the idea that spending money on luxuries was stupid and irresponsible. Given my circumstances, this was irrational, but I still found it hard to pay $30 for a continental breakfast. I would often feign an excuse to skip breakfast and ask Sabrina to bring back a few rolls because I felt so guilty about "wasting money."

This specific holiday could not have come at a worse time. The markets were moving up and down 5 percent a day, and I shouldn't have been more than a few feet from my desk. But if I'd canceled, it would have thrown my marriage into complete crisis. So in mid-August I flew to Milan, got in a car, and met Sabrina and David at Lake Como.

The contrast between Lake Como and Moscow was staggering. Where everyone was aggressive, angry, and tense in Russia, everyone was tanned, relaxed, and happy in Italy. We checked into our lavish two-bedroom suite, and after getting settled I went to sit on the terrace. I saw the crystal-clear alpine lake and the rolling foothills of the Alps and watched as people splashed and laughed in the water. The air was still and warm and smelled of pine trees. None of it seemed real.

I tried to clear my head and not obsess about every twist and turn in the market, but it was impossible. The only peaceful moments came at the crack of dawn, when David woke up. I would dress him and fill his bottle with milk, and we would share a couple of quiet hours, walking around the hotel's manicured grounds while Sabrina slept.

I really enjoyed these intimate moments, but then on August 18, after our morning walk, when David and I were both on the balcony overlooking the lake while Sabrina was taking a bath, Vadim called in a state of panic from Moscow.

"Bill, it all seems to be happening."

"What's happening?" I asked, not understanding the context.

"The ruble is in a free fall. The government is no longer support-ing the currency. Analysts are saying it'll level out at seventy-five percent down."

"Oh my God." I put my water bottle on the metal table. I was utterly shocked. A dark bird whisked past, banking hard toward the water. David made a small, happy sound.

"It gets worse, Bill. They also announced they're defaulting on domestic debt."

"What? Why would they default when they can just print money to pay it back? That doesn't make any sense."

"Bill, nothing these guys do makes any sense," Vadim said in a resigned tone.

"How are the markets taking it?" I asked, preparing for the worst.

"It's a complete meltdown. The bids have evaporated. A few spo-radic trades are going through anywhere from eighty to ninety-five percent down."

I ended the call without saying anything else, picked up David, and walked inside. Not in my worst nightmares had I seen this coming. Before my conversation with Vadim, I thought the market had hit bottom.

I knew in that instant that I *had* to get back to Moscow.

When I told Sabrina, she asked why I couldn't just take care of it from the hotel. I tried to explain the gravity of the situation and that it was imperative that I be in Moscow, but she just couldn't understand. I packed hastily, and when I was ready to leave, I tried to hug Sabrina, but she rebuffed me. I picked David up and gave him a tight squeeze.

I got back to Moscow that night, and when the dust finally settled the fund was nursing a $900 million loss—a 90 percent drop. *That* was bottom.

It's hard to describe what it's like to lose $900 million. I could feel it in the sides of my stomach, as if I had been emptied out from the inside. For weeks afterward, my shoulder blades tingled unpleasantly, as if I literally carried the loss on my back. And it wasn't just a financial loss. I had spent the previous two years extolling the virtues of investing in Russia and now I had let all of my investors down in spectacular fashion.

It was also a public humiliation. The same journalists who'd clamored to showcase me on the way up were now desperate to go into all the gory details of my downfall. It was as if I were the victim of a horrible car accident and every passerby was slowing down to see the carnage and the burning wreck of metal.

Yet in my mind, I had only one choice: to stay. I had to make back all the money I had lost for my clients. I wasn't going to leave Russia with my tail between my legs. That was simply not how I wanted to be remembered.

15

And We All Fall Down

I hated myself for all that had gone wrong, but remarkably many of my clients didn't. They had much bigger problems. Because domestic Russian government bonds had yielded more than 30 percent before the crisis, and most people viewed bonds as less risky than stocks, the average investor in my fund had five times as much invested in the Russian bond market as in the Hermitage Fund. Before things went off the rails, the bond returns were so enticing that many investors used leverage to buy even more. While my clients understood that in the worst case their investment in Hermitage could go down to zero, never did they think that their Russian bond portfolios could drop to nothing. Yet this is exactly what happened to many of them.

One of the biggest casualties was Beny Steinmetz, the Israeli diamond magnate who'd set me up with Edmond. As a result of his bond losses, he had to divest his interests in the Hermitage Fund and the company. Losing Beny as a partner was unfortunate, but, thankfully, Edmond was still in the picture.

Or so I thought.

In May 1999, as I was on a weekend trip to London, I picked up the *Financial Times* and read that Edmond Safra had sold Republic National Bank to HSBC, one of Britain's largest banks. Like Beny, Edmond's bank had also bet heavily on Russian bonds and lost. In an earlier phase of his life, Edmond, who had been through more market cycles than I could count, would have ridden this out, but over the previous few years he had become sick with Parkinson's disease. In the time that we were partners, I could see a steady deterioration in his condition, to the point that it was difficult even to have a conversation with him. For some reason Edmond hadn't drawn up a succession plan, so if he bowed out, there was nobody to take over. Because of this, he was forced to sell the bank as quickly as he could and HSBC stepped in to conclude a deal.

Edmond's departure hit me hard. He was one of the world's most brilliant financiers—and he was no longer involved in my business.

My personal life was also disintegrating. Things with Sabrina had gone from bad to worse since my flight from the Villa d'Este. The separation, the stress, and the distance weighed heavily on our relationship. Every time I returned to London for the weekend, we would fight. We were clearly heading toward divorce, though I tried to do everything I could to stop it. I suggested we go for counseling. We went to three different therapists, but none of them gelled for us. I tried extending my trips home to three- and four-day weekends, but she was more annoyed by my presence than pleased by it.

In spite of all this, she still planned a family break for us in August 1999. Sabrina chose a resort in Greece called the Elounda Beach Hotel. She was excited about staying there and, from the moment we arrived, was incredibly happy and nice to me. She was even sweet. This caught me off guard. I got no cold looks or arguments about work or Russia or my clients, and on the second night we even got a babysitter and left David behind to go to a local taverna. Over dinner I told her a little about Russia, and she went on and on about how wonderful David was, and for those few hours I thought, *This isn't so bad. It's like how it used to be.* I nearly asked her if anything had happened to make her demeanor change so drastically, but I decided to just go with it. I even remember her laughing at some stupid joke I made over dessert.

The following day was more of the same. We spent the whole day at the beach, playing in the sand and ordering lunch right to our chairs. As the sun set that evening with the three of us returning to the hotel room early to get David into bed, I thought that maybe, for some unknown reason, Sabrina had turned a corner and everything would work out.

After David fell asleep, I went into the bathroom to wash off the day's sunscreen and sand. When I was finished, I went to the sink, ran the hot water, and began to shave. Sabrina, who'd freshened up while I was telling David a bedtime story, was in the bedroom reading a magazine. It was the picture of a perfect family vacation.

As I was finishing up, sliding the razor up the length of my neck, Sabrina appeared in the doorway. "Bill, we have to talk."

I lowered the razor into the sink to rinse it, watching her in the mirror. "Sure. What is it?"

Calmly she said, "I no longer want to be married to you."

The razor slipped out of my hand and I fumbled to pick it up. I turned off the water, grabbed a towel, and turned to her. "What?"

"I no longer want to be married to you. I just can't do it anymore."

"But we seem to be having such a good time," I said feebly.

"We were—we are. I've been nice because, well, I've made up my mind. I don't see the point in being angry any longer." She gave me a weak smile, turned, and went back to the bed, leaving me alone with my thoughts.

I was devastated, but also relieved. We'd reached a stalemate. I didn't want to live a "normal life with a normal job" in London as she wished, and she wanted nothing to do with the crazy life I lived in Moscow. We didn't have a partnership by any objective measure, and staying together because I didn't want the marriage to fail was the wrong reason *to* stay together. In a way, I was oddly thankful that she had the guts to end it when I didn't.

We finished the rest of our Greek vacation and, in spite of the cloud hanging over our marriage, continued to enjoy each other's company and the company of our little boy. It was as if we were suddenly free to be friends again instead of estranged spouses who could barely stand each other. When the vacation was over, we went to the airport and, before parting to go to separate gates, Sabrina said, "Bill, I know this was my fault. I'm really sorry."

"It's all right," I said, thinking that while it was gracious of her to say that, I knew that I shared at least an equal portion of the blame.

"We're good people, Bill. You're a good father and I think I'm a good mother. It just wasn't meant to be."

"I know."

She kissed me on the cheek, said good-bye, and walked away, pushing David in his stroller. As I watched them leave, the feeling of loss that I was so familiar with overcame me. Once again, I had that visceral and empty feeling in my stomach, but this time it was worse. Losing love was a lot harder than losing money.

I returned to Russia. As autumn set in, Moscow felt as cold and lonely as anywhere I'd ever been. The one consolation was that in spite of the gigantic losses, my firm managed to stay up and running. Strangely, in the hedge fund business, if you're down 30 percent or 40 percent your clients will withdraw all their money and you'll be shut down in no time. However, when you're down 90 percent, as the Hermitage Fund was in 1999, most clients said to themselves, "What the hell. Might as well hold on and ride it out to see if it recovers." In spite of my disastrous performance, the fund still had $100 million under management after the crash. This generated enough fees to pay the rent and a small staff and to keep the operation running.

Except that there was literally nothing to do. From the height of the market to early 1999, trading volumes had declined 99 percent from $100 million a day to $1 million a day, and most of the fund's positions had become so illiquid that they couldn't be sold even if I'd wanted to sell. It was also impossible to arrange any meetings with existing or prospective clients. The people who had been so eager to invite me to their yachts didn't even have fifteen minutes for a cup of tea in their offices.

The most difficult part of the day was at 6:00 p.m., when business wrapped up and I made my way home. I lived in an expensively refurbished apartment not far from the Kremlin. It was fitted with a Poggenpohl kitchen and had a Jacuzzi and sauna in the bathroom. It could have been a great home, but it lacked a woman's touch and I kept almost no personal belongings there. It was a cold, sterile, and uninviting place, which just added to my isolation.

Each day bled into the next, but on December 3, after spending another day watching a moribund market, the phone rang. It was Sandy Koifman, Edmond's right-hand man. Sandy had quit Republic after HSBC took over, but we had stayed in touch. Normally his voice was deep and assertive, but as he greeted me he sounded totally different.

"Bill, I have some very bad news to share with you."

It seemed as if bad news was all I got lately. "What is it?"

"Edmond is dead." The last word was clearly hard for him to say and I could hear that Sandy—the ex–Israeli fighter pilot—was fighting back tears.

"What?"

"He's dead, Bill."

"H-how?"

"He died in a fire in his apartment in Monaco yesterday."

"A fire? What do you mean a fire?"

"The news is still sketchy," Sandy said, pulling himself together. "The police aren't releasing any details and Lily"—Edmond's wife—"is in a state of shock. From what we understand, one of his night nurses—a man—staged a false home invasion, started a fire, and Edmond and another of his nurses died of smoke inhalation in a safe room."

I was speechless. Sandy was too.

"My God, Sandy," I finally said. "This is such terrible news. . . . I'm so sorry. So, so sorry."

"Thanks, Bill. I'll be in touch when we know more. I just wanted you to hear it from me."

I hung up the phone carefully and quietly. This felt like the last straw. I'd already accepted that I'd lost Edmond as a partner, but he had been more than a partner. Edmond Safra had become my mentor and role model.

And now he was gone.

16

Tuesdays with Morrie

The year of 1999 was the worst of my life, and I hoped that the new millennium would bring some positive changes. But as New Year's came and went, it was hard to see how anything was going to get better.

It didn't help that everyone I knew in Moscow had left. I'd had a Thursday night poker game with expats and English-speaking Russians, and, at its height in mid-1997, thirteen people regularly attended. But by January 2000, I was the only one left. It was like being the last passenger at an airport baggage carousel. Everyone else had gotten their luggage and gone home, but I was standing there all by myself, watching the creaking metal track go around and around, waiting for my bag—knowing it was lost and would never show up.

I'd stayed in Moscow for one simple reason: I was going to make my clients' money back no matter what it took.

In theory, the post-crash economic conditions should have made that easy. The fund held big positions in most of Russia's oil and gas companies. These companies sold their oil in dollars but paid their costs in rubles. Their sales had not decreased, but their costs had gone down by 75 percent because of the currency crash. In simple terms, when a company's costs go down, its profits go up. I estimated that the profits of companies in our portfolio would rise by anywhere from 100 to 700 percent because of the devaluation. All else remaining equal, this should have led to a spectacular recovery in the shares of these companies.

Except all else *didn't* remain equal.

Prior to the crash, the oligarchs, who were the majority shareholders of these companies, had for the most part acted honestly toward minority shareholders. Why? Because they wanted to get what they viewed as "free money" from Wall Street. Back then, Western investment bankers told them, "We can raise lots of money for you, but if you want it, don't scandalize your investors." So, they didn't.

This arrangement worked before the crash, generally keeping the oligarchs in line. But after the crash, all the bankers who had anything to do with Russia were fired and those who weren't put their hands on their hearts and swore to their bosses that they had never even heard of Russia. When the oligarchs called their bankers in 1999 looking for that "free money," nobody answered. Overnight, they'd become pariahs. Wall Street was closed for business for the Russian oligarchs.

With no more incentive to behave, and with all these profits piling up after the devaluation, there was no longer any incentive *not* to steal. Why share the profits with minority investors? What had they done to help? Nothing.

With the brakes off, the oligarchs embarked on an orgy of stealing. The tools they used were many and with no law enforcement to stop them, their imaginations ran wild. They engaged in asset stripping, dilutions, transfer pricing, and embezzlement, to name but a few of their tricks.

This was a huge problem that every business person in Russia was obsessed with, and because I'd developed a reputation after my fight with Sidanco, in early January 2000 I was invited by the American Chamber of Commerce in Moscow to give a presentation to the local business community about corporate-governance abuse. It seemed as though I was the only person in Moscow crazy enough to speak publicly about the misdeeds of the Russian oligarchs.

I decided to use the Yukos oil company as my case study. I could have picked any Russian company, but Yukos was attractive because it had had so many minority-shareholder scandals. I called my presentation "The Armed Forces of Corporate Governance Abuse" to describe the many ways that the oligarchs went about ripping off their minority shareholders. The "Army" was transfer pricing; the "Navy," asset stripping; and the "Marines," shareholder dilutions.

The presentation was scheduled for 8:00 on a snowy morning in January. As my alarm went off at 6:30, I could barely pull myself out of bed. The temperature outside was minus-twenty degrees Celsius, the streets were covered with a fresh coat of snow, and the sun had not yet risen. Because the Moscow stock exchange didn't open until 11:00 a.m., I didn't normally get to the office until 10:30. I simply wasn't used to getting up so early. Besides, who would go to a presentation at 8:00 a.m. on a snowy morning in Moscow? I wouldn't have gone myself except that I was the speaker.

Alexei picked me up at 7:45 and drove me the short distance to the American Chamber of Commerce. When I arrived, I was surprised to find the conference room completely full. I made my way in and mingled with the crowd of indistinguishable middle-aged men in gray suits. I couldn't help but notice that in the midst of this sea of gray was a beautiful young woman in a red-and-orange dress, her hair pulled into a tight bun that rested on top of her head like a ballerina's. All of a sudden I felt that I had gotten up at the crack of dawn for a good reason. As I made my way toward the front of the room, I gravitated toward her.

When I reached her, I stuck out my hand. "Hi, I'm Bill Browder."

Her grip was firm, her fingers a little cool. "I'm Elena Molokova," she said professionally.

"What brings you here at such an early hour?"

"I'm interested in the Russian investment climate."

I handed her my business card. She reluctantly opened her purse and handed me hers. I looked down and saw that she worked for a US public relations firm that advised Mikhail Khodorkovsky, none other than the CEO of Yukos. It now made sense. I was about to rake her company's biggest client over the coals and they had sent someone to assess the damage.

"You're interested in the investment climate?" I asked, the tone of my voice perhaps betraying a bit too much surprise.

"Of course we are, Mr. Browder," she answered with a straight face.

"In that case, I'm glad you came."

I walked away with a strange feeling, as if she were pulling me back to her ever so slightly. I couldn't be sure, but there seemed to be a spark between us, and even though it was way too early in the morning, I felt newly motivated to do a good job with my speech. I went through the presentation with a lot more flair and drama than I would normally have, and it was well received. Elena, however, appeared unmoved. I glanced at her far more often than I should have while speaking, and her expression never changed: professional and unsmiling. I wanted to talk to her again when I was finished, but I was accosted by several men in the room, who acted as a barrier to Elena. I watched her colorful dress from the corner of my eye as she slid out of the door and out of my life.

But I still had her card.

It practically burned a hole in my wallet. I wanted to call her as soon as I got back to the office, but had the good sense to wait an hour. I felt a bit like a high school kid strategizing the best way to ask out a girl without appearing to be too desperate.

Her phone must have rung seven times before she picked up. She didn't sound nearly as eager to hear from me as I was to talk to her, but I still succeeded in inviting her to lunch, even if her tone of voice made it clear that she considered it to be a business meal and nothing more. What the hell, I had to start somewhere. At least my foot was in the door.

Our lunch took place a week later at a Swedish restaurant called Scandinavia, just behind Tverskaya Street near Pushkin Square. The meeting was slightly uncomfortable because neither of us knew what the other person's agenda was. I supposed she expected me to talk to her about Russian business, Yukos, and corporate governance, and she was clearly confused when I started asking more personal questions, all of which she artfully declined to answer. By the middle

of the meal we both understood that we were operating on different wavelengths, but even so, my persistence began to pay off. She didn't open up entirely, but by the time the bill came I'd learned that Elena was not merely beautiful but incredibly smart. She'd graduated at the top of her class at Moscow State University (the Russian equivalent of Harvard) and had a pair of PhDs, one in economics and the other in political science. That she was working for the enemy made her fiercely attractive to me, even more than she had been when I first laid eyes on her.

One way or another I had to find a way to get her.

If she'd been any other Russian woman, this would not have been a tough get. In Moscow, Western men, and especially those with money, were the male equivalents of supermodels. Russian girls would throw themselves at you—and into your bed—almost upon meeting. There was no sport to it at all, no chase, no courting. Just "Hi," and the next thing you knew, some slender vixen with perfect lips and mysterious eyes was wrapping herself around you as your mind calculated where the nearest bed—or private room of any kind—was.

Elena was different. She was like a professional woman you might meet in London, Paris, or New York. She didn't need a man for money, and certainly not to make her feel better about herself. Winning her would not be so easy. I wasn't discouraged, though. Soon after our lunch date I called and asked her out again, this time to dinner. I must have been doing something right. Although she didn't jump at the chance, she did agree.

We went to a Chinese restaurant called Mao and she was even more aloof than she had been before. She knew I had ulterior motive and she was being cautious. As we walked through the restaurant our table and took our seats, she seemed disinterested.

Which naturally made me want her that much more.

We made small talk for a while, and then I asked, "Have you the article in *Foreign Affairs* by Lee Wolosky? About how America should treat the oligarchs like pariahs?"

Elena wrinkled her nose in a subtle gesture of disapproval. "No, I haven't."

"It's very interesting." I took a sip of red wine. "The writer suggests that the US government should take away the oligarchs' visas so they can't go to America."

Elena had flawless porcelain-white skin and a long, regal neck, and as I spoke, little red blotches began to break out across her skin. "Why would the Americans single out Russians like that? There are plenty of bad people all over the world. It would be hypocritical," she declared, as if I'd insulted her.

"No, it wouldn't. The oligarchs are monsters and you have to start somewhere," I countered matter-of-factly.

I'd struck a nerve, and the tone of our dinner changed. Why had I brought up this *Foreign Affairs* article? I wanted to gain Elena's trust and affection, not upset her. I dropped it and tried to change the subject, but the damage was done. We parted that evening with a perfunctory double-cheek kiss. It didn't matter how much I liked her, I'd taken an unwarranted swipe at her homeland. As I walked away that night, I felt sure that I would never see her again.

For the rest of the night I couldn't stop chiding myself for screwing up the date, nor could I shake the idea that my feeble attempt at romance was a reflection of my other troubles. The fund was still struggling, the Russian economy was on its knees, and it looked as if the oligarchs were about to steal every last penny left in the fund. I was screaming into the wind, not only with my work but with this unattainable woman as well. I climbed into bed racked by anxious energy. After about an hour of tossing and turning I picked up the phone and dialed my friend Alan Cullison from the *Wall Street Journal*. It was around midnight but that didn't matter. Alan was always up late and I could count on him to talk. I told him about my unsuccessful date and he played along, offering me the usual condolences. Then, about midway through my story, I mentioned Elena by name.

"Wait—you got a date with Elena Molokova?" Alan interrupted.

"Two dates, actually."

"Shit, Bill, that's an accomplishment in itself. Lots of people are after her."

"Yeah, well, I guess they'll get her. I blew it."

"Eh, who cares. . . . There's a million good-looking girls in Moscow."

I shrugged and said quietly, "Yes, but not like this one."

Alan didn't have much sympathy for me, and after a while longer we hung up. I eventually fell asleep and woke the next morning determined to go about my life. I would simply try to forget about Elena. I was a busy guy who had a lot of work to do, and there *were* other women out there, if that's what I wanted. . . .

Only that wasn't what I wanted. Try as I might, I could not forget Elena, and a week after our dinner at Mao I decided that I had to do something to salvage the situation.

But what? How could I reach out without seeming desperate or pathetic? All I could remember, other than her disappointment in my beliefs regarding the oligarchs, was the story of how Elena's father died. It had happened three years earlier when he'd suffered a sudden and unexpected heart attack. His death caught her completely off guard, and I remembered her saying that the worst thing about it was that she never got to say good-bye. Too many things were left unsaid.

The story of her father's death reminded me of a book I'd recently read called *Tuesdays with Morrie*. I wrote a short note to Elena and stuck it in the front cover of my copy. I wrapped it up and had Alexei deliver it to her office. The note read:

Dear Elena,

After you told me about your father, I couldn't help but think of you in relation to this book. It's about a dying man who's trying to say all the things he wants to say before he no longer would be able to. I don't know if you have the time to read it, but I hope you do because it might touch you the way it touched me.

Warmly,

Bill

Frankly, this was a long shot, even though the book truly did have a great effect on me. It was simple, direct, and incredibly moving. But as I sent it to her, I was afraid she would see it as something different, like a small Trojan horse I was using to try to infiltrate her heart.

Another week passed with no word and I was sure that I'd missed the mark entirely. But then a week later, Svetlana leaned across her desk and said, "Bill—there's a phone call from Elena Molokova."

My heart jumped and I took the call. "Hello?"

"Hello, Bill."

"Hi, Elena. Did you . . . did you get the book I sent?"

"I did."

"And did you have a chance to read it?"

"I did." Her voice was softer than it had been before. I couldn't be sure, but it sounded as if a layer of toughness had been peeled back.

"And did you like it?"

She sighed. "I liked it a lot, Bill. I just finished it. Just now. It really spoke to me. Thank you."

"I'm glad. I mean, you're welcome."

"It was surprising too." Her tone changed ever so slightly, wandering into a personal space where she hadn't yet led me.

"Oh? How's that?"

"Well, I didn't take you for such a sensitive man, Bill. Not at all." I could hear her smile through the phone.

"I'm not sure I am very sensitive, to be truthful." There was a pause. "Tell me, would you . . . would you like to have dinner again?"

"Yes, I would. I would like that very much."

A couple nights later I met Elena at Mario's, an expensive Italian restaurant frequented by the Russian Mafia, but which also featured

Moscow's best Italian food. I arrived first and took a seat at the bar, and when the maître d' brought Elena over, I had to look twice. She was transformed. Her flaxen hair was no longer tied in a bun but rested softly on her shoulders. Her lipstick was redder than before, and her black dress was simultaneously tighter and classier than anything I'd seen her in before. She wasn't just beautiful. She was sexy. It was clear that for her, this was *really* our first date.

We sat and had dinner. We didn't talk about Russian oligarchs or corporate governance or business practices; we just talked about our families and our lives and our aspirations—what everyone talks about when they're getting to know someone. It was great. Before we said good-bye that night, I grabbed her around the waist and pulled her toward me, and without any resistance we shared our first real kiss.

After that we spoke every day, and I would have been happy to see her every day too, but she had time to see me only once a week or even once every two weeks. We carried on like this for three months—nice dinners, nicer conversation, a real kiss before going our separate ways. I wanted more and it seemed that she did too, but I couldn't figure out how to get past her defenses. So I decided that I had to do something rash and romantic.

The May holidays—a big deal in Russia, when everything shuts down for ten days—were fast approaching. One afternoon I called her. "How would you like to go to Paris with me for the holiday?"

She hesitated. I surely wasn't the first man to ask if I could whisk her away for an impromptu getaway, and we both knew what would happen if she said yes. After a few seconds she said, "Let me think about it, Bill."

Ten minutes later she called back. "I'd love to come with you if I can get a visa." A warm feeling welled in my chest and stomach as I heard *I'd love to*, but it was quickly tempered by the words *if I can get a visa*. Getting West European visas for Russian girls under the age of thirty was no small feat. It usually required a few weeks and a mountain of documentation to show that the applicant had no intention of staying in the West. Making it worse, we had only four days before the start of the holidays to sort it out.

Elena called some travel agents. Luckily, one was organizing a group tour to Paris and was on her way to the French embassy that afternoon with thirty passports for visas. If Elena could deliver the paperwork in time, she had a shot at getting her visa quickly. She put everything together and, amazingly, her application was approved the next day. Less than a week after I'd asked her, we were sitting next to each other on an Air France flight bound for Paris.

In an attempt to impress Elena, I booked a suite at the Hôtel Le Bristol, one of the nicest and most lavish hotels in France, if not the world. A pair of white-gloved bellhops took our two small bags and escorted us to our room. I walked behind Elena down the blue-carpeted halls decorated with Louis XV armchairs and wall sconces, peeking over her shoulder to gauge her response. She had a slight smile on her face, but she always seemed to have a slight smile on her face, no matter what her mood. We reached our room. The first bellhop opened the door, and we walked into one of the most impressive hotel rooms I'd ever been in, and by then I'd been in quite a few. I tipped the bellhops and uttered my thanks in my regrettable French and turned to Elena.

She was not impressed, or if she was, the same slight smile masked it perfectly. "Let's go out," she said.

We freshened up and made our way downstairs to Avenue Matignon. Paris is made for strolling, so we walked slowly, talking now and then about nothing in particular. We held hands at intervals, but never long enough to give me comfort that I'd finally won her over. The sky grew more ominous as we walked, and as we turned onto the Champs-Élysées, the clouds overhead were heavy and looked ready to let loose. "I can smell the rain coming," Elena said.

"Me too."

We picked a café that had umbrellas over its outdoor tables and sat. The waiter brought warm bread and I ordered a bottle of Bordeaux. We had mussels in white wine and a big bowl of *frites*. The rain held off. I ordered a crème brûlée and a pot of English breakfast tea, and when the dessert arrived, fat raindrops began to pelt the sidewalk and the umbrellas in a staccato rhythm. The umbrella was not big, so I scooted my chair around the table and wrapped my arm around Elena's waist in an attempt to keep her dry. We giggled like schoolkids as the sky opened up and the rain fell in a heavy spring downpour. I pulled Elena directly into my lap, and she wrapped her arms over mine and we squeezed each other.

At that moment I knew that she was all mine, and that I was all hers.

17

Stealing Analysis

It's amazing how being in love changes things. When Elena and I
returned to Moscow, I was totally reenergized. With Elena at my side,
I felt as though I could take on any challenge.

At the time, my overriding concern was to stop the massive theft
taking place in the companies in the fund's portfolio. The Hermitage Fund had already lost 90 percent of its value from the Russian
default, and now the oligarchs were in the process of stealing the
remaining 10 percent. If I didn't do something, the fund would be left
with absolutely nothing.

These thefts were happening in every business sector, from banking to natural resources, but the company that truly distinguished itself was Russia's largest—the oil and gas giant Gazprom.

In terms of output and strategic significance, Gazprom was one of
the world's most important companies. Yet the entire market value of
the company—$12 billion—was smaller than your average midsize
US oil and gas firm. In terms of hydrocarbon reserves, Gazprom was
eight times the size of ExxonMobil and twelve times bigger than BP,
the largest oil companies in the world—yet it traded at a 99.7 percent
discount to those companies per barrel of reserves.

Why was it so cheap? The simple answer was that most investors
thought that 99.7 percent of the company's assets had been stolen.
But how could virtually all of one of the world's largest companies
even *be* stolen? No one knew for sure, but everyone accepted it as
fact.

Even though I knew how crooked the Russians could be, I couldn't accept that Gazprom's management had stolen the whole thing. If I could somehow prove that the market was wrong, then there was a lot of money to be made. I needed to study this company and figure out what was really going on. What I needed to do was a "stealing analysis."

But how do you do a stealing analysis of a Russian company? This wasn't something they taught at Stanford Business School. I obviously couldn't confront Gazprom's management directly. I also couldn't ask the research analysts at any of the major international investment banks. All that mattered to them was fee-paying work, meaning their lips were so firmly planted on the asses of Gazprom's management that they would never publicly acknowledge the egregious thefts going on under their noses.

As I thought about how to proceed, I realized that my experience at BCG was worth something in this situation. As a management consultant I'd learned that the best way to answer difficult questions was to find the people who knew the answers and interview them.

So I made a list of people who knew things about Gazprom: competitors, customers, suppliers, ex-employees, government regulators, and so on. I then invited each of them to a breakfast, lunch, dinner, tea, coffee, or dessert. I didn't want to scare them off prematurely, so I didn't tell them my whole agenda. I just said that I was a Western investor interested in talking to them. Surprisingly, about three-quarters of the roughly forty people I invited agreed to meet.

My first meeting was with the head of planning at one of Gazprom's small domestic competitors. Bald and slightly overweight, he wore a Soviet watch and a rumpled gray suit. Vadim and I met him for lunch at an Italian restaurant called Dorian Gray, directly across the Moscow River from Bolotnaya Square.

After the usual introductory chitchat, I said bluntly, "We wanted to talk to you because we're trying to figure out what's been stolen from Gazprom. You're one of the experts in the field, and I was wondering if you might be willing to share some of your knowledge with us?"

There was a moment of silence and I thought maybe I'd crossed a line. But then his face lit up. He placed his hands on the white table-cloth and leaned forward. "I am so glad you've asked. Gazprom management is the biggest bunch of crooks you could imagine. They're stealing everything."

"Such as?" Vadim asked.

"Take Tarkosaleneftegaz," the man said, banging his spoon on the table. "They took it right out of Gazprom."

Vadim asked, "What's Tarko—"

"Tarko Saley," the man said, cutting Vadim off. "It's a gas field in the Yamalo-Nenets region. It has something like four hundred billion cubic meters of gas."

Vadim got out his calculator and converted this number into barrels of oil equivalent.[1] The number he got—2.7 billion barrels of oil—meant that Tarko Saley was bigger than the reserves of the US oil company Occidental Petroleum, a $9 billion company.

I have pretty thick skin, but taking a company worth $9 billion right out of Gazprom shocked me. As the man went through the details, he named names, gave dates, and told us about other major gas fields that were being stolen. We followed up with as many questions as we could think of and filled seven pages of a Black n' Red notebook. We eventually had to end lunch after two hours, otherwise he would have gone on forever.

Without knowing it, I'd stumbled upon one of the most important cultural phenomena of post-Soviet Russia—the exploding wealth gap. In Soviet times, the richest person in Russia was about six times richer than the poorest. Members of the Politburo might have had a bigger apartment, a car, and a nice dacha, but not much more than that. However, by the year 2000 the richest person had become *250,000 times* richer than the poorest person. This wealth disparity was created in such a short period of time that it poisoned the psy-

---

1   Barrel of oil equivalent, or BOE, is a unit of energy used to compare cubic meters
    of gas to barrels of oil.

chology of the nation. People were so angry that they were ready to spill their guts to anyone who wanted to talk about it.

Most of our other meetings went roughly the same way. We met a gas industry consultant who told us about another stolen gas field. We had a meeting with a gas pipeline executive who recounted how Gazprom had diverted all of its gas sales in the former Soviet Union to a murky intermediary. We met with an ex-employee who described how Gazprom had made large, below-market loans to friends of management. In all, we filled two notebooks with damning allegations of theft and fraud.

If you were to believe all the information we collected, this was probably the largest theft in the history of business. Only there was one big catch. We had no idea if any of these allegations were true. The things people were saying could easily have been sour grapes, exaggeration, or deliberate misinformation. We needed to find a way to verify what we had heard.

But how could we verify anything in Russia? Wasn't that the essence of the problem we were facing with Gazprom in the first place? Wasn't Russia a place that was so extremely opaque that you sometimes felt as though you couldn't even see your hand in front of your face?

It appeared that way, but in reality, it wasn't so opaque at all. All you needed to do was scratch the surface to find that Russia was strangely one of the most transparent places in the world. You just needed to know how to get the information, and we learned this almost by accident a few weeks after we'd finished the Gazprom interviews.

Vadim was driving his VW Golf to work when traffic ground to a halt where the Boulevard Ring meets Tverskaya at Pushkin Square. At that junction, every car has to turn either left or right, creating near-permanent gridlock at most times of the day. With motorists stuck in their cars for as long as an hour, a small army of enterprising street urchins had popped up to sell anything from pirated DVDs to newspapers to cigarette lighters.

While Vadim sat there that day, a boy approached the car brandishing his wares. Vadim wasn't interested, but the boy persisted.

"All right, what are you selling?" Vadim asked warily.

The boy held open his dirty blue parka to reveal a collection of CD-ROMs in a plastic portfolio. "I've got databases."

Vadim's ears perked up. "What kind of databases?"

"All kinds. Mobile phone directories, tax return records, traffic violations, pension fund info, you name it."

"Interesting. How much?"

"Depends. Anywhere from five to fifty dollars."

Vadim squinted at the small print on the collection of discs in this kid's portfolio and spotted one entitled "Moscow Registration Chamber Database." Vadim did a double take. The Moscow Registration Chamber is the organization that tracks and collects information about who owns all Moscow-based companies.

Vadim pointed to the disc. "How much for that one?"

"That? Eh . . . five dollars."

Vadim gave the boy a $5 bill and took the disc.

As soon as Vadim got to the office, he went to his computer to see if he'd just spent $5 on a blank disc. But just as the boy had promised, a menu appeared allowing Vadim to search for the beneficial ownership of every single company in Moscow.

It was at that moment that we discovered the second most interesting cultural phenomenon in Russia—that it was one of the most bureaucratic places in the world. Because of Soviet central planning, Moscow needed data on every single facet of life so its bureaucrats could decide on everything from how many eggs were needed in Krasnoyarsk to how much electricity was needed in Vladivostok. The fact that the Soviet regime had fallen hadn't changed anything— Moscow's ministries continued to exist, and their bureaucracies took great pains to account for everything for which they were responsible.

After Vadim's chance run-in on Pushkin Square, we quickly became adept at finding all sorts of other data to help us cross-check the allegations we'd collected in the Gazprom interviews. Using these databases, we calculated that the management of Gazprom had sold seven major gas fields between 1996 and 1999 for next to nothing.

These asset transfers weren't merely huge, they were brazen, and they were done without the slightest sense of shame. The new owners of the stolen property did nothing to even try to hide their ownership.

One of the more blatant examples was the story of Sibneftegaz, a subsidiary of Gazprom. Sibneftegaz, a Siberian gas producer, obtained licenses for a gas field containing 1.6 billion barrels of oil equivalent in 1998. Based on an extremely conservative estimate, we determined this subsidiary was worth about $530 million, yet a group of buyers was allowed to buy 53 percent of Sibneftegaz for a total of $1.3 million—a 99.5 percent discount to our calculation of its fair value!

Who were these fortunate buyers? One was Gennady Vyakhirev, the brother of Gazprom's CEO, Rem Vyakhirev. Gennady, along with his son Andrey, used a company to buy 5 percent of Sibneftegaz for $87,600.

Another 18 percent block was bought for $158,000 by a company partially owned by a Victor Bryanskih, who was a manager in Gazprom's strategic-development department. A further 10 percent of Sibneftegaz was bought by a company owned by Vyacheslav Kuznetsov and his wife, Natalie. Vyacheslav was the head of Gazprom's internal audit department, the very department that was supposed to detect and stop this type of thing from happening in the first place.

We uncovered six other major asset transfers using similar techniques. When Vadim added up all the oil and gas reserves that had left Gazprom's balance sheet, he found that Gazprom had effectively given away reserves equivalent to the size of Kuwait's. Full-scale wars had been fought over far less.

What was most astonishing, though, was that while these oil and gas reserves were huge, Vadim determined they represented only *9.65 percent* of Gazprom's total reserves. In other words, more than 90 percent of Gazprom's reserves had *not* been stolen. No other investors understood this. The markets had assumed that literally every last cubic meter of gas and every drop of oil had been pilfered from the company, which was why it traded at a 99.7 percent discount to its Western peers. But we had just proved that *more than 90 percent was still there*—and no one else knew it.

What should an investor do in a situation like this? I'll tell you what: you buy the shit out of that stock.

In a world where people fight tooth and nail to make 20 percent, we'd just found something that might generate 1,000 percent, or even 5,000 percent. It was so obvious, that the fund increased its investment in Gazprom right up to the 20 percent limit, the largest percentage for a single stock that the fund allowed.

For most investment professionals, this is where you would stop. You do your analysis, make your investment, and then wait for others to discover what you've learned. But I couldn't do that. Our discoveries about Gazprom were too great. I had to share them with the world.

I then did something very unusual in my profession. I divided the Gazprom dossier into six sections and gave each one to a major Western news outlet. The reporters and editors at these outlets immediately saw the impact this story would have, and our research was so exhaustive that they couldn't resist. We'd saved them months of investigative work, and it didn't take long for them to turn our research into a slew of staggering articles.

The first appeared in the *Wall Street Journal* on October 24, 2000, entitled "Gas Guzzler?" It described how the stolen gas fields had enough natural gas "to keep all of Europe going for five years." The next day, the *Financial Times* came out with its story, "Gazprom Directors to Meet over Governance." This article detailed all of the "friends and family" transactions at Gazprom. On October 28, the *New York Times* published "Directors Act on Asset Sales at Gazprom" in its international-business section. Less than a month later, on November 20, *BusinessWeek* published "Gazprom on the Grill." And on December 24, the *Washington Post* published "Asset Transfers May Provide Challenge to Putin."

The public in Russia and abroad was shocked by the level of corruption at Gazprom. Over the next six months, there were more than 500 articles in Russian and 275 in English, all reporting what we had exposed at Gazprom.

This coverage had a noticeable effect in Russia. Russians accepted the concept of corruption and graft in the abstract, but when they were given concrete examples of who was getting money and how much they were getting, they were furious. So furious, the Russian Parliament called for debates in January 2001 about the situation at Gazprom. These led to a recommendation for the Audit Chamber, Russia's equivalent to the US General Accounting Office, to conduct its own investigation of Gazprom.

Responding to the Audit Chamber's investigation, Gazprom's board of directors commissioned PricewaterhouseCoopers, the big American accounting firm, to conduct an independent review.

After several weeks, the Audit Chamber announced the results of its investigation. Perhaps not too surprisingly, it said that they hadn't found anything wrong with the conduct of Gazprom's management. It justified the asset transfers by saying, "Gazprom was capital constrained and needed the outside capital."

All that was left was the PwC report. This accounting firm was making millions of dollars off Gazprom as its auditor, so any indictment of Gazprom would have been an indictment of itself. Sure enough, it also exonerated Gazprom's actions. It came up with obtuse and irrational arguments to explain why all the things that we'd exposed were reasonable and legal.

While these were not completely unexpected outcomes, I was so fed up with everything that I didn't want to be anywhere near Moscow when Gazprom held its annual general meeting on June 30, 2001. I knew that in spite of all we'd exposed, the management would strut around like proud peacocks, telling the world how well managed the company was.

I wanted to avoid the whole spectacle, so I asked Elena if she wanted to get away from Moscow for a long weekend. She had just finished a big project at work and agreed, so I booked two tickets to Istanbul, one of the few desirable places we could go without Elena's having to get a visa.

We flew on the day of Gazprom's annual meeting, and after arriving at Atatürk Airport we took a taxi to the Ciragan Palace Hotel, a former sultan's palace on the European side of the Bosporus. It was a beautiful summer day. We went to the veranda next to the pool and ate lunch under a huge white umbrella, with the sun beating down. Ships of all sizes slowly passed below as they made their way in and out of the Sea of Marmara. It had only been a three-hour flight, but the exotic sights and sounds of Turkey, combined with Elena's soothing presence, made me feel a million miles away from the dirty dishonesty of Russia.

As we ordered mint tea and dessert, my mobile phone rang. I didn't want to answer, but it was Vadim, so I did.

And he had the most amazing news.

Gazprom's management wasn't strutting around their annual general meeting at all. Rem Vyakhirev had just been fired as CEO by none other than President Vladimir Putin.

Putin replaced Vyakhirev with a virtually unknown man named Alexey Miller. No sooner had Miller taken office than he announced that he would secure the remaining assets on Gazprom's balance sheet and recover what had been stolen. In response to that, the stock price went up 134 percent in one day.

In the following two years, it doubled again. Then, it doubled again . . . and *again*. By 2005, Gazprom was up a hundred times from the price at which the Hermitage Fund had purchased its first shares. Not 100 percent—*one hundred times*. Our little campaign had gotten rid of one of the country's dirtiest oligarchs. It was, without question, the single best investment I have ever been involved with in my life.

18

Fifty Percent

Aside from work and spending time with Elena, one of the things I most enjoyed in Moscow was playing tennis, which I did often.

One cold Saturday in February 2002, I was running late for a game with a broker friend. Alexei was driving fast, and Elena and I sat in the backseat of the Blazer holding hands. As the car approached the final stretch of road that led to the tennis bubble, I saw a large, dark object in the middle of the street. Cars were swerving left and right to avoid it. I thought it was a canvas bag that had fallen off a truck, but as we got closer, I saw that it was not a bag at all, but a man.

"Alexei, stop," I shouted.

He didn't say anything or show any indication of slowing down.

"Goddammit, stop!" I insisted, and he reluctantly pulled the car next to the man. I opened my door and jumped out. Elena followed, and when Alexei saw there was no way out of this situation, he got out too. I knelt next to the man, cars zipping by and horns honking. He wasn't bleeding but was unconscious, and I noticed that he was twitching and foam was bubbling from his mouth. I didn't know what had happened, but at least he was alive.

I bent down and looped my arm under one of his shoulders. Alexei took his other shoulder, and Elena grabbed his feet. Together we moved him to the side of the road.

Once we were on the sidewalk, we found a soft bank of snow and gently laid him down. He started to come around. "Epilepsia," we heard him mumble. "Epilepsia."

"You're going to be okay," Elena told him in Russian, patting his arm.

Somebody must have called an emergency number because just then three police cars arrived. Shockingly, the officers paid no attention to the man and started thumping across the sidewalk looking for someone to blame. After hearing me speak in English and concluding I was a foreigner, they moved on to the Russians in the crowd who'd gathered around. The cops then converged on Alexei, whom they accused of hitting the man with our car. The injured man, who was at this point completely conscious, tried to explain that he hadn't been hit and that Alexei was trying to help, but the police ignored him. They demanded Alexei's documents and forced him to puff into a Breathalyzer. They then had a heated argument with Alexei that lasted fifteen minutes. Finally, when they were satisfied that nothing was wrong, they got back in their squad cars and drove off. The man thanked us and got into an ambulance that had arrived while Alexei was speaking with the police, and we piled back into the Blazer.

As we drove off, Alexei explained why he'd been so reluctant to help, as Elena translated: "This is what always happens in Russia. It doesn't matter if that guy was even hit or not. Once the police get involved, they will blame someone and that's the end of the story."

Thankfully, because Alexei had been a colonel in the traffic police, he was able to extricate himself. But for the average Muscovite, a single act of Good Samaritan–ship could lead to a seven-year prison sentence. And every Russian knew this.

This was the story of Russia.

I went to my tennis match, but as hard as I tried, I couldn't get the incident out of my head. What if we hadn't stopped? Sooner or later a car wouldn't have swerved and the man would have been severely injured or killed. Similar situations must have played out all over Russia every day, and this thought made me shudder. This perverse scenario wasn't just confined to road safety, either. It happened in all walks of life: business, real estate, health care, the school yard, you name it. Anywhere that bad things happened, people would not get involved in order to save their own skin. It wasn't that people weren't civic-minded, it was just that the price for intervention would be punishment, not praise.

Perhaps I should have viewed this incident as an omen. Perhaps I should have minded my own business in Russia and not tried to fix the corrupt companies in which I was investing. But I believed that I could help. Because I wasn't Russian—the police had ignored me as soon as they heard me speaking English—I believed I could do things that a Russian in my position would have never been allowed to do.

• • •

Which explains why, after seeing how well our campaign worked at Gazprom, I decided to go after corruption in other big companies in our portfolio. I went after UES, the national electricity company, and Sberbank, the national savings bank, to name just two. As with Gazprom, I spent months investigating how the stealing was taking place. I packaged the results into easily understandable presentations and then shared these presentations with the international media.

As with Gazprom, once the campaigns reached a fever pitch, Putin's government would generally step in to flex its muscles.

After I revealed that the CEO of UES was trying to sell his company's assets at a huge discount to various oligarchs, the Kremlin put a moratorium on asset sales. After I sued Sberbank and its board of directors for selling cheap shares to insiders and friends at the exclusion of minority shareholders, Russia changed the law on abusive share issues.

You may wonder why Vladimir Putin allowed me to do these things in the first place. The answer is that for a while our interests coincided. When Putin became president in January 2000, he was granted the title of President of the Russian Federation, but the actual power of the presidency had been hijacked by oligarchs, regional governors, and organized-crime groups. As soon as he took office, it became his highest priority to wrest power from these men and return it to its rightful place in the Kremlin, or more accurately, into his own hands.

Basically, when it came to me and my anti-corruption campaigns, Putin was operating on the political maxim of "Your enemy's enemy is your friend," so he would make regular use of my work as a pretext to knock his oligarch enemies off-balance.

I was so wrapped up in my own success and the runaway returns of the fund that I didn't understand this. I naively thought that Putin was acting in the national interest and was genuinely trying to clean up Russia.

Many people have asked why the oligarchs didn't just kill me for exposing their corruption. It's a good question. In Russia, people get killed for a lot less. It was a completely lawless society where anything could happen, and where anything often did happen.

What saved me was not anyone's fear of the law, but paranoia. Russia is a country that lives on conspiracy theories. There are layers upon layers of explanations for why things happen, and none of them is straightforward. In the mind of an average Russian, it was inconceivable that an unassuming American guy who barely spoke Russian would aggressively be going after Russia's most powerful oligarchs on his own. The only plausible explanation was that I must have been operating as a proxy for someone powerful. Considering how each of my battles with the oligarchs led to an intervention by Putin or his government, most people assumed that this someone was none other than Vladimir Putin himself. It was a ridiculous thought. I had never met Putin in my life. But because everyone thought I was "Putin's guy," no one touched me.

The upshot of our campaigns and Putin's interventions was a spectacular recovery in my fund. By the end of 2003, the fund had gone up more than 1,200 percent from the bottom of the market. I'd recovered all of the losses from 1998. It had taken five years and a Herculean struggle, but I'd achieved my goal of pulling my clients out of that terrible hole. In addition to vindicating myself, I also felt that I'd discovered the perfect business model: not only was I making lots of money, but I was also helping to make Russia a better place. There are very few jobs in the world that allow you both to make money *and* do good at the same time, but I had one of them.

It seemed as if it was all too good to be true, and it was.

Early one Saturday morning in October 2003, as I was running on the treadmill in my apartment watching CNN, a breaking-news headline came across the screen saying that Mikhail Khodorkovsky, the CEO of Yukos and Russia's richest man, had been arrested.

I jumped off the treadmill, wiped the sweat from my brow, and hurried to the kitchen, where Elena was preparing breakfast. "Have you heard the news?" I shouted, still out of breath.

"Yes. I just heard it on the radio. It's unbelievable."

"What do you think will happen?"

"I don't know. I can't imagine that he'll be in jail by Monday morning. Rich people don't tend to spend much time in jail in Russia."

My emotions were mixed about Khodorkovsky's arrest. In the short term, the Russian market would take a big hit and my fund would lose money if he stayed in jail for even a few days. Longer term, however, if he miraculously stayed in jail and this was to be the beginning of a crackdown on the oligarchs, it meant that Russia had a chance at becoming a normal country. Ultimately, that would be a good thing, not just for the fund, but for everyone living in Russia.

When I arrived at the office on Monday morning, Khodorkovsky was still in jail, and the market opened at 10 percent down. His arrest and detention was on the front page of every major newspaper in the world. My clients started panicking, and I fielded calls from them all day. What did this mean? What was going to happen next? Should they take their money out of Russia?

I didn't know—nobody did. It all came down to the personal negotiation between Vladimir Putin and Mikhail Khodorkovsky, a negotiation in which neither law nor logic played any role.

For reasons that no one will ever really know, this negotiation went badly for Khodorkovsky, and he was still in jail by the end of the week. Then the Russian government escalated matters by seizing Khodorkovsky's 36 percent block of Yukos.

This was unprecedented. Not only was it a personal disaster for Khodorkovsky, but for the whole financial market. The fear of expropriation sat at the back of every investor's mind, and now it was happening under Vladimir Putin. Over the next four business days, the market slid a further 16.5 percent, and Yukos lost 27.7 percent of its value.

Why was Putin doing this? The most popular theory was that Khodorkovsky had broken Putin's golden rule: "Stay out of politics, and you can keep your ill-gotten gains." Khodorkovsky had violated this maxim when he'd sent millions of dollars to the opposition parties for the upcoming parliamentary elections, and when he had begun to make statements that were clearly anti-Putin. Putin is a man who believes in symbols, and since Khodorkovsky had overstepped the mark, Putin had to make an example out of him.

As if to drive this home, Putin engaged in a full-scale witch-hunt against anyone connected to Khodorkovsky. In the weeks that followed his arrest, Russian law enforcement agencies went after the political parties he'd financed, his charities, and scores of his employees.

In June 2004, Khodorkovsky and his business partner, Platon Lebedev, were put on trial and convicted of six counts of fraud, two of tax evasion, and one of theft. Each was sentenced to nine years in prison. Since this was all about symbolism, Putin did something unprecedented: he allowed television cameras in the courtroom to film Russia's richest man as he sat silently in the courtroom cage.

It was a powerful image. Imagine you're Russia's seventeenth-richest oligarch. You're on your yacht moored off the Hôtel du Cap in Antibes, France. You've just finished screwing your mistress and you wander out of your stateroom to the galley to pick up two glasses of Cristal champagne and some caviar. You grab your remote and switch on CNN. There, right before your eyes, you see one of your peers—a man who is far richer, smarter, and more powerful than you—sitting in a cage.

What would your natural reaction be? What would you do?

Anything to make certain that you don't end up in that cage.

After Khodorkovsky was found guilty, most of Russia's oligarchs went one by one to Putin and said, "Vladimir Vladimirovich, what can I do to make sure I won't end up sitting in a cage?"

I wasn't there, so I'm only speculating, but I imagine Putin's response was something like this: "Fifty percent."

Not 50 percent to the government or 50 percent to the presidential administration, but 50 percent to Vladimir Putin. I don't know this for sure. It could have been 30 percent or 70 percent or some other arrangement. What I do know for sure was that after Khodorkovsky's conviction, my interests and Putin's were no longer aligned. He had made the oligarchs his "bitches," consolidated his power, and, by many estimates, become the richest man in the world.

Unfortunately, I wasn't paying enough attention to see that Putin and I were on a collision course. After Khodorkovsky's arrest and conviction I didn't alter my behavior at all. I carried on exactly as before—naming and shaming Russian oligarchs. There was a difference this time, though. Now, instead of going after Putin's enemies, I was going after Putin's own economic interests.

You might wonder why I couldn't see this. It all came back to that incident with the man in the road. The police had ignored me that day because I wasn't Russian. I believed that, because I was a foreigner, I was somehow exempt from the informal rules that governed everyone else's lives in Russia. If I had been a Russian citizen engaging in my anti-corruption work, I would certainly have been arrested, beaten, or murdered.

But Putin was not as brazen then as he is now. Back then killing a foreigner would have been too drastic a move. And putting me in prison would have made Putin just as much of a hostage to the situation as I was. If he did this, every Western head of state would have been forced to spend a third of their meetings with Putin arguing for my release. In the end, Putin came up with a compromise that satisfied everyone in his circle—on November 13, 2005, upon returning to Moscow from London, I was stopped in the VIP lounge at Sheremetyevo-2, detained for fifteen hours, and expelled from the country.

19

A Threat to National Security

As soon as I got off my deportation flight from Moscow, I began making calls to try to figure out what had gone wrong. Elena, who was eight months pregnant, tried helping me in any way she could. I'd spent the previous ten years painstakingly building my business brick by brick, forgoing a social life, obsessing about every move in the stock market, treating weekends like workdays, all to create a $4.5 billion investment-advisory business. I couldn't let the cancellation of my visa destroy it in one fell swoop.

My first call was to a well-connected immigration lawyer in London. He listened to my story and was intrigued. He'd just heard that another British citizen, Bill Bowring, a human rights lawyer, had been denied entry to Russia on the day after me and suspected that my expulsion was a case of mistaken identity. I thought that was pretty far-fetched, but this *was* Russia we were dealing with.

My next call was to HSBC, my business partner after Edmond had sold the bank. As an enormous bureaucratic bank, it'd been wholly uninspiring when it came to moneymaking, but it was world-class when it came to dealing with the British establishment.

I first spoke to the CEO of HSBC's private bank, Clive Bannister. Within fifteen minutes he connected me to Sir Roderic Lyne, a former British ambassador to Russia who was on retainer to HSBC for issues like these. Sir Roderic promised to help me navigate the departmental maze of the British government. Fifteen minutes after speaking to him, I had an appointment with Simon Smith, head of the Russia Directorate of the Foreign and Commonwealth Office, Britain's version of the State Department.

A couple of days later I made my way to the Foreign Office building in London, an ornate and imposing neoclassical building on King Charles Street, just down the road from No. 10 Downing Street. After announcing myself at the reception area, I was escorted across a big courtyard to the main entrance. Inside were vaulted ceilings, marble columns, and Victorian imperial details. The place had been designed at the height of the British Empire to intimidate and awe visitors, and although I had met with many corporate CEOs, politicians, and billionaires, it had that same effect on me.

Simon Smith arrived a few minutes later. He was about five years older than me with thick, graying hair and wireless glasses that framed a ruddy face. "Hello, Mr. Browder. So glad you could make it," he said jovially with an educated British accent. We sat and he poured tea from a blue-and-white china pot for each of us. As the smell of Ceylon tea filled the room, Smith said, "So, it sounds as if you've got yourself into a bit of trouble with our friends in Moscow."

"Yes, it seems that way."

"Well, actually, you'll be happy to know that we're already on the case," he said professionally. "Our minister for Europe is in Moscow right now. He's planning to raise your case tomorrow with Putin's foreign policy adviser, Sergei Prikhodko."

That sounded reassuring. "Wonderful. When do you think we might know something from that meeting?"

Smith shrugged. "Soon, I hope." Then he leaned in and held his cup with both hands. "Bill, there's one important thing here, though."

"Yes?"

"I watched your shareholders' rights campaigns with great admiration when I was at the embassy in Moscow, and I know how successfully you used the press to advance your causes. But in this situation you absolutely *must* keep this away from the press. If this story is given a public airing, we won't be able to help you. The

Russians will dig in their heels and your issue will never be resolved. Russians always need a way to save face."

I put down my tea and tried not to show my discomfort. Following this advice would be a totally unnatural thing for me to do. But here I was facing the biggest problem in my professional career, with the British government ready to weigh in on my behalf. I understood that I had to honor Smith's request, so I agreed and we wrapped up the meeting.

The next afternoon, Smith called with an update. "Prikhodko said he has no idea why you were deported, but promised to look into it." Smith said this as if he were delivering good news. I thought it was pretty unlikely that Putin's top foreign policy adviser would be unaware of the expulsion of the largest foreign investor in Russia.

"And Bill," Smith continued, "we've decided to get our ambassador in Moscow, Tony Brenton, involved. He'd like to speak with you as soon as possible."

The next day I called Ambassador Brenton. I started to tell him my story, but after a few seconds he cut me off. "No need to carry on, Bill. I know all about you and Hermitage. I think the Russians are being quite stupid in alienating an important investor like you."

"I'm hoping it's a mistake."

"Me too. I have to say, I'm reasonably optimistic this visa situation will be resolved once I speak to the right people. Sit tight. You're in good hands."

I couldn't help but feel that I *had* indeed landed in good hands. I liked Ambassador Brenton. Like Smith, he sounded genuine in wanting to solve this problem. I didn't know if losing my visa was a case of mistaken identity, or if one of the targets from my anti-corruption campaigns was exacting revenge, but I felt that with the British government on my side, I would ultimately prevail.

The first thing Ambassador Brenton did was to send a request to the Russian Foreign Ministry asking for a formal explanation. If my visa cancellation was indeed due to a mix-up of names, this would become apparent immediately.

A week later, Ambassador Brenton's secretary called to say that they'd received a reply from the Foreign Ministry. She faxed me a copy. As soon as it came off the machine, I handed it to Elena to translate.

She cleared her throat and read, "We have the honor to inform you that the decision to close entry to the Russian Federation to a subject of Great Britain William Browder has been made by competent authorities in accordance with section one, article twenty-seven, of the federal law."

"What's article twenty-seven of the federal law?"

Elena shrugged. "I have no idea."

I called Vadim, who was in Moscow, and asked him.

"Hold on a sec." I heard him type something into his computer. After about a minute, he came back on the line. "Bill, article twenty-seven allows the Russian government to ban people who they deem a threat to national security."

"What?"

"A threat to national security," Vadim repeated.

"Shit," I said quietly. "This is not good."

"No. It's not."

With that one letter I understood that my visa denial definitely wasn't a mix-up of names. I hadn't been confused with Bill Bowring at all. Someone serious wanted me banned from Russia.

20

Vogue Café

When I told Ambassador Brenton that the Russians had declared me a threat to national security, he said, "That's unfortunate, Bill, but don't worry. We'll continue to work the diplomatic channels. I have a meeting scheduled with one of Putin's top economic advisers, Igor Shuvalov. I'm guessing he'll be sympathetic. However, at this point it wouldn't hurt for you to get your own contacts involved as well."

I agreed, and Vadim and I began to compile a list of Russian officials we knew who might be helpful.

Since meeting in Moscow five years before, Elena and I had moved in together, gotten married, and she was pregnant with our first child. She stayed in London in the two-month period before her due date. As I sat in bed on the evening of December 15, 2005, adding names to this list, Elena emerged from the bathroom, her robe tied tightly around her bulging pregnant belly. "Bill," she said with a shocked look on her face, "I think my water just broke."

I jumped up, paperwork scattering over the bedcovers and onto the floor, not knowing what to do. My ex-wife Sabrina had delivered David via a scheduled cesarean section, so I had just as little experience with natural childbirth as Elena, a first-time mother. We'd read all the books and gone to all the classes, but once it actually started, all that stuff went out the window. I grabbed our prepacked hospital bag with one hand and wrapped the other around Elena, quickly shepherding her to the elevators and then to the garage near our apartment building, where I helped her into our car. The St. John and St. Elizabeth Hospital was only a short drive away, but in my panic I took a wrong turn on Lisson Grove and ended up in a one-way system that I had no idea how to get out of. As I looked desperately left and right, Elena, normally pleasant and unflappable, started to scream words I'd never heard come out of her mouth. Evidently, the contractions had started.

Ten minutes later we arrived at the hospital. Thankfully, she hadn't given birth in the passenger seat. The rest was a whirlwind, but after ten hours, our daughter, Jessica, was born, a healthy, seven-pound, six-ounce baby. The joy I experienced from Jessica's birth completely overwhelmed any negative thoughts I had about my visa situation.

We left the hospital two days later. Friends started arriving at our apartment with flowers, food, and baby presents. David, who'd just turned nine, immediately took to having a little sister. Watching him hold Jessica all wrapped up in a little hospital waffle blanket and giving her kisses for the first time remains one of my most cherished memories. Christmas—which we celebrate in spite of the fact that David and I are Jewish—came and went, and for a week or more, my troubles disappeared.

The New Year passed in equally blissful and uneventful fashion. There was no news from Russia because the whole country was shut down for the Orthodox Christmas holiday, but then, early on the morning of January 14, 2006, Vadim called from Moscow. "Bill, I just got off the phone with Gref's deputy."

German Gref was the minister for economic development and one of the most visible reformers in Putin's government. Vadim had approached his deputy before Christmas to ask for his help with my visa.

"And? What did he say?"

"He said that Gref managed to get pretty high up—in fact, he got to Nikolai Patrushev, the head of the FSB, to discuss your case."

"Wow," I said, both impressed and a little frightened. The FSB was Russia's Federal Security Service, its secret police, which during Soviet times was universally known as the infamous KGB. If this weren't ominous enough, Patrushev was reputed to be one of the most ruthless members of Putin's inner circle.

"Apparently, he told Gref, and I quote, 'Stay out of this. You shouldn't put your nose in things that aren't relevant to you.'" Vadim paused as this news sank in, then he added, as if it weren't obvious, "There are some pretty serious people behind this stuff, Bill."

Hearing this was like stepping into an ice-cold shower. All the good feelings of the holidays and Jessica's birth and my expanding family were pushed to the back of my mind, and I was dropped harshly back into reality.

A week later, Ambassador Brenton called with similarly discouraging news. "Shuvalov *was* sympathetic, but said that there was nothing he could do."

While these messages were disappointing, we still had the head of Russia's version of the Securities and Exchange Commission, Oleg Vyugin, working on my case. He'd written to the deputy prime minister asking for my visa to be reinstated. He was due to be in London in mid-February for an international investment conference, and I hoped that he would bring some better news.

We arranged to meet in Mayfair at the bar of Claridge's Hotel on the first night of his trip. But when I laid eyes on him, I could immediately tell that something was wrong. We sat on the low velvet stools and ordered drinks. While we waited, I said, "Thank you for the strong letter you wrote to the deputy prime minister."

"There's no need to thank me, Bill," he said in excellent English. "But I'm afraid it achieved nothing. The government's position on your visa is entrenched."

My heart sank. "How entrenched?"

He stared at me and raised his eyebrows ever so slightly. He then pointed a slender finger at the ceiling and said nothing more. Was he saying Putin? It wasn't clear, but that was the only way I could interpret his mysterious gesture. If this really was Putin's decision, then I had no chance of fixing it.

When I told Vadim about the meeting, he wasn't as disappointed as I was. "If Putin really is behind this he must have been fed false information about you. We'll find someone close to Putin so he can hear the truth."

It was nice of Vadim to find such a positive way to spin this bad situation, but I didn't buy it. "Who could possibly do that for us?" I asked skeptically.

"How about Dvorkovich?" Vadim suggested. Arkady Dvorkovich was Putin's chief economic adviser, and Vadim had met him during our campaign to stop asset stripping at the national electricity company. Dvorkovich had been friendly to us, and most importantly, he had the president's ear.

"It's worth a shot," I said.

Vadim contacted Dvorkovich, and surprisingly, he said he would try to help.

In spite of Vadim's deliberate hopefulness, we were clearly running out of options.

Several days after I shared the bad news from the securities commissioner, Vadim got a call in our Moscow office from a man who refused to identify himself and who claimed to have important information regarding my visa refusal. He would share the information only in person and wanted to know when they could meet.

Vadim asked what he should do. Normally, we would have steered a million miles away from a Russian cold-caller seeking a meeting, but with all the obstacles we were hitting, I felt like we needed some kind of break. "Can you meet him somewhere public?" I asked.

"I don't see why not," Vadim said.

"Then maybe it's worthwhile," I said tentatively.

A day later, the stranger called again and agreed to meet Vadim at the Vogue Café on Kuznetsky Most, a trendy spot frequented by Russian oligarchs and their twenty-year-old model girlfriends. Standing around them were countless armed bodyguards, making it an ideal location.

As they had their meeting, I paced my apartment in London waiting for news. It lasted more than two hours, and Vadim called shortly after 11:00 a.m. London time. His voice was low and grave. "Bill, it was very disturbing. This guy, he had a lot of things to say."

"Okay—but first of all, who was he?"

"I don't know. He wouldn't give me his real name, but told me to call him Aslan. He was someone in the government for sure. Probably FSB."

"Why should we believe someone who refuses to identify himself?" I asked.

"Because he knew everything. I mean everything, Bill. He knew about our attempts with Gref, Vyugin, Shuvalov, Prikhodko. He had a paper in front of him with all the details of your detention at the airport, a copy of the letter from Brenton, everything. It was scary."

A chill ran up my spine. "What *exactly* did he say?"

"He said this whole thing is under FSB control, and your visa cancellation is just the beginning."

"Just the beginning?"

"That's what he said. He said that the FSB is interested in, quote, depriving Hermitage of its assets, unquote."

"Fuck."

"Yeah. And it gets worse. It's not just the company. It's us. It's me. Apparently the FSB is tracking everything I do, and he claimed that I'm going to be arrested imminently." Vadim said this calmly— he said everything calmly—as if he were describing events that were happening to someone else.

I stood quickly, knocking over my chair. "Do you believe him?"

"I'm not sure, but he sounds very credible."

"Why would this Aslan be sharing their intentions with us?"

"He claims there's a war going on inside the government, and his group is in conflict with the people doing this to us."

I had no idea if this was real or if we were being played, but I was sure of one thing: Vadim had to leave Russia. "Listen, I think it would be best if you came here as soon as possible. If there's even a small chance that this guy's telling the truth, we can't have you getting arrested."

My grandfather, Earl Browder, flanked by his intellectual sons. From left are my father, Felix, who became chair of the University of Chicago mathematics department and received the National Medal of Science in 1999, and his younger brothers, Andrew and Bill, both renowned mathematicians in their own right. Bill was president of the American Mathematical Society and chair of the mathematics department at Princeton, and Andrew was chair of the mathematics department at Brown University. *(© Lotte Jacobi)*

Earl Browder, who for a decade was America's top-ranking Communist, running for president of the United States on the Communist ticket in 1936. *(© AP Photo)*

My brother, Tom, and I at our house on the South Side of Chicago around 1970. I'm the one with the guitar. *(Courtesy of the Browder family archives)*

High school graduation with my mother, Eva, in 1981. Now you can see why I was nicknamed "Brillo" in college. *(Courtesy of the Browder family archives)*

Me, my father, Felix, and my brother, Tom, at home in New Jersey for Christmas in 1988. *(Courtesy of the Browder family archives)*

On the Tube in London, headed to my first day of work with the Boston Consulting Group in 1989. *(Courtesy of the Browder family archives)*

By 1991, I was finally hitting the big time and flying by helicopter from Budapest to a provincial Hungarian city to look at a deal for Robert Maxwell. *(Courtesy of the Browder family archives)*

Crossing Red Square in 2004, at the height of the Hermitage Fund's success. *(© James Hill)*

Sergei Magnitsky in 2008– the bravest man I've ever known. *(Courtesy of the Magnitsky family archives)*

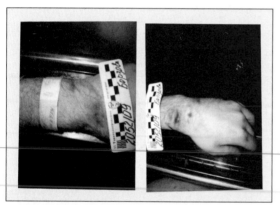

Post-mortem photographs of the wrist and hand of Sergei Magnitsky taken on November 17, 2009, a day after his death. The deep lacerations and bruises attest to a desperate fight for his life. *(Courtesy of the Magnitsky family archives)*

Sergei's mother, Natalia Magnitskaya, grieves over her son's body at his burial at a Moscow cemetery on November 20, 2009. *(© Reuters/Mikhail Voskresensky)*

At a press conference in November 2010, one day before the first anniversary of Sergei's murder, the Interior Ministry spokeswoman, Irina Dudukina, holds up a makeshift chart that "proves" Sergei was guilty of the crimes he exposed. (© Dmitry Kostyukov/ AFP/Getty Images)

Major Pavel Karpov of the Russian Interior Ministry. Major Karpov was the lead investigator on the case and was responsible for the documents used in the $230 million tax refund fraud that Sergei Magnitsky uncovered. His attempt to silence me through a British libel suit in 2012 failed. (© Sergey Kiselyev/ Kommersant/Getty Images)

Investigator Oleg Silchenko of the Russian Interior Ministry at a press conference in December 2011. Silchenko, who was responsible for much of Sergei's torture, rejected Sergei's desperate request for medical treatment. Just before the one-year anniversary of Sergei's murder, he was given a prestigious "Best Investigator" award by the Interior Ministry. (© Reuters/ Anton Golubey)

United States President Barack Obama signs the Sergei Magnitsky Rule of Law Accountability Act on December 14, 2012. The law sanctions Russian officials who were responsible for Sergei's detention, torture, and murder, as well as other Russian human rights abusers. (© *Mandel Ngan/AFP/Getty Images*)

Russian President Vladimir Putin at his annual press conference in 2012. Putin responds shrilly to repeated questions regarding a new Russian law that would ban the adoption of Russian orphans by American families, a law that was carried out in direct retaliation to the Magnitsky Act. Putin publicly mentioned me by name for the first time at this press conference. (© *Sasha Mordovets/Getty Images*)

The empty, yet carefully guarded, defendant's cage at the posthumous 2013 trial of Sergei Magnitsky, where I was also tried in absentia on trumped-up charges of tax evasion. This show trial was universally denounced by the international community. *(© Andrey Smirnov/AFP/Getty Images)*

Senate staffer Kyle Parker, who helped to make the Magnitsky Act a reality, shows Sergei's mother around the Capitol rotunda in April 2013. *(© Allison Shelley)*

A reception in Washington, D.C., in 2013, marking the passage of the Magnitsky Act. With me are Congressman Jim McGovern (who introduced the Magnitsky Act in the House of Representatives), Sergei's mother, Natalia, and his widow, Natasha. *(© Allison Shelley)*

Senator Ben Cardin recognizing the courage of the Magnitsky family at a press conference in 2013 in the Capitol building. With him are Sergei's widow, Natasha; Sergei's son, Nikita; Sergei's mother, Natalia; and Vadim Kleiner. (© Allison Shelley)

Thanking Senator John McCain in a meeting with Sergei's family in 2013 for his unrelenting fight for justice on Sergei's behalf. (© Allison Shelley)

Natasha, Nikita, and I meeting members of the European Parliament at the European Parliament plenary session on April 2, 2014, in Brussels, Belgium. Moments after this picture was taken, the European Parliament passed a Magnitsky sanctions list, creating further consequences for the Russian officials responsible for Sergei's murder. From left are Estonian MEP Kristiina Ojuland, British MEP Edward McMillan-Scott, Nikita Magnitsky, Natasha Magnitsky, Belgian MEP Guy Verhofstadt, and me. (© ALDE Group)

"Wait, wait, Bill. Let's not overreact."

"Are you kidding, Vadim? Get out. You're in Russia. Russia! There's no such thing as overreacting in Russia."

We hung up, but Vadim refused to leave. He knew that if he left Russia at that moment, he might never go back. In his mind, he couldn't just go into exile because of what this anonymous stranger told him that afternoon. He wanted more information.

I saw things differently, and I implored Vadim to talk to Vladimir Pastukhov, a Moscow lawyer Hermitage had used as outside counsel over the years. Vladimir was the wisest man I knew and like no one else I'd ever met. He was nearly blind, and the Coke-bottle glasses he wore made him look like a scribe from a Dickens novel. Because of his disability, however, Vladimir's mind was sharper, bigger, and more well rounded than that of anyone else I've ever known. He had a rare gift: the ability to read any complex situation to the deepest level and the smallest detail. He was like a great chess player, able to anticipate an opponent's every move not merely before it was made but also before his opponent even realized it was available.

Even though Vadim wouldn't leave, he did agree to see Vladimir. When Vladimir opened the door to his apartment just before midnight, Vadim put a finger to his lips, indicating that they shouldn't talk—just in case Vladimir's apartment was bugged. He stepped aside and Vadim entered. They made their way in silence to Vladimir's computer. Vadim sat and started to type.

I've been warned by somebody in the government that I'm going to be arrested. Can they do that?

Vladimir took a turn at the keyboard. *Are you asking me as a lawyer, or as a friend?*

Both.

As a lawyer, no. There are no grounds to arrest you. As a friend, yes. Absolutely. They can do anything.

Should I leave?

How credible is your source?

Very. I think.

Then you should leave.

When?

Right away.

Vadim went home, hastily packed a suitcase, and made his way to the airport for the 5:40 a.m. British Airways flight to London. I couldn't sleep at all that night until I got a text at 2:30 a.m. London time that Vadim was on the plane and about to take off.

He arrived in London that morning and came directly to my apartment. We were both in shock. We couldn't believe how quickly things had gone from bad to worse.

As we sat in my study discussing the previous day's drama, Vadim got a message that Arkady Dvorkovich, Putin's economic adviser, had taken our request for help seriously. Dvorkovich said he'd convinced several people in the presidential administration that it would be damaging for the Russian investment climate if my visa wasn't reinstated. Most significantly, the message stated that my visa issue would be put on the agenda at the National Security Council meeting with President Putin the following Saturday.

After this call Vadim and I tried to make sense of the conflicting news coming out of Russia. How could it be that people like the minister of economics or the head of the Russian securities commission were relaying messages that my situation was hopeless, while the president's economic adviser seemed to think that he could help me get my visa fixed at the National Security Council?

It occurred to me that perhaps everyone was telling us what they thought to be true, but the Russian government was full of different factions expressing their own opinions.

Whatever was really happening, all I could do was hope that Dvorkovich's faction was going to win and the National Security Council meeting would bear fruit for me.

But then, just four days before the big meeting, a new factor entered the equation when I received an email from the *Washington Post*'s Moscow bureau chief, Peter Finn. It read:

Hi Bill,

Hope all is well. Sorry to bother you with a rumor, but there's one floating around that you're having some visa difficulties. Anything to this? And if so, are you willing to talk about it? For an investor of your stature it would be significant.

Cheers,
Peter

Shit! How had this guy heard about my visa? This wasn't good. All I could think of was Simon Smith's warning about how the Russians would dig in their heels if my story got out. I didn't respond to Finn, and thankfully he didn't follow up.

Unfortunately, another reporter, Arkady Ostrovsky from the *Financial Times*, called me on Thursday. He'd heard the rumors too. "Is it true you've been denied entry to Russia, Bill?"

I tensed my stomach. "Arkady, I'm sorry, but I can't comment on that."

"C'mon, Bill. This is big news. I need to know what's going on."

Arkady and I were on a first-name basis because he was one of the journalists who'd been instrumental in the Gazprom exposé. While I couldn't deny to Arkady what was happening, I had to delay him. "If it were true," I said, "and I gave you an exclusive on this, can you give me four more days?"

He didn't like that, but it was better than no story at all, and we agreed that I'd call him on Monday.

I was completely on edge after talking with Arkady. Reporters were catching wind of what was going on, and all I had to do was get through the next thirty-six hours without any more of them calling. But then, at 10:30 a.m. on Friday, a Reuters reporter named Elif Kaban left me a message on my voice mail. She didn't say what she was calling about, but she called again at 11:45 a.m.

I had a lunch scheduled with an old friend from Washington that afternoon and left the office without returning either of her calls. I met my friend at a dim sum restaurant in Chinatown and turned off my phone, but I put my BlackBerry on the table to monitor the Reuters issue just in case. After my friend and I collected a few dishes off the cart, my BlackBerry started to blink with a message from my secretary:

Bill, Elif Kaban is still trying to get through to you. She says Reuters has received solid information about you not being allowed into Russia and they'd like to give you an opportunity to make the first statement. Please get back to them as soon as possible. This is their fourth call today. Elif Kaban is being VERY persistent!!

I stared blankly at the email for several seconds, stuffed my Black-Berry in my pocket, and tried to enjoy the rest of my lunch. I knew that the shit was about to hit the fan, but I wanted a few last minutes of peace.

After leaving the restaurant I took a detour through Green Park. It was a bright, crisp spring day, one of those days when it felt good to be a Londoner. I breathed the fresh air and looked around at all the carefree people walking in the park, people who weren't about to have their worlds turned upside down.

I finished my walk and got to my desk. A few minutes later Reuters published a red headline: "Hermitage CEO Browder Barred From Russia."

The secret was out. My phone immediately lit up like a Christmas tree. Calls came from the *Wall Street Journal*, the *Financial Times*, *Forbes*, the *Daily Telegraph*, the *Independent, Kommersant, Vedomosti*, Dow Jones, AP, the *New York Times*, and about twenty other news organizations. This was exactly what Simon Smith had warned me about, and now it was happening. There would be no way for the Russians to save face, no way to back down. Nothing would come of Russia's National Security Council meeting anymore. My fate had been decided, and from that moment I knew that it was official: I was done with Russia.

Except Russia was not done with me.

21

The G8

When the Russian government turns on you, it doesn't do so mildly— it does so with extreme prejudice. Mikhail Khodorkovsky and Yukos were prime examples. The punishment for presenting a challenge to Vladimir Putin went beyond Khodorkovsky to anybody who had had anything to do with him: his senior managers, lawyers, accountants, suppliers, and even his charities. By early 2006, ten people connected to Yukos were in jail in Russia, dozens more had fled the country, and tens of billions of dollars of assets had been seized by the Russian authorities. I took this as an object lesson, and I was not going to allow the Russians to do similar things to me. I needed to move my people, and my clients' money, out of Russia as quickly as possible.

I brought Hermitage's chief operating officer, Ivan Cherkasov, to London to help do these things. Ivan had joined Hermitage five years earlier from JP Morgan, and he was the one who hounded brokers, chased banks, and organized the payroll. He was thirty-nine, tall and telegenic, spoke flawless American English, and did his job perfectly.

Ivan set up a war room in our serviced offices on Tavistock Street in Covent Garden and got to work. Getting our people out was relatively easy. Within a month everyone at Hermitage whom I thought was at risk, as well as their families, was safely outside of Russia.

The harder part was selling billions of dollars' worth of Russian securities without anyone knowing. If the market caught wind of what we were doing, brokers and speculators would engage in a practice called "front-running." In our case, if brokers learned that Hermitage was going to sell all of its Gazprom holdings, those brokers would try to sell their shares first, driving down the price and potentially costing Hermitage clients hundreds of millions of dollars in that one stock alone.

To avoid this, we needed to find a broker who could execute the fund's sell orders with complete confidentiality and discretion. However, brokerage firms are generally not a trustworthy bunch, and local Russian brokerage firms are *particularly* untrustworthy. We also couldn't choose a major Western brokerage house that we had previously done business with because, as soon as it started executing our orders, the other brokers would put two and two together and conclude that Hermitage was selling, causing them to start dumping their shares.

This didn't leave us with many options. We looked at who was left and zeroed in on an affable thirty-two-year-old broker who headed a two-person trading desk at one of the big European banks in Moscow. He'd tenaciously been trying to get some business from us for years, and now we were going to give him his shot.

Ivan called him up and told him that his persistence was about to pay off. "There's one thing, though. We can only do this if you can swear to complete secrecy."

"Of course," he said. "I won't let you down."

The next day the broker received a sell order for $100 million. He was probably expecting $1 million—$5 million max—but never in his wildest dreams $100 million. It was likely the biggest order anyone had given him in his career.

Over the next week, he sold $100 million of our shares without any market impact or any information leak. He reported his results proudly, thinking he had completed the job, but was completely surprised when he got another $100 million sell order. Again, he executed this flawlessly. He continued to receive large orders from the fund over the next two months, and in the end he sold billions of dollars' worth of Russian stocks for us without any leaks. This virtuoso performance transformed his little operation from total obscurity into his bank's most successful European trading desk. Most importantly,

Hermitage had successfully removed its money from Russia without our enemies ever knowing.

With our people and money safe, we had eliminated the main levers that the Russian government could use to harm us. Whatever their next move might be, it couldn't be that daunting.

I felt better after achieving this, but dealing with the loss of confidence from my clients was a different matter. Most had invested in Hermitage because I was on the ground in Moscow. When I was there, I could identify profitable investments and protect their capital if something went wrong. Now, all of a sudden, I could do neither.

The first person to point this out was Jean Karoubi, the man I'd first approached as an investor back in 1996. Jean had become one of my closest confidants over the years and always had his finger on the pulse of the markets. When Reuters broke my visa story on March 17, Jean called me almost immediately and said in an uncharacteristically serious tone, "Bill, we've done great together. But I'm having a hard time coming up with a reason why I should keep my money in the fund when you've fallen out with the Russian government."

Hearing this from one of my earliest and most enthusiastic supporters was a bit of a shock, but he was right. The last thing I wanted to do was try to convince him to keep his money in the fund only to have things go further off the rails with the Russians. The only logical thing for him to do was take his winnings off the table.

In the following days I had similar conversations with many other clients who'd come to the same conclusion.

I knew what was coming: redemption orders, and lots of them.

The next available date that investors could withdraw money from the fund was May 26, and they had to submit their redemption requests eight weeks before that. So on March 31 I would get my first look at how bad the situation was.

At 5:20 p.m. that day, I received the redemption spreadsheet from HSBC, the fund's administrator. Normally, the subscriptions and redemptions were listed on a single page. In a busy quarter it might be two or three pages. But this spreadsheet was ten pages long with 240 line items of people requesting their money back. I quickly flipped to the end and added it all up. More than 20 percent of the fund was redeeming!

That was a huge number by any measure, and I knew it was just the beginning. I was standing on the precipice. Everything I'd worked for was starting to fall apart. The only thing that might possibly change the situation was getting my Russian visa reinstated. But I had given up on that.

Surprisingly, the British government hadn't. In mid-June 2006, I got a call from Simon Smith, head of the Russia desk at the Foreign Office: "We're working an interesting angle for sorting out your visa problem, Bill. But we wanted to make sure you're still interested in returning to Russia before we move forward."

"Of course I'm interested, Simon!" I said enthusiastically. "But I thought you wouldn't do anything more after the media circus."

"The press didn't help, that's for sure. But we haven't given up," Smith said reassuringly.

"What do you have in mind?"

"As you probably know, Russia is hosting the G8 summit in Saint Petersburg on the fifteenth of July. We were thinking of putting your case on the prime minister's agenda to discuss directly with Putin."

"Really. . . . That would be amazing, Simon."

"Don't get your hopes up too much. It's not a done deal, Bill, but we are working on it."

We hung up and I stared out the window. How could I not get my hopes up? Just as easily as my visa refusal had ruined my business, a visa reinstatement could restore it.

As the G8 drew nearer, I was a bundle of nerves. A positive outcome from Prime Minister Tony Blair's intervention would be life-changing. However, as the days and weeks passed, I began to have my doubts. I hadn't been able to get in touch with Smith. I tried to keep a cool head, but I couldn't figure out why he had been so encouraging before and then suddenly gone quiet.

When I couldn't stand it any longer, I called Sir Roderic Lyne, the former British ambassador to Russia who advised HSBC, to see if he had any insights. He was surprised that Smith had even suggested putting my issue on the prime minister's agenda and encouraged me to keep my expectations low. Based on his experience, issues always emerged at summits that trumped the carefully crafted agendas.

I tried to take his advice, but six days before the summit, Elena and I went to have lunch at Richoux, a restaurant on Circus Road in St. John's Wood. As we sat at our table, she casually picked up the *Sunday Observer* and flipped through it. Her eyes lit up as she said, "Bill, look at this headline: 'Blair to Raise Fund Manager's Case with Putin'!" I grabbed the paper from her and started reading. It was a total confirmation of what Smith had discussed with me. The most salient sentence was to the point: "The prime minister will use the G8 summit in Saint Petersburg next weekend to ask Russia's president to lift all restrictions on Browder."

Elena looked at me in shock. "This is amazing," she said.

The *Observer* article also surprised my clients, and some started to postpone their redemption decisions until after the G8.

My spirits were as high as they could be, but then, three days before the summit, Vadim pulled me aside. "Bill, you need to see this." He pointed to a Bloomberg headline on his computer screen. I leaned forward and scanned a story about Hezbollah militants in Lebanon who'd fired antitank missiles into Israel. Three Israeli soldiers were dead, and five others had been kidnapped and taken into Lebanon.

"What does this have to do with us?" I asked incredulously.

"I'm not sure, but this looks like a war's starting in the Middle East. That may distract Blair from bringing up your visa discussion at the G8."

Sure enough, the following day Israel launched air strikes on targets in Lebanon, including the Beirut airport, resulting in forty-four civilian deaths. Russia, France, Britain, and Italy immediately criticized Israel for a "disproportionate" use of force, and the United States publicly condemned the Hezbollah militants. Vadim was right.

The G8 summit might well disintegrate into a frantic Middle East peace summit, with Blair's intended agenda jettisoned.

As the summit began on Saturday, I didn't know what was going to happen, and I couldn't reach anyone in the British government over the weekend. The summit dragged on, but all the news reports were about Israel and Lebanon—nothing about my visa.

As the summit wrapped up, Putin was scheduled to give the concluding press conference. The room was packed. Hundreds of journalists from across the globe were all hoping for their chance to ask Putin a question.

After about twenty minutes of softball questions, Putin called on Catherine Belton, a pretty, diminutive, thirty-three-year-old British journalist at the *Moscow Times*. She took the microphone and tentatively addressed Putin. "Bill Browder was recently denied a Russian entry visa. Many investors and Western diplomats are concerned about this and don't understand why this happened. Can you explain why he was denied an entry visa without any explanation?" She then sat, held her notebook on her knees, and awaited his answer.

The room went quiet. Everyone knew that Putin had been caught off guard. He let a couple seconds pass before uttering, "Please say it again. Who exactly was denied a visa?"

Catherine stood back up. "Bill Browder. He is CEO of the Hermitage Fund, which is the biggest investor in the Russian stock market. And I believe the prime minister of the United Kingdom might have discussed this with you today."

Putin frowned and replied tartly, "Well, to be honest I don't know for what reasons any particular individual may be denied entry into the Russian Federation. I imagine that man may have violated our country's laws."

That was it. When I saw this, I knew Blair hadn't brought up my case, and that my visa wasn't going to be reinstated. More importantly, if I translated this from Putin-speak into plain English, what he was saying was crystal clear: "We never mention enemies by name, and that includes Bill Browder. I am now instructing my law enforcement agencies to open up as many criminal cases against him as possible."

If you think this interpretation is paranoid or an exaggeration, it wasn't. If anything, I wasn't being paranoid enough.

22

The Raids

After Putin's remarks, my clients had their answer. Nothing good was going to happen in Russia. The next redemption date was August 25, and this time another 215 clients withdrew more than 30 percent of the assets from the fund. In my business this is what's called a run on the fund, and like a run on a bank, once it starts it's almost impossible to stop. Unless I could somehow pull a rabbit out of a hat, the Hermitage Fund was quickly going to be forced out of business.

I'd handled hundreds of ups and downs throughout my career. Stocks rise and fall often for no reason, and I'd had to develop a thick skin to absorb bad news and not lose confidence. I hadn't lost confidence after the fund lost 90 percent of its value in 1998, and I was rewarded for sticking it out when the fund fully recovered.

But this time was different.

My whole professional life had been geared toward being an investor in Russia. I'd never thought about anything else. But now, since I could no longer operate in Russia, I *had* to think about something else. What were my options? I couldn't imagine returning to America to compete against thousands of people just like me. Nor could I imagine setting up in a new place such as China, only to spend a decade trying to establish myself.

And I certainly wasn't going to retire. I was forty-two years old and had fire in my belly. None of my options seemed attractive, and the more I thought about my situation, the more hopeless it seemed.

The fact that Hermitage was probably going out of business was even more upsetting for the people who worked for me. After all the excitement and impact from our activities in Russia, no one on our team wanted to disband and be forced to return to regular jobs at investment banks or brokerage firms.

As I pondered our strengths, it was obvious that we were good at finding undervalued investments. We were also experienced at protecting those investments from crooked managers. It seemed to me that we could take those two skills and apply them to other emerging markets.

I decided to put Vadim and four other analysts on planes to Brazil, the United Arab Emirates, Kuwait, Turkey, and Thailand to see if they could come up with interesting investing ideas. They met with representatives from the twenty cheapest companies in each country. They went to a hundred meetings, did serious analyses on ten companies, and ultimately identified three solid opportunities.

One was a phone company in Brazil that had a valuation of three times its previous year's earnings, the lowest in the world for a telephone company; the second was a Turkish oil refiner that traded at a 72 percent discount to the asset price of other refineries; and the third was a UAE-based real estate company that traded at a 60 percent discount to its net asset value.

I began investing the firm's money in these stocks and shared the analysis with my friend Jean Karoubi. I could always rely on him to be a good sounding board, and he had a much more positive reaction than I expected: "Bill, I like these ideas a lot. I think this is the type of business you should be developing more broadly."

He was right. My skills were as an investor, and they could be applied anywhere, particularly in countries that faced issues similar to Russia's. I didn't need to be in Russia to succeed.

As I shared these investment ideas with other clients, most had the same reaction as Jean. By the fall of 2006, my confidence had grown so much that I started drafting a prospectus for a new fund called Hermitage Global.

The plan was to have this prospectus ready in time for the World

Economic Forum in Davos at the end of January 2007. There is no better place in the world to raise capital than Davos.

My fortunes had changed since my first foray there in 1996. I no longer had to sleep on the floor or linger in hotel lobbies hoping to meet important people. Since 2000 I had been a proper member of the forum and had been going every year since.

This time, I decided to bring Elena with me. She was in the first trimester of her second pregnancy, and I thought the interesting lectures and receptions of Davos would be a welcome break from looking after our one-year-old at home. We flew to Zurich and took the train to Davos, just as Marc Holtzman and I had done so many years back, and checked into the Derby Hotel. I began taking meetings almost as soon as we arrived.

As Jean predicted, investors were very receptive to Hermitage Global. On the second day, after going through the presentation with one of my old clients, he said, "Hey, Bill, are you going to the Russian dinner tomorrow night?"

"What Russian dinner?" I knew a large contingent of Russians were in Davos, but so many things were going on that I hadn't heard about this event.

"It's a big deal. All the main Russian officials will be there."

"I doubt they'd allow me anywhere near it," I said with a smile.

"That's the beauty of it, Bill. It's not the Russians who decide who goes, it's the World Economic Forum. You can just sign up."

This was an intriguing idea. After our meeting, I headed straight for the computer bank where you can sign up for events. I logged on and, with several clicks of the mouse, registered Elena and myself for the dinner.

The following evening we arrived ten minutes early, only to find that nearly every table was full. We scoured the room and took the last two empty seats that were together. Each table was hosted by a Russian VIP, and as I looked around, I was appalled to discover that our table host was the CEO of Gazprom's export division. I could not have found a more awkward place for us to sit. Hermitage's anti-corruption work at Gazprom was probably the catalyst that had led to my Russian expulsion, and here I was getting ready to have an elegant meal of veal escalope, *rösti*, and carrot cake with one of the company's most senior officials.

The Gazprom executive and I spent the meal avoiding eye contact, and as dinner progressed, Russian officials and oligarchs took turns giving speeches. Each speech was more insipid, ingratiating, and full of platitudes than the last. The Russians have great skill in talking without saying anything, and this was on full display that evening.

Toward the end of the event, as silverware clinked and waiters came and went, there was a big commotion near the entrance as twenty tough-looking security men walked into the room, forming a mobile cordon around a small man. I couldn't tell who it was until he reached his table—but it was none other than Dmitri Medvedev, the first deputy prime minister of Russia. Medvedev was running for president to replace Putin, whose second term would end in June 2008, and Davos was Medvedev's first chance to present himself to the international community.

After the main course was cleared, Medvedev rose and took the microphone at the front of the room. He spoke for several minutes in Russian (I listened to the translation on an earpiece), and his speech was even more tedious and devoid of substance than the others. I couldn't wait for it all to be over.

As soon as Medvedev finished, waiters glided across the room delivering plates of carrot cake and cups of coffee and tea. As I drank my tea and picked the icing off the cake, Elena tugged my jacket and whispered, "Bill, I've just had a great idea. Why don't you ask Medvedev to help with your visa?"

I gave her a sideways glance. "Don't be ridiculous." I'd exhausted every possibility of getting my visa back, right up to Putin. After the G8, I considered that chapter in my life to be well and truly over. Moreover, I couldn't imagine anything more humiliating than walking up to Medvedev to beg for my visa.

I tried to tell Elena this but she wouldn't listen. She was insistent. "Seriously, look. No one's talking to him. Let's just do it."

She stood and stared at me intently. Defying Elena was more frightening than having an unpleasant encounter with Medvedev, so I stood too. I reluctantly followed her across the room, and when we reached Medvedev, I stuck out my hand and said, "Hello, Mr. Deputy Prime Minister. I'm Bill Browder. Maybe you remember me?"

Elena translated. Medvedev stood and shook my hand. There was a general bustle as other people in the room took notice. If I could talk to Medvedev, then they could too. People started to stand and move in our direction.

"Yes, of course I remember you. How are you, Mr. Browder?"

"I'm fine, but as you probably know, I haven't been allowed into Russia for more than a year. I was wondering if you could help me get my visa back?"

As I said this, a group of people, including a reporter from Bloomberg and another from the *New York Times*, pressed in on us. If Davos was Medvedev's international debut, then this conversation was going to be one of the most interesting moments of the whole conference.

Medvedev glanced at the people gathering around him and had to make a snap decision. He could reject my request, which would be interesting and newsworthy, or he could be helpful, which would be less so. He paused for a moment before saying, "Gladly, Mr. Browder. If you give me a copy of your visa application, then I'll submit it to the Federal Border Service with my recommendation to approve it."

That was it. The reporters pressed in on Medvedev, and as Elena and I slid away from the crowd, she squeezed my hand. "You see? I was right."

We went straight back to the hotel and got on the phone to London. Normally it takes three or four days to gather all the documents needed for a Russian visa application, but the team stayed up all night working on it, and by 8:00 a.m. the fax machine at the hotel spewed out the paperwork.

I had back-to-back meetings with investors that morning, so Elena went to a room at the conference center where Medvedev was due to give a speech and stood near the podium. With all the security, it was unlikely that she would be able to make direct contact with Medvedev, but she spotted Arkady Dvorkovich, Putin's adviser who had tried to help me before. She asked if he would deliver the application. Dvorkovich took it and promised he would.

The forum ended the next day, and Elena and I returned to London, proud of our fortuitous high-level intervention.

The results took a few weeks, but on February 19 I received a message from Moscow about my visa. Only it wasn't from the Federal Border Service. It was from a Lieutenant Colonel Artem Kuznetsov at the Moscow branch of the Interior Ministry. This was odd. The Interior Ministry dealt with criminal investigations, not visas. Since I didn't speak Russian, I asked Vadim to return Kuznetsov's call.

After Vadim explained that he worked for me, Kuznetsov said, "Okay. I'll explain to you what the situation is."

"Great."

"As far as I understand, Mr. Browder sent in an application requesting permission to enter the territory of the Russian Federation."

"Yes, yes, we sent those documents."

"I just wanted to drop by and discuss it, if that's possible," Kuznetsov said casually.

"You see, the thing is, I'm not in Moscow right now," Vadim responded. "So if you could send me the questions, then we could try to answer them for you."

"I can't just send them over, I'd prefer to discuss them in person," Kuznetsov said testily.

This wasn't a normal inquiry. In a legitimate investigation, Russian officials always sent their questions in writing. What had become apparent to me from my decade in Russia was that when an official asks to meet informally, it means only one thing: they want a bribe. In the many instances where officials had tried to shake me down, I'd uniformly ignored them and they always went away.

Kuznetsov finished the conversation by saying, "The sooner you answer these questions, the sooner your problems will disappear."

As with similar requests in the past, I decided to ignore it.

This phone call might have upset me more if the launch of Hermitage Global wasn't going so well, and I quickly forgot about it. One by one, my old clients and a number of new ones started subscribing to the fund. By the end of April 2007 I had raised $625 million. This didn't replace the amount of money withdrawn from the Russian fund, but it meant that I had stopped the bleeding and that my company would stay in business.

On June 4, 2007, I was scheduled to present the results of the launch of Hermitage Global to our board of directors at the Westin Hotel in Paris. After all the bad news in the previous two years, it was the first time since I had been expelled from Russia that I had some good news to share with the board.

Ivan and I arrived on the evening of the third to get prepared. I got up at six the next morning, went to the gym, showered, and ate a light breakfast. By 8:00 a.m. I was on the phone arguing with my trader over a Dubai stock he was supposed to have sold several days earlier. There'd been a technical problem at the Dubai exchange that had held up the sale. Now the share price was plummeting, and I was furious that he hadn't been able to sell it before we started losing money. He was making excuses and I was growing more and more agitated.

As he and I argued, my call waiting beeped. I looked at the caller ID only because I was worried that it might be Elena, who was due to give birth to our second child later in the month. It wasn't Elena, though—it was Emma, the Hermitage Fund secretary in Moscow. Emma was a pleasant twenty-one-year-old Russian girl from the provinces who looked several years younger. She was honest and hardworking and managed the office vigilantly. She rarely called me directly, so I told the trader to hold on and clicked over. "Emma, can this wait?"

"No, it can't, Bill," she said in perfect English. "There are twenty-five plainclothes police officers raiding our office!"

"What?"

She repeated what she'd just said.

"Shit. Hold on." I clicked back to the trader, told him I had to call back, and returned to Emma. "What are they after?"

"I don't know but there's a guy—Artem Kuznetsov—who's in charge and—"

"Did you say Kuznetsov?"

"Yes."

This had to be the same Artem Kuznetsov who'd tried to shake us down us a few months earlier! "Does he have a search warrant?"

"Yes. He showed it to me, but he won't let me keep it."

"Can you write down what it says?"

"I'll try."

I hung up and called Ivan to tell him what was going on. He was equally alarmed and called Emma back. Then I called my lawyer in Moscow, Jamison Firestone. Jamison—a fit, good-looking, forty-one-year-old American with bright eyes, brown hair, and an incredibly boyish face—was a Russophile who'd been in Russia since 1991. He was the managing partner of Firestone Duncan, the law firm he founded with another American, Terry Duncan. In 1993, during the attempted Russian coup, Terry had gone to the Ostankino TV Tower to help protesters. As the authorities opened fire on them, he tried to evacuate the wounded, but he was shot and later died. Afterward Jamison carried on by himself.

I liked Jamison from the moment I met him, not just because he was a straight-talking American, but also because unlike most lawyers he never overcharged me. We'd done a lot of business together over the years, and our stars had risen together.

As soon as he picked up the phone, I skipped all pleasantries. "Jamie, I just got a call from our secretary in Moscow. There's—"

"Bill! You were my next call—"

"Jamie, there are twenty-five cops raiding our office!"

"You too?"

"What're you talking about, Jamie?"

"There're two dozen plainclothes officers here tearing my office apart as well. They've got a search warrant for Kameya."

This was like being punched in the face. *"Jesus Christ!"*

Kameya was a Russian company owned by one of our clients whom we advised on investing in Russian stocks. Since the police were conducting simultaneous raids at our office and at Jamison's, I could only conclude that the police were targeting Hermitage.

"Shit, Jamie. What do we do?"

"I don't know, Bill. They're holding us captive in our conference room. They won't even let people use the bathrooms. The warrant doesn't appear to be valid. The cops aren't allowed to search until our defense lawyers get here, but they're ripping the place apart anyway."

"Can you call me as soon as you learn anything more?"

"I will."

We hung up. Now I was late for the board meeting. I grabbed my file with the agenda and presentations and quickly made my way downstairs. Adrenaline pumped through my veins—all I could think about were these raids.

I entered the room and our four board members—men in their fifties and sixties who'd come in from different points in Europe—were looking relaxed and happy as they sipped coffee, ate croissants, and gossiped about the markets. I broke the mood by telling them what was going on in Moscow. As I spoke, Ivan burst into the room looking like a ghost. One of the board members asked what else we knew. Since we didn't know anything else, I decided to call Emma and put our phone on speaker.

She answered and put her phone on speaker too. We listened from seventeen hundred miles away to a live blow-by-blow of boxes being emptied, men shouting, feet stomping, and even our safe being drilled into.

Ten minutes passed. Twenty. Thirty. We were shocked and impressed as Emma tried to take charge, shouting at the officers: "You can't drink our coffee! . . . Put that computer down! . . . Leave him alone! That guy has nothing to do with Hermitage!" She was talking about a Deutsche Bank employee who was unfortunate enough to have shown up that morning to deliver some documents. The police had forced him to stay, and he was holed in up in the conference room, shitting himself with fear.

This raid was both disturbing and riveting. I assured the board members in Paris that there was nothing for the police to take from our office—no relevant information, no confidential files, and most importantly no assets. Everything that mattered had been safely removed from the country the previous summer.

While we continued to listen to the raid at the Hermitage office, my phone rang. It was Jamison. I stepped out of the room to take the call.

"B-Bill. Something terrible has hap-happened!"

"Jamison, slow down." He was upset and emotional. He was a corporate lawyer with fifteen years' experience, and I'd never heard him like this. "What's going on?"

"Maxim, one of my junior lawyers, pointed out that their warrant wasn't valid and that they couldn't take things unrelated to Kameya."

"And what happened?"

"They beat the shit out of him! He's going to the hospital right now."

"Fuck. Is he okay?"

"I don't know."

A lump formed in my throat. "Jamie, you've got to document everything these guys are doing. We're not going to let these bastards get away with this."

"Bill—it's not just Maxim. They're taking almost everything."

"What do you mean 'everything'?"

"They're grabbing client files that have nothing to do with Kameya. They have two vans out front. They've taken almost all of our computers, our servers, all the corporate stamps and seals we hold for our clients' companies. None of this makes any sense. It'll be hard for some of our clients to operate without their documents and seals. I don't even know how we're going to be able to work after this. We can't even get emails!"

I was at a loss for words. "I . . . I'm so sorry, Jamie. We're going to get through this together. I promise. More importantly, let me know how Maxim's doing as soon as you know anything."

"Okay. I will."

I walked back into the conference room completely stunned. Everybody looked at me. "Hang up the phone." Ivan said good-bye to Emma and clicked off. I then told them what was happening at Firestone Duncan. None of us could speak.

We were in deep shit, and if I knew anything about Russia, this was just the beginning.

23

Department K

Ivan and I took the 3:00 p.m. Eurostar back to London. We needed to talk out of earshot, and the only place available was between cars, where we sat uncomfortably on fold-down jump seats. Northern France churned by just outside the door, a blur of green and gray. We tried to call Moscow and London, but the connection kept dropping out as the train zipped in and out of tunnels, so we gave up and went back to our seats, where we sat in silence for the rest of the journey. Although I'd known Russia was a violent place, since the day that I'd set foot on Russian soil in 1992 it had never touched me, or anyone close to me. Now, all of a sudden, it was all too real.

My first concern was Maxim. As soon as I got home, I called Jamie and asked for an update. After Maxim had been beaten, the police had arrested and fined him, even before he was taken to the hospital. Thankfully, his injuries were not life-threatening. I implored Jamie to file a complaint, but he resisted. "Maxim's scared, Bill. The officers who beat him said that they'd accuse him of pulling a knife on them, rearrest him, and put him in jail if he says anything."

How could I argue with that? At least he was going to be all right.

I arrived at the office early the next morning. Ivan was already there, inspecting a handwritten copy of the search warrant that Emma had faxed over. Her handwriting was obsessively clear and still had the bubbly letters of a schoolgirl's, but the content of the warrant was anything but innocent. It said that the tax crimes department of the Moscow Interior Ministry had opened a criminal case against Ivan, accusing him of underpaying $44 million in dividend withholding taxes for Kameya. They came up with an arbitrary tax claim for the company, and because Ivan administered the entity for our client, the police blamed Ivan.

No matter how illegitimate the Russian criminal justice system may seem from the outside, Russia is still a sovereign state that most Western governments cooperate with on extradition requests, Interpol Red Notices, and international asset freezes. Even though we were in London, ignoring a criminal case like this could lead to all sorts of terrible things for Ivan.

The warrant was baseless—Kameya had paid the same rate of tax as everyone else—and accusing Ivan of any crime was plainly unjust. If there was ever a person who lived by the rules, it was Ivan Cherkasov. He was a good husband, father, friend, and colleague. His suits were always pressed, his hair was always trimmed, and he was always on time. Watching him pace the office because of this trumped-up charge was infuriating, and I promised I would do whatever I could to help him sort out this mess.

The first thing I did was to retain the best tax lawyer I knew in Moscow, a thirty-five-year-old attorney named Sergei Magnitsky. Sergei was the head of the tax practice at Firestone Duncan, and his knowledge of Russian tax law was encyclopedic. Since he'd begun working there, he was rumored never to have lost a case.

Once Sergei was on board, we asked him to analyze whether we'd done anything wrong. Ivan had always been vigilant, and I assumed that our taxes were correctly paid, but since the Interior Ministry was making such grave allegations, we needed to be absolutely sure.

Sergei requested all of Kameya's tax filings and supporting documents. He stayed up late into the night and called the next morning with his analysis: "Guys, I've looked at every aspect of Kameya's tax situation. Ivan's done nothing wrong."

While Sergei could help us understand tax law, Ivan also needed a criminal lawyer to deal with the police. We then hired Eduard Khayretdinov, a former police investigator and judge who'd been a defense attorney since 1992. He was forty-eight years old, six feet two, with gray hair, a thick mustache, and big hands. He reminded me of a Russian version of the Marlboro Man. He was the type of man you wanted to have on your side in Russia if things ever went horribly wrong. He'd defended and won some of Russia's most high profile and seemingly hopeless criminal cases—in a country whose conviction rate is over 99 percent, that was a true miracle.

Eduard volunteered to go to the police station to find out what the cops were up to. When he arrived, he was directed to the lead investigator on the case, a thirty-year-old major named Pavel Karpov. Eduard asked Karpov for a copy of some of the case files, which under Russian law the defense attorney is entitled to see. Karpov refused. This was very unusual. In Eduard's fifteen years as a defense lawyer, it had never before happened.

Eduard was frustrated by Karpov's stonewalling, but I actually saw it as a positive sign. I thought that if Karpov was afraid to show us the case files, it must mean that he simply *had* no case.

Unfortunately, my optimistic theory started to unravel almost immediately. On June 14 I got a call from Catherine Belton, the reporter from the 2006 G8 summit who'd asked Putin why I was kicked out of the country. She was now working for the *Financial Times* and wanted to know if I had any comment on the raids by the Interior Ministry. I gave her my response and hoped the article would accurately reflect our side of the story.

The next morning I went to the front door to pick up the papers and was greeted by a headline on the front page of the *FT* that read, "Russia probes Browder firm over taxes." I sat on the bench in my hallway and read the article three times. It was full of Interior Ministry fabrications and innuendo, but the one thing that jumped out at me was a single sentence in the middle of the story: "Investigators are targeting Mr. Browder as being behind the scheme."

These guys weren't backing off at all. They had much bigger plans. Clearly, whatever was happening with Ivan and Kameya was just a prelude to a much bigger plan to go after me.

This was disturbing, and we were at a complete disadvantage.

We arguably had the best lawyers in Russia, but that didn't matter because our opponents were law enforcement officials working outside the law. What we needed more than anything was intelligence, the kind of intelligence that the FSB would have. What we needed was Vadim's source Aslan, the man who'd warned Vadim to leave Russia back in 2006, after things got hot following my expulsion from the country.

We had no idea whether the internal governmental conflict that had motivated Aslan to come to Vadim in the first place was still going on or if he would be willing to help us again, but it was worth a try.

Vadim sent him a simple message asking to talk.

Thirty minutes later we had a response: "What do you want to know?"

"I'm hoping you could tell me who's behind last week's raids, and if you might know what they're planning next?" Vadim wrote.

A few minutes later another message arrived: "Yes, I know. Department K of the FSB is behind everything. They want to take Browder down and seize all of his assets. This case is only the beginning. Many other criminal cases will follow."

When Vadim translated this message for me, my leg started to twitch uncontrollably. Aslan's message was unequivocal and chilling, and I desperately hoped he was wrong.

I had a million questions, starting with, What was Department K?

I asked Vadim, but he didn't know. We walked to his desk on the off chance we could find some reference on the Internet. Remarkably, after clicking several links, we were staring at an official organizational chart on the FSB website. Department K was the FSB's economic counterespionage unit.

I stumbled back to my desk and fell into my chair. I told my secretary to hold all calls. I needed to process this. The thought of being pursued by Department K was almost too much to take in.

As I sat there, I thought, *I am being pursued by the Russian secret police, and there is nothing I can do about it. I can't file a complaint with them and I can't request my case files. They are the* secret police. *Worse, they have access to every tool imaginable, both legitimate and illegitimate. The FSB doesn't just issue arrest warrants and extradition requests—it dispatches assassins.*

24

"But Russian Stories Never Have Happy Endings"

As I sat at my desk trying to take everything in, my secretary quietly placed a message at my elbow: "Elena called. Not urgent." Normally I would have called Elena back right away, but I had so much on my mind that I didn't.

About an hour later, Elena called again. I answered. Before I could say anything she yelled, "Why haven't you called?"

"What do you mean? You said it wasn't urgent."

"No—I said it *was* urgent. Bill, I'm in labor. I'm at the hospital!"

"My God! I'm coming right away!" I jumped up and ran for the door. I didn't wait for the elevator and rushed down the stairs, nearly slipping in my smooth-soled loafers as I turned a corner. I ran outside into the midafternoon sun, suddenly forgetting about Department K, the FSB, and Russia.

Covent Garden is a maze of tiny roads that leads to a central pedestrian square. Hailing a taxi there was pointless because it would take twenty minutes just to get out of the neighborhood, so I sprinted toward Charing Cross Road, but when I arrived, there wasn't an unoccupied taxi in sight. I kept running in the direction of the hospital, looking over my shoulder for cabs along the way. I dodged through pedestrians and the mixture of London traffic with its trucks, double-decker buses, and motor scooters. It seemed as if every London cab was already taken. It was too far for me to go on foot, so I kept on running and finally found a free taxi on Shaftesbury Avenue.

Fifteen minutes later I burst through the hospital doors. I was a complete mess as I made my way up to the delivery suite on the fourth floor. Elena was in the final stages of labor. She was screaming and red-faced from the contractions. She didn't have time to be mad at me—she didn't have time to think about me at all. I took her hand and she gripped mine so hard I thought her nails might draw blood. Twenty minutes later, our second daughter, Veronica, was born.

Unlike with Jessica's birth, when the joy of a new baby overcame my thoughts of problems in Russia, this time my troubles were so monumental that I couldn't get away from them. As soon as it was clear that Elena and Veronica were healthy, my Russian problems reinvaded my mind like a horde.

I wasn't going to share the bad news about Department K with Elena, not then, anyway. I decided to let her rest and bond with our newest daughter. We went home the following day, and I put on a brave face as friends came to meet the baby and congratulate us. But I could never shake what was going on in the background. Up until then, the main reason I'd been able to hold up psychologically had been Elena. In our relationship, we had this strange rhythm of emotions. Whenever I panicked, she was calm, and vice versa. It had worked perfectly up until now, but this news was so disturbing that I couldn't imagine the pattern would hold.

Two days after we got home, I couldn't wait any longer to tell her. That night, after rocking Veronica to sleep, I went to our bed and sat at Elena's side. "I have something I need to talk to you about."

She took my hand and looked into my eyes. "What is it?"

I told her about the latest message from Aslan about Department K.

Veronica, sleeping in the bassinet, interrupted me now and then with a coo or one of those staccato exhales that newborns make—*ah-ah-ah-ahhh*. When I was finished, I asked Elena, "What do you think we should we do?"

The expression on her face never changed, and she had the same remarkable calm that she had always had in the past. She said quietly,

"Let's see what they do next and then we'll deal with it. These people may be nasty, but they're only human, just like everybody else. They'll make mistakes."

Elena squeezed my hand and gave me one of her soft smiles.

"What about our vacation?" I asked. We had a family trip planned for August, as soon as the baby could travel.

"That's simple, Bill. We go. We carry on with our lives."

Thankfully the next few weeks were quiet at work, with no more alarming Russian information. In mid-August 2007, we boarded a plane to make the short flight to Marseille in the south of France. Veronica slept most of the way, and Jessica and I played a little game with a plastic bottle and a bag containing half a dozen wads of paper. David handed us bottles and rags and favorite toys and snacks and did his homework in between. We touched down in Marseille, and I automatically turned on my BlackBerry to see if I'd received any calls or emails. There was nothing—nothing important, anyway—and I took this to be a good omen for the trip.

We disembarked and made our way through the airport. We collected our bags and went outside to wait for our van. As soon as we stepped outside, the heat—thick and full and pleasant—washed over us. Our driver helped us load our things and we piled in. As we pulled away from the curb, my mobile phone rang. It was Ivan.

"Bill, it's happening again," he said, panic-stricken.

Without even knowing what he was about to say, my leg started twitching. His panic was contagious. "What's happening?"

"The police are raiding Credit Suisse in Moscow."

"What does that have to do with us?"

"They're searching for anything that belongs to Hermitage."

"But we don't have anything there," I pointed out.

"True, but the police don't seem to know that."

"What are they looking for then?"

"Hold on. I've got a copy of the search warrant." He dipped off the line and was back in half a minute. "They're searching for anything that belongs to Hermitage Capital Management, Hermitage Capital

Services, Hermitage Capital Asset Management, Hermitage Asset Management. . . . It goes on for two more pages. Should I continue?"

"No."

Apparently, the police were playing some strange game of Battleship, using every possible formulation of our company's name in hopes of landing a direct hit. I almost had to laugh at the amateurishness of it.

"Who's leading the raid?" I asked.

"That's the really fucked-up part, Bill. It's Artem Kuznetsov."

Goddammit! Artem Kuznetsov? He seemed to have his hands in everything bad that was happening to us in Russia.

We hung up, but I knew that we had just turned another corner. Aslan, our source, had been right—these people were indeed after our assets. The only thing I couldn't understand was why they didn't know that we no longer had any assets in Russia. Weren't the Russian secret police smarter than that? Perhaps not. As Elena had pointed out, maybe they really were just as fallible as everyone else.

Kuznetsov left Credit Suisse empty-handed, but he kept trying to find Hermitage assets. Over the next two weeks, as I tried to enjoy the warmth of southern France, Kuznetsov raided more banks in Moscow. He raided HSBC, Citibank, and ING; in each instance he came away with nothing.

As I learned about each of these raids, I was drawn further and further from my family. Instead of decompressing, singing lullabies to Veronica and Jessica, and playing with David in the pool, I spent most of my holiday on conference calls as we tried to figure out what our enemies were going to do next.

When my "vacation" was over, I went back to London and huddled with the team to plan our next steps. The key legal issue was the criminal case against Ivan. I didn't really care about the bank raids, but I profoundly cared about anything that might lead to Ivan's being arrested or extradited.

Since Eduard had found Major Karpov to be so unforthcoming about Ivan's case, Sergei came up with an interesting idea of how we might get more information. "If the police won't tell us what they're doing, why don't we go directly to the tax authorities and see what they have to say?"

This was a good idea, and we instructed our accounting firm to send a letter to the Moscow tax office where Kameya had submitted its returns, asking if Kameya owed any taxes.

On September 13, Sergei called Ivan back almost giddy with excitement. "The accountants got a reply to the letter. You won't believe this, but it says that Kameya doesn't owe any money at all. In fact, it says that Kameya actually *overpaid* its taxes by a hundred and forty thousand dollars!"

When Ivan told me this, I was amazed. This was ironclad proof that the charges against him were utterly bogus. It was as if members of the New York City Police Department had raided a Manhattan office on suspicion of tax evasion when the IRS had no problem with the taxes in question. No matter how distorted the Russian legal system was, this letter completely exonerated Ivan.

After this, I began to relax for the first time in months. As September moved into October, no more bad news came out of Russia. I had been operating in full-blown crisis mode, but over that fall, little by little my Russian crisis meetings started to be replaced by regular investment meetings. It was a great relief to talk with analysts about stocks instead of lawyers about raids.

One country that kept on coming up in these meetings was South Korea.

South Korea is hardly a developing country like Thailand or Indonesia, but its stock market traded at a 40 percent discount to the United States on a price-earnings ratio basis. This made it interesting for an investor like me. If I could find no good reason for this discount, then certain Korean stocks could potentially re-rate. I decided to get on a plane in October to visit some Korean companies to determine why their equities were so cheap.

I arrived in Seoul on the evening of Sunday, October 14. After a twelve-hour flight and a two-hour drive from Incheon Airport into town, I checked into the Intercontinental and unpacked. Even though it was 11:00 p.m. in Seoul, my body thought it was early afternoon. I spent most of that night trying and failing to go to sleep and eventually gave up. I pulled myself out of bed and sat at the window overlooking the lights of Seoul. The city—bright and twinkling and distinctly foreign—stood outside like a scene from a movie. Whether in Tokyo, Beijing, Hong Kong, or Bangkok, every Western traveler seems to have one of these jet-lagged, late-night moments upon arriving in Asia.

I got only a few hours of sleep that night and had a painful time getting out of bed in the morning to meet Kevin Park, a thirty-five-year-old Korean broker who was taking me to visit various companies. He'd arranged meetings with banks, a real estate company, and an auto parts supplier. The jet lag made every meeting drag, and I practically had to pinch myself under the table to stay awake. It was a hard day.

By the evening, I was ready to collapse, but Kevin insisted on taking me to a Korean barbecue. He had been so helpful and earnest in planning the trip I couldn't turn him down. I drank two Diet Cokes in my room, splashed some cold water on my face, and met him in the hotel lobby. At the restaurant we ordered bulgogi, bibimbap, and kimchi. At the end of dinner, just when I thought I could finally go back to the hotel and fall into bed, Kevin told me we were meeting some of his work colleagues for drinks at a nearby karaoke bar. It was excruciating as he and his friends tried to ply me with Johnnie Walker Black Label as they took turns at the karaoke machine. Finally, at midnight, when I could no longer keep my eyes open, he took pity on me and put me in a taxi back to the hotel.

The next day consisted of more meetings and more food, yet in spite of the jet lag and overbearing hospitality, I was having fun being a regular investment analyst again and I savored being momentarily removed from the grave things going on in Russia.

I returned to the Intercontinental at the end of the day to check my messages. British mobile phones don't work in Korea, so my office was forwarding my messages to the hotel. As I leafed through a little stack of white paper in the elevator, I saw one from Vadim that read, "Call me when you get this. Urgent."

Vadim never overreacted, so when he said "urgent," it really was urgent. My heart started pounding as I raced to my room to make the call.

He picked up on the first ring. "Bill, we got a call from a bailiff at the Saint Petersburg court early this morning. He said there's a judgment against one of our Russian investment companies, and he wants to know where he can find the money to satisfy it." Although we had sold all of our shares in Russia, we had to keep the empty investment holding companies in place for three years in order to liquidate them properly.

"Judgment? What judgment? What's he talking about?"

"I don't know."

"Do you know if this person is even real?" It was perfectly plausible that this was some kind of clumsy setup.

"No, but I don't think we should ignore it."

"Of course not. How much money was he talking about?" I imagined that we had misplaced a $200 courier bill and this had somehow found its way to court.

"Seventy-one million dollars."

Seventy-one million dollars? "That's insane, Vadim! What is this about?"

"I have no idea, Bill."

"Vadim, get Eduard and Sergei on this ASAP. We need to find out what's going on."

"I will."

My week of distraction had been shattered. The Russians hadn't given up at all.

This whole bailiff thing was ludicrous. Where the hell did this claim come from? Who was behind it? How could they make a claim on assets that were no longer even in Russia? They couldn't. Or could they?

I could barely think about Korea anymore. I had to get back to London as soon as possible. I called Kevin, apologized profusely that I wouldn't be able to make dinner, and asked him to cancel the rest of my meetings. I then called Korean Air and booked the first flight to London the next morning.

After the long flight, I went straight to the office to meet Vadim and Ivan. We settled into the conference room and they debriefed me on what they'd learned while I was in the air.

The first thing was that the judgment was indeed real. Eduard had taken the train to Saint Petersburg, gone to the court, retrieved the case file, and taken pictures of the documents with his digital camera. Vadim pulled one of these pictures from a stack of papers and laid it in front of me. He pointed at a word on the page. "This says Mahaon," which was one of the fund's dormant investment holding companies. "And this is the amount." It was in rubles, but I did a quick mental calculation and could see that it was roughly $71 million.

"How could we not have known about this?" I demanded, thinking it was some colossal oversight on our side.

"Sergei was wondering the same thing," Vadim said. "While Eduard was in Saint Petersburg, Sergei checked the company ownership database."

"And?" I asked with a sinking feeling.

Ivan sighed. "Mahaon's been stolen, Bill."

"What do you mean stolen? How do you steal a company?"

Ivan, who knew a bit about the company registration process, said, "It's not simple. But basically a company's owners can be illegally changed without you knowing if the person taking control of the company has the company's original seals, certificates of ownership, and registration files."

This hit me hard. "Those are the documents that were seized by the police," I said quietly. "When they raided Jamie's office."

"Exactly," Ivan confirmed.

He explained that once this was done, the new owners could act just like any other owners of a company. They could run it, liquidate it, take its assets, relocate it—anything they wanted.

Everything had now become clear. We had become the victims of something called a "Russian raider attack." These typically involved corrupt police officers fabricating criminal cases, corrupt judges approving the seizure of assets, and organized criminals hurting anyone who stood in the way. The practice was so common that *Vedomosti*, the independent Russian newspaper, had even published a menu of "raider" services with prices: freezing assets—$50,000; opening a criminal case—$50,000; securing a court order—$300,000; etc. The only way to fight these Russian raiders effectively was to retaliate with extreme violence, which was obviously not an option for us.

Sergei spent the night doing research and called us the next day to explain how it had all happened: "Mahaon, plus two other companies that belonged to you, have been reregistered to a company called Pluton, located in Kazan." Kazan is the provincial capital of Tatarstan, a semiautonomous republic located in central Russia.

"Who owns Pluton?" I asked.

"A man named Viktor Markelov, who, according to the criminal records database, was convicted for manslaughter in 2001."

"Unbelievable!" I exclaimed. "So the police raid our offices, seize a ton of documents, and then use a convicted killer to fraudulently reregister our companies?"

"That's exactly what happened," Sergei said. "And it gets worse. Those documents were then used to forge a bunch of backdated contracts that claim your stolen company owes seventy-one million dollars to an empty shell company that you never did any business with."

"My God," I said.

"Wait. It gets *even* worse. Those forged contracts were taken to court, and a lawyer who you didn't hire showed up to defend your companies. As soon as the case started, he pleaded guilty to seventy-one million dollars in liabilities."

As rotten and incomprehensible as this was, everything now made sense. As the story crystallized in front of my eyes, I started laughing.

At first a little, then loudly. There was nothing funny about what was going on, but I was laughing out of sheer relief. At first everyone else was silent, but then Ivan joined me, followed by Vadim.

We now knew exactly what they were up to, and they had completely failed. They wanted the Hermitage money, but none of it was there. Based on the published price list of corporate raiding, these guys had spent millions bribing judges, cops, and clerks only to get nothing.

The only person who didn't laugh was Sergei. "Don't relax, Bill," he said ominously over the speakerphone. "This is not the end of the story."

"What do you mean?" Vadim asked.

"I don't know," Sergei answered, his phone line crackling slightly. "But Russian stories never have happy endings."

25

High-Pitched Jamming Equipment

We could have walked away from the situation right then and there. Except for one big wrinkle: a criminal case was still open against Ivan.

We decided the best way to defend Ivan was to go after Kuznetsov and Karpov, both of whom were obviously involved in both Ivan's case and the theft of our companies. To do that, we decided to file criminal complaints against them with the Russian authorities. Because our legal team was so stretched, we brought in Vladimir Pastukhov, the lawyer who had urged Vadim to flee Russia in 2006, to help out.

He came to London and installed himself in the conference room of our new offices. With the successful launch of Hermitage Global, we had moved into a newly refurbished building on Golden Square, just behind Piccadilly Circus, and were no longer crammed together in a warren of serviced offices in Covent Garden.

Vladimir surrounded himself with our files, and over several days interviewed each of us. He then started drafting a long complaint about the theft of our companies and the creation of these huge fake liabilities. A special section described the fraud's reliance on the documents and electronic files that were seized during the police raids led by Kuznetsov and which Karpov kept in his custody.

While Vladimir was working on offense, Eduard was in Russia working on defense. For five months he'd been trying to get the relevant parts of the case file on Ivan to prepare his defense, and for five months Major Karpov had steadfastly refused to hand them over.

Eduard had been filing complaints with prosecutors and Karpov's superiors, but they'd achieved nothing. With every refusal his frustration mounted. It wasn't just professional for Eduard, it was starting to get personal.

But then, on November 29, Eduard received an unexpected call from Karpov, who said that he was finally willing to provide some of the documents that Eduard had been requesting for months. Eduard cleared his schedule and rushed to the Moscow Interior Ministry headquarters on Novoslobodskaya Ulitsa. Karpov met him at the entrance, and when they reached his small office, Karpov waved his hand toward an empty seat.

Eduard sat.

"I know you've been asking for the Cherkasov documents, and I'm prepared to share some of them with you today," Karpov said with a magnanimous smirk.

Eduard regarded Karpov with a mix of exasperation and contempt. "You should have given them to me a long time ago."

"Whatever. I'm giving them to you now. Be grateful." Karpov then stood, took a ten-inch stack of paper in both hands, walked to the other side of his desk, and plonked them in front of Eduard. "There's one thing, however. The copier is broken, so if you want any copies, you'll have to do them by hand."

Eduard is normally dispassionate and professional, but here was a thirty-year-old police officer strutting around in a $3,000 Italian suit, with an expensive watch and manicured nails, taunting Eduard like a high school bully. After five months of trying to get this information, this behavior was simply too much for Eduard. He'd been an Interior Ministry investigator himself and had never treated anyone this way.

Eduard was so frustrated that he shouted, "I don't know what you think you're doing! We've caught you. We know everything about what happened in Saint Petersburg!"

Karpov turned white. "W-what? What happened in Saint Petersburg?" he stammered, playing dumb.

"We have all the evidence. The documents in your custody were used to steal three companies and create huge fake liabilities. As a criminal lawyer, I can tell you that this will be an easy case to prove."

Karpov crossed his arms and leaned forward, his eyes darting around the room. After several seconds he motioned for Eduard to come to his side of the desk. Eduard did so. Without saying a word, Karpov started typing furiously into his laptop, apparently thinking that his office was bugged.

After Karpov finished, Eduard leaned forward to read the message. *It wasn't me. This is Kuznetsov's project.*

Karpov then deleted everything on the screen.

In seconds, Karpov had gone from being arrogant to submissive, and he even selected some of the more important documents from Ivan's file for Eduard to copy.

Eduard wasn't sure what to make of this turn of events, but he wasn't going to miss this opportunity to get the documents for Ivan. He furiously hand-copied the papers, but then had to stop when Karpov announced he had to leave for another meeting. Karpov took the unusual step of escorting Eduard to the front door of the building and even continued walking with him to his car. Karpov seemed to be hoping that Eduard would say something more about what we knew as they walked.

Once Eduard got into his car, he realized that he had just made a big mistake. We hadn't authorized him to talk about our discoveries with anybody. By losing his cool, he'd let the bad guys know that we were onto them.

After regaining his composure, Eduard called London to tell us what happened. It was definitely a mistake, but given how obstinate Karpov had been, I could hardly be angry with Eduard. After apologizing, Eduard advised us that we needed to file our complaints as soon as possible since our secret was out. When I asked Vladimir how much more time he needed, he told me, "Four days," which meant Monday, December 3, 2007.

Meanwhile, I had to go to Geneva for a client lunch on November 30. With everything that was going on, I would have preferred to stay in London, but the meeting was too important to cancel. I flew out in the morning and returned the same evening to London City Airport. As my taxi wound its way through the back streets of Canary Wharf on my way home, my secretary called with my messages.

She took me through the list and at the end said, "Someone named Igor Sagiryan called for you. Would you like me to get him on the line now?"

"Sagiryan?" I searched my memory. I knew that name. As I looked through my contacts in my BlackBerry, I remembered that he was one of the main guys at Renaissance Capital, the same firm that Boris Jordan ran when I was fighting Sidanco. I'd met Sagiryan only once, at an investment conference a few years earlier, so I wondered why he was trying to reach me.

"Sure. I'll talk to him."

She called him up and put him through. "Igor. Bill Browder here. How are you?"

"I'm okay, as much as one could be okay these days. Listen, when are you going to be in London? I want to see you and have a short meeting, preferably face-to-face rather than over the phone."

This was a strange request. I barely knew the guy and he was proposing to fly from Moscow to meet with me. "Sure. What's up?"

"Not much, but as you know, everybody is under certain pressures, so I just wanted to discuss with you what other steps we can take because we are working a lot with you, so I mean we're now having some small difficulties, but it's better to have none."

His answer made no sense. I had no idea what "pressures" and "small difficulties" he was referring to and began to suspect this had something to do with Eduard's meeting with Karpov.

"Is there anything specific you want to talk about right now?"

"Well, the question is that honestly I'm on a mobile phone. You are a lucky guy, you live in the UK, but I'm in Russia and I would prefer to meet in person."

Something unusual was going on. Perhaps Sagiryan was trying to deliver a message from the bad guys or negotiate with me on their

behalf. Whatever his agenda was, his request didn't seem coinciden-
tal, so I agreed to meet him at the Dorchester Hotel on December 11,
which was right after I returned from a business trip to the Middle
East that I was embarking on the next day.

I flew to Saudi Arabia the next morning, and the following Mon-
day our legal team filed our 244-page criminal complaints with the
Russian authorities. Two copies went to the general prosecutor (Rus-
sia's attorney general); two to the head of the State Investigative
Committee (Russia's FBI); and two to the head of the Internal Affairs
Department of the Interior Ministry.

I expected to see a reaction to these complaints sometime after
the New Year, but two days later, as I was walking through the lobby
of the Four Seasons in Riyadh, I got a call from an agitated Jamison
Firestone, who was still in Moscow. "Bill, are you on a clear line?"

"What?"

"Is your phone safe?"

"I have no idea. I'm in Saudi Arabia. Why?"

"I just had the strangest meeting with a guy named Igor Sagiryan."

"Sagiryan?"

"Yeah. He's the president of Renaissance Capital—"

"I know who he is. Why did he call you?"

"He wanted to talk about *you*, Bill."

"What?"

"It was weird. He knew everything about your situation. When I
went to his office, he had a stack of papers on his desk about you. He
picked up a sheet and made a strange gesture showing that the situation was serious. He said that the people involved are very bad. The
kind who hurt people. Guys with criminal records."

"What did he want?" I asked.

"That's the interesting part. He wanted me to convince you to
allow Renaissance to liquidate your stolen companies."

"Liquidate our stolen companies? That's absurd. Why would he
want to do that? *How* would he do that?"

"I have no idea. I don't understand how liquidating these things would help Ivan. Besides, how could Sagiryan liquidate something he doesn't control?"

We hung up. This development was very odd indeed. Where did Sagiryan get this information? It certainly hadn't been from us. This meant that my upcoming meeting with him might be a crucial opportunity to learn more about what our enemies were up to.

I hastened to finish my business in the Middle East. When I returned to London, I prepared for my meeting with Ivan and Vadim. If possible, I wanted to catch Sagiryan off guard.

It was also essential to record our conversation so that we could analyze every word he said. Two days before the meeting, I called Steven Beck, a former British Special Forces officer and security specialist whom I used for these kinds of situations. He came to the office with two surveillance specialists. One of them asked for my cashmere blazer. I reluctantly handed it to him and cringed as I watched him roughly cut the seam of the lapel, insert a microphone, and sew it back up. He then ran a wire through the jacket into my left-hand pocket, where he placed a slim digital recorder.

This is what I would use to record the meeting with Sagiryan.

The day of the meeting arrived. I left our offices on Golden Square, hopped into a black taxi, and turned on the recording device as we pulled away from the curb. I was a ball of nerves. I was about to go face-to-face with someone I suspected to be connected to a major criminal conspiracy. I'd confronted countless financial crooks and other rogues in my business dealings, but never in my life had I walked willingly into such a potentially dangerous and hostile situation. It took every ounce of effort for me to keep my cool.

The taxi arrived at the Dorchester Hotel on Park Lane and pulled into the triangular driveway between a silver Bentley and a red Ferrari. These were not out of place given the ostentatious nature of the Russian oligarchs and Middle Eastern sheikhs who favored the hotel. I was early. I went inside and settled into an olive-green armchair in the lobby, scanning the room with its red marble columns and matching drapes, trying to pick Sagiryan out of the crowd. At about 7:10 p.m., he rushed in, looking as if he were late for a normal business meeting. Taller than me, Sagiryan was a fifty-five-year-old businessman with gray hair, jowly cheeks, and a soft double chin that ran straight into his neck. He looked like an indulgent grandfather, not someone I suspected of having been involved in our troubles in Russia.

For a while we made small talk about London, the weather, Moscow, and politics, dancing around the real reason we were here. Finally, I asked what was so important that he was ready to come all the way to England to see me.

He took a breath and told me how Renaissance had been recently raided by the police. He claimed the raid had happened because Renaissance had done business with us. He repeated what he said to Jamison, proposing that if I allowed him to liquidate Hermitage's stolen companies, it would somehow solve all of the problems that he and Renaissance were having.

None of this made any sense. First, Hermitage hadn't done any business with Renaissance in years. Second, how could I give him permission to liquidate our companies if we didn't own them anymore? And third, even if I could give him permission, how would that benefit us, and specifically Ivan, who still had a criminal case open against him? I silently concluded that Sagiryan was either stupid or that he had another agenda. I suspected the latter.

I tried to draw him out as far as I could for the recording. Unfortunately, every direct question I asked was countered with an evasive or incomprehensible answer, similar to the way he'd spoken to me on the phone when he'd first called.

Our conversation ended when he looked at his watch and stood abruptly. "I'm late for dinner, Bill. I hope you have a happy holiday." We shook hands, and just as quickly as he had arrived, he left. I followed him through the lobby, went out the door, and hopped into a taxi to return to the office to share the recording.

When I got to Golden Square, the entire team, plus Steven and one of his surveillance guys, was waiting for me in the conference room. I pulled the recorder from my pocket, disconnected it from the wire, and handed it to Steven. He placed it on the table and hit play.

We leaned in. We heard the sounds of me talking to the first cab-driver and the ride to the Dorchester. We heard my footsteps on the pavement and the greeting from the hotel's doorman. We heard the sounds of the Dorchester's lobby. And then, at 7:10, we heard a burst of white noise that drowned out everything.

Steven took the recorder, thinking something was wrong with it. He rewound it a few seconds and pressed play again. The result was the same. He fast-forwarded, hoping to pick up something later in the conversation, but the white noise persisted. It disappeared only when I left the hotel and asked the doorman for a taxi. Steven hit stop again.

I looked at him. "What was that?"

He frowned, turning the recorder over in his hand. "I don't know. It could either be that this thing is faulty or that Sagiryan was using some kind of high-pitched jamming equipment."

"Jesus Christ. Jamming equipment. Where do you even get that?"

"It's not easy. But it's commonly used by special services like the FSB."

I found this extremely unsettling. I thought I was being clever by hiring Steven and playing the spy, but it turned out that I might just have sat down with an *actual* spy. I decided then and there that this would be the end of my naive foray into cloak-and-dagger tradecraft.

Sagiryan was a dead end, and we were no closer to understanding what the bad guys were up to. All of our hopes now rested with the complaints we'd filed with the Russian authorities.

The day after the Sagiryan meeting, we received our first official reply from the Saint Petersburg branch of the Russian State Investigative Committee. Vadim printed it, skimmed the legalese, and got to the punch line. "Listen to this, Bill. It says, 'Nothing wrong happened in the Saint Petersburg court, and the request to open a criminal case is declined due to lack of a crime.'"

"'Lack of a crime'? Our companies were stolen!"

"Wait, there's more. They helpfully point out that they won't prosecute our lawyer, Eduard, for filing our complaint," Vadim said sarcastically.

The next day we received another response. This time it was from the Internal Affairs Department of the Interior Ministry, which should have been *very* interested in Kuznetsov's and Karpov's dirty business.

"Get this," Vadim said, reading over it. "Internal Affairs is passing our complaint to Pavel Karpov himself to investigate!"

"You can't be serious."

"I am. It says so right here."

Over the next week we received three more responses, all of them equally unhelpful.

By the New Year, only one complaint was left outstanding. I had no reason to think the response would be any different. But on the morning of January 9, 2008, Eduard got a call from an investigator named Rostislav Rassokhov from the Major Crimes Department of the Russian State Investigative Committee.[1] Rassokhov had been put in charge of dealing with the complaint and asked Eduard to come to the Investigative Committee's headquarters to go over it.

When Eduard arrived, he was greeted by a man roughly his age. Rassokhov wore a wrinkled polyester suit and a cheap watch and had a bad haircut—all encouraging signs in a land as corrupt as Russia. They walked to Rassokhov's office, sat down, and went line by line through the complaint. Rassokhov asked detailed questions with a look of stone-cold seriousness. At the end of the meeting he indicated he was going to open a preliminary investigation into our allegations against Kuznetsov and Karpov and bring them in for questioning.

This was excellent news. I could only imagine the looks on Kuznetsov's and Karpov's faces when they were invited to the Investigative Committee for questioning. After all the terrible things they had done to us, it felt as if the tables were about to be turned.

I enjoyed this feeling for nearly two months, until one evening in

---

1   Russia's FBI.

early March when Vadim walked into my office looking very anxious. "I just got a message from my source Aslan."

"What about?" I asked nervously. I was getting uncomfortably used to Vadim being the constant bearer of bad news, especially when it came from Aslan.

He thrust Aslan's message in front of me and pointed at the Russian words. "This says, 'Criminal case opened against Browder. Case No. 401052. Republic of Kalmykia. Tax evasion in large amounts.'"

I felt as if someone had just knocked the air out of me. It looked as if Kuznetsov and Karpov were getting their revenge for being called in for questioning. I had a hundred questions I wanted to ask, but it was 7:30 p.m. and, annoyingly, Elena and I were obligated to be at a dinner in half an hour that had been planned for months. An old friend from Salomon Brothers and his fiancée had made a big deal of securing an impossible-to-get reservation at a new London restaurant called L'Atelier de Joël Robuchon, and I couldn't cancel on such short notice.

On the way to the restaurant I called Elena to share Aslan's message. For the first time since this crisis started, our emotional rhythms were in sync and we panicked simultaneously. When we arrived at the restaurant, our friends were already there, sitting in a booth and smiling. They announced that they'd taken the liberty of ordering the seven-course degustation menu for the four of us, which would take at least three hours to consume. I soldiered through dinner, trying to hide my raw panic as they blithely talked about wedding venues, honeymoon plans, and other fantastic London restaurants. I couldn't wait to leave. The moment the *second* dessert course was served, Elena squeezed my knee under the table and made an excuse about getting home to our children. We rushed out. On the way home, Elena and I just sat in the cab in silence.

This new criminal case against me required immediate attention. The next morning, I told Eduard to drop everything and go straight to Elista, the capital of Kalmykia, to find out as much as he could.

Early the next day Eduard flew to Volgograd, hired a taxi, and made the four-hour trip to Elista. The landscape of Kalmykia—a southern Russian republic on the Caspian Sea populated by Asiatic Buddhists—was the most desolate he had ever seen. It was flat and barren with no grass or trees, just brown land and gray skies for as far as the eye could see. The only breaks in the monotony were a few dilapidated buildings every ten or twenty miles.

When he arrived in Elista, he went straight to the Interior Ministry building on Pushkina Ulitsa. The clean, modern four-story building was across from a public square containing a golden pagoda.

He entered, introduced himself to the receptionist, and asked if he could see the investigator in charge of criminal case number 401052. A few minutes later, a short, middle-aged Asiatic man with bowlegs and a leather vest emerged and said, "How can I help you?"

Eduard shook his hand. "Do you have a case opened against William Browder?"

The investigator, Dmitry Nuskhinov, gave Eduard a searching look. "Who are you?"

"I'm sorry. I've just come down from Moscow. I'm Mr. Browder's lawyer." Eduard then showed the investigator his power of attorney and asked, "Can you please tell me about the case against my client?"

The investigator relaxed. "Yes, yes, of course. Please come to my office." The two men walked down a long corridor to a small and cluttered room, where the investigator allowed Eduard to inspect the case file.

The Russian authorities were charging me with two counts of tax evasion in 2001. Kalmykia had tax breaks not unlike those in Delaware or Puerto Rico, and the fund had registered two of our investment companies there. The case was clearly trumped-up. Inside the file Eduard found audits from the tax authorities that showed that everything had been correctly paid.

Eduard pointed this out to the investigator, who sighed heavily. "Listen, I didn't want to have anything to do with this. They forced me back from vacation to meet with a high-level delegation from Moscow."

"What high-level delegation?"

"There were four of them. They demanded that this case be opened. They said it was an instruction right from the top, and it had to do with worsening relations between Britain and Russia. I didn't have any choice," Nuskhinov said, clearly worried about all the laws he'd broken by following their orders. We later learned that the delegation consisted of Karpov, two of Kuznetsov's subordinates, and an officer from Department K of the FSB.

"So what's the status of all this?" Eduard asked.

"It was opened here and we issued a federal search warrant for Browder."

When Eduard got back to Moscow the next evening, he called and told us everything. Aslan had been absolutely right. The criminal case against Ivan was just the beginning, and we had to believe that many more would follow.

26

The Riddle

On October 1, 1939, Winston Churchill made a famous speech in which he discussed Russia's prospect of joining the Second World War: "I cannot forecast to you the action of Russia. It is a riddle wrapped in a mystery inside an enigma; but perhaps there is a key. That key is Russian national interest."

Fast-forward to 2008. Churchill's observations about Russia were still correct, with one big proviso. Instead of the national interest guiding Russia's actions, they were now guided by money, specifically the criminal acquisition of money by government officials.

Everything about our situation was a riddle. Why would Karpov and three of his colleagues jump on a plane and fly hundreds of miles to Kalmykia to open a criminal case against me just for revenge? Why would they pursue the case against Ivan if it accomplished nothing for them? Why go through the trouble of raiding all those banks if the Hermitage assets weren't in Russia?

I couldn't figure it out.

The more I thought about it, the more convinced I was that the answer to this riddle lay in the remains of our former investment companies that had been fraudulently reregistered. They didn't have much economic value, but if we could somehow regain ownership of them, we would have the right to request all the relevant information from the government. From that, we could piece together exactly who—for this clearly went beyond Kuznetsov and Karpov—was behind the fraud.

To do this, we took legal action in the Moscow arbitration court to have our companies returned to us. This must have come as a surprise to the people behind the fraud because they immediately countersued us in the Kazan arbitration court, forcing the case to be relocated to Tatarstan. Presumably, they thought that the Kazan court would be friendlier to them.

I wasn't sure about our chances in a provincial Russian court, but I was happy to see our opponents reacting so quickly and defensively. We'd obviously touched a nerve. Eduard and one junior lawyer immediately got on a plane to Kazan. They arrived there on a cold day in March and went to the courthouse, an elegant building inside the "Kremlin" of the Republic of Tatarstan. Eduard was used to spending his time in grimy criminal courts where people were aggressive and tension permeated the air, but this was a civil court. The surroundings were nicer and the people were, well, much more civil.

On the day before the hearing, Eduard went to the clerk to request the case file. She typed the names of our companies into her database and helpfully said, "There are two lawsuits involving these companies. Would you like both of them?"

This was the first time Eduard had heard of a second lawsuit, but he deliberately showed no reaction to her question and only smiled. "Yes. I'd like both, please."

She went into the file room and returned with a box full of documents, suggesting that Eduard might find it easier to study them at a table down the hall. He thanked her, walked to the table, and went through the case files. The first case was the countersuit for which Eduard was there. But the second case was one he had never seen. A *$581 million* judgment against Parfenion, another of our stolen investment companies.

He rifled through the paperwork completely mesmerized. The judgment was a carbon copy of the Saint Petersburg one. They'd used the same bogus lawyer and the same forged contracts containing the same information seized by the police.

The moment I heard about the additional $581 million judgment,

I wondered how many other Russian courts had similar fraudulent judgments against our stolen companies. I shared my concerns with everyone on the team, and Sergei began searching the court databases throughout Russia. Within a week he discovered one more— a $232 million judgment in the Moscow arbitration court.

In total, roughly $1 billion of judgments had been awarded against our stolen companies using the same exact scheme.

These discoveries only made the riddle that much more complicated. It still wasn't clear how the criminals would make any money out of these claims. Just because they were "owed" this money didn't mean it would magically appear in their bank accounts. *There was no money to pay them!* I was convinced that they had another agenda. But what was it?

It wasn't obvious, and I realized that I needed to take a step back and have another look at everything to see if I could spot any patterns or connections that we might have missed.

On a Saturday morning at the end of May 2008, I asked Ivan to come to the office and bring all of our new legal documents, the bank statements, and the warrants to our big boardroom. We unloaded the box with all the documents on the long wooden table and made a number of piles. One for each judgment, one for each bank raid, and one for each criminal case. When it was all laid out, we started constructing a timeline of what had happened.

"When was the last Kuznetsov raid on our banks?" I asked.

Ivan shuffled through the stack of papers. "August seventeenth."

"Okay. What were the dates of the fake court judgments?"

"Saint Petersburg was September third, Kazan was November thirteenth, and Moscow was December eleventh."

"So let me get this straight—the bad guys went to all the courts and spent all sorts of money to get these judgments, even *after* they knew there were no assets or money left in our companies?"

"Apparently so," Ivan said, noticing this inconsistency for the first time.

"Why would they do that?"

"Maybe they wanted to use the judgments as collateral to borrow money," Ivan suggested.

"That's ridiculous. No bank would lend money off the back of one of these amateurish judgments."

"What about them trying to seize your personal assets abroad?"

The thought was horrifying, but I knew it was impossible. I'd confirmed this with my British lawyers as soon as we learned about the claims in Saint Petersburg.

We sat in silence for several moments, then a lightbulb went on over my head. "How much were the Hermitage profits in 2006?"

"Just a sec." Ivan opened his laptop and retrieved a file. "Nine hundred and seventy-three million dollars."

"And how much did we pay in taxes that year?"

He consulted his laptop again. "Two hundred and thirty million dollars."

"This may sound crazy. But do you think . . . do you think they're going to try to get that two hundred and thirty million dollars refunded to them?"

"That *is* crazy, Bill. The tax authorities would never do that."

"I don't know. I think we should ask Sergei."

That Monday, Ivan called Sergei to test this theory. But like Ivan, Sergei was completely dismissive. "Impossible," he said without even thinking about it. "The idea that someone could steal past taxes is preposterous."

But an hour later, Sergei called back. "Perhaps I was too hasty. I've looked at the tax code, and what you're describing is theoretically possible. Although in practice, I can't imagine it ever happening."

During those weeks, while I was sitting in my office dreaming up theories, Sergei was in the trenches conducting his own investigation. More than anything else, he wanted to know about everyone who was involved with this crime. He'd written to the government office in Moscow where our stolen companies were registered, demanding all the information it had. While he got no response, the perpetrators did something telling. They immediately moved the stolen companies to an obscure town in southern Russia called Novocherkassk. Sergei's letter had obviously spooked them. He then wrote to the registration office in Novocherkassk, requesting the same information. While the officials there were just as silent as they were in Moscow, the criminals moved the companies again. This time to Khimki, a suburb of Moscow. This game of cat and mouse was clearly getting to the bad guys, so Sergei kept it up and wrote to the Khimki registrar too.

Sergei understood that while the people we were fighting had no respect for the law, they had an almost slavish respect for procedure and bureaucracy. Just as he'd rattled the bad guys into moving the companies around, he thought he would rattle the police by inserting more evidence about their own involvement in the crime into the case file. Sergei knew that once something went into the case file, procedure dictated that it would stay there forever. Sergei hoped that, even though the investigation into our stolen companies was going nowhere, in the future an honest investigator might take over and do the right thing. This mere possibility would leave the conspirators constantly on edge.

Sergei set up an appointment at the Investigative Committee for June 5, 2008. When he arrived at its building, he was met by the detective in charge and taken to his office. Just before the detective opened the door, Sergei noticed that the man's hand was shaking nervously.

He pushed open the door, and it immediately became apparent why. There, sitting at the desk, was Lieutenant Colonel Artem Kuznetsov.

Sergei was startled. He looked straight into the eyes of the detective and said, "What's he doing here?"

The detective avoided Sergei's glare and said, "Lieutenant Colonel Kuznetsov has been assigned to assist the investigative team for this case."

First Karpov had been assigned to investigate himself, and now Kuznetsov was doing the same!

"I won't talk to you in front of him," Sergei said forcefully.

"Okay," the detective said uncertainly. "Then you'll have to wait in the hall until we finish our meeting."

Sergei sat on an uncomfortable metal chair for an hour, clutching his files in his lap. Kuznetsov and the detective probably hoped that Sergei would abandon his plan, but he didn't. When Kuznetsov finally left, Sergei rose and went inside. He sat in the chair, provided the evidence, and gave his witness statement, explicitly naming Kuznetsov and Karpov in the crimes. Following procedure, the detective had no choice but to accept this and put it into the case file.

Sergei left the Investigative Committee's headquarters and hopped on the Metro. What had just happened was beyond comprehension. Sergei had expected his testimony to go nowhere. He had expected his witness statement to be ignored. He had even expected to be treated rudely. What he hadn't expected was to find the very man he was giving evidence against to be part of the investigation team.

It took the whole ride back to the office and a couple of laps around the block for Sergei to calm down, but when he returned to his desk at Firestone Duncan, he found something else he didn't expect. A letter from the Khimki tax office, one of the registration offices he had previously sent a letter to looking for information on our stolen companies.

Sergei tore it open. For once, someone had actually done his or her job. There was information, there were names, but most importantly the letter showed that the people who'd stolen our companies had set up accounts at two obscure banks: Universal Savings Bank and Intercommerz Bank.

This was a huge breakthrough. Why would three companies with $1 billion of fake liabilities and no assets need bank accounts? Sergei immediately logged on to the Russian Central Bank website. He typed in Universal Savings Bank and found that it was so small that it had capital of only $1.5 million. Intercommerz was only slightly bigger, with $12 million of capital. They could hardly even be called banks.

But then he noticed something extremely interesting. Because these two banks were so small, the moment they received any money, he could see the spike in deposits right there on the website. And indeed, there were some big inflows. In late December 2007, shortly after these bank accounts were opened for our stolen companies, Universal Savings Bank received $97 million in deposits, and Intercommerz received $147 million.

It was then that Sergei remembered our question about the tax rebates. The amount these two banks had received was roughly the same amount the Hermitage companies had paid in taxes in 2006. This couldn't just be coincidence. He quickly gathered all of the judgments and laid them side by side with our companies' tax filings. At that moment everything crystallized for Sergei.

The Saint Petersburg judgment against Mahaon was for $71 million, and sure enough Mahaon's profits for 2006 were exactly $71 million. Parfenion's judgment in Kazan was for $581 million, and the 2006 profits were identical. It was the same story in Moscow with our third stolen company, Rilend. In total, the conspirators had created $973 million of judgments to offset $973 million of real profits.

Sergei called Ivan immediately, and after a few minutes of explanation Ivan jumped up and waved over Vadim and me. "Look at this, guys," Ivan said excitedly, pointing toward his screen.

Ivan brought the Central Bank website up, and we looked at the two spikes in deposits that Sergei had uncovered.

"Son of a bitch," I said.

"Bill, Sergei figured it out," Ivan said.

"This is great, but how can we prove that this money actually came from the tax authorities?" I asked.

Vadim said, "I'll ask several sources in Moscow if they can verify the wire transfers. Now that we know the names of the banks, we can probably figure out where the money came from."

Two days later, Vadim rushed into my office and laid out several sheets of paper on my desk. "These are the wire transfers," he said with a satisfied grin.

I grabbed the papers, which were all in Russian. "What do they say?"

He flipped to the last page. "This confirms a tax refund payment of one hundred and thirty-nine million dollars from the Russian tax service to Parfenion. This one is for seventy-five million for Rilend. And this is sixteen million dollars for Mahaon. That's two hundred and thirty million dollars in total."

This was the same amount of money—$230 million—that we had paid in taxes. *The same.*

We assembled in my office and called Sergei to congratulate him on his amazing detective work, but even though he'd solved the riddle, he was distraught. These people had stolen from the Russian taxpayers—from him, his family, his friends. Everyone he knew.

"This has to be the most cynical thing I've ever seen," he said.

It was the largest tax refund in Russian history. It was so big and so brazen that we were sure we had them. This had to be a rogue operation, and we now had the evidence to expose it and bring these guys to justice.

Which was exactly what we intended to do.

27

DHL

In my opinion, Vladimir Putin had authorized my expulsion from Russia, and he probably approved the attempts to steal our assets, but I found it inconceivable that he would allow state officials to steal $230 million from his own government. I was convinced that as soon as we shared the evidence of these crimes with the Russian authorities, then the good guys would get the bad guys and that would be the end of the story. In spite of all that had happened, I still believed that there were some good guys left in Russia. So on July 23, 2008, we started filing detailed complaints about the tax rebate fraud, sending them to every law enforcement and regulatory agency in Russia.

We also gave the story to the *New York Times* and to Russia's most prominent independent news outlet, *Vedomosti*. The articles were explosive, and the story quickly got picked up widely, both in Russia and internationally.

Several days after the story broke, I was invited by Echo Moscow, Russia's leading independent radio station, to give a forty-five-minute phone interview. I accepted and, in a live broadcast on July 29, methodically went through the whole ordeal: the raids, the theft of our companies, the false court judgments, the involvement of ex-convicts, the police complicity, and most importantly, the theft of $230 million of taxpayer money. The interviewer, Matvei Ganapolsky, a veteran reporter who had years of experience with Russian venality and corruption, was noticeably shocked. When I had finished, he said, "If our broadcast hasn't been switched off, then tomorrow some arrests must be carried out."

I thought so too—except nothing was done. The hours passed into days, and there was nothing. The days passed into weeks, and there was still nothing. It was hard to believe that such a huge story about the theft of government money would elicit no response.

But then there *was* a response—just not the one I was expecting. On August 21, 2008, during an unusually still and hot summer day in London, the phone in my office started to ring. First it was Sergei, calling from Firestone Duncan; then it was Vladimir Pastukhov, calling from his home office; then it was Eduard, calling from his dacha just outside Moscow. Each of our lawyers had the same message: a team from the Russian Interior Ministry was raiding his office.

Eduard's message was the most disturbing. While he wasn't at his office, a DHL package arrived at 4:56 p.m. Thirty minutes later, a large group of police officers showed up to his workplace to conduct a search. No sooner had they started their search than they "found" the DHL package and seized it. As soon as they had it in their possession, they concluded their raid and left.

Obviously, the whole episode was constructed around the arrival of this mysterious package. Thankfully, Eduard's secretary had had the foresight to make a copy of the waybill and faxed it to us. We were shocked when we logged on to the DHL website, entered the waybill number, and got the return address for the package: Grafton House, 2-3 Golden Square, London W1F 9HR.

Our address in London.

Of course, it hadn't actually been sent from our office. The waybill, though, showed it *had* been sent from a DHL depot in south London, so we immediately contacted London's Metropolitan Police and explained the story. Later that day, Detective Sergeant Richard Norten, a young officer in a leather jacket and aviator sunglasses, strutted into our offices.

I introduced myself and asked whether he had had any luck figuring out who'd sent the parcel.

He shrugged and slid a DVD out of his jacket. "No, but I've got

the CCTV from the Lambeth DHL," he said. "Maybe you can identify them."

I indicated my desk. Vadim, Ivan, and I gathered in front of it as
Norten loaded the disc into my computer. He grabbed the mouse,
opened the file, and fast-forwarded through low-resolution video
footage of people coming and going at DHL's shipping desk. Then
he let it play. "Here it is."

We watched as two East European–looking men arrived at DHL.
One carried a plastic bag emblazoned with the logo of a retail store in
Kazan, Tatarstan. The bag was full of papers. The man stuffed these
documents into a DHL box and closed it, while the other man filled
out the waybill and paid in cash to have it shipped to Eduard's office.
When they were done, they turned their backs on the camera and
walked out of frame.

When it was finished, Norten asked, "Do you recognize either of
them?"

I looked at Ivan and Vadim. They shook their heads. "No," I answered. "We don't."

"Well, if you give me the names of the people who are making
problems for you in Russia, I can cross-reference them with flight
manifests out of Heathrow and Gatwick for the past week to see if
anything comes up."

I wasn't particularly hopeful, but we gave him a list of names and
he left.

I didn't have time to dwell on DHL, though, because the Russian
authorities were moving quickly. In addition to raiding our lawyers'
offices, they also summoned Vladimir and Eduard to appear at the
Kazan Interior Ministry's headquarters three days later on a Saturday
for questioning.

Not only was this summons illegal—lawyers cannot be compelled
to give evidence about their clients—it was ominous. Kazan's police
force had the reputation of being one of the most medieval and corrupt in Russia. They made the prison in *Midnight Express* look like
a Holiday Inn. The men who worked there were notorious for tortur-

ing detainees, including sodomizing them with champagne bottles, to extract confessions. Moreover, by inviting Eduard and Vladimir on a Saturday, they would be off the grid until the following Monday, and during that time the Kazan Interior Ministry could do anything it wanted, more or less in the dark.

I was absolutely terrified. This was a whole new level of escalation. I'd taken Ivan, Vadim, and other Hermitage people out of Russia to prevent exactly this kind of thing from happening, but never in my worst nightmares had I imagined that my lawyers could be targets.

Because of Vladimir's frail health, I was especially concerned about him being taken into custody. I called him right away. "I'm worried about you, Vladimir," I said anxiously.

But Vladimir was strangely unconcerned. He approached this situation as if it were an academic problem, one that he could examine and analyze, not one that was actually happening to him. "Don't worry, Bill. I'm protected as a barrister. They can't summon me for questioning. I've spoken to the Moscow bar association, and they will reply on my behalf. I won't go anywhere near Kazan."

"Let's assume for a second that you're wrong and they take you anyway. You wouldn't survive a week in jail given the state of your health."

"But Bill, it's just too outrageous. They can't start going after lawyers."

I was unmoved. "Listen, Vladimir. You were the one who convinced Vadim to evacuate in the middle of the night a couple of years ago—now it's your turn. At least come to London so we can talk about it in person."

He paused for a moment. "Let me think about it."

Vadim had a similar conversation with Eduard, who also didn't intend to leave. Both lawyers knew that these summonses were illegal and that they had strong grounds to reject them, so neither showed up for questioning.

Saturday came and went, and nothing happened. Same for Sunday. On Monday morning, I called Vladimir. "Okay, you survived the weekend and you've thought about it—when are you coming to London?"

"I don't know if I am. Everybody has told me the same thing. If I leave Russia, it would be the worst thing I could possibly do. It would appear as though I was guilty of something. Moreover, my life is here. All my clients are here. I can't just get up and leave, Bill."

I understood his reluctance, but I felt that the danger for him in staying was reaching a critical level. The people behind this were criminals, and they acted as if they had full control of the police. "But Vladimir, if they frame you, it doesn't matter whether you're innocent or guilty. You've got to get out of there. If not permanently, then at least until this all stops. It's crazy for you to stay!"

Despite my logic, he was resolute about staying—until he called me that Wednesday, sounding much less confident. "Bill, I've just received a new summons from Kazan."

"And?"

"I called the investigator who signed it and told him it was illegal. He responded that if I didn't show up, they would bring me in forcibly. I tried to talk to him about my health, but he wouldn't listen. He was talking like a gangster, not a police officer!"

"Now will you—"

"That's not even the worst of it, Bill. From all this stress, I had a problem with my eye last night. It's like a fireball in my head. I need to see my specialist as soon as possible, but he's in Italy."

"So go to Italy, then."

"I will as soon as I'm well enough to fly."

Later that day we found out that Eduard had also received a second summons. He thought that the Moscow bar association could deflect it, but there was nothing they could do either.

Since Eduard had been an investigator and a judge in his past life, he thought he might be able to use his network to find out who was behind these attacks, but nobody knew the answer.

One by one they said, "Until you can figure it out, you'd better disappear, Eduard."

For the first time in his life, Eduard was out of his comfort zone. He was the kind of person whom everyone went to for help, not the other way around. Since 1992, Eduard had been a criminal defense lawyer, representing a wide array of clients, and he had one of the most successful track records of any lawyer in Russia. Yet while he knew how to work the legal system, he didn't know how to disappear. Luckily, Eduard had many former clients who *did*, and when they heard of his troubles, several offered to help.

On Thursday, August 28, 2008—two days before he was due to appear in Kazan—Eduard called Vadim. "You may not hear from me for a while. If that happens, don't worry. I'll be all right." Vadim asked him what he meant, but Eduard interrupted him and said, "I have to go." He hung up.

After that call, Eduard removed the battery from his mobile phone and went to his apartment near Vorobyovy Hills in southern Moscow. He knew that he'd been under surveillance for several weeks. The people following him hadn't even bothered to hide it. A car was sitting outside his building night after night, with two men constantly watching his apartment. This was ominous because he didn't know whether they were the Russian Mafia or the police. Either way, he didn't want to find out.

After eating a quick dinner that evening, Eduard and his wife headed out for their regular evening stroll. The surveillance team didn't follow them because Eduard and his wife went on this walk every night, and they always came back.

They walked slowly along the wide street for about half a mile holding hands, but instead of turning back where they normally would, Eduard pulled his wife by the hand and they quickly crossed the street. There, waiting for him, was a large black Audi A8 sedan with tinted windows. Eduard's wife knew things had been getting bad for her husband, but she was totally unaware of his plan. He turned to her, took her by the hand, and said quickly, "Now's the time."

Tonight was the night he would disappear.

She took him by the shoulders and leaned in to give him a kiss.

Neither of them knew when they would see each other again. When their kiss ended, Eduard jumped into the backseat of the sedan, lay down, and the car was off.

His wife went back across the street, pushed her hands into her pockets, and walked home alone, blinking the tears from her eyes. She didn't notice when the surveillance team perked up. But perk up they did. It took them a few hours to process what had happened, but around midnight three people showed up at the apartment asking for Eduard.

But his wife had no idea where he was, and that was exactly what she told them.

If Eduard, with all his connections and knowledge of criminal law, had decided to go into hiding, then there was no question that Vladimir, an academic with severe disabilities, had to leave Russia right away.

I called Vladimir immediately, annoyed that he was still in Moscow. "Vladimir, Eduard is gone. When are you leaving?"

"Bill, I'm sorry, I'm still not well enough to travel. But your points are well taken." I didn't know exactly what he meant and he refused to elaborate, but it sounded as if he was going to leave.

I certainly hoped so. I was pretty sure that when he and Eduard didn't show up in Kazan on Saturday for their second summons, the corrupt cops would issue arrest warrants for both of them.

What Vladimir couldn't tell me was that he was assessing his options for getting out of Russia. The most attractive ones involved a land- or sea-based border crossing. The Russian border service was so antiquated that many of the remote crossings didn't have up-to-date technology for detecting fugitives. These posts were generally staffed with the rejects of the border service. Laziness and drunkenness were practically requirements for these positions, and they routinely let people slip by who were on the wanted list. Using these criteria, the two best crossings were the Nekhoteevka crossing into Ukraine and the ferry from Sochi to Istanbul. Unfortunately for Vladimir, the car journey to either of these far-flung places could easily push his eye problems over the edge. Roads in Russia are notoriously bad, with huge potholes and unpaved sections, and a bumpy trip could make Vladimir, suffering from problems with his retina, permanently blind.

After rejecting these options, Vladimir spotted the one opportunity that had any chance of working. The Russian summer holiday was ending on Sunday, August 31. Hordes of people would be entering and leaving the country. In that chaos, Vladimir hoped that the border service might not be able to check all the passports properly. It was a long shot, and any able-bodied person would have rejected it outright, but Vladimir didn't have that luxury.

Saturday, August 30, came—the day that Vladimir and Eduard were due for questioning in Kazan—and I sat on the edge of my seat waiting for a call from Vladimir's wife saying they had come to arrest him. But I got no calls from Russia. I was tempted to call early on Sunday morning, but I didn't want to alert anyone who might be listening to Vladimir's phone that he was still there.

That day, Vladimir, his wife, and his son booked an Alitalia flight for 11:00 p.m. from Sheremetyevo Airport to Milan. They left their home at 4:40 p.m. with simple carry-on bags. Unlike with Eduard, no shady characters were watching him. The family took a taxi to the airport, but because of the end-of-summer traffic, it took two and a half hours to get there. They arrived at Sheremetyevo at seven in the evening and took their place in the check-in line. The airport was absolute chaos. People were everywhere, nobody was queuing properly, and large suitcases blocked most of the hallways. Tempers flared as whole groups of people fretted over the possibility of missing their flights.

This was just the scenario Vladimir had been hoping for. Check-in took over an hour. Then came security. Another hour just to get through the screening area. It was already 10:00 p.m. when Vladimir and his family stood in the passport control line. This was just as congested as the previous lines: people crowded in front of one another, jockeying for position and arguing for the right to be next.

As Vladimir and his family approached the front of the line, the gravity of the situation hit him hard. If this didn't work, he was likely to be arrested. And if he was arrested, he would likely die in prison. It wasn't overly dramatic to conclude that, for Vladimir, this normally mundane border crossing was a matter of life and death.

With less than forty minutes until their flight took off, Vladimir and his family crossed the red line on the floor and stepped up to the border guard's booth. The agent was a young man with red cheeks, bright eyes, and a sheen of sweat on his forehead.

"Papers," he said in Russian without looking up from his computer terminal.

Vladimir dug into his travel wallet for his family's passports and boarding passes. "Crazy night here at the airport," he said, trying to sound casual.

The border guard grunted something incomprehensible. He looked at Vladimir with a frown, waiting for the documents.

"Here you are." Vladimir handed everything over.

This was probably the five hundredth set of documents the border guard had seen that day. Normally, Russian immigration officers are fastidious about processing every passport. They type the details into the computer, wait for a result, then stamp the passport. But if they'd applied that level of attention on this day, there would have been twelve-hour delays and half the passengers would have missed their flights.

Without going through any of these normal steps, the guard took up his stamp, leafed through each passport, and stamped the pages with his exit stamp in red ink. He then handed everything back to Vladimir. "Next!" he shouted.

Vladimir looped his hand through his son's arm, and together the three of them hustled away. They reached the plane with only fifteen minutes to spare. They boarded, strapped in, and said prayers of thanks. The plane pulled away and took off, and within hours they were in Italy.

He called me as soon as he landed, late that night. "Bill—we're in Milan!" he exclaimed.

Vladimir was safe, and I couldn't have been more relieved.

28

Khabarovsk

But while Vladimir was safe, Eduard was still somewhere in Russia, and we had no idea where.

Not even his wife knew. After he left her on Universitetsky Prospekt, Eduard was taken to a friend's apartment on the eastern side of the city, just outside the Garden Ring. He stayed there that night and the next. He never went out, never made a phone call. He just paced the apartment and, when his friend was home, discussed his situation and considered his options. He still wasn't prepared to leave the country. Not yet.

Just before dawn on the third day, Eduard got into a different friend's car and was taken to another apartment. They took a circuitous route. Eduard lay in the backseat, and only after they were sure they weren't being followed did they go to the next location.

Eduard spent two nights there. The moving around was getting to him. Eduard was used to getting things done on his own, and now all of a sudden he was completely dependent on others. He couldn't use his phone or send emails. All he could do was scan the news and pace the apartment like a caged animal, feeling more and more stressed.

Toward the end of the first week, Eduard received a message from one of his friends. It was grim. The number of men searching for Eduard had increased.

The people after him were closing in and Moscow was getting too hot.

He wasn't ready to leave Russia and admit defeat, so he needed to find another city in which to hide. He considered going to Voronezh or Nizhny Novgorod, which were both overnight train rides away. But in either place he would be on his own. He was a skilled lawyer, not a skilled fugitive, and he probably wouldn't have lasted a week. He realized that he needed two things: a location far from Moscow, and someone trustworthy with the resources to hide him.

He looked through his contacts, and one stood out: a man named Mikhail who lived in the city of Khabarovsk in the Russian Far East. A decade earlier, Eduard had gotten Mikhail out of a major legal jam and saved him from a long prison sentence.

He called Mikhail on a prepaid mobile phone and explained the situation. When he was finished, Mikhail said, "If you can find a way to get to Khabarovsk, I can keep you hidden for as long as you need."

Khabarovsk certainly satisfied the requirement of being far away. It was more than 3,800 miles from Moscow, nearly 500 miles *farther* than the distance between New York City and Anchorage, Alaska. The problem was getting there. Driving would take too long, and Eduard would likely get pulled over at some point along the way and shaken down by some corrupt local cops, which could end in disaster. The train was also problematic because he would have to buy a ticket and put his name into the system, then sit in a moving metal box for a week while the bad guys put two and two together.

The best option by far was to fly. Even though this would also put his name into the system, the trip would be over in eight hours, giving the people who were after him little time to react.

To increase his chances of doing this safely, Eduard decided to travel late on a Friday night. He hoped that the people who were monitoring him would already have started their weekend drinking, making it unlikely that they would receive the information, process it, and then act on it before he landed.

He arrived at Moscow's Domodedovo Airport, from where most regional flights operated, ninety minutes before the flight and went to the counter to buy a ticket. The desk agent told him the price— 56,890 rubles, about $2,350—and Eduard got out his wallet and counted out the amount in cash. He handed it to the woman as nonchalantly as he could, his heart pounding fast. It was a large amount of cash to be handing over, but she took it without any reaction, continued typing, handed him his ticket with a smile, and said, "Have a good trip."

First hurdle cleared.

Next was security, then check-in at the gate, and then just getting off the ground. All of these hurdles were cleared too, but there was one more. The purchase of this ticket could have tripped a wire, and it was entirely possible that some of the bad guys would be waiting for him at the Khabarovsk airport when he landed. He tried to sleep on the overnight flight that crossed seven time zones, but it was impossible.

Finally, exhausted and frayed, Eduard landed in Khabarovsk. The plane taxied to a stop. A stairway on a truck was driven to the side of the plane. The door opened, and the few passengers got off and made their way into the terminal. When Eduard ducked his tall frame under the plane's door, he saw a car waiting right there on the tarmac. His heart skipped a beat, but then he saw Mikhail standing next to it, a welcoming smile on his face.

Eduard walked down the stairway, his small carry-on in hand and, without ever setting foot in the terminal, was whisked to a nondescript hotel in a suburb where Mikhail checked him in under an assumed name.

• • •

We had no idea where Eduard was, what he was doing, or if he was safe. But while we were powerless to help him in Russia, that didn't mean we couldn't find out more about what was being used to frame him.

In early September, we received copies of materials from the court in Kazan. The most ominous document was a witness statement from Viktor Markelov, the convicted killer who'd stolen our companies. He'd sworn he'd done everything at the direction of a man named Oktai Gasanov, who'd died of a heart attack two months before the theft. Furthermore, Markelov claimed that Gasanov took all of his instructions from Eduard Khayretdinov, and that Eduard received all of his orders from me.

We now understood exactly what would happen if Eduard stayed in Russia. The corrupt officers at the Interior Ministry would eventually find him and arrest him. Once in custody, he would be tortured until he gave testimony implicating both of us in the theft of the $230 million. If he complied, they might go easy on him and make him serve only a few years in a penal colony. If he refused, they would kill him, and everything Markelov, the convicted killer who stole our companies, claimed would be accepted as the official "truth" in Russia.

We had to find a way to get this information to him. Vadim gave some of Eduard's contacts in Moscow a simple message in case they were in touch with him: "New information has come to light. Your life is in danger. Please leave as soon as possible."

• • •

Unbeknownst to us, Eduard eventually received this message. But even then, he was not ready to give in. He thought that if our complaints about the theft of the $230 million were reviewed by someone high enough in the government, then everything could still be resolved.

But even Mikhail, his host, was getting nervous and thought that it was becoming too dangerous for Eduard to stay in Khabarovsk. He assigned Eduard two armed bodyguards, who moved him to Mikhail's dacha in the woods, a hundred miles from town. There, Eduard had electricity from a generator, a satellite phone, and a car. It was picturesque country, blanketed by softwoods and birch, and dotted with fish ponds.

After two weeks in the country, Eduard got a message from Mikhail. One of Eduard's most trusted confidants was making a special trip to Khabarovsk to deliver a message to Eduard in person. Eduard took this as a good sign—why would someone come all the way to the Far East only to deliver bad news? Two days later Eduard and the guards got into the car and left the dacha to meet the man from Moscow at a café on the outskirts of Khabarovsk. When his friend arrived, Eduard's hopes were almost immediately dashed. His friend shook his hand with a grave look of concern. They sat and ordered tea and began to talk.

"We've tried everything," the man said. "There are some very powerful people involved. Nothing is going to change. This is not going away."

"But why come all the way here just to tell me that?"

The man leaned forward. "Because, Eduard, I wanted to tell you face-to-face—you *must* leave Russia. You're in danger of being killed. These people who are after you will stop at nothing."

This shook Eduard to the core. After this meeting, he called Mikhail and said, "I need to get out of Russia. Can you help?"

"I'll do what I can," Mikhail said.

Since Russia is such a decentralized country, the power of an influential businessman in some areas could rival that of the Moscow Interior Ministry. Mikhail was one of the most important businessmen in the region, and Eduard had no choice but to put his faith in Mikhail's influence. He had to hope that it would help him navigate the security and immigration checkpoints that every traveler had to pass through on their way out of the country.

Mikhail arranged to have a local fixer escort Eduard through the airport all the way to the gate. Eduard asked over and over if this fixer would be able to get the border agents to let him pass. Mikhail just told him not to worry. Of course, Eduard couldn't help *but* worry.

On October 18, 2008, at 10:00 a.m., Eduard went to the airport and was met by the fixer, a short man with friendly eyes in a well-tailored, gray suit. Eduard already had a UK visa, so he went to the Asiana ticket desk and bought a round-trip economy ticket to London via Seoul. Eduard checked in and waited until an hour before the flight to go through security and passport control. When he couldn't wait any longer, he and the fixer walked toward security.

They walked straight to the front of the security line and went through. The fixer stayed with Eduard the whole time, nodding and winking at the security people, and even shaking a few hands. Eduard put his bags on the scanning belt, presented his boarding pass, and went through the metal detector.

They then moved toward passport control, and when they reached the immigration booth, the fixer shook hands with the border guard and they exchanged pleasantries.

The guard then took Eduard's passport. He placed it on his desk, looked at Eduard, looked back to the fixer, found a blank spot in the passport, slammed his stamp onto a red-ink pad, and punched the stamp onto the paper. He didn't even bother to look at his computer. He closed the passport and handed it back. Eduard's eyes met those of the fixer. He winked. "Thank you," Eduard said. He turned and hurried to his gate. He had only a few minutes until the doors closed.

He made the flight, and the plane took off. Not until two hours later, when Eduard could see that the plane was flying over the Sea of Japan and was therefore out of Russian airspace, did he finally, after all these weeks, feel at ease.

He was out.

• • •

Later that day in London, Vadim's phone rang with a number whose country code he didn't recognize. He picked up. "Hello?"

"Vadim! It's Eduard."

Vadim jumped from his chair. We hadn't heard from Eduard in nearly two months. Every day we'd swung between hope and despair, wondering if he was safe or dead or somewhere in between. "Eduard!" Vadim exclaimed. "Where are you? Are you okay?"

"Yes, I'm fine. I'm in Seoul."

"Seoul?"

"Yes, Seoul. I'm coming to Heathrow on the next Asiana flight. I'll be there tomorrow."

"So you're safe?"

"Yes, yes. We have a lot to talk about. I'll see you soon."

The next evening at 7:00 p.m., a car picked up Eduard at Heathrow and brought him straight to the offices on Golden Square. As soon as he walked through the door, we took turns giving him big, backslapping hugs. Though I'd met him only once before in my life, it was as if I were being reunited with a long-lost brother.

When we finally settled down, Eduard told us his story, with Vadim and Ivan taking turns translating. We were rapt, and when he finished, I said, "That's amazing, Eduard. Truly amazing. Thank God you made it."

He nodded. "Yes, thank God is right."

That evening, I allowed myself a moment to savor that Eduard was safe, but our problems were nowhere near over.

While Eduard had been underground, Sergei was still fully exposed in Moscow. In late September, we'd come across an article in an obscure Moscow business weekly called *Delovoi Vtornik*. The title of the piece was "Purely English Fraud." It repeated the now familiar claim—that Eduard and I were the masterminds behind the fraud—but it slipped in a name we'd never seen in print before: Sergei Magnitsky.

After this, Vadim tried to convince Sergei to leave, but Sergei steadfastly refused. He insisted that nothing would happen to him because he had done nothing wrong. He was also indignant that these people had stolen so much money from his country. He was so adamant and believed so faithfully in the law that, on October 7, he actually *returned* to the Russian State Investigative Committee to give a second sworn witness statement. Once again, he sought to use procedure to insert more evidence into the official record, and this time he provided a number of additional details about the fraud and who was behind it.

This was a bold move. It was also a worrying one. While I couldn't help but be impressed by Sergei's determination and integrity, given what they had tried with Eduard and Vladimir, I was terrified that they would just detain him on the spot. Remarkably, they didn't.

On the morning of October 20, 2008, Ivan made another attempt to convince Sergei: "Listen, all of our lawyers are being targeted. Eduard is here. Vladimir is here. We've seen materials with your name on them. I believe that something very bad is going to happen to you if you stay, Sergei."

"But why would anything happen?" Sergei asked, sticking to his guns. "I haven't broken any laws. They're only after Eduard and Vladimir because they fought the fraudulent lawsuits in court. I never did that. There's no reason for me to leave."

"But you *must* leave, Sergei. They'll arrest you. Please. I beg you."

"I'm sorry, Ivan. The law will protect me. This isn't 1937," Sergei said, referring to Stalin's purges, when people were disappearing left and right at the hands of the secret police.

There was no changing Sergei's mind. He was staying in Russia and we could do nothing about it. He was of a different generation than Vladimir and Eduard. Both of them had been adults during the Soviet era and had seen firsthand how capricious the government could be. If powerful people wanted you arrested, then you were arrested. The law didn't matter. Sergei, on the other hand, was thirty-six years old and had come of age at a time when things had started to improve. He saw Russia not how it was but how he wanted it to be.

Because of this, he didn't realize that Russia had no rule of law, it had a rule of men.

And those men were crooks.

29

The Ninth Commandment

Early on the morning of November 24, 2008, three teams of Interior Ministry officers reporting to Lieutenant Colonel Artem Kuznetsov moved out across Moscow. One team made its way to Sergei's home. The other two were headed to the apartments of junior lawyers who reported to Sergei at Firestone Duncan.

When Irina Perikhina, one of those junior lawyers, heard the knock on her door, she was sitting at her vanity. Like any self-respecting thirtysomething Russian woman, she wouldn't be caught dead talking to anyone without her makeup on. Instead of answering, she continued to brush on mascara and apply lipstick. When she was finally done and went to the door, no one was there. The police had given up and left, thinking the apartment was empty.

Boris Samolov, another of Sergei's lawyers, was luckily not living at his registered address when the knock came. He avoided the police altogether.

Sergei, however, was at home with Nikita, his eight-year-old son. Sergei was getting himself ready for work and Nikita for school. His eldest son, Stanislav, was already gone. Sergei's wife, Natasha, hadn't been feeling well that morning and had gone to see the doctor.

When the knock came, Sergei opened the door and was faced with three officers. He stepped aside and let them in.

The Magnitsky family lived in a modest two-bedroom apartment on Pokrovka Street in central Moscow. Over the next eight hours the officers turned the apartment upside down. When Natasha returned from the doctor, she was shocked and scared, but Sergei wasn't. As they sat in Nikita's bedroom, he whispered, "Don't worry. I've done nothing wrong. There's nothing they can do to me." The police were still there when Stanislav returned home from school. He was angry, but Sergei, in his calm voice, assured him that everything would be fine.

The police finished their search at 4:00 p.m. They confiscated all of Sergei's personal files and computers, family photos, a stack of children's DVDs, and even a paper airplane collection and sketchbook that belonged to Nikita. They then arrested Sergei. As he was being led away, he turned toward his wife and children, forced a smile, and said he'd be back soon.

$$\bullet \quad \bullet \quad \bullet$$

Thus began the tragic ordeal of Sergei Magnitsky. I learned about it in fits and starts over several months, but it's an ordeal that I have never stopped thinking about.

I learned about the search of his home in real time. In the midafternoon of November 24, Vadim rushed to my desk with a panicked look on his face. "Bill, we need you in the conference room now!"

I followed him. I knew what he was going to tell me. Ivan, Eduard, and Vladimir were already there. As soon as I closed the door, Vadim said, "Sergei's been arrested!"

"Shit." I fell into the nearest chair, my mouth suddenly dry. Dozens of questions and images ran through my head. Where was he being held? On what grounds had they arrested him? How did they frame him?

"What's going to happen next, Eduard?" I asked.

"He'll be given a detention hearing where he'll either be granted bail or put into a detention center. Almost certainly the latter."

"What are those like?"

Eduard sighed and avoided my eyes. "They're not good, Bill. Definitely not good."

"How long can they hold him?"

"Up to a year."

"A *year*? Without charging him?"

"Yes."

My imagination launched into overdrive. I couldn't help but think of the American TV show *Oz*, about a Harvard-educated lawyer who gets thrown in jail with horrific and violent criminals at a fictional New York State correctional facility. It was only a TV show, but the unspeakable things that happened to this character made me shudder when I considered what Sergei was about to face. Were the authorities going to torture him? Would he be *raped*? How would a gentle, erudite, middle-class lawyer deal with a situation like this?

I had to do whatever I could to get him out of there.

My first move was to get Sergei a lawyer. He requested a well-known attorney from his hometown named Dmitri Kharitonov. We hired him immediately. I assumed Dmitri would share any information he learned about Sergei's situation, but he turned out to be extremely guarded. He was certain his phone was being tapped and his email monitored. He wanted to communicate with us only in person, and that could only happen when he would be in London, in mid-January. I found this arrangement highly unsatisfactory, but if this was the lawyer Sergei wanted, I couldn't possibly argue.

My next move was to see the new head of the Russia desk at the Foreign Office, Michael Davenport, a Cambridge-educated lawyer roughly my age. Unlike his predecessor, Simon Smith, I didn't warm to Davenport. I'd met him several times before to brief him on our troubles with the Russians, but he seemed to view me as a businessman who'd gotten what he deserved in Russia and didn't merit the attentions of the British government.

Now that a vulnerable human being was involved, I hoped his attitude would change.

I went to his office on King Charles Street and he ushered me in. He pointed to his wooden conference table and we sat opposite each other. He asked his assistant to bring us some tea, then said, "What can I do for you, Mr. Browder?"

"I have some bad news from Russia," I said quietly.

"What's happened?"

"One of my lawyers, a man named Sergei Magnitsky, has been arrested."

Davenport stiffened. "One of your lawyers, you say?"

"Yes. Sergei discovered the massive tax-rebate fraud I told you about earlier in the year. And now the Interior Ministry officers who committed the crime have taken him into custody."

"On what grounds?"

"We're still trying to figure that out. But if I had to guess, it would be tax evasion. That's how these guys operate."

"That's very unfortunate. Please, tell me everything you know."

I gave him all the details as he took notes. When I was finished, he promised authoritatively, "We will raise this issue at an appropriate time with our counterparts in Russia."

I'd met enough diplomats by that point to know this was standard Foreign Office speak for "We're going to do jack shit for you."

The meeting didn't last much longer. I hurried out, hopped into a black taxi, and headed back to the office. As we drove through Trafalgar Square, my phone rang. It was Vadim.

"Bill, I just got some bad news from my source Aslan."

"What is it?"

"He told me that the Interior Ministry has assigned nine senior investigators to Sergei's case, Bill. *Nine!*"

"What does that mean?"

"A normal criminal case gets one or two. A big one might get three or four. Only a huge political case like Yukos would have nine."

"Shit!"

"There's more. He also said that Victor Voronin, the head of Department K of the FSB, was personally responsible for Sergei's arrest."

"Fuck," I muttered, and hung up the phone.

Sergei was in big trouble.

• • •

Sergei's bail hearing took place at the Tverskoi District Court in Moscow two days after his arrest. The police had no evidence of a crime and no legal basis for keeping him in custody. Sergei and his lawyers thought that with such a flimsy case, bail would be granted for sure.

As they assembled in court, they were confronted with a new investigator from the Interior Ministry, a thirty-one-year-old major named Oleg Silchenko, who was so boyish-looking that he didn't even appear qualified to give evidence to a court. He could have been an intern in Sergei's tax department at Firestone Duncan, or a graduate student at Moscow State University. But Silchenko was wearing a crisp blue uniform, and as he aggressively presented his "evidence," he showed that he was every inch an officer at the Interior Ministry.

Silchenko argued that Sergei was a flight risk and waved around a "report" from Department K as his evidence, claiming that Sergei had applied for a UK visa and had reserved a plane ticket to Kiev. Both allegations were fabricated. Sergei pointed out that he hadn't applied for a UK visa, which could easily be proven by contacting the British embassy. Sergei then addressed the made-up Kiev reservation, but the judge wouldn't let him finish. "I have no reason to doubt the information provided from investigative bodies," the judge said. He then ordered Sergei to be held in pretrial detention. Sergei was hustled out of the court, handcuffed, and put in a prison transport. He spent ten days at an undisclosed location and was then taken to the place where he would be held for at least the next two months, a jail known simply as Moscow Detention Center No. 5.

When he got there, he was put in a cell with fourteen other inmates but only eight beds. The lights were left on twenty-four hours a day and the prisoners slept in shifts. This was clearly designed to impose sleep deprivation on him and the other detainees. Silchenko probably thought that after a week of fighting hardened criminals for a mattress, Sergei, a highly educated tax lawyer, would do anything Silchenko wanted.

Silchenko was wrong.

For the next two months Sergei was moved again and again and again. Each cell was worse than the last. One cell had no heat and no windowpanes to keep out the arctic air. It was so cold that Sergei nearly froze to death. Toilets—which consisted of holes in the ground—were not screened from the sleeping area. Sewage often bubbled up and ran over the floor. In one cell, the only electrical outlets were located directly next to the toilet, so he had to boil water with the kettle while standing over the rank latrine. In another cell, Sergei fixed a blocked toilet with a plastic cup, but it was chewed away by a rat in the night, and so much sewage covered the floor by morning that he and his cellmate had to climb up on the bed and chair like monkeys.

Worse than the physical discomfort for Sergei was the psychological torture. He was a devoted family man, and Silchenko tormented Sergei by refusing to allow him any contact with his family. When Sergei applied for his wife and mother to visit, Silchenko replied, "I reject your application. It's not expedient for the investigation."

Sergei then applied for permission to speak to his eight-year-old son on the phone. "Your request is denied," Silchenko said. "Your son is too young for you to have a phone conversation." Silchenko also refused a request for Sergei's aunt to visit because Sergei "couldn't prove" she was a relative.

The purpose of everything Silchenko did was simple: to compel Sergei to retract his testimony against Kuznetsov and Karpov. Yet Sergei never would, and every time he refused, Silchenko made Sergei's living conditions increasingly worse, further isolating him from the life he knew and the freedom he had so recently enjoyed.

. . .

It wasn't until Sergei's detention hearing in January 2009 that we learned of his horrible living conditions, his complete isolation from his family, and his mistreatment at the hands of Silchenko. It wasn't until then that we heard of his steadfast refusal to recant. It wasn't until then that a picture of Sergei's strength began to take shape.

While most of the information we received that January was extremely grim, there was one bit of positive news. As Sergei was being moved around, he ended up sharing a cell with an Armenian accused of burglary. The Armenian was preparing for trial and desperately needed legal help. Without any law books or other resources, Sergei was still able to write a comprehensive defense for his cellmate. When the Armenian went to court, he was surprisingly acquitted and set free. As news of this spread, Sergei's stock with the other prisoners shot up like a rocket. Overnight he became one of the most popular and well-protected inmates in the detention center.

The terrible images from *Oz* at least partially faded from my mind, and I slept a little easier after hearing that Sergei's fellow inmates were not mistreating him.

Unfortunately, the authorities were.

In late February, Silchenko secretly moved Sergei to a special facility called IVS1. This was a temporary holding facility outside the main detention system where the police could do whatever they wanted to detainees. We suspected this was where Silchenko and the FSB were trying to coerce Sergei into signing a false confession. We had no idea what they did to Sergei there, but we assumed the worst.

For the next two or three months we didn't hear much more. All we knew for certain was that no matter what Silchenko and the other officers at the Interior Ministry did to Sergei, he refused to sign anything that they put in front of him. When Silchenko told him to expose somebody, Sergei would say, "I will expose those officers who have committed the crimes." Eventually Silchenko must have realized that he had seriously underestimated this gentle tax lawyer.

The more they did to Sergei, the stronger his spirit became. In a letter to his mother he wrote, "Mama, don't worry about me too much. My psychological resilience surprises me sometimes. It seems as if I can endure anything."

Sergei would not break. But while his will was unbreakable, his body was not. In early April he was moved again, this time to a detention center called Matrosskaya Tishina. There, he began to suffer from acute pains in his stomach. The episodes would last for hours and result in violent bouts of vomiting. By mid-June he had lost forty pounds.

Sergei was sick. But with what, we had no idea.

. . .

As Sergei's detention dragged through the spring, a part of me wished that he would just give the Interior Ministry what it wanted. His doing so might have increased my problems with the Russian authorities, but that would be nothing if Sergei could have gotten out of that hell-hole and ended up back in the arms of his family.

As each day passed, I became increasingly desperate to get him out of jail. Since I had no capacity to do anything in Russia, my only option was to pull out all the stops in the West.

The British government had made it clear that it was going to do next to nothing to help Sergei, so I began looking for international or-ganizations that might be able to help. The first solid lead came from the Council of Europe, a multilateral organization that dealt specifi-cally with human rights issues. Headquartered in Strasbourg, France, it was composed of forty-seven European countries, including Rus-sia. A German MP and former justice minister, Sabine Leutheusser-Schnarrenberger, had recently been appointed by the Council to conduct an investigation into Russia's criminal justice system, and she was looking for high-profile cases for her report.

We were aware that we were competing with many other Russian victims for her attention. At the time, there were roughly 300,000 people who had been unjustly imprisoned in Russia, so we didn't have high hopes, but our lawyers contacted her office and she agreed to a meeting. Prior to that meeting, I spent a week putting together a presentation outlining each step of the crime and how it led to Ser-gei's being taken hostage and mistreated in detention. When she saw the facts laid out so clearly and with so much evidence, she immedi-ately agreed to take up his case.

In April 2009, she approached the Russian law enforcement agencies with a long list of questions. It was a positive development because the mere process of the Council of Europe asking the Russian government about Sergei could potentially free him—or at least get him better conditions.

Unfortunately, it did neither.

The Russian authorities refused a face-to-face meeting with Leutheusser-Schnarrenberger, so she was forced to send her questions in writing. After a long silence, she received her answers.

Her first question was simply, "Why was Sergei Magnitsky arrested?"

The answer: "Sergei Magnitsky was not arrested."

Of course he was arrested. He was in *their* prison. I couldn't imagine what the Russians were thinking when they said this to her.

Her second question was, "Why was he arrested by Interior Ministry officer Kuznetsov, who he testified against before his arrest?"

She got an equally ridiculous answer. "The officer with such a name doesn't work in the Moscow Interior Ministry."

We had proof that Kuznetsov had worked in the Interior Ministry for many years! They must have thought Leutheusser-Schnarrenberger was stupid.

Nearly all the other answers were similarly absurd and untrue.

Leutheusser-Schnarrenberger would put all of these lies and absurdities in her final report, but a draft wouldn't be ready until August, and Sergei didn't have the luxury of time. I continued to canvass other organizations and found two powerful legal groups that might get involved: the International Bar Association and the UK Law Society. After hearing Sergei's story and reviewing our documentation, each organization sent letters to President Medvedev and to General Prosecutor Yuri Chaika, asking for Sergei's release.

Again, I had high hopes that these interventions would help, but again they fell flat. The General Prosecutor's Office replied to the Law Society by saying, "We considered your application and found no grounds for prosecutorial intervention." The Russian authorities didn't even bother to reply to the other letters.

Continuing my search, I looked to America. In June 2009, I was invited to Washington, DC, to testify in front of the US Helsinki Commission, an independent government agency whose mission is to monitor human rights in former Soviet Bloc countries. At the time, it was headed by the first-term Democratic senator from Maryland, Ben Cardin. The purpose of the hearing was to decide which cases would go into President Obama's briefing package for an upcoming summit with President Medvedev.

This was the first opportunity I'd had to share Sergei's case with such a high-profile group in the US political arena. I made my presentation, and the senators and congressmen were appropriately shocked by Sergei's ordeal. Unfortunately, one of the staffers at the Helsinki Commission, a young man named Kyle Parker, decided not to include Sergei's story in the commission's letter to President Obama. Parker thought too many other issues were more pressing.

After this I realized that what we needed most to get Sergei's story above the fray was media attention. Only a handful of articles about Sergei had appeared, and all of them were written shortly after his arrest. As much as I tried, journalists simply weren't interested. With all the evil going on in Russia, they didn't see the newsworthiness of a story about a jailed lawyer. Any attempt to share the complicated details of Sergei's case just made journalists' eyes glaze over.

I'd exhausted my list of Russia correspondents when I hit upon a young *Washington Post* reporter named Philip Pan. Unlike the others, he was new to Moscow and wasn't jaded. He immediately recognized the resonance of Sergei's story.

From early July until August 2009, he interviewed members of our team, verified our documents, and tried as best as he could to get the Russian authorities to respond. By early August, he had put together a truly damning exposé.

On August 13 the *Washington Post* published his feature story, entitled "3 Lawyers Targeted After Uncovering Seizure of Firms." He accused the Russian government of a major financial fraud and explained how it had targeted Sergei, Eduard, and Vladimir to cover up the crime.

Normally, a corruption exposé like this would cause a big stir, but in this case, there was dead silence. The Russians were totally unmoved and unashamed. Even worse, the Russian press didn't pick it up at all. Journalists in Russia seemed too scared to write about anything to do with me. I was simply radioactive.

At roughly the same time that the *Washington Post* article came out, Leutheusser-Schnarrenberger published her report. Like Pan, she went step-by-step through all of the Russian lies, the tax-rebate fraud, and how Sergei had been falsely arrested and mistreated in Russian custody. She concluded, "I cannot help suspecting that this coordinated attack must have the support of senior officials. These appear to make use of the systemic weaknesses of the criminal justice system in the Russian Federation."

Her report was definitive and damning, but it also had no impact whatsoever. The Russians met it with more deafening silence. The people tormenting Sergei simply didn't care.

We had a big debate internally about what to do next. We were getting nowhere with traditional advocacy tools and running out of ideas. But then our twenty-four-year-old secretary popped her head in my office and said, "Sorry to interrupt, but I couldn't help overhearing your conversation. Have you guys ever thought of doing a YouTube video?"

I barely knew what YouTube was in 2009, so she brought in her laptop and showed us how it worked.

Given our lack of success elsewhere, it seemed worth a try. We organized our information about the fraud, wrote a script, and produced a fourteen-minute video. It explained in simple terms how the police and criminals had succeeded in stealing $230 million from the Russian Treasury, and how they'd arrested Sergei when he exposed the crime. We made two versions—one in Russian and one in English. It was clearer and more understandable than anything we'd done before, and I suspected it would make a big impression when we released it.

I was keen to get it online as quickly as possible, but first I needed Sergei to approve it, since he was the one who was most exposed to any repercussions. I passed a copy of the script to his lawyer and waited anxiously to hear whether I had his blessing.

But Sergei was dealing with more pressing issues.

• • •

By the summer of 2009, Sergei's health had seriously deteriorated. The doctors in the medical wing of Matrosskaya Tishina diagnosed him with pancreatitis, gallstones, and cholecystitis. They prescribed an ultrasound examination and possible surgery for August 1, 2009.

One week before this scheduled exam, however, Major Silchenko made the decision to move Sergei from Matrosskaya Tishina to Butyrka, a maximum-security detention center that in Soviet times had been a way station to the gulags. The place was infamous throughout Russia. It was like Alcatraz, only worse. Most significantly for Sergei, Butyrka had no medical facilities that could deal with his illnesses.

What Sergei was forced to endure at Butyrka was worthy of Solzhenitsyn's *Gulag Archipelago*.

As soon as he passed through the doors of Butyrka on July 25, Sergei asked the prison authorities to arrange for the medical treatment he was supposed to receive. But they simply ignored him. For weeks, he languished in his cell, the pain growing steadily with each passing day.

Then, at 4:00 p.m. on August 24, the pain in his stomach became so acute that he couldn't lie down. Every position sent fiery pains through his solar plexus and chest. The only respite came when he pulled up his knees and rolled into a ball, rocking from side to side.

At 5:30 p.m. that day, his cellmate, Erik, returned from an interrogation. Sergei was on the bed in this balled-up position, whimpering quietly. Erik asked what was wrong, but Sergei was so consumed with pain that he couldn't respond. Erik shouted for a doctor. The guard heard him and promised to find one, but nothing happened. Half an hour later, Erik banged on the bars to get the guard's attention, but still there was no response.

An hour later, Erik heard some male voices: "Which cell?"

Erik shouted, "Two sixty-seven! Please come now!" But no one came.

Sergei's pain became even more excruciating over the next few hours. He was holding himself tight, tears streaming down his face, when, finally, at 9:30 p.m. two guards showed up, opened the cell door, and took him to the infirmary.

When he arrived, he was made to wait for half an hour while the nurse slowly finished her paperwork. He crouched with his knees close to his chest to alleviate the pain. When the nurse was finally done, she barked in an accusatory tone, "Okay. Why are you here?"

Sergei was practically shaking, and through clenched teeth he said slowly, "I'm in unbearable pain. I've asked over and over, but no doctor has examined me since I arrived last month."

The nurse was visibly annoyed. "What do you mean you haven't been examined? You were examined at your previous detention center!"

"Yes, and they prescribed treatment and surgery. But nothing has happened here."

"When did you come to us? Only one month ago! What do you want? To be treated every month? You should have had treatment when you were free."

"I wasn't sick when I was free. I developed these illnesses in detention."

"Don't tell me fairy tales." She then dismissed him, without providing any treatment. Her final words were, "If you need medical attention, write another letter to the doctor."

The guards took him back to his cell. Eventually the pain subsided and he was able to drift into a fitful sleep.

It was now clear that the authorities were deliberately withholding medical attention from Sergei. They were using illnesses he had contracted in detention as a cudgel against him. They knew that gallstones were one of the most painful conditions anyone could suffer from. In the West, you might last two hours before you crawl to the emergency room, where the doctors will immediately give you a dose of morphine before treating you. Sergei, though, had to deal with untreated gallstones for *four months* without any painkillers. What he had to endure was unimaginable.

Sergei and his lawyer wrote more than twenty requests to every branch of the penal, law enforcement, and judicial systems of Russia, desperately begging for medical attention. Most of these petitions were ignored, but the replies he received were shocking.

Major Oleg Silchenko wrote, "I deny in full the request for a medical examination."

A Tverskoi District court judge, Aleksey Krivoruchko, replied, "Your request to review complaints about withholding of medical care and cruel treatment is denied."

Andrei Pechegin from the Prosecutor's Office replied, "There's no reason for the prosecutor to intervene."

Judge Yelena Stashina, one of the judges who ordered Sergei's continued detention, said, "I rule that your request to review the medical records and conditions of detention is irrelevant."

While Sergei was being systematically tortured, he began to receive regular visits from a man who refused to identify himself or his organization. Whenever this man came, the guards would drag Sergei from his cell to a stuffy, windowless room. The meetings were short because the man had only one message: "Do what we want, or things will continue to get worse for you."

Every time Sergei would stare across the table at this man and refuse to do what he wanted.

Nobody knows how much hardship one can endure until one is forced to endure it. I don't know how I would have handled this situation, and Sergei probably didn't know either until he faced it. Yet at every turn, no matter how bad it got, he refused to perjure himself. Sergei was religious, and he would not violate God's ninth commandment: "Thou shalt not bear false witness." Under no circumstances would he plead guilty to a crime he did not commit, nor would he falsely implicate me. This, it seems, would have been more poisonous and painful to Sergei than any physical torture.

Here was an innocent man, deprived of any contact with his loved ones, cheated by the law, rebuffed by the bureaucracy, tortured inside the prison's walls, sick and becoming sicker. Even in these most dire circumstances, when he had the best possible reasons to give his tormentors what they wanted, he wouldn't. In spite of the loss of his freedom, his health, his sanity, and possibly even his life, he would not compromise his ideals or his faith.

He would not give in.

30

November 16, 2009

As Sergei endured this living nightmare, I was living in a daze. Saturday mornings were the worst. I would wake early and roll over to look at Elena in our comfortable king-size bed. Beyond the edge of our bed was a window, and beyond that London. I was free and comfortable and loved. I could still touch and feel what love meant, while Sergei could only remember. It made me feel sick. My desire to reconcile my family's communist background with my own capitalist ambitions had brought me to Russia, but, naively, I never imagined that this pursuit would result in a human tragedy.

On these days, I would get up, shuffle to the bathroom, turn on the shower, and get in. The hot water was meant to be cleansing, only it wasn't. The dirt fell free, but the guilt coated me like tar. Sergei got to shower once a week at most, sometimes having to wait as long as three weeks. The water falling over his body was cold, and the soap, if there was any, was rough. His prison cells were rank and his health was failing. More than once I fought back fits of nausea. Even today I can't step into my bathroom without thinking of Sergei.

But I did shower, and I did get up on Saturdays, and I did love my family, and after getting more dire news about Sergei's condition, I fought even harder for him. His situation was becoming grave.

In October 2009 I returned to Washington and New York to continue advocating for him. Nobody was particularly interested, but I kept trying. Somehow I needed to find a way to make what was happening to Sergei important for the whole world. For the life of me, though, I couldn't see how.

Then, as I was boarding an overnight British Airways flight back to London, my phone rang. It was Elena.

I answered, and before she could even speak, I said, "Sweetie, I'm just getting on the plane. Can this wait?"

"No, it can't. The Interior Ministry just issued a formal indictment!"

I stepped aside to allow the other passengers by. "Against Sergei?"

"Yes." She paused. "And you. They're going after both of you."

This scenario had always been lurking, but to hear the words was still shocking. "They're actually going through with it?"

"Yes. They're going to have a big show trial."

I took a moment before asking, "Do we have any idea what happens after that?"

"Eduard thinks Sergei will get six years and you'll get the same in absentia. He said Russia will then issue an Interpol Red Notice for you and try to extradite you from the UK."

An Interpol Red Notice is an international arrest warrant. If one was issued in my name, I could be detained at any border crossing the moment I presented my passport. The Russians would then apply for my extradition, which would most likely be granted. I would then be sent to Russia to face the same type of ordeal as Sergei.

"Bill, we need to put out a press release to contradict their lies right away."

"Okay." The idea that I was going to be put on trial had a physical effect on me, and I was jittery as I rejoined the throng of people making their way onto the plane. "I'll write something in the air and we'll go over it as soon as I land."

"Have a safe flight, sweetheart. I love you."

"I love you too."

I found my seat and stared in front of me, lost in thought. I knew what was coming: a bunch of unpleasant headlines that would say things like "Browder and Magnitsky on Trial for Tax Evasion," or "Russia to Issue Interpol Red Notice for Browder." Any rebuttal we offered would be found in the last paragraph of these articles, which almost always goes unread. That, in essence, was the beauty of how corrupt Russian police worked—they abused their official status to steal money and terrorize their victims. They hid behind a wall of legitimacy granted by their status as law enforcement agents. The press would always report official statements as if they were the truth because in most countries law enforcement agencies don't openly lie. This was a big problem for us. Somehow, I had to find a way to get the real story out.

The plane reached cruising altitude, the lights went out for the night, and I tried to get comfortable in my seat. As I stared at the dim light of the NO SMOKING sign, I suddenly remembered the YouTube video we'd made. Sergei had given us the green light only a week before, and it was ready to go. I thought, *Why issue a press release when we have a much better way to tell the story?*

When I landed in London, I got in a cab and rushed to the office. I pulled the hard drive with the video on it off the shelf and uploaded the film to YouTube. I named it "Hermitage Reveals Russian Police Fraud," and it quickly spread everywhere. By the end of the first day, it had eleven thousand views; after three days, over twenty thousand; and after a week, more than forty-seven thousand. For a video about a complicated crime and human rights case, these were big numbers. In the past, I'd had to brief people one by one about our case in an endless series of forty-five-minute meetings. Now thousands were learning about it all at once.

As soon as the video was posted, I began fielding calls from friends, colleagues, and acquaintances. Each of them expressed their amazement at just how twisted the tale was. They'd heard about Sergei's situation, but they didn't really understand it until they saw that video. Mixed in with these calls were others from reporters. The film quickly *became* the story. For the first time people understood that the Russian Interior Ministry was not a reputable police organization, but rather a collection of officials abusing their positions to perpetrate massive financial frauds. With this one film, we gained our first foothold in explaining the truth of what had happened and were able to push back against our enemies.

From inside his prison cell, Sergei was also bravely trying to explain the truth even after all the torture he had been subjected to.

On October 14, 2009, he submitted a formal twelve-page testimony to the Interior Ministry in which he documented the full extent of the financial fraud. He provided names, dates, and locations, and left nothing to the imagination. At the end, he wrote, "I believe all members of the investigation team are acting as contractors under someone's criminal order."

It was a remarkable document, and he was incredibly brave to have filed it. It's hard to describe to someone who doesn't know Russia just how dangerous it was for him to do this. People in Russia are regularly killed for saying much less. That Sergei was saying it from jail, where he was at the mercy of the people who had put him there and whom he had testified against, showed how determined he was to expose the rot in the Russian law enforcement agencies and go after his persecutors.

In the middle of all this, I'd committed to giving a big speech at Stanford about the dangers of investing in Russia. I decided to take my son, David, who was twelve at the time. He'd never been to my alma mater, and with all these bad things going on, I wanted to share with him one of the places where I had spent some of the happiest years of my life.

We boarded the flight to San Francisco, and I tried to take my mind off everything going on in Russia. But it didn't matter what time zone or part of the world I was in. Sergei's situation followed me everywhere, shrouding me with sadness and guilt. The only thing that would give me any respite was seeing him free.

I gave my speech the day after we arrived. I told the audience my story of doing business in Russia, culminating with the events that had been consuming my life for the past year. I also showed the Hermitage YouTube video, which even elicited a few tears.

David and I left the lecture hall and walked into the warm California air, and in that moment I felt slightly better. Even though the video had been viewed tens of thousands of times on the Internet, I'd never interacted with the people who were watching it. Sharing Sergei's story with a roomful of people, and then being able to see on their faces and hear in their voices just how appalled they were, made me feel less alone in this fight.

But then, as David and I walked across the campus, my phone rang. It was Vladimir Pastukhov and he didn't sound good. "Bill, something really awful just happened."

"What is it?"

"I just got a text message on my BlackBerry. It's in Russian. It says, 'What's worse, prison or death?'"

I began to pace. "Was it directed at you?"

"I don't know."

"Could it be directed at me, Vadim . . . Sergei?"

"I don't know. Maybe."

"Who's it from?"

"It's not clear."

"How'd they get that number? Nobody's got your BlackBerry number."

"I don't know, Bill."

David stared at me, concerned. I stopped pacing and tried to reassure him with a weak smile. "Can we trace it? Figure out who sent it?"

"Maybe. I'll try. I'll call you back as soon as I hear anything more."

"Thank you."

Any positive feelings I had evaporated in that sixty-second call. The return trip to London was long and bleak. I had no idea how to assess this threat, whom it was directed at, or what to do about it. It sounded serious, and it was extremely worrying.

Within days, Vladimir received a second text message, also in Russian. "Trains, trains through the night, trains, trains never stopping." Vladimir explained that it was a line from a famous Russian prisoners' poem that alluded to trains running endlessly to the gulags in the Urals, their packed cars carrying human fodder to their ultimate deaths.

A few days later I got an unexpected call from an old client named Philip Fulton. He'd been my friend and confidant since the Gazprom days. He and his wife were in London and wanted to see Elena and the kids. We had a lovely brunch at the fifth-floor restaurant at Harvey Nichols, and I managed to put aside my worries for a couple of hours. Philip and his wife fawned over my small children and we had a great visit. I hated to admit it, but for a little while I felt okay. I knew our problems weren't going away, but I also knew that it was acceptable—maybe even preferable—to forget about them for a few moments and pretend I had a normal life.

When we were leaving, though, Vladimir called again. "A new message came in, Bill."

"What is it?"

"It's a quote from *The Godfather*: 'History has taught us that anyone can be killed.'"

I paused. "Fuck!" I said, my hands starting to shake.

We hung up.

I was completely spooked. Early the next morning I gathered the three messages from Vladimir's BlackBerry, with time stamps, and reported them to SO15, the antiterrorism unit at Scotland Yard. It sent in a team of investigators to interview me and Vladimir, and its technicians traced the calls. Each call came from an unregistered number in Russia, which was unusual. Steven Beck, our security specialist, later told us that the only people in Russia who had access to unregistered numbers were members of the FSB.

•   •   •

Sergei was due to appear in court on Thursday, November 12, for another detention hearing. Getting to court was never straightforward. It usually started at 5:00 a.m., when the guards pulled the men from their cells and brought them to a prison transport. Twenty or so prisoners were then herded into a van that was designed for half as many people. For the next few hours, the truck would sit in a parking lot as some clerk filled out paperwork in the detention center's office. Sergei and the other prisoners were forced to stand in this tightly packed van and wait. They had no access to water, fresh air, or a toilet. This same process would be repeated after their day in court, and the men wouldn't get back to their bunks until after midnight. Throughout the day, they would be given no food, and often prisoners would go without eating for up to thirty-six hours. In essence, going to court was itself a form of torture designed to break and demoralize the prisoners as they fought for their all but nonexistent chance of being acquitted.

That day, Sergei arrived at court in midmorning. He was taken to a hallway and chained to a radiator. As he sat there going over the petitions he'd spent the previous two weeks preparing, Silchenko appeared and said with a smirk, "I've given the court the documents you've been asking for."

Sergei had requested a number of case documents on five different occasions over the previous six weeks. He needed them to put up a proper defense, but now, with only ten minutes to go before the hearing, Silchenko was finally adding them to the case file, and Sergei would not be able to see them before the hearing got started. Before this could sink in, the guards unchained Sergei, walked him into the courtroom, and put him in the defendant's cage.

As Sergei sat, he saw his mother and his aunt in the first row of the gallery. He gave them a small wave, trying to put on a brave face. They hadn't seen him in the two months since his last court appearance.

The judge, Yelena Stashina, brought the hearing to order. Sergei first read his complaint about not receiving adequate medical care. Judge Stashina rejected it. He then read his complaint about the fabrication of evidence in his case file. She rejected this as well. As he began to read the complaint about his false arrest, Stashina cut him off midsentence and rejected it too. In total, she rejected more than a dozen of Sergei's complaints. When Sergei asked for more time to go over the "new materials" that Silchenko had brought to court, Stashina told him to be silent.

But Sergei wouldn't be silent. Instead he stood in the cage and, in a booming voice that defied his physical state, accused her of violating the law and his rights. He finished his speech by saying, "I refuse to take part in and listen to today's court hearing because all my petitions to uphold my rights have been simply ignored by the court." He sat and turned away from the judge, and the hearing proceeded without him. Stashina was unmoved. She went through a few technical issues and then coldly extended Sergei's detention. The hearing ended and the guards came into the cage for Sergei. He couldn't muster the strength even to smile at his family as they led him away.

He was taken back to the hallway and chained to the same radiator. Neither his lawyer nor his family was allowed to see him for the rest of the evening. His mother and his aunt waited for hours outside in the cold for the van that would take him back to Butyrka, so that they could try to give him a little wave and tell him that they loved him. But by 9:00 p.m. the prison van had still not emerged. The cold, the despair, the sadness, ate into them. Finally, they gave up and went home.

• • •

I found out about all of this the next morning. When I told Elena, she became distressed. "I don't like this, Bill. I don't like this one bit."

I agreed.

"We have to get someone to Butyrka," she insisted. "Someone needs to see Sergei—today."

But no one could. His lawyer, who was the only person permitted to see him, was out of town and wouldn't be back until Monday.

That night, at 12:15 a.m., the voice mail alert on my BlackBerry vibrated. Nobody ever called my BlackBerry. No one even knew the number. I looked at Elena and dialed into voice mail. There was one message.

I heard a man in the midst of a savage beating. He was screaming and pleading. The recording lasted about two minutes and cut off mid-wail. I played it for Elena. Afterward, we sat in bed, unable to sleep, pondering all sorts of gruesome scenarios.

As soon as the sun came up, I called everyone I knew. They were all okay. The only person I couldn't call was Sergei.

. . .

On Monday, November 16, 2009, Sergei's lawyer, Dmitri, went to Butyrka to see him. However, the prison officials said they wouldn't bring Sergei out because he was "too unwell to leave his cell." When Dmitri asked for Sergei's medical report, he was told to go to Silchenko. He called and asked for a copy, but Silchenko told him that the report was "an internal matter for the investigation" and re-fused to give Dmitri any details.

They were deliberately giving Dmitri the runaround; Sergei was more than "unwell." After months of untreated pancreatitis, gall-stones, and cholecystitis, Sergei's body finally succumbed, and he went into critical condition. Although the prison officials at Butyrka had previously rejected his numerous requests for medical attention, that day they finally sent him to the medical center at Matrosskaya Tishina to receive emergency care.

However, when he arrived, instead of being taken to the medical wing, he was taken to an isolation cell and handcuffed to a bedrail. There, he was visited by eight guards in full riot gear. Sergei de-manded that the lead officer call his lawyer and the prosecutor. Sergei said, "I'm here because I've exposed the five-point-four billion ru-bles that were stolen by law enforcement officers." But the riot guards weren't there to help him, they were there to beat him. And they laid into him viciously with their rubber batons.

One hour and eighteen minutes later, a civilian doctor arrived and found Sergei Magnitsky dead on the floor.

His wife would never hear his voice again, his mother would never see his easy smile, his children would never feel the squeeze of his soft hands.

277

"Keeping me in detention," Sergei had written in his prison diary, "has nothing to do with the lawful purpose of detention. It is a punishment, imposed merely for the fact that I defended the interests of my client and the interests of the Russian state."

Sergei Magnitsky was killed for his ideals. He was killed because he believed in the law. He was killed because he loved his people, and because he loved Russia. He was thirty-seven years old.

31

The Katyn Principle

In April 1940, at the beginning of the Second World War, a Soviet NKVD[1] officer stationed in Belarus named Vasili Mikhailovich Blokhin was assigned the task of executing as many Polish POWs as he could. To do this efficiently and without alerting the prisoners to their fate, Blokhin had a special shed built at the POW camp. It had an entry door and an exit door and was surrounded on all sides by sandbags. Prisoners were taken into the shed by the entry door one at a time and told to kneel. Blokhin would then hold his pistol to the back of the prisoner's head and shoot. The corpse would be dragged out the exit door and put into a truck. When the truck was full, it was driven into a forest, where the bodies were dumped into mass graves.

Blokhin was good at his job. He was a night owl and worked tirelessly from sunset to sunrise. When he first started his assignment, he used his standard-issue Soviet service revolver, but later switched to a German-made Walther PPK. It had less recoil and didn't hurt his hand as much. Over twenty-eight days, and only taking time off for the May holidays, Blokhin murdered some seven thousand Polish prisoners. A prolific executioner, he was nevertheless just one man in a vast Soviet-sponsored and Stalin-directed massacre of Polish servicemen and officers that saw the deaths of twenty-two thousand men. The vast majority of these men were buried in the Katyn forest.

When the war was over and the mass graves were discovered, the Soviets claimed the Germans were responsible for this atrocity. The

---

1   The predecessor organization of the KGB and FSB.

world knew of all the terrible and unthinkable things the Germans had done during the war, so this lie was eminently plausible. To back it up, the Soviets manufactured evidence, issued official reports, and repeated their allegations so many times and in so many places, including at the famous Nuremberg trials, that their version of events became unchallenged. Only decades later, in early 1990, when the Soviet Union was on the verge of collapse and no longer had the fortitude to maintain the cover-up, did they admit the truth of what had happened in the Katyn forest.

One might think that as Russia entered the twenty-first century, the government would have stopped this type of behavior. But when Vladimir Putin came to power in 2000, instead of dismantling this machine of lying and fabrication, he modified it and made it all the more powerful.

Sergei Magnitsky's murder would become the prime example of this approach, and we had a unique opportunity to see how every gear and piston in this machine worked.

• • •

On the morning of November 17, 2009, hours before sunrise, Sergei's mother, Natalia, made her weekly trip to the Butyrka detention center to deliver a parcel of food and medicine to her son. She assembled with the other prisoners' family members at a small side entrance at 5:30 a.m. They arrived early because the prison accepted items only between 9:00 a.m. and 11:00 a.m. on Tuesdays. If Natalia missed that window, she would have to wait until the following week. Since most prisoners couldn't survive without these parcels, Natalia was never late.

The line moved slowly that morning. Natalia jostled with the fifty or so other family members in the narrow, dank passageway that led to the desk where two prison officers accepted the parcels. She finally made it to the front of the line at 9:40 a.m. She handed the prison officer a form listing the items she was delivering.

The woman looked at the form and shook her head officiously.

"That prisoner is no longer at this facility. He was moved to Matros-skaya Tishina last night."

"To the hospital there?" Natalia asked nervously. Given Sergei's frail appearance at the court hearing a few days before, she was worried about his health and hoped that he hadn't had some kind of emergency.

"I don't know," the officer said sternly.

Natalia tucked Sergei's parcel under her arm and hurried out. She hopped on the Metro and arrived at the parcel desk at Matrosskaya Tishina at 10:30 a.m. Fortunately, only three people were in line there. When she got to the desk, she said to the attendant, "I was told my son Sergei Magnitsky is here."

Without looking at a logbook or typing his name into a computer, the prison official responded, "Yes, he was transferred here last night in very bad condition."

Natalia started to panic. "Is he okay? What's happened to him?"

The attendant didn't respond for a few seconds. Then she said, "I'm afraid not. He died at nine last night."

Natalia shrieked. "W-w-what? What happened?"

"He died of pancreonecrosis, rupture of the abdominal membrane, and toxic shock," the attendant said in a monotone. "I'm very sorry for your loss." Natalia started to shake, but she couldn't move her feet. She leaned against the desk as this news hit her. Tears welled in her eyes.

"Woman, please step aside. I need to take care of the next person in line," the attendant said coldly.

Natalia couldn't even look at her.

"You need to step aside," the attendant repeated, and pointed to a hard plastic chair against the wall. Natalia followed her finger and shuffled to the chair, the other people in line staring at her, none of them sure what to do.

Natalia collapsed into the seat and broke down. After a few minutes she pulled herself together just long enough to call Sergei's lawyer, Dmitri, whose office was nearby. When Dmitri got there fifteen minutes later, Natalia was no longer able to speak. Dmitri took charge and asked for the doctor on duty. A few minutes later, a man in a lab coat appeared. He repeated the cause of death and said that Sergei's body had been transferred to Morgue No. 11, and if they wanted to know anything more, they should go there.

• • •

That morning my home phone rang at 7:45, 10:45 a.m. in Moscow. I picked up. It was Eduard, speaking in hasty Russian. I passed the phone to Elena. She listened. She gasped. Tears filled her eyes. Then she began to scream. Not in Russian, not in English, just a primal howl. I had never heard anyone make a sound like that in my life.

When she told me that Sergei had died, I jumped up and turned circles like a wild animal caught in a cage.

Sergei's death was so far beyond my worst nightmares that I had no idea how to cope. The pain I felt was physical, as if someone were plunging a knife right through my gut.

After a few minutes of hyperventilating, pacing, and choking back tears, I regained enough composure to make some calls. My first was to Vladimir. He always knew what to do, what to say, whom to approach—but not this time. When I told him the news, there was just silence on the other end of the phone. There was nothing he could say. Eventually he whispered meekly, "Bill, this is terrible."

Without showering, I pulled on my trousers, grabbed a shirt, rushed out the front door, and hopped in a cab to go to the office. I was the first to arrive, but within twenty minutes everyone else was there, disheveled and grief-stricken.

In any major crisis, what you do in the first few hours defines it forever. We quickly drafted a press release in English and Russian. With it, we included a forty-page, handwritten document that Sergei had prepared detailing his torture, the withholding of medical attention, and the intense hardship to which the prison authorities had subjected him. We then hit send, hoping and praying that this time people would care.

And this time, everyone did.

Most major newspapers took up the story, and they put calls in to the Russian authorities for comment. The press officer at the Interior Ministry was a plump blond woman in her early forties named Irina Dudukina. Shortly after the calls started coming in, she released the Interior Ministry's version of events. According to her, Sergei hadn't died of pancreonecrosis and toxic shock as the prison official had told Natalia earlier, but rather of "heart failure, with no signs of violence."

Later that day Dudukina went further, posting an official statement on the Interior Ministry's website saying, "There has not been a single complaint from Magnitsky about his health in the criminal case file" and "his sudden death was a shock for the investigators."

This was completely untrue. Not only were there many complaints in his case file, but there were also specific refusals from Major Silchenko and other senior officials denying him any medical attention.

Dudukina also lied about the time and place of Sergei's death. She claimed that Sergei died at 9:50 p.m. on a bed in Matrosskaya Tishina's emergency room as doctors tried to resuscitate him. This was directly contradicted by the civilian doctor who was first on the scene, who said that Sergei had died around 9:00 p.m. on the floor of an isolation cell.

I had never known Sergei's mother or wife. My contact had always been either with Sergei directly or, during his imprisonment, with his lawyer, but now his family and I were about to become inextricably linked forever.

I made my first call to his mother, Natalia, on November 17. Vadim translated. I not only wanted to express my most profound condolences, but also to tell her that I felt responsible for what had happened to her son and that she wasn't alone. It remains one of the most difficult conversations I've ever had in my life. Natalia was inconsolable. Sergei was her only child and meant everything to her. Every time she started talking, she would break down in tears. I didn't want to cause her more pain, but I wanted her to know that I was going to step into Sergei's shoes and look after her and the family. More importantly, I needed to tell her that I was going to make sure that the people who tortured and killed Sergei would face justice, and I wouldn't rest until they did.

Unfortunately, I couldn't be in Moscow to help them, so the family had to deal with the grim aftermath of Sergei's death on their own. The day after he died, they requested that an independent pathologist attend the state autopsy, but the prosecutor immediately denied their request, saying, "All our pathologists are equally independent."

Two days later, Natalia asked for his body to be released so the family could conduct their own autopsy. This was also denied on the grounds that "there is no reason to doubt the results of the state autopsy."

Later that day, Natalia went to Morgue No. 11. When she arrived, she was told that Sergei's body wasn't being stored in a refrigeration unit because the morgue had too many corpses, and that Sergei's body would decompose if he wasn't buried immediately. When Natalia asked whether Sergei's body could be released to the family so they could conduct a religious service with an open casket, the official categorically refused: "The corpse will only be released to the cemetery."

Sergei's family had to organize the burial for the next day. Natalia, along with Sergei's widow and aunt, went to the morgue to deliver a dark suit, a crisp white shirt, and a striped blue tie. They hoped they would be able to see Sergei one last time. The coroner reluctantly agreed. He led them down a flight of stairs and along a hallway to a room in the basement. The room was dark and had an overpowering and nauseating smell of formaldehyde and death. Fifteen minutes later, the coroner wheeled in Sergei's body on a gurney and said, "Now you can say good-bye."

Sergei was covered to the neck in a white sheet. Natalia had a candle that she wanted to put between his fingers in the Orthodox tradition for his burial. When she pulled back the sheet, she was shocked to see dark bruises on his knuckles and deep lacerations on his wrists.

At the sight of this, all three women lost their composure and broke down.

They kissed Sergei on the forehead, cried, and squeezed his injured hands. They gave the coroner Sergei's clothing and left.

On November 20, 2009, a brown wooden casket emerged from Morgue No. 11 and was put in a van. The family followed the van to the Preobrazhensky Cemetery in northeast Moscow. Sergei's friends pulled the casket from the transport and placed it on a cart. The procession went to the burial plot, many of his friends and family members carrying large bouquets of flowers. Once the casket was resting safely near the plot, the lid was pulled back and leaned against the foot of the box. Sergei was perfectly dressed. He was covered with a crisp cotton shroud that came up to his chest. His color was good. Even though everyone there could see the signs of violence on his wrists and knuckles, he looked at peace, and that was how he would be buried.

His family and friends took turns to say good-bye and lay red roses at his feet. Natalia and his widow, Natasha, placed a garland of white roses around his head. They cried and cried and cried and put the lid back on and lowered him into the ground.

• • •

The cover-up blossomed at every branch of Russian law enforcement from the moment that Sergei died. On November 18, the Russian State Investigative Committee announced, "No ground has been identified to warrant launching a criminal investigation following Magnitsky's death." On November 23, three days after his burial, the Russian General Prosecutor's Office issued a statement saying it had found "no wrongdoing by officials and no violations of the law. Death occurred from acute heart failure." Finally, on November 24, the head of Matrosskaya Tishina declared, "No violations have been found. Any investigations into Magnitsky's death should end and his case be filed in the archive."

But Sergei's case would not just go away. Every prisoner has his own way of dealing with the adversity of being in jail, and Sergei's had been to write everything down. In his 358 days in detention, he and his lawyers filed 450 criminal complaints documenting in granular detail who did what to him, when, how, and where. These complaints and the evidence that has since surfaced make Sergei's murder the most well documented human rights abuse case to come out of Russia in the last thirty-five years.

I completely suppressed my emotions in the week following Sergei's death. I'd tried to do as much as possible to achieve some sort of justice in Russia, but the consistent chorus of denial was demoralizing. When I came home on the evening of November 25, I sat at the dinner table with Elena. I put my head in my hands and closed my eyes. I hoped she might rub my neck or say something to make it all better, just as she had so many times before. But at that moment, she was distracted.

I looked up to find her intensely reading an email on her BlackBerry. "What's going on?"

She held up a hand, read some more, then said, "Medvedev just called for an investigation into Sergei's death!"

"*What?*"

"President Medvedev is going to launch an investigation!"

"Truly?"

"Yes. It says that he was briefed about this case by his human rights commissioner and that he asked the general prosecutor and the justice minster to launch a probe."

My mobile phone rang almost as soon as Elena had told me. It was Vladimir. "Bill, have you seen the Medvedev news?"

"Yes, Elena and I are reading it right now. What do you think?"

"You know, Bill, I never believe a word these people say—but how can this be bad?"

"I suppose it can't," I said. Although nothing could change the fact that Sergei was dead, this at least indicated that there might be some crack in Russia's evil foundation. Maybe, just maybe, Russia wouldn't operate on the Katyn principle of lying about everything in Sergei's case.

Two weeks later, on December 11, Medvedev's spokeswoman announced that twenty prison officials were to be fired "as a result" of Sergei's death. When I heard this, I started to picture Sergei's torturers being arrested at their homes and thrown into the same cells to which Sergei had been consigned.

Unfortunately, later that day, Vadim approached my desk with a grim look, clutching a handful of papers.

"What's this?" I pointed my chin at the paperwork.

"The names of the fired prison officials. Nineteen had absolutely nothing to do with Sergei. Some worked in prisons as far away as Vladivostok and Novosibirsk"—both of which were thousands of miles from Moscow.

"Were *any* associated with him in any way at all?"

"One. But this is bullshit. It's a complete smoke screen."

On top of the denials and fake firings was the reaction to the Moscow Public Oversight Commission (MPOC) report that came out on December 28. The MPOC is a nongovernmental organization whose mandate is to investigate brutality and suspicious deaths in Moscow prisons. Shortly after Sergei died, it launched its own independent investigation into his death, headed by an incorruptible man named Valery Borschev. He interviewed guards, doctors, and inmates who had had anything to do with Sergei. He and his team also read Sergei's complaints and the official files written about him. Their conclusions were definitive. The MPOC report stated that Sergei "was systematically denied medical care"; that he "was subjected to physical and psychological torture"; that his "right to life was violated by the state"; that "investigators, prosecutors, and judges played a role in his torturous conditions"; and finally, that "after his death, state officials lied and concealed the truth about his torture and circumstances of his death."

Borschev filed this report with five different government agencies, including the Presidential Administration, the Ministry of Justice, and the General Prosecutor's Office.

None of them ever replied.

It didn't matter to the authorities that *Novaya Gazeta* had published Sergei's unedited prison diaries on its front page, and that everyone read them.

It didn't matter that Sergei's name had been mentioned in 1,148 articles in Russia and 1,257 articles in the West since his death.

It didn't matter that Sergei's murder violated the social contract everyone had accepted: if you didn't get involved in anything controversial—politics, human rights, or anything to do with Chechnya—then you could get on with life and enjoy the fruits of the authoritarian regime.

The Russian authorities were so wrapped up in their cover-up that they ignored the most emotive aspects of Sergei's story. He was just a middle-class tax lawyer who bought his Starbucks coffee in the morning, loved his family, and did his tax work in his cubicle. His only misfortune was to stumble across a major government corruption scheme and then behave like a Russian patriot and report it. For that he'd been plucked out of his normal life, incarcerated in one of Russia's darkest hellholes, and then slowly and methodically tortured to death.

It didn't matter that any Russian could just as easily have been Sergei Magnitsky.

I'd suspended disbelief, wishfully thinking that Russia was beyond the Katyn principle of massive state-sponsored lying, but it wasn't. Evil hadn't withered under the bright lights of publicity.

If I wanted to get any justice for Sergei, then I was going to have to find a way to get it outside of Russia.

32

Kyle Parker's War

But how does one get justice in the West for torture and a murder that took place in Russia?

Since the British government had proved to be so unhelpful, I needed to broaden my scope. Given my personal history, the next logical place to turn was the United States.

I made several appointments for early March 2010 in Washington, DC, arriving on the second of the month. Washington was cold and drizzly. My first meeting was with Jonathan Winer, a top international criminal lawyer. Before going into private practice, Jonathan had been the deputy assistant secretary of state for narcotics and law enforcement—commonly referred to in Washington as the "DASS for drugs and thugs." He'd been responsible for US foreign policy regarding narco-traffickers and the Russian Mafia. He'd been effective, and a real tough customer.

I went to his downtown office on the morning of March 3. Based on his reputation, I was expecting a tall, rugged Clint Eastwood type of character, so when I arrived at his office I thought I'd gone to the wrong place. The person before me was a five-feet-six-inch, middle-aged, balding man with a long, narrow face who reminded me of one of my favorite economics professors from college. He hardly looked like the crime-fighting superhero I'd been imagining.

Jonathan ushered me into his office. We sat and he politely asked me to go through the whole story. He listened intently, periodically scribbling notes on an index card, not saying a word. Only when I was done did he start talking, which was when I began to see how he'd earned his reputation.

"Have you been to the Senate Foreign Relations Committee on this yet?" he fired at me in a low, staccato voice.

"No. Should I have?"

"Yes. Add them to the list." He put a check mark next to one of the notes on his index card. "What about the House Committee on Investigations?"

"No. Who are they?" I was starting to feel inadequate.

"It's a House committee that has virtually unlimited subpoena powers. Add them to the list too. What about the US Helsinki Commission?"

"Yes, I'm seeing them on my last day in Washington." I felt a little better that I wasn't totally failing the test. I somehow wanted this man's approval even though I'd only just met him.

"Good. They're important. I want to hear about that meeting when it's over." He put another check mark in his notes. "What about the State Department? Are you seeing anyone there?"

"Yes, tomorrow. Someone named Kyle Scott. He runs the Russia desk."

"That's a start. They won't give you anyone more senior until later, but it works for now. It's important that you know what you're going to say to Kyle Scott." Jonathan paused. "Do you have a plan?"

Every question he asked made it more and more clear that I had no idea what I was doing. "Well, I'd intended to tell them the story of what happened to Sergei," I said meekly.

Jonathan smiled benevolently, as if he were talking to a child. "Bill, Scott will have a detailed intelligence report on you and Sergei. With the resources of the US government, he'll probably know more about your story than you do. As far as the State Department is concerned, the primary purpose of this meeting is damage control. They'll be trying to figure out if this situation is serious enough to force the government to act. Your objective is to show them that it is."

"All right. How do I do that?"

"It all depends on what you want from them, Bill."

"What I really want is to create consequences for the people who killed Sergei."

Jonathan rubbed his chin for a few seconds "Well, if you really want to put the cat among the pigeons, I'd ask them to impose Proclamation Seventy-seven Fifty. It allows the State Department to impose visa sanctions on corrupt foreign officials. Bush created it in 2004. It would really get under the Russians' skin if they were slapped with that."

The 7750 idea was brilliant. Visa sanctions would cut right to the core of what it meant to be a Russian crook. When communism ended, corrupt Russian officials spread across the globe, filling up every five-star hotel from Monte Carlo to Beverly Hills, spending their money as if it were their last day on earth. If I could convince the US government to restrict their travel, then it would send shock waves through the Russian elite.

"Would the State Department actually do that?" I asked.

Jonathan shrugged. "Probably not, but it's worth a shot. Seventy-seven Fifty has rarely been used, but it's on the books, and it'll be interesting to see how they justify *not* implementing it with the evidence you have on this case."

I stood. "Then I'll do it. Thanks so much." I left Jonathan's office feeling empowered. I was still a Washington outsider, but now at least I had a plan—and an ally.

I arrived at the State Department on C Street the following morning. The plain, hard-angled building looked more like an elongated cinder block than the seat of US diplomatic power. After passing through a lengthy security screening, I was greeted by Kyle Scott's secretary, who led me down a series of drab, linoleum-covered corridors, her black high heels clicking rhythmically. Finally, we reached a door labeled OFFICE OF RUSSIAN AFFAIRS.

She opened the door and held out her hand. "Please." I went into a small suite, and she led me to the corner office. "Mr. Scott will be right with you."

Normally a corner office is meant to convey some sort of seniority, but as I settled in, I realized that it was the only sign that Kyle Scott had any status. His room was cramped and only big enough for a desk, a love seat, a small coffee table, and a couple of chairs. I took the love seat and waited.

After a few minutes Kyle Scott entered, an assistant in tow. "Hello, Mr. Browder." Kyle Scott was about my height and age and had close-set, brown eyes. His white shirt, red tie, and gray suit were standard-issue US government bureaucrat. "Thank you so much for meeting me today," he said, generously not acknowledging that I was the one who had asked for the meeting.

"No, thank you for making the time for me," I replied.

"I have something here that I think will make you very happy," he said with a conspiratorial smile. The assistant—a young woman wearing a gray pantsuit and a bright red silk scarf tied around her neck—wrote notes in a spiral notebook. Scott twisted to grab an overstuffed manila folder off his desk—a folder, no doubt, that contained all of his briefing material on Sergei and me, just as Jonathan had predicted. Scott brought his knees together, placed the folder on his lap, and removed a sheet of paper from it.

I was intrigued. "What is it?"

"Mr. Browder, each year the State Department publishes a human rights report, and this year, there are two *very strong* paragraphs in the report about the Magnitsky case."

I'd heard that organizations such as Human Rights Watch and Amnesty International had whole teams working throughout the year on strategies for getting their cases into this document—and here was Kyle Scott handing it to me on a silver platter.

While this may have been a big deal in other cases, it wasn't in ours. The Russian government couldn't have cared less about a couple of paragraphs in a US government human rights report. The Russians were actively covering up a massive crime, and the only thing they cared about—the only thing that would get their attention—was real-life consequences.

Kyle Scott watched me expectantly for my reaction.

"Can I read what's been written?"

He handed me the sheet of paper. The paragraphs were reasonably punchy, but they were just words.

I looked at Scott and said politely, "These are really great. Thank you very much. But there's something else I wanted to ask you."

Scott shifted uncomfortably in his chair, and the assistant peeked up from her notes. "Sure, what is it?"

"Actually, Mr. Scott, I've been studying the US statutes and have come across something I think would work very well in the Magnitsky case: Proclamation Seventy-seven Fifty, the one that can be used to ban corrupt foreign officials from coming into America."

He sat up stiffly. "I'm aware of that order. But how is it applicable here?" he asked defensively.

"It's applicable here because the people who killed Sergei are obviously corrupt, and therefore would be captured under the proclamation. The secretary of state should ban their entry into the US."

The assistant wrote feverishly, as if I'd spoken three times as many words. This was not how they had expected the meeting to go. Jonathan Winer had been right.

This was not what they wanted to hear because ever since Barack Obama had become president in 2009, the main policy of the US government toward Russia had been one of appeasement. The administration had even created a new word for it: *reset*. This policy was intended to reset the broken relations between Russia and the United States, but in practical terms it meant that the United States wouldn't mention certain unpleasant subjects concerning Russia so long as Russia played nice in trade relations and nuclear disarmament and various other areas. Sure, the US government could put a few paragraphs in a report to demonstrate "concern" over human rights abuses, but the main policy was for the United States to do absolutely nothing about them.

I was asking for something completely at odds with this policy, and Scott was suddenly in uncomfortable territory. "I'm sorry, Mr.

Browder, but I still don't see how Seventy-seven Fifty applies to the Magnitsky case," he said evasively.

I knew Scott was in a tough spot, but instead of backing down I pushed harder. "How can you say that? These officials stole two hundred and thirty million dollars from the Russian people and then killed the whistle-blower. They've laundered all of that money, and now parts of the Russian government are engaged in a massive cover-up. Seventy-seven Fifty is tailor-made for a case like this."

"But, Mr. Browder—I don't—it would be impossible to prove that any of these people did any of the things that you claim," he said firmly.

I tried to keep calm but was finding it more and more difficult. "The two paragraphs you just showed me mention several of these officials by name," I said pointedly.

"I—I—"

My voice started to rise. "Mr. Scott, this is the most well documented human rights abuse case since the end of the Soviet Union. It's been independently recognized that a number of Russian officials were involved in Sergei's death. I'd be happy to take you through it."

This meeting had gone completely off track for Scott, and now he wanted it to end. He motioned to his assistant, who stopped writing, and stood. I stood too. "I'm sorry, Mr. Browder," he said, ushering me toward the door, "but I have to get to another meeting. I'd be glad to discuss this with you another time, but I simply can't at the moment. Thank you again for coming in."

I shook his hand knowing full well that I wouldn't be returning to his office anytime soon. His assistant awkwardly escorted me out of the building without saying a word.

I left the State Department frustrated and upset. I wandered east, toward my next meeting near the Capitol, and eventually found myself strolling along the National Mall under slate-gray skies. Two heartland-looking young men, all of twenty years old, in blue blazers with brass buttons and khaki slacks, walked toward me in the middle of a heated discussion. They still had pimples, yet here they were in

Washington playing government. This wasn't my world. Who was I to think that I had a chance of making things happen in Washington? It had been obvious how little I knew when I met Jonathan, and it was confirmed by this unpleasant meeting with Kyle Scott.

I had several more meetings that day, but went through them in a daze, and none produced any real results. All I could think about was flying back home to London.

Before leaving Washington, I had my last appointment, this one with Kyle Parker at the US Helsinki Commission. This was the same man who had failed to put Sergei's case in President Obama's briefing packet back when Sergei was still alive, so I wasn't expecting a warm reception. I kept the meeting only because Jonathan Winer had made such a big deal about it when we went through my list of meetings.

I remembered Kyle Parker as a man in his early thirties who had weary eyes that appeared to have seen much more than his age suggested. He spoke perfect Russian and had a firm grasp of everything that was going on inside Russia. He could just as easily have worked for the CIA as for this obscure congressional human rights committee.

I made my way to the Ford House Office Building on D Street, one block away from the train tracks and the interstate. This ugly gray box of a building with zero architectural charm was far from the center of Capitol Hill in arguably the US government's worst piece of real estate. As I made my way into the building, I couldn't help but think that this was where they stuck all the orphan congressional institutions that weren't part of mainstream power circles.

Kyle Parker met me at security and brought me to an underheated conference room with all sorts of Soviet memorabilia displayed on the bookshelves. He sat at the head of the table in an awkward silence. I took a breath to break it, but he cut me off.

"Bill, I just want to say how sorry I am that we didn't do more to help Sergei last year. I can't tell you how often I've thought about him since he died."

I wasn't expecting that, and I took a moment before saying, "We tried, Kyle."

He then said something so un-Washington-like that I still can't believe it to this day. "When you sent out the tribute to Sergei after he died, I rode the Red Line home reading it over and over. I was heartbroken. You'd just been here four months earlier pleading for help. I cried, right there on the train. I read it to my wife when I got home. She cried too. This murder—it's one of the worst things that's happened since I started my career."

I was stunned. I had never heard anyone in government speak in such an emotional and human way. "Kyle, I don't know what to say. It's been the worst thing for me too. The only way I can get up in the morning is to go after the guys who did this to Sergei."

"I know, and I'm going to help you."

I took a deep breath. This Kyle was completely unlike anyone I had ever met in Washington.

I wanted to tell him about what had happened at the State Department, but before I could, Kyle launched into a one-sided brainstorming session. "Bill, I want to make a list of every person involved in Sergei's false arrest, torture, and death. Not just Kuznetsov and Karpov and the other thugs at the Interior Ministry, but the doctors who ignored Sergei's pleas, the judges who rubber-stamped his detention, the tax officials who stole Russian money. Everyone who's directly culpable in Sergei's death."

"That's easy, Kyle. We have that information and the documents to back it up. But what would you do with it?"

"I'll tell you what I'd do. I'd organize a congressional fact-finding trip to Moscow and have the US embassy call each person on that list requesting a meeting to discuss the Magnitsky case. I'm not sure many would agree, but it would shock the Russian authorities to no end that the United States is paying such close attention to Magnitsky's death."

"I like that idea, but I could see a lot of reasons why it wouldn't get off the ground. However, we could use the list in a different way."

"I'm listening."

I told him about Jonathan Winer, Proclamation 7750, and the meeting with Scott at the State Department.

As I spoke, Kyle wrote everything down. "That *is* a great idea." He tapped the point of his pen on his notepad. "How did the person at the Department react?"

"Not well. As soon as I said 'Seventy-seven Fifty,' he deflected and obfuscated and shooed me out of his office."

"I'll tell you what. I'm going to talk to Senator Cardin and ask him to send a letter to Secretary Clinton requesting her to invoke Seventy-seven Fifty." Kyle paused and looked me straight in the eye. "Let's see if they treat a United States senator the same way."

33

Russell 241

On returning to London I gathered the team to tell them about what had happened in Washington. I knew they needed good news. Everything we'd done inside Russia had gone nowhere. I didn't try to cheer them up as they took their seats. Instead I just told them the entire Washington story, ending with the idea of visa sanctions and Senator Cardin's letter to Hillary Clinton.

"Bill, you realize the significance of this, don't you?" Ivan asked when I was done. "If this happens, it means that we'll have the US government on our side!"

"I know, Ivan. I know."

This was a huge morale boost, especially to the Russians on the team. As anyone who has read Chekhov, Gogol, or Dostoyevsky will tell you, and as Sergei himself once reminded us, Russian stories don't have happy endings. Russians are familiar with hardship, suffering, and despair—not with success and certainly not with justice. Not surprisingly, this has engendered in many Russians a deep-seated fatalism that stipulates that the world is bad, it will always be bad, and any attempt to change things is doomed.

But now a young American named Kyle Parker was challenging this fatalism.

Unfortunately, a week passed, then two, and finally three without so much as a peep from Kyle. Every day I could see Ivan, Vadim, and Vladimir reverting to fatalistic form, and by the third week even I was being infected with this Russian gloom. I resisted the urge to pick up the phone for fear of scaring Kyle off. As I got further and further from my meeting with Kyle, I grew more and more uncertain that I'd read him correctly.

Finally, in late March 2010, I couldn't take it any longer. I dialed Kyle's number and, as if he were hanging over the phone, he answered on the first ring.

"Hello?" he said cheerfully.

"Hi, Kyle. It's Bill Browder. I'm sorry to bother you, but I was wondering if you had any idea when Senator Cardin's letter might go out? It would make a huge difference for the campaign. . . . In fact, I think it would completely change it."

"I'm sorry, but things don't always work on a schedule over here. But don't worry, Bill, just be patient. I'm serious about this."

"All right, I'll try," I said, barely put at ease. "But if there's anything—*anything*—I can do to help, then please let me know."

"I will."

As much as I believed that Kyle was genuinely shocked by Sergei's death, I thought this talk of being patient was a way of letting me down slowly. I was sure that lots of people in Washington didn't want sanctions and that in the end there would be no Cardin letter.

A few weeks later on a Friday, in one of my few moments of doing something unrelated to the campaign, I took Elena and David to the movies at Leicester Square. Perhaps fitting to my situation, it was a political thriller—*The Ghost Writer*, directed by Roman Polanski. As we sat in the dark watching previews and eating popcorn, my phone vibrated. I looked at the number. It was Kyle Parker.

I whispered to Elena that I would be back in a second and went out to the lobby.

"Hello?"

"Bill, I've got some good news for you. It's ready. It's going to Secretary Clinton on Monday morning."

"The letter? You're doing it?"

"Yep. We're just putting the finishing touches on it right now. I'll send it over in an hour."

We hung up. I "watched" the movie but could barely keep track of what was going on. After the film ended, we rushed home and I ran to my computer and printed the letter addressed to Hillary Clinton. Clutching it in both hands, I read it several times over.

The language was beautiful, succinct, and compelling. Its concluding paragraph read:

> *I urge you to immediately cancel and permanently withdraw the US visa privileges of all those involved in this crime, along with their dependents and family members. Doing so will provide some measure of justice for the late Mr. Magnitsky and his surviving family and will send an important message to corrupt officials in Russia and elsewhere that the US is serious about combating foreign corruption and the harm it does.*

I called Kyle immediately. "This is amazing. I can't tell you how much this means to me and to everyone who knew Sergei. . . ."

"I told you we were going to do it, Bill, and I meant it. It broke my heart when Sergei was killed. I want to make sure his sacrifice wasn't in vain," Kyle said, his voice cracking slightly.

"What happens now?"

"The letter will go to Clinton on Monday. We'll post it on the commission's website as soon as we send it."

"That's great. Let's speak Monday. Have a great weekend."

It took me nearly two hours to fall asleep that night. Was Cardin really going to do this? Could these things be stopped at the last minute? And if it did happen—what would Clinton do? What would the Russians do?

Monday morning came. I got to the office early, sat at my desk, and opened up the Helsinki Commission website. There was nothing, but London was five hours ahead of Washington so it was reasonable to expect that the letter would be published later in the day.

I checked again at noon London time, but there was still nothing. As I paced through the office, I noticed that I wasn't the only one compulsively checking the US Helsinki Commission website.

Vadim, Ivan, and Vladimir all had the home page on their screens, but no matter how many times any of us pressed the refresh button, the same page kept coming up.

Finally, at 2:12 p.m.—9:12 a.m. in Washington—a new page appeared. There, staring back at me, were two mug shots, one of Kuznetsov and one of Karpov, along with Senator Cardin's letter to Secretary of State Hillary Clinton. Attached to the letter was the list of the sixty officials involved in Sergei's death and the tax fraud, and next to each name was his or her department affiliation, rank, date of birth, and role in the Magnitsky case. Cardin was requesting that all sixty have their US travel privileges permanently revoked.

I fell back into my chair.

It was real. It was here, right in front of the world's eyes. Something had finally been done to hold the people who'd killed Sergei to account. As I stared at the screen, a lump formed in my throat. If Sergei was looking down on us, he would see that his heartbreaking prison letters, in which he'd pleaded for help, were finally being heard.

Within ten minutes, the Russian newswires started reporting the story. Within thirty minutes, the Western press picked it up. By the end of the day a new term had been created and repeated over and over: the Cardin List.

Nobody in Russia had heard of Ben Cardin before, but after April 26, 2010, the conventional wisdom in Russia was that this senator from Maryland was the most important politician in America. Russian human rights activists and opposition politicians jumped onto the bandwagon, writing letters to President Obama and the head of the EU supporting the Cardin List. Not since Ronald Reagan had Russians witnessed a foreign politician act so decisively on a Russian human rights issue. The sad fact was that most Russian atrocities were never noticed by the outside world, and in the rare instances that they were, foreign governments almost never reacted to them. But now, all of a sudden, a US senator was calling for sixty named Russian officials to have their US visas revoked for their involvement in a human rights atrocity. It was totally unprecedented.

While average Russians were celebrating, Putin's top officials were apoplectic. All of his key lieutenants had used their jobs to become enormously wealthy, and many had done some very nasty things to get rich. In theory, the Cardin List opened the door so that these people could be sanctioned in the future. As far as they were concerned, the list changed everything for them.

But, at least initially, they needn't have worried. Back in Washington, the State Department wanted to do nothing in response to the Cardin letter and hoped that by just sitting on the letter and ignoring Cardin, the problem would go away.

But it didn't. If the State Department was going to ignore Senator Cardin, then Kyle was going to up the ante. He arranged for me to testify about the Magnitsky case in front of the Tom Lantos Human Rights Commission in the House of Representatives in early May.

The hearing was scheduled for May 6 at the Rayburn House Office Building, which sits just to the southwest of the Capitol. Completed in 1965, the building is in the stripped-down style of the neoclassical architecture you see all over Washington, although the inside is not like other congressional buildings. It has no soaring marble columns or domes or cherrywood panels on the walls. Instead, there are linoleum floors, low ceilings, and chrome details on the clocks and in the elevators.

I'd never been there before, so I arrived well before the 10:00 a.m. start time in order to get a feel for the place. I entered from Independence Avenue, going through the small security checkpoint manned by a pair of Capitol police. I found my way to room 2255 and had a quick look inside. The large hearing room had a horseshoe dais for the commission members, two long tables for the guest speakers, and an audience gallery behind the speakers with seats for about seventy-five people. The chairman—a Massachusetts congressman named Jim McGovern—hadn't arrived yet, but aides, staffers, and various others milled around making small talk. I retreated to the hall and went over Sergei's story in my head.

When I reentered the room, little papers folded into upside-down Vs had been placed on the speakers' tables. There were representatives from prestigious human rights organizations—the Committee to Protect Journalists, Human Rights Watch, and the International Protection Centre—and I felt a bit out of place as a businessman amid all of these professional human rights activists.

I spotted Kyle Parker, who sat off to one side of the gallery, just as Congressman McGovern entered. McGovern was a congenial man with a prominent bald spot and a pleasant, boyish face. He greeted all the witnesses with a firm handshake and spoke with a Boston accent. I was drawn to him immediately. He asked us to sit, and the hearing commenced promptly.

The first speaker was an advocate for persecuted journalists in Russia. She read from a statement and was knowledgeable, citing numerous facts and figures about killings and abductions of journalists who'd exposed the crimes of the Russian regime. I was intimidated by both the enormity of her testimony and her grasp of policy issues. I was just speaking about one case, one man, and didn't even have a prepared statement to read from.

The next speaker was from Human Rights Watch, and she repeated many of the same points in the litany of Russian rights abuses that her organization had documented. She also referred to a number of notorious cases, including the murders of Anna Politkovskaya and Natalia Estemirova. I remembered both stories well, and I was impressed by this speaker. When she was finished I felt even more inadequate.

The preppy staffers scattered around the room were less moved. They'd sat through many such hearings and had heard it all before. Their noses were turned downward to tiny screens cupped in their hands, thumbs dancing over BlackBerry keypads, and they'd barely noticed as the first presenter wrapped up and the next one took the stage.

At last it was my turn. I didn't have any statistics or spreadsheets or policy recommendations. I just stood uncomfortably, pulling at the cuffs of my jacket, and started talking. I gave a little background on myself and then told the committee Sergei Magnitsky's deep, dark story. I looked Congressman McGovern straight in the eye, and he returned my gaze. Step-by-step, I told him and the others how Sergei had uncovered the crime, how he was arrested after testifying, how he had been sadistically tortured in prison, and how, finally, he had been killed.

As I spoke, I noticed that the fresh-faced staffers had stopped tapping away at their BlackBerrys. I concluded my speech by asking the commission to support Senator Cardin in his call to the State Department to impose visa sanctions on Sergei's killers. In closing, I said, "Sergei Magnitsky is one individual case, but there are thousands upon thousands of other cases just like his. And the people who do these things will continue doing them unless there is some way of challenging them and showing them there is no impunity."

I sat and glanced at my watch. My speech had taken eight minutes. I smoothed my hands over the table and looked around. Several people in the room had tears in their eyes, including some of the human rights activists. I waited for someone to speak, but the room remained still.

Finally, after about twenty seconds, McGovern laced his fingers together and leaned forward. "I have had the privilege of being the cochair of this commission for almost two years, and I have learned an awful lot. We have been inundated with so many statistics and facts that sometimes we lose the human ability to actually feel them, Mr. Browder. That is why I am grateful you were here to talk about the case of Mr. Magnitsky. That is a really tragic story. I think people who commit murder should not have the right to travel here and invest in businesses here. There should be a consequence. So one of the things I would like to do, we will not only send a letter to Hillary Clinton, but I think we should introduce legislation and put those sixty people's names down there and move it to the committee and make a formal recommendation from Congress, pass it on the floor, saying to the administration, This is a consequence. You have got to do this, because if you don't, nothing is going to happen. You have my pledge that we will do that."

When the hearing was over, Kyle and I walked out of the room in silence. Had Jim McGovern just promised to introduce a Magnitsky law? Yes, he had. It was so far above my most optimistic expectations that it seemed unbelievable.

When we got downstairs, I said, "Kyle, do you think Cardin would do the same thing in the Senate?"

Kyle stopped walking. "Given what just happened, Bill, I can't imagine that Cardin *wouldn't.*"

Later that afternoon, Kyle called to confirm that, yes, Cardin would be happy to be the original cosponsor in the Senate. All of a sudden, there was a small but real chance of making a US law in Sergei's name—the Sergei Magnitsky Act.

However, there was a lot of work between the idea of a law and making it a reality. First we needed an actual document that Cardin and McGovern could introduce. When this was ready, it would have to be approved by committees in both the Senate and the House of Representatives. After that, it would then go for a full vote in front of each chamber of Congress. If both chambers passed the bill, then it would go to the president for his signature.

Thousands of draft laws are brought before Congress every year, and only a few dozen actually make their way onto the books. Therefore it was essential that the draft document Cardin and McGovern presented to their colleagues be bulletproof against any potential detractors. Kyle spent that entire summer working on the draft law, and as he did, we developed a close friendship. We spoke every day, sometimes twice a day, as we both learned as much about US sanctions law as we could.

By early September, a good draft of the bill was ready.

When Kyle sent it to me, I asked, "How quickly can Cardin schedule a vote in the Senate?"

Kyle laughed. "It's not as simple as that, Bill. To get any bill passed in Washington you need bipartisan support. We're going to need a senior and powerful Republican senator to cosponsor this to get it off the ground. Only then can we begin the process."

"Will Cardin find that person?"

"Possibly, but if you want this to happen quickly, you could try as well. Your personal story with Sergei is very persuasive."

I didn't want to leave it to chance, so after talking to Kyle, I began reviewing the list of Republican senators who might be cosponsors, and one name jumped right off the page: John McCain.

If there was one senator who could truly empathize with being tortured in prison, it was John McCain. He'd been a navy fighter pilot during the Vietnam War, and when his plane was shot down, he was taken prisoner. He was held and tortured at a POW camp for five years before being freed. He would surely understand the horror that Sergei had experienced and want to do something about it.

But how on earth was I going to get a meeting with John McCain? Access in Washington is closely guarded, and the more important the person, the more inaccessible he or she is. A whole industry of lobbyists has been built around this fact. When I started asking around for someone who could introduce me to McCain, people looked at me as if I were asking them to give me a million dollars for nothing.

But then I remembered that I knew one person who might be able to make this happen. Her name was Juleanna Glover, a tall, attractive woman with wavy auburn hair, impeccable style, and an easy manner. I'd met Juleanna through a mutual friend in Washington in 2006, shortly after my Russian visa had been revoked. She'd invited me to a large group dinner at Cafe Milano, a trendy Italian restaurant in Georgetown. We exchanged cards at the end of the meal, but only when I got back to my hotel and typed her name into Google did I realize I'd been sitting next to one of Washington's most influential lobbyists.

Juleanna had quite a résumé. She'd served as Vice President Dick Cheney's press secretary and then as Attorney General John Ashcroft's senior policy adviser. She went with Ashcroft when he left government to run the Washington office of his law firm, the Ashcroft

Group. She was so well regarded that in 2012, *Elle* magazine named her one of Washington's ten most powerful women.

Apparently, after dinner that night she also went home and typed my name into Google and learned about my escalating problems with the Russian government. She called me the next day and offered to help in any way she could, and from that moment we became friends. When Sergei died, one of the first calls I received was from Juleanna and John Ashcroft to express their condolences. "We know how bad you must feel, Bill," Ashcroft had said. "But you should know that you're not alone in this. If there's anything we can do to help you or Sergei's family, we'll do it. Just call."

Now, I did need help. I needed help getting a meeting with John McCain.

I called Juleanna and told her the situation. She said that she'd have no problem getting me in with McCain. Was it really that easy for her? We hung up and she called back inside of ten minutes.

"Bill, Senator McCain will see you at three fifteen on September twenty-second."

Yes, for her it *was* that easy.

I flew to Washington on September 21, and Juleanna met me at my hotel the next afternoon. We shared a taxi to Capitol Hill, cleared security, and made our way to McCain's office—Russell 241. Given his stature in the Senate, his office was in a prime location, taking up a series of high-ceilinged rooms. We announced ourselves and were ushered into a waiting room by an assistant. McCain's chief foreign policy adviser—a tall, thin, redheaded man with a friendly grin named Chris Brose—greeted us and made small talk while we waited for the senator. After half an hour, Senator McCain was ready to see us.

McCain met us at the door with a hearty handshake and a warm smile. He led us into his office—a comfortably furnished room with a leather couch, warm lighting, and a long and full bookcase. It had a definite Americana West feel. If it weren't for the soaring ceiling and the tall window framing his desk, it could have been mistaken for the comfortable home office of a bibliophile executive in Phoenix.

I sat on the sofa and he perched on a chair at the head of the coffee table. He cleared his throat. "Thanks for coming in, Mr. Browder. I've been told you want to tell me about some of the things going on Russia." He probably expected me to lobby him about some Russian business issue.

"Yes, I do, Senator."

I then began my story about Sergei, and it quickly became clear to McCain that this wasn't going to be like his other meetings. Less than two minutes in, he held up a hand to ask the date of Sergei's arrest. I answered and continued. A short time later he interrupted again to get clarification on Sergei's prison conditions. I answered and continued until he interrupted me again. We carried on like this until my fifteen minutes were up, when his secretary poked her head in to say that his next appointment was ready. I froze. I couldn't lose this opportunity to ask him to cosponsor the law.

"I need some more time with Mr. Browder," McCain said softly. His secretary left and McCain turned his attention back to me. "Please continue."

I did. More questions, more answers. After another fifteen minutes his secretary reappeared. Again, McCain politely waved her off. We repeated this sequence once more, and by the time I was finished, I'd been sitting in McCain's office for nearly an hour.

"Bill, Sergei's story is shocking, truly terrible. I am so sorry for what happened to him, for you and for everybody else involved."

"Thank you, Senator."

"Tell me—what can I do to help?"

I told him about Cardin and McGovern and the early drafts of the Magnitsky Act. Then I said, "Since Senator Cardin is a Democrat, it would be hugely helpful to have an important Republican cosponsor on this bill. I was hoping that this could be you, sir."

McCain leaned back in his chair, his face thoughtful and serene. "Of course I will do that. It's the least I can do." He turned to his aide Chris Brose, who'd been sitting there throughout. "Chris, please coordinate with Senator Cardin right away to make sure you get me on that bill." McCain then turned back to me. "You've been a real friend to Sergei. Not many people would do what you're doing, and I deeply respect that. I will do everything in my power to help you get justice for Sergei. God bless you."

34

Russian Untouchables

While I was flying back and forth to Washington working the political angles, the team was in London working the Russian angles.

Ever since we'd posted our first YouTube video in October 2009, we'd been receiving unsolicited phone calls and emails from ordinary Russians with tips related to our case. One of these came from a young woman named Ekaterina Mikheeva, who told us a horrifying story.

Kuznetsov and Karpov hadn't victimized just us. According to her, both officers were involved in a raid on her husband's office in 2006. After the raid, her husband, Fyodor, was arrested and taken to the same police station where Sergei had been held. But instead of being kept there, Fyodor was escorted to a car outside. He was shoved into the backseat and, without any explanation, driven to a house thirty miles from Moscow. Fyodor soon figured out that he was being held hostage. Ekaterina told us that one of these kidnappers was Viktor Markelov, the same convicted killer who took control of our stolen companies in 2007.

Shortly after arriving at the house, the kidnappers called Fyodor's boss to issue the terms of his release: $20 million. Ekaterina also got a call from one of the kidnappers. She was warned that if she went to the police, Fyodor would be hurt and she would be visited by some of the kidnappers' friends and gang-raped.

Ekaterina was terrified, but she bravely defied the warnings. She found a different police unit, which located her husband. They stormed the house and freed Fyodor, taking Markelov and his accomplice into custody.

Unfortunately, her story didn't end there. A month later, Fyodor was arrested again by the same group of officers and thrown into a cell with one of his former kidnappers. We don't know what happened to him there or who was involved, but we do know that Fyodor was eventually convicted of fraud and sentenced to eleven years at a prison camp in the Kirov region, five hundred miles from Moscow. Ekaterina was thirty-four years old, and she and Fyodor had two small children. Their family was torn apart. Suddenly, this young woman was forced to take care of herself and raise the children on her own, while her husband wasted away in jail.

I knew we were dealing with some nasty people, but when I heard her story, it became that much more imperative to see that corrupt officers like Kuznetsov and Karpov were stopped.

From that point on, our team focused all of its energy on finding anything they could about Kuznetsov and Karpov. They rummaged through bank statements, court filings, judgments, registration documents, letters, and briefs, trying to identify any assets belonging to these two officers. We were sure we'd find something. Kuznetsov and Karpov dressed in expensive suits, wore fancy watches, and drove luxury cars, even though they each earned less than $1,500 a month. Finding any evidence of their extravagances would give us a big advantage in our battle with these two men.

We began our investigation by running their names through the same type of databases we used during our corporate governance campaigns in Russia. Unfortunately, nothing came up using their specific names. However, searching for their parents' names in the databases generated a number of direct hits. Kuznetsov's and Karpov's lack of discretion was remarkable, especially considering that they were police officers.

One of the most interesting discoveries was a property registered to Kuznetsov's mother, a 1,660-square-foot condominium in the prestigious Edelweiss high-rise just off Kutuzovsky Prospekt, the Champs-Élysées of Moscow. It had views over Victory Park and was worth about $1.6 million.

We also found that Kuznetsov's father was the registered owner of a nine-hundred-square-foot condominium that had a market value of roughly $750,000, in a building called the Capital Constellation Tower.

In addition to these upscale properties, Kuznetsov's mother had three land plots in her name located in the Noginski district just outside Moscow, which were worth almost $180,000.

Theoretically, the ownership of all this real estate could have been legitimate, but Kuznetsov's parents' monthly income was only $4,500, which wasn't nearly enough to account for these properties. In our minds, there was only one possible explanation: the properties had been paid for by their son, Artem.

The Kuznetsov family didn't just own expensive real estate. According to the records of the Moscow Traffic Police, Kuznetsov's mother had a brand-new $65,000 Land Rover Freelander, while Kuznetsov's wife owned a $115,000 Range Rover and an $81,000 Mercedes-Benz SLK 200.

The Russian Border Control database presented an even more interesting glimpse into Kuznetsov's lifestyle. In 2006, Artem and his wife started traveling the world like global jet-setters. Over five years they made more than thirty trips to eight different countries, including Dubai, France, Italy, and the United Kingdom. When they went to Cyprus, they even flew by private jet.

According to our research, the total value of assets owned by the Kuznetsov family was roughly $2.6 million. To put this in perspective, Kuznetsov would have had to work for *145 years* on his official Interior Ministry salary to make this sum of money.

The information we dug up on Karpov was equally shocking and followed the same pattern: a $930,000 luxury condo registered to his pensioner mother; a brand-new Audi A3, a Porsche 911 registered in his mother's name, and a Mercedes-Benz E280 in his name. His travel records showed that since 2006 he had gone to the United Kingdom, the United States, Italy, the Caribbean, Spain, Austria, Greece, Cyprus, Oman, Dubai, and Turkey. He frequented the best and most expensive nightclubs in Moscow, having his picture taken with gorgeous girls and well-dressed friends. Clearly he wasn't shy about sharing any of this, because he had posted pictures of his grinning face all over the Internet.

These guys were disgusting. If an ordinary Russian person could see images of Kuznetsov's and Karpov's lives—the houses, the vacations, the cars—they would be apoplectic. The images would go further than any newspaper article or radio interview ever could. We had to *show* how these midlevel police officers profited from what they did. They couldn't have it both ways. They couldn't get to ruin lives in the morning and go to Michelin star restaurants at night.

I decided to make some more YouTube videos, this time starring Artem Kuznetsov and Pavel Karpov. We got right to work, and they were ready by June 2010, just as the Magnitsky Act was being drafted in Washington. All we were waiting for was the right moment to launch them.

That moment came when Oleg Logunov, the Interior Ministry general who'd authorized Sergei's arrest, began a publicity campaign to justify Sergei's arrest and death. When he was asked by a popular radio station whether Sergei was pressured while in custody, Logunov stated blandly, "The fact that investigators are interested in obtaining testimony is normal. They do it in all countries," as if what had happened to Sergei were the most mundane thing in the world.

Their cover-up was gaining momentum and we had to do something, so on June 22 I uploaded the Kuznetsov video to YouTube. At the same time, our campaign launched a new website called www.russian-untouchables.com, where we provided the documents and evidence supporting our allegations of the unbelievable lifestyles of these officials for the world to see.

In its first day, the Kuznetsov video got more than fifty thousand views, which was more than the *total* number of views for the first YouTube video we did about the fraud. Within a week, 170,000 people had seen the Kuznetsov video, and it was the top political video in Russia on YouTube. The *New Times* magazine (a Russian opposition weekly) wrote a big story entitled "Private Jets for the Lieutenant Colonel." Kuznetsov's wealth was such a sexy story that it even got a write-up in the UK tabloid the *Sunday Express*, which almost never reports on things occurring outside Britain.

While everyone talked, wrote, and blogged about the video, a group of Russian activists took matters into their own hands. They showed up at Kuznetsov's building and pasted a picture of Sergei on every apartment door with the words *Kuznetsov murderer!* below his face. They also unfurled a massive banner on the high-rise facing his apartment with the same words.

To keep the pressure on the Russian authorities, just before releasing the movie, Jamie Firestone also filed criminal complaints with the General Prosecutor's Office and the Internal Affairs Department of the Interior Ministry, challenging Kuznetsov's unexplained wealth.

In spite of the overwhelming evidence, the authorities circled the wagons around this midlevel police officer. They trotted out Deputy Interior Minister Alexei Anichin, who said it was "not part of our remit" to investigate Kuznetsov's wealth.

In spite of the official nonreaction to the video, it clearly touched a nerve. On July 11, 2010, Pavel Karpov filed a criminal defamation complaint in Russia against my colleagues and me. In his complaint he said, "William Browder, Eduard Khayretdinov, Jamison Firestone, and Sergei Magnitsky conducted an information campaign to discredit me and Artem Kuznetsov, and also to cover up the traces of their own criminal activity." He went on to say, "The only person who stood to benefit by the theft of his own companies, the tax refund, and the death of Magnitsky was William Browder."

That's right: Karpov was now saying that I was responsible for Sergei's death.

Maybe Karpov thought that if he attacked me, I would back down, but it had the exact opposite effect. The day after we learned of his complaint, we released the movie starring him. Cinematically, this one was even better than the Kuznetsov video. It had all the images of property and cars, and also lots of Karpov's own photos from nightclubs, restaurants, and discotheques that had been taken all over Moscow. If you were an honest, middle-class Russian and saw how this ordinary cop lived, you would have been shocked—and they all were.

Jamie also filed another set of criminal complaints against Karpov. This time the Internal Affairs Department of the Interior Ministry actually questioned Kuznetsov and Karpov, but in the end claimed that the department lacked the authority to check their parents' incomes and found nothing wrong.

Kuznetsov and Karpov may have been untouchable by Russian law enforcement, but they were anything but untouchable in the court of public opinion. Within three months, more than four hundred thousand people had watched the videos. No matter how many lies the Russian authorities told, a person could always hold up a finger and say, "Yes, but if Kuznetsov and Karpov are not corrupt, then how did they get so rich? Can you answer that? *How* did they get so rich?"

35

The Swiss Accounts

That August, I took David for a father-son trip to the English countryside. One day, as we were hiking up a cliffside trail in Cornwall, an unexpected gift fell in my lap. It came in the form of a phone call from Jamie Firestone.

Jamie was so excited he could barely get the words out. "Hey, Bill—can I make your day?"

"Always ready for that." I caught my breath from the steep trail while David stopped in a patch of shade to drink some water. "What's happening?"

"I just got an email from someone who claims to have proof that a woman at Moscow Tax Office Number Twenty-eight got *millions* from the fraud."

"Who sent the email?"

"Someone named Alejandro Sanches."

"That doesn't sound very Russian. How do you know it's not bullshit?"

"I don't. But he sent me some Swiss bank statements and some offshore company documents in his email."

"What do they say?"

"They show a bunch of wire transfers going to bank accounts that seem to belong to the husband of Olga Stepanova, the lady at the tax office who signed the refund check."

"That's amazing! Do you think they're real?"

"I don't know. But Sanches said that if we're interested, he's willing to meet."

"Are you comfortable doing that?"

"Sure," Jamie said almost dismissively. Even after all that had happened, Jamie hadn't lost his optimism. "Don't worry, Bill."

We hung up and I took a few sips of water. David and I put our heads down and kept walking up the trail, but I hardly noticed the beautiful views over the beach. My head was spinning. The campaign needed a break like this, but I was worried about sending Jamie into harm's way.

Nowhere was safe, especially London, which was rife with Russians. In 2006, Alexander Litvinenko, a former FSB agent and well-known Putin critic, was poisoned by FSB agents at London's Millennium Hotel, just across the street from the American embassy.

Jamie and Sanches exchanged a few more emails and agreed to meet each other on August 27, 2010. The plan was for them to sit down, and if Sanches appeared legitimate, Jamie would call Vadim to join them to go over the documents.

Sanches suggested the Polo Bar at the Westbury Hotel in Mayfair, which was ominously close to where Litvinenko had been poisoned. Terrified that something awful would happen, I called our security guy, Steven Beck, to come up with a plan.

Steven surveyed the location and decided to bring in four men to watch over Jamie and Vadim. Two were ex–Special Forces and two were former British intelligence officers. At 2:30 p.m. on the twenty-seventh these men began to show up in the Polo Bar one at a time. They took up strategic positions—two by the exits, one near the table where the meeting would occur, one at the end of the bar. They blended in seamlessly. One carried a device that could detect and jam any surveillance equipment similar to the kind that we thought Sagiryan might have used for the meeting at the Dorchester Hotel. Another did a discreet walk-through with a Geiger counter to check for any radiation, since Litvinenko had been poisoned with a highly toxic radioactive isotope of polonium.

There were no guarantees, but I knew that if things got ugly, Steven's guys would get Jamie and Vadim out of there in a hurry.

Jamie got to the Polo Bar early, entering through one of the steel-and-glass double doors. He walked through the low-ceilinged art deco lounge to the reserved table. He sat in one of the blue velvet club chairs with his back to a wall, a picture of the Empire State Building hanging over his shoulder. The position was strategic, deemed by Steven to be the safest place in the room. Jamie tried to pick out the guards from the crowd of tourists but was at a loss. He looked along the length of the green-and-black marble bar as the bartender shook a martini and poured it into a frosted glass. A waitress brought him a small tray of complimentary snacks, and he eyed the smoked almonds before thinking better of it. He ordered a Diet Coke with a slice of lemon. When it arrived, he let it sit on the table untouched.

Anything could be poisoned.

Sanches arrived fifteen minutes late. In his early forties, he was about five feet ten inches and had a paunch. He was wearing a tan sport jacket, dark slacks, and a white shirt with no tie. His brown hair was unkempt. His skin was milky, his eyes nervous and intense. As soon as he spoke, it was evident that he was no Alejandro Sanches.

"Please excuse the alias, Mr. Firestone," he said in Russian, "but I have to be careful."

"I understand," Jamie answered, also in Russian, wondering if all the other people in the bar were security personnel for Sanches.

"My real name is Alexander Perepilichnyy."

Jamie motioned for the waitress as Perepilichnyy dropped into a chair. He ordered green tea as Jamie tried to size him up. Perepilichnyy did the same to Jamie.

The tea was served.

Perepilichnyy said, "Thank you for agreeing to see me."

"Of course. We're very interested in what you have to say."

Perepilichnyy lifted the teacup and took a careful sip. He put the cup down. Both men stared at each other in awkward silence. Then Perepilichnyy said, "I got in touch with you because I saw the videos about Kuznetsov and Karpov. Magnitsky's death was shocking.

Every Russian accepts corruption, but torturing an innocent man to death is crossing the line."

Bullshit, thought Jamie. He knew that these days most Russians didn't operate on high-minded principles like these. Everything in Russia was about money. Making it, keeping it, and making sure no one took it. Jamie had no idea what Perepilichnyy's real agenda was, but he was confident that the man wasn't sitting here because he cared about Sergei.

"The information in your email is good but incomplete," Jamie said. "Do you have any more documents?"

Perepilichnyy said, "Yes, but not with me."

Jamie leaned back in his chair, the ice in his Diet Coke shifting as it melted. "Would you mind if one of my colleagues joined us? I'd like him to go over the documents you provided. When we're sure we understand them, we'll tell you what else we need."

Perepilichnyy agreed. Jamie pulled his phone from a pocket and texted Vadim, who was waiting on New Bond Street right around the corner. Two minutes later, Vadim pushed through the entrance, made his way to the table, and introduced himself.

As Vadim sat, Jamie pulled out Perepilichnyy's documents. Vadim leafed through them and asked, "Do you mind walking me through these?"

"Sure. This is a Credit Suisse bank statement for an account owned by Vladlen Stepanov, husband of Olga Stepanova." Perepilichnyy indicated a line midway down the page. "Here's a transfer for one point five million euros on May twenty-sixth. Here's one for one point seven on June sixth. And here's another for one point three million on June seventeenth." He ran his finger over several other transactions. All told, in May and June of 2008, €7.1 million had been transferred into this account.

Jamie squinted at the documents. "Where did you get these?"

Perepilichnyy shifted uncomfortably. "Let's just say I know some people."

Jamie and Vadim didn't like this, but they didn't want to spook Perepilichnyy so they didn't press him.

Vadim flipped through the papers. "This could be very useful, but I don't see Vladlen Stepanov's name in any of the bank statements. How are they connected to him?"

"That's simple. The account belongs to a Cypriot company owned by Vladlen." Perepilichnyy pointed to an ownership document with Vladlen's name on it, but not his signature.

Vadim lowered his glasses. He'd been investigating corporate fraud for over thirteen years, and his standard practice was to assume everything was a lie until he saw evidence to prove otherwise. "Thank you. But without proof that Stepanov actually owns this company, there's not much we can do with this. We need copies of these ownership papers with his signature."

"I understand," Perepilichnyy said. "This was just meant to be a first meeting. I can come back with what you're asking for if you'd like to meet again."

"Yes, that'd be great," Jamie said. With that they finished the meeting and shook hands, and Perepilichnyy got up and left.

When Vadim returned to the office to report what had happened, I was suspicious and said, "It sounds like a scam."

"Maybe. But if what he's saying is true, this would be the first time we could show exactly how some of these people got money from the tax-rebate fraud."

"Fair enough. Let's see if Perepilichnyy can produce what he promised."

A week later, they agreed to meet again. This time they would be joined by Vladimir Pastukhov, who, because of his near blindness, had an amazing sixth sense for people.

The following Tuesday, Vadim and Vladimir met Perepilichnyy back at the Polo Bar. True to his word, Perepilichnyy produced a copy of a signed document showing that Vladlen Stepanov owned the Cypriot company with the Credit Suisse bank statements.

When Vadim and Vladimir came back to the office and showed me the document, I was not impressed. It looked like a simple piece of paper with some illegible signatures on it. Anyone could have made it or forged it.

"What is this? I can barely read it."

"This is from Stepanov's auditor," Vadim said.

It seemed to me that they were too ready to believe Perepilichnyy. "This could be anybody's signature. Do you really think we should trust this guy?"

"I do," Vadim said. "I think he's for real."

"What do you think, Vladimir?"

"I believe him too. He seems honest."

They continued to meet over the following weeks, and we learned some interesting things. In addition to the Swiss accounts, Perepilichnyy told us how the Stepanovs had purchased a six-bedroom villa and two luxury condominiums in Dubai on the Palm Jumeirah, a massive man-made archipelago shaped like a palm tree. The market value of these properties was around $7 million. In Russia, the Stepanovs built a mansion in the most fashionable suburb of Moscow that was valued at $20 million. In total, they'd amassed bank accounts and properties worth nearly $40 million.

To help illustrate just how lavish and ridiculous these expenditures were, Vadim got hold of the Stepanovs' tax filings, which showed that since 2006 their average annual income was only $38,281.

This information was so good that I was sure it would go viral if we produced another YouTube video. Adding Olga Stepanova to our collection of "Russian Untouchables" would shake the Russian elite right to the core.

There was one problem, though.

Perepilichnyy's story wasn't just good. It was *too* good.

It was entirely plausible that Perepilichnyy was working for the FSB, and that this was a well-planned operation to destroy my credibility. It was right out of their playbook: create a character with a believable story; have this person pass valuable information to his target; wait for the target to disclose this information publicly; then show how the information is false.

If this scenario played out, it would entirely compromise all the work we had done over the last three years with journalists and governments throughout the world. It wouldn't take long for policy makers to ask, "Why are we backing this liar at the expense of our important relationship with Russia?"

If we were going to make a video about the Stepanovs, I had to be certain that what Perepilichnyy said was true—and I also needed to know how he'd gotten his information.

For a long time he was cagey on this point, but finally, he let down his guard. He told us the reason he had so many of these financial documents was that he'd been a private banker for a number of wealthy Russians, including the Stepanovs.

This vocation worked well for Perepilichnyy until 2008, when the markets crashed and he lost the Stepanovs a lot of money. According to Perepilichnyy, instead of accepting these losses, the Stepanovs accused him of stealing the money and demanded he repay them. Since Perepilichnyy had no intention of covering their market losses, Olga Stepanova used her position as head of the tax office to get a criminal tax-evasion case opened against Perepilichnyy.

Perepilichnyy promptly fled Russia to avoid arrest. He moved his family to a rented house in Surrey, a fashionable London suburb, where he lay low. He first watched the Kuznetsov and Karpov videos there and came up with an idea. If he could get us to make a Russian Untouchables video about Olga Stepanova and her husband, then it could possibly compromise them to such an extent that it would make his problems go away.

When Vladimir told me this, it made sense, and I was finally ready to go ahead and use his information to make a video.

But just as we started to get comfortable with Perepilichnyy, we received a new message from our source Aslan: "Department K furious about Kuznetsov and Karpov videos. Large new operation being planned against Hermitage and Browder."

We asked for clarification, but Aslan didn't have any more details. My fears that Perepilichnyy was part of an FSB plot came roaring back. Maybe everything *was* going according to plan. It didn't matter how compelling his information was. Before going forward I had to be doubly sure that we weren't falling headfirst into an FSB trap.

36

The Tax Princess

One of our top priorities starting in the fall of 2010 was to be certain that Perepilichnyy wasn't scamming us.

We began by verifying the property outside Moscow and quickly found that the sixty-four-thousand-square-foot lot that their suburban mansion was built on belonged to Vladlen Stepanov's eighty-five-year-old pensioner mother. She had an income of $3,500 per year, but was somehow sitting on this plot of land with a market value of $12 million, and that was before anything had even been built on it.

But the Stepanovs *had* built something on it. They'd hired one of Moscow's leading architects to design two hard-angled, modernist buildings totaling twelve thousand square feet. These were made of German granite, structural glass, and polished metal. When I saw the pictures of the houses, I thought they looked more like they belonged to a top hedge fund manager than a midlevel Russian tax collector and her husband.

Next, we turned to Dubai. Using an online property database, we confirmed that the villa there, which was bought for $767,123, was indeed registered to Vladlen Stepanov. Unfortunately, the other two condominiums, which together were worth more than $6 million, were still under construction and hadn't been registered. We knew about them only because of some wire transfers from the Stepanovs' Swiss accounts.

The Swiss accounts were the strings that tied everything together. Not only had they been used for these lavish purchases, but they also held more than $10 million in cash that, according to Perepilichnyy, was wired in after the tax-rebate fraud occurred. If we could confirm that these accounts were real, then we could make a Russian Untouchables video about Olga Stepanova and her husband that would light up the Moscow sky.

Everything now hinged on the authenticity of the Swiss accounts.

In an ideal world I could just have gone to Credit Suisse and asked if the statements were genuine, but Swiss bankers are so secretive that they would have told me nothing.

I could also have approached acquaintances at Credit Suisse, but they wouldn't have helped. Divulging confidential client information was a fireable offense, and I didn't know anybody well enough that he or she would take that risk for me.

Our only remaining option was to file a complaint with the Swiss authorities and see where that led. My London lawyer drafted the complaint, and when it was ready to go, I asked how long he thought it would take to hear back.

"I don't know," he said. "Anywhere from three months to a year."

"*Three months to a year?* That's way too long. Is there some way to make them go faster?"

"No. In my experience the Swiss authorities can take a long time. They'll get to it when they get to it."

January and February passed with no news, and March did too. By mid-March 2011, the Stepanova video was finished and was better than anything we'd done before. I wanted to move ahead, but the Swiss authorities were holding me back.

Then, in late March, we learned of an entirely new twist to the Russian cover-up. The Russian authorities convicted an ex-felon, a man named Vyacheslav Khlebnikov, for his role in the tax-rebate fraud. They could have put a hundred ex-cons in jail as fall guys for the crime and it wouldn't have mattered to me, but what did matter was what was written in the official sentencing documents. The documents stated that the tax officials were completely innocent and had been "tricked" and "misled" into granting the single largest tax refund in Russian history in one day on Christmas Eve 2007.

Tax officials such as Olga Stepanova.

I decided, *Enough is enough. They can't continue lying like this. Perepilichnyy's information is good. I know it, the Swiss know it, and soon the world will know it too.*

The video went live on April 20, 2011. The reaction was immediate and huge—bigger than anything we'd done before. By the end of the first day, it had over 200,000 views. By the end of the week it had nearly 360,000. And by the end of the month, more than 500,000 people had watched it. Olga Stepanova became known around the world as the Tax Princess, and reporters from every corner of Russia harangued her and her husband. NTV, one of the state-controlled television stations, even staked out Vladlen Stepanov's eighty-five-year-old mother, who lived in a one-room hovel in a Soviet apartment complex. When asked about the lavish property she nominally owned, she answered that she agreed to put it in her name in exchange for a cleaning lady to help her tidy up her apartment once a week. Her millionaire son wouldn't even take care of his elderly mother properly.

Best of all, three days after we launched the video, the Swiss attorney general announced that he'd frozen the Stepanovs' accounts at Credit Suisse. Unbeknownst to us, the Swiss authorities had opened a full criminal money-laundering case soon after they received our complaint.

I felt completely vindicated. Perepilichnyy's information had been genuine and the money had been frozen. We'd hit the criminals in the place they cared about most—their bank accounts.

37

Sausage Making

Our YouTube videos caught these corrupt Russian officials completely off guard, but the real coup de grâce that would destroy the equilibrium of the Russian authorities would be passing sanctions legislation in the United States.

In the fall of 2010, just as we were establishing contact with Perepilichnyy, Kyle Parker finished drafting the Magnitsky Act. On September 29, Senators Ben Cardin, John McCain, Roger Wicker, and Joe Lieberman introduced the bill in the Senate. The language was simple and direct—anyone involved in the false arrest, torture, or death of Sergei Magnitsky, or the crimes he uncovered, would be publicly named, banned from entering the United States, and have their US assets frozen.

When the bill's introduction was made public, the Russian authorities were furious and had to devise some way to counter what was happening in Washington.

They found their first opportunity on November 10, less than a week before the first anniversary of Sergei's death. That date was National Police Day in Russia, and the Interior Ministry held an annual awards ceremony for their most outstanding officers. Of the thirty-five awards given, five went to key figures in the Magnitsky case. These included Best Investigator awards for Pavel Karpov and Oleg Silchenko, the officer who organized Sergei's torture in prison, and a Special Award of Gratitude for Irina Dudukina, the Interior Ministry spokeswoman who'd loyally spouted all the lies about Sergei just after he'd died.

Then, to really push their point, five days later the Interior Ministry held a press conference to "reveal new details about the Magnitsky case." Dudukina presided. Her bleached hair was a little longer and more teased out than it had been the year before, but she was still plump and tired-looking and still had a lower jaw that appeared to belong to a ventriloquist's dummy. She unfolded a makeshift poster of twenty sheets of taped-together A4 paper and stuck it to a dry-erase board. Despite its being a jumbled mash of numbers and words, most of them too small even to be legible, this poster "proved" that Sergei had committed the fraud and received the $230 million tax rebate. When journalists started asking the most basic questions about her display, she had no credible responses and it was clear to everyone present that it was a fabrication.

While these tactics were aggressive and crude, they confirmed that our legislation had touched a nerve. I wasn't the only one who recognized this. Many other victims of human rights abuses in Russia saw the same thing. After the bill was introduced they came to Washington or wrote letters to the Magnitsky Act's cosponsors with the same basic message: "You have found the Achilles' heel of the Putin regime." Then, one by one, they would ask, "Can you add the people who killed my brother to the Magnitsky Act?" "Can you add the people who tortured my mother?" "How about the people who kidnapped my husband?" And on and on.

The senators quickly realized that they'd stumbled onto something much bigger than one horrific case. They had inadvertently discovered a new method for fighting human rights abuses in authoritarian regimes in the twenty-first century: targeted visa sanctions and asset freezes.

After a dozen or so of these visits and letters, Senator Cardin and his cosponsors conferred and decided to expand the law, adding sixty-five words to the Magnitsky Act. Those new words said that in addition to sanctioning Sergei's tormentors, the Magnitsky Act would sanction all other gross human rights abusers in Russia. With those extra sixty-five words, my personal fight for justice had become *everyone's* fight.

The revised bill was officially introduced on May 19, 2011, less than a month after we posted the Olga Stepanova YouTube video. Following its introduction, a small army of Russian activists descended on Capitol Hill, pushing for the bill's passage. They pressed every senator who would talk to them to sign on. There was Garry Kasparov, the famous chess grand master and human rights activist; there was Alexei Navalny, the most popular Russian opposition leader; and there was Evgenia Chirikova, a well-known Russian environmental activist. I didn't have to recruit any of these people. They just showed up by themselves.

This uncoordinated initiative worked beautifully. The number of Senate cosponsors grew quickly, with three or four new senators signing on every month. It was an easy sell. There wasn't a pro-Russian-torture-and-murder lobby in Washington to oppose it. No senator, whether the most liberal Democrat or the most conservative Republican, would lose a single vote for banning Russian torturers and murderers from coming to America.

The Magnitsky Act was gathering so much momentum that it appeared it might be unstoppable. From the day that Kyle Scott at the State Department stonewalled me, I knew that the administration was dead set against this, but now they were in a tough spot. If they openly opposed the law, it would look as if they were siding with the Russians. However, if they publicly supported it, it would threaten Obama's "reset" with Russia.

They needed to come up with some other solution.

On July 20, 2011, the State Department showed its cards. They sent a memo to the Senate entitled "Administration Comments on S.1039 Sergei Magnitsky Rule of Law." Though not meant to be made public, within a day it was leaked.

I got a copy and nervously skimmed the document. It was the height of Washington hypocrisy. The State Department's main argument was that the sanctions proposed by the Magnitsky Act already existed under executive powers, so why bother passing a new law?

In an effort to be clever, it threw the senators a bone. It said that the other main reason the Senate shouldn't support the law was that the people who killed Magnitsky had already been banned from entering the United States. Therefore, the law was unnecessary.

I wasn't sure whether this was a positive development. I called Kyle Parker to see what he thought.

"We don't understand it either, Bill. Cardin had me call the Department to see who was on the visa sanctions list, and they wouldn't tell me."

"Did they at least tell you how many people were on it?"

"Nope. They wouldn't tell me that either."

"What about asset freezes?"

"They were pretty clear on that one. They don't support asset freezes."

"So what's Cardin's reaction?"

"It's pretty straightforward. We're not going along with this and he'll continue to push for the law."

On August 8, 2011, Cardin publicly rejected the administration's position and reconfirmed his commitment to passing the Magnitsky Act in a strongly worded *Washington Post* op-ed entitled "Accountability for Sergei Magnitsky's Killers." This was an important signal of his resolve, since Obama and Cardin were in the same party. He was publicly throwing down the gauntlet to the president.

When the administration read Cardin's op-ed, it seemed to become even more agitated. The White House was so afraid of offending the Russians and derailing the "reset" that it contacted Cardin and the other cosponsors and suggested that the bill should apply globally, not just to Russia.

The senators loved that idea. What started out as a bill about Sergei had morphed into a historic piece of global human rights legislation.

After this, Cardin concentrated on bringing the bill before a full vote in the Senate. To do that, one last hurdle had to be cleared: the Senate Foreign Relations Committee. All bills have to be passed by a Senate committee before they can come to a vote in the full Senate, and since the Magnitsky Act involved visa bans, it had to go through the Foreign Relations Committee. Since the bill had so much support generally, and there was no Senate opposition, this seemed like a simple formality.

Cardin requested that the committee chair, Senator John Kerry, add it to the agenda for the committee's next business meeting on September 9. For some reason, Kerry refused. Cardin made the same request for the October 12 meeting, but once again Kerry didn't bring it to the table. It wasn't clear what Kerry's problem was, but there seemed to be one.

Meanwhile, we received some macabre information from Moscow. Sergei's mother, Natalia, had finally been granted access to information from Sergei's autopsy report. Among the documents she was allowed to copy were six color photos taken of Sergei's body shortly after he died. While they were not a surprise, they showed deep bruising along his legs and hands, as well as deep cuts in his wrists—the same injuries that Natalia had seen when she went to view her son's body in the morgue. She was also able to copy a protocol, signed by the head of Matrosskaya Tishina, authorizing the use of rubber batons on Sergei by riot guards on the night of November 16.

What we knew—that Sergei had died violently at the hands of the state—was now undeniable and backed up by documentary evidence.

After seeing these photos and documents, Natalia filed a new complaint requesting that the Russian authorities open a murder investigation. Like everything else we tried to do in Russia, it was denied.

When I spoke with her on the phone, the only consolation I could offer her was that we were getting close to some form of justice in the United States. I promised that I was doing everything I could, and although prohibiting travel and freezing accounts in America were hardly commensurate punishments for what these people had done to Sergei, it was better than total impunity, which is what we had so far.

On November 29, 2011, the Senate Foreign Relations Committee convened its next business meeting. When the agenda went up on the committee's website that day, I clicked on the link hoping to see Sergei's name. I scrolled down. The first item was "A resolution calling for the protection of the Mekong River Basin."

I scrolled a little further and saw its next order of business: "A resolution expressing the sense of the Senate regarding Tunisia's peaceful Jasmine Revolution."

I scrolled to the bottom. There was no Magnitsky.

I called Kyle immediately. "What the hell's going on? I don't see the bill."

"I don't know, we're trying to figure that out ourselves."

I began to suspect that some ugly horse-trading was going on behind the scenes. Kerry seemed to be stonewalling.

Since this problem appeared to be with Kerry specifically, I figured that if I could get a meeting with him, then the power of Sergei's story might sway him the way it had McCain and McGovern.

I called Juleanna. She'd been batting a thousand when it came to getting meetings for me with senators—but when she tried Kerry, she struck out. The best she could do was get me an audience with his adviser on Russian issues, a Senate staffer named Jason Bruder.

I flew to Washington and the day after I arrived, Juleanna and I went to the Dirksen Senate Office Building to meet Bruder outside the Foreign Relations Committee room. Bruder, a thirtysomething man of average height with a close-cropped goatee, led us into the room, a cavernous chamber with a U-shaped arrangement of tables and desks. Finding no good place for us to sit comfortably, we each dragged a chair from the audience area and arranged them in a little circle in the middle of the floor.

After thanking Bruder for taking the time to meet, I began to tell Sergei's story. Three sentences in, Bruder cut me off. "Yes, yes. I know everything about this case. I'm very upset by what happened. He and his family deserve justice."

"That's why we're here."

"Listen, I've given this a lot of thought. The senator and I would really like to help with the Magnitsky case."

"That's great. Will Senator Kerry support the bill and push it through committee?"

Bruder leaned back, his chair creaking. "Well, I really don't think the Magnitsky Act is the right approach to dealing with these problems, Mr. Browder."

Here we go again, I thought, thinking back to Kyle Scott and all the other nervous careerists in the US government. "What do you mean it's not the 'right approach'?"

He then repeated the same tired State Department script nearly word for word. I tried to argue with him, but he wouldn't listen.

Finally Bruder said, "Listen, Bill, this case *is* important to us. I'd like to get Senator Kerry to bring up Magnitsky directly with the Russian ambassador the next time they meet."

Bring it up with the Russian ambassador? Was he fucking kidding? Sergei's name had been on the front page of every major newspaper in the world! The Russian president and his senior ministers had spent countless hours trying to minimize the fallout from the Magnitsky case, and Bruder thought that a quiet conversation with the ambassador might help?

I left the meeting cursing under my breath.

It turned out that Kerry's opposition to the Magnitsky Act had nothing to do with whether he thought it was good or bad policy. The rumor in Washington was that John Kerry was blocking the bill for one simple reason: he wanted to be secretary of state after Hillary Clinton resigned. According to the story making the rounds, one of the conditions for his getting the job was to make sure that the Magnitsky Act never saw the light of day at the Senate Foreign Relations Committee.

For the next few months nothing happened with the Magnitsky Act. But then, in the spring of 2012, we were handed an unexpected gift. After nearly twenty years of negotiating, in August of that year Russia was finally going to be admitted to the World Trade Organization (WTO). The moment Russia became a WTO member, every other member could trade with Russia on the same terms, without tariffs or other costs. Only one country would be excluded: the United States, thanks to something called the Jackson-Vanik amendment.

This thirty-seven-year-old piece of legislation, put in place in the mid-1970s, imposed trade sanctions on the Soviet Union to punish it for not allowing Soviet Jews to emigrate. At first, the Soviets dug in their heels, but after several years they realized that the costs of the sanctions were simply too great, and eventually 1.5 million Jews were allowed to leave the country.

Thirty-seven years later the Soviet Union no longer existed, and Russian Jews could freely emigrate, but Jackson-Vanik was still on the books. If it remained, then it would effectively prevent American businesses such as Boeing, Caterpillar, Ford, and American beef exporters from enjoying the same trade benefits with Russia as every other WTO member in the world.

As far as the US business community was concerned, Jackson-Vanik had to go, and the Obama administration fully supported this idea. If the president could have repealed Jackson-Vanik by himself, he would have. But in order to get the law off the books, he needed an act of Congress.

I was in Washington working with Juleanna on our campaign during the week that the administration began its campaign to repeal Jackson-Vanik. After a morning of meetings, Juleanna and I were breaking for lunch at the snack bar in a basement hallway of the Hart Office Building. As I sat at a flimsy aluminum table and ate my salad, Juleanna tapped me on the arm and pointed discreetly down the hall. There, walking with a small group of aides, was Senator Joe Lieberman, one of the most high-profile cosponsors of the Magnitsky Act.

She whispered, "Bill, there's Lieberman. I think you should talk to him about this whole Jackson-Vanik situation."

"What, now? He's just walking down the hall. How am I going to have a proper conversation with him?"

While I've learned to be assertive when necessary, to this day I'm still uncomfortable with foisting myself on unsuspecting strangers, especially those who are constantly bombarded by the public.

But Juleanna ignored my obvious discomfort, stood, and practically pulled me out of my seat. "Come on, Bill. Let's go talk to him." Side by side, we crossed the hallway and headed toward Senator Lieberman.

As soon as we got within earshot of Lieberman, Juleanna held out her hand and said, "Sorry to interrupt you, Senator, but I was wondering if I could introduce you to Bill Browder, the man behind the Magnitsky Act."

Lieberman and his aides stopped. Senators have hundreds of things on their minds, and it sometimes takes them a few seconds to figure out who belongs to what. When the phrase *Magnitsky Act* clicked for him, his face brightened. "Ah, Mr. Browder." He turned to me. "It's a pleasure to meet you. Thank you for the important work you've been doing."

I was flattered that he had any idea who I was. "I wouldn't have been able to achieve anything without your support," I said truthfully. "There's a problem, though. I'm sure you know that the administration is pushing for the repeal of Jackson-Vanik."

"Yes, we're hearing that."

"I think it's unconscionable that while the administration is repealing one of the most important pieces of human rights legislation ever, they're blocking Magnitsky."

He took a moment, then said sincerely, "You're absolutely right. We need to do something about this."

"What can be done?"

"I'll tell you what. We'll tell the administration that we'll block Jackson-Vanik repeal unless they stop blocking Magnitsky. I'm sure John, Ben, and Roger[1] would join me on this."

"That would be powerful. Thank you."

"No, Bill. Thank you for everything you've done." Lieberman

---

1   That is, Senators McCain, Cardin, and Wicker.

then turned to his aides, told one of them to remind him to get on this letter, and walked off, leaving Juleanna and me standing there, the bustle of the hallway buzzing all around us.

After a few seconds I turned to her. "Did that really just happen?"

"It sure did. That's how things get done in Washington, Bill. Congratulations."

True to his word, a few days later, Lieberman and the other original cosponsors of the Magnitsky Act sent a letter to Montana senator Max Baucus, the chairman of the Senate Finance Committee. Just as Foreign Relations had to clear the way for passage of the Magnitsky Act, the Finance Committee had to okay the repeal of Jackson-Vanik. The letter said, "In the absence of the passage of the Magnitsky legislation, we will strongly oppose the lifting of Jackson-Vanik." Given the way the Senate operates, this letter was as good as a veto.

Senator Baucus was keen to get Jackson-Vanik repealed. Many of his constituents in Montana were cattle farmers and beef exporters. They wanted to sell their steaks and hamburgers to Russia—the world's sixth-largest importer of US beef—without fear of being at a disadvantage.

This meant that the only way to repeal Jackson-Vanik was also to pass Magnitsky, and after some deliberation the Senate decided to combine the two bills into one. First the bill would be brought up at the Senate Foreign Relations Committee to pass Magnitsky, then it would go before the Finance Committee to repeal Jackson-Vanik, and then, at long last, it would go before the full Senate for a vote.

A famous expression goes, "The less people know about how sausages and laws are made, the better they sleep at night." Our human rights campaign made strange bedfellows with Montana beef farmers, Russian human rights activists, and Boeing airplane salesmen, but by working together it appeared as if we had the strength to overpower any remaining resistance to getting the law passed.

With the prospect of Jackson-Vanik being blocked, Kerry took his foot off the brakes. He called for a meeting of the Senate Foreign Relations Committee on June 26, 2012, with the sole purpose of approving the Magnitsky Act. I flew to Washington specifically to be there. The meeting was open to the public and scheduled to start at 2:15 p.m., and I arrived at the Capitol forty-five minutes early to get a good seat. But as I approached security, I was surprised to see more than three hundred people lined up, waiting to get in. Journalists, activists, student volunteers, staffers, Russian embassy officials—you name it, they were all there.

I got in the back of the line and a few minutes later heard someone shouting my name. I recognized a senior from Columbia University who'd volunteered on our campaign. He had one of his friends hold his spot while he came back to me and said, "Mr. Browder, please come up to the front with me."

He pulled me aside and we started walking past everybody, but then one of the Capitol policemen stopped us and said, "Hey, fella, what do you think you're doing?"

I felt slightly embarrassed and didn't say anything, but the student said enthusiastically, "Officer, this is the man who's responsible for the Magnitsky Act. He needs to be at the front of the line."

"I don't care what he's done." The officer pointed at me. "Back of the line."

"But—"

"Back of the line!"

I told the student it was okay and walked to my old spot, noticing along the way a Russian embassy official I knew by sight. Judging by the smirk on his face, he enjoyed watching me get slapped down.

When I finally got to the hallway outside the committee room, I found a giant scrum of people. The room could hold only around sixty, and I realized if I didn't get in at the beginning, then I wasn't going to get in at all. The door was opened at 2:15 sharp by a short, stocky woman with brown hair and a booming, authoritative voice. She called for members of the press. A full third of the people surged forward, and I tried to get swept up with them. But this formidable woman, who took her job very seriously, stopped me when it was my turn and said, "Where're your credentials?"

"Uh . . . I don't have any. But I've been deeply involved in the Magnitsky Act and it's important that I be in there."

She shook her head as if to say, *Nice try, pal*, and pointed back at the crowd.

What could I do? For the second time that day I slunk away feeling like the total outsider that I was. I stepped behind a velvet rope as the senators and their aides suddenly appeared. The crowd parted for them and cameras flashed from every corner. One of the last senators to arrive was Ben Cardin, who didn't notice me.

But his senior aide, Fred Turner, did.

As they approached the door, I saw Fred stop to say something to the brown-haired gatekeeper. He pointed in my direction, and the woman came over and said, "Mr. Browder, I'm very sorry. We have a space for you. Please follow me."

She led me into the packed chamber, the most ornate of all the Senate committee rooms, and showed me to the last empty chair.

Senator Kerry entered through a side door and called the meeting to order. His body language made it clear that this was the last place he wanted to be. He began the meeting with a strange speech about how America is not a perfect country, and that the people in that room should be "very mindful of the need for the United States not to always be pointing fingers and lecturing and to be somewhat introspective as we think about these things."

He gave the floor to some of the other senators, all of whom made supportive comments about the bill, and when they were finished, Kerry addressed Cardin directly: "I don't view this as a completely finished product, and I don't want it judged as such." Kerry then carried on in his condescending Boston Brahmin voice with a lot of barely intelligible thoughts about how the Magnitsky Act could potentially compromise classified information, and that while it was "very legitimate to name and shame," he was "worried about the unintended consequences of requiring that kind of detailed reporting that implicates a broader range of intelligence equities."

Kerry's fuzzy diplospeak made it clear that he was there only because he had to be, and that he couldn't reconcile himself with what had to be done. Everything he said seemed to be a badly disguised attempt to postpone a vote on the bill so that it lapsed into the next Congress. If that happened, then this whole sausage-making exercise would have to restart from square one. Everything rode on this moment. Would Cardin, a first-term senator, stand up to Kerry, a twenty-seven-year veteran of the Senate and a Democratic powerhouse?

When Kerry was done droning on, all eyes turned to Cardin, who appeared to be nervous as he braced himself for what he was about to say.

But Cardin didn't budge. He refused to revisit the bill later and called for an immediate committee vote. After five minutes of back-and-forth, Kerry had had enough and even cut Cardin off midsentence to ask, "Any further debate? Any further comment, discussion?"

The room was silent.

Kerry called for a vote. Not a single voice stood with the nays.

Kerry announced a unanimous decision and called the meeting to a close. It took all of fifteen minutes. Everyone filed out.

I was walking on air. I had spent every day of my life since November 16, 2009, working in the service of Sergei's memory. On this day in June 2012, it felt as if there wasn't a person in Washington—the most important city in the most powerful country in the world—who didn't know the name Sergei Magnitsky.

38

The Malkin Delegation

All the planets seemed to be lining up for a smooth passage of the Magnitsky Act. The business community was on board, the human rights community was on board, the Obama administration was on board, Republicans, Democrats, everyone. I had a hard time seeing how anything could stand in the way.

But then, on July 9, 2012, less than two weeks before the joint bill was to come before the Senate Finance Committee, the Russian government made a last-ditch effort to derail the bill. It was sending a high-level delegation to Washington to present a "parliamentary investigation into the Magnitsky case." It indicated that it wanted to establish a joint commission between the US Congress and the Russian Parliament to review the case, but like Kerry before them, its real objective was to slow down the bill so it slipped into the next Congress and died a slow death.

This delegation consisted of four members of the Federation Council, Russia's upper chamber of Parliament, and was led by a parliamentarian named Vitaly Malkin, a Russian billionaire who was number 1,062 on the *Forbes* list.

When I looked up Malkin, I discovered that in 2009 he had been named as a "member of a group engaging in trans-national crime" by the Canadian government and that despite his fierce denials, he was banned from entering Canada. I didn't understand how someone with this kind of reputation could be leading a delegation to Washington, but then I found a picture of him on the steps of the Capitol shaking hands in connection to a $1 million gift to the US Library of

Congress. I guess $1 million buys a certain amount of tolerance in Washington.

In spite of his background, I could imagine how earnest members of Congress would want to learn whatever "new details" this parliamentarian possessed about the Magnitsky case. I knew that Malkin's presentation would include forgeries and other fabrications from the FSB, but how would a member of Congress be able to understand that in a thirty-minute briefing?

I spent most of the day on July 9 calling different congressional offices, trying to find out who'd agreed to meet the delegation. Kyle told me that Cardin had refused, but that McCain, Wicker, and Mc-Govern had all agreed. Kyle also heard that the delegation would be given an audience at the president's National Security Council and at the State Department. When these meetings were finished, the Malkin delegation was going to hold a press conference on July 11 at the Russian embassy to announce "new details of the case."

Most of Malkin's meetings took place on July 10, and I frantically called everyone I knew in Washington to try to get some feedback on how they went, but I didn't have any luck. Even Kyle was unavailable that day.

I would have repeated this exercise on the eleventh, but unfortunately I was flying with my family for a trip to San Diego. This couldn't have come at a worse time, but I wasn't going to cancel it. As I'd promised Elena when this whole mess started, we weren't going to let the Russians ruin our lives.

We boarded the flight at noon, and even though I was distracted, I helped Elena with our children in whatever way I could. We settled in, and Jessica and I played a game of make-believe with a pair of stuffed giraffes as the plane taxied and took off. As we climbed higher, she suddenly blurted, "Daddy, who is Magnitsky?"

I'd never explicitly spoken with Jessica about Sergei, but she'd heard his name so many times that it was part of her daily vocabulary. I thought carefully before I answered, "Sergei Magnitsky was a friend."

"Did something happen to him?"

"Yes. Some very bad people put him in jail and hurt him and asked him to tell a lie."

"Did he?"

"No, he didn't. And because of that they made his life hard and kept him from seeing his family."

"Why did they want him to lie?" she asked, making her giraffe dance on the armrest between us.

"Because they stole lots of money and wanted to keep it."

She let the giraffe fall in her lap. After a few moments she asked, "What happened to Magnitsky?"

"Well, sweetie . . . he died."

"Because he wouldn't lie?"

"Exactly. He died because he wouldn't lie."

"Oh." She then picked up her giraffe and turned it around, saying something inaudible to it in her private child's language. I sat there for a few seconds with my thoughts before she said, "I hope that won't happen to you."

I blinked, fighting back a tear. "It won't, sweetie. I promise."

"Okay." The seat-belt light went off and Jessica got up to talk to Elena about something, but our conversation hit me hard. It saddened me, but more than anything else, it made me angry. I needed to know what was going on in Washington with the Malkin delegation as soon as possible.

As soon as we were on the ground eleven hours later, I switched on my phone and called Kyle, bracing for the worst. He picked up on the first ring with the same casual voice I'd grown accustomed to. "Hey, Bill. What's up?"

"I've been on a plane all day. What's happening with the Russians? Do we still have a law?"

"Absolutely. Their intervention, if that's what you can call it, was a complete clusterfuck," he said with a chuckle. "You should have seen it."

He told me that the first point Malkin made to the senators was that

Sergei was a drunk and out of shape, and that his death was somehow due to his "alcoholism." Not only was this offensive, but the senators knew it to be untrue. They were familiar with the independent reports that determined that Sergei died because he was tortured and beaten, and because he hadn't received proper medical attention.

Malkin's second point came after he plonked a pile of redacted documents in Russian in front of the senators declaring that these papers constituted "absolute proof" that Sergei and I were crooks and had stolen the $230 million. This ploy didn't move them either. Many of the senators had seen the Russian Untouchables videos and knew all about the unexplained wealth of Kuznetsov, Karpov, and Stepanova, not to mention the Swiss money-laundering case and the frozen millions belonging to Stepanova's husband. The senators reminded Malkin of these inconvenient facts, and he responded that the Russian authorities had looked into all of these allegations and found nothing wrong.

Kyle then told me that the press conference had been an even bigger disaster. When a *Chicago Tribune* reporter asked for a comment about the documents that proved Sergei had been beaten by riot guards, Malkin replied dismissively, "Yeah, maybe he was kicked one time, maybe two, but this is not the reason for his death."

When news of Malkin's Washington fiasco reached Moscow, the chairman of Russia's Foreign Affairs Committee of the Federation Council completely disowned Malkin and his delegation, saying that there had been "no parliamentary investigation. These were his personal views and were not approved by anybody."

For all the noise and drama that had built up around this last desperate attempt by the Russians, it achieved the exact opposite of its goal. Instead of driving people away from the Magnitsky Act, it drove them even closer. Our support was now rock solid, and there was no way that Magnitsky wouldn't pass in the Finance Committee.

Without incident, on July 18 the Magnitsky Act did just that. The next step was a full vote in both chambers of the US Congress, which would happen after the summer recess.

Things quieted down during the recess, and I enjoyed a properly relaxing vacation with my kids for the first time in years. I couldn't remember the last time I'd been able to just let go and unwind. In the middle of our trip, my kids begged me to take them camping. We borrowed a tent and some sleeping bags, and I drove the family to Palomar Mountain State Park, an hour and half drive north of San Diego, where we got a campsite for the night. We brought wood from the ranger station and made a campfire and explored the forest. David cooked and we ate a dinner of spaghetti, tomato sauce, and hot dogs off plastic plates. As night fell, owls hooted and other birds cooed in the treetops, and the smell of burning wood filled the air. It was one of the best evenings I'd had in a long time.

When I returned to London, I was recharged and ready for the final push.

But the Russians were too. On my very first day back, a large, registered-mail envelope arrived. Inside was a 205-page lawsuit, *Pavel Karpov v. William Browder*, on the letterhead of a British law firm, Olswang, one of the UK's most prestigious and expensive firms. Karpov was suing me for libel in Britain's High Court. The lawsuit alleged that our YouTube videos about Karpov, Kuznetsov, and Stepanova defamed him and caused him moral suffering.

I had to laugh. "Moral suffering"? Was he kidding?

Moreover, Karpov earned less than $1,500 a month, while the law firm he hired charged around £600 *an hour*. This meant that just to have this document drawn up and delivered, Karpov would have burned through several years of his official salary.

This appeared to me to be a last-ditch attempt to silence our campaign, and it fit squarely into Putin's instructions to his government. Days after he resumed office in May 2012 after having been reelected as president in March, he issued an executive order stating that one of his top foreign policy priorities was to stop the Magnitsky Act from becoming law in America. In my mind, this explained how Karpov could miraculously afford the services of this expensive London law firm.

I'm sure that Olswang was happy to take the case. I could imagine some silver-tongued lawyer lecturing a bunch of unsophisticated Russians on what spending £1 million on this lawsuit would do for all their problems with Bill Browder and the Magnitsky Act. What Olswang might not have realized was that a Russian police officer, who didn't speak English and had been to the United Kingdom only twice for vacation, hardly had standing in the British libel court.

I hired lawyers to contest the suit, but I didn't let it distract me from my main objective of getting the Magnitsky Act passed. The summer recess ended at the beginning of September, and I called Kyle as soon as he was back in his office to find out when the bill would be voted on.

Kyle laughed. "Bill, we're nearing peak political silly season right before the presidential election. Magnitsky is too much of a win-win for the leadership to schedule a vote."

"But we have full bipartisan support. This seems to be the one thing in Washington that everyone agrees on."

"That's the point, Bill. Now that the election is in full swing, no one wants to talk about things that everyone agrees on. None of these guys can afford to make the others look good."

"What are you saying, then?"

"I'm saying that the earliest Magnitsky can come up is after November sixth."

I did some mental math. "So that means we'll only have seven weeks between the election and when Congress ends."

"Not even seven weeks. With the holidays it's much less."

While I was concerned about this delay, I could do nothing but wait. I spent September and October catching up with my staff on the Hermitage investment business, which was a shadow of its former self. To build my fund back to what it had been would have required month after month of marketing trips and investment conferences. When I put the idea of doing this against that of getting justice for Sergei, justice won in a heartbeat.

The weeks passed slowly, and finally the US presidential election took place on November 6. Obama easily defeated Mitt Romney, and the day after the election I called Kyle and asked again when Magnitsky would come up for a vote.

To my surprise, he said, "I was just going to call you—the House just announced it's going to vote a week from Friday."

"Are you serious?"

"Yes. It's finally happening!"

I looked at my calendar. "That's November sixteenth. . . ."

Kyle paused as he realized the significance of this date. November 16, 2012, would be the third anniversary of Sergei's death. "Yes," he said quietly. "It is . . . but there's one more problem. The House is insisting that Magnitsky go back to a Russia-only bill, and that's what they're going to vote on."

When Senator Cardin made it a global human rights bill, he had become so enthusiastic about its historic, precedent-setting nature that he was ready to risk the whole deal to keep it a global piece of legislation.

"Does that mean Cardin won't accept the Russia-only version in the Senate?"

"He might not."

If the Senate had a different version of a law than the House, then they would have to reconcile them, and this would take more time— the one thing we didn't have. If Cardin didn't back down, then there was a good chance that we would have no law at all.

Naturally, I wanted Cardin's global version of the bill to pass. Having Sergei's name on a piece of legislation as broad and meaningful as what Cardin had proposed would have been an ideal way to honor him. But more than that, I wanted the bill to get passed into law, and if that meant going with this Russia-only version, then I thought it was the right thing to do.

I hoped Cardin would too.

Finally, November 16 arrived. It was due to be a big day. Not only was the US House of Representatives going to vote on the Magnitsky Act, but that night, I was hosting the London premiere of a play entitled *One Hour Eighteen Minutes*, an independent, award-winning production by Russian playwright Elena Gremina that detailed the last one hour and eighteen minutes of Sergei's life.

In the late afternoon every single person in the office logged on to C-SPAN's website for the live feed from the US House of Representatives. Before the vote began, members of Congress came to the floor and gave speeches, beautifully telling and retelling Sergei's story, and calling for justice. This watershed moment was happening right before my eyes in this cavernous room steeped in American history. This was the same chamber where the amendments to abolish slavery and give women the right to vote were passed, and where landmark civil rights laws were approved. I was awed to think that everything that happened had led to this.

Finally, the voting commenced. One by one, the votes trickled in—nearly all were in favor. Whenever there was a vote against, I would hear boos in the office, but these outbursts were few and far between. The bill was going to sail through the House.

When the roll call was about halfway done, my phone rang. Without looking at the caller ID I picked it up, thinking it was Elena or some other well-wisher wanting to talk about what was happening in Washington.

"Bill, it's Marcel." I recognized the voice as that of an accountant we'd introduced to Alexander Perepilichnyy, the Russian whistle-blower who'd exposed the Swiss accounts.

I was surprised to hear from Marcel because he had nothing to with the Magnitsky Act or anything else I was working on at that moment. "Hey, Marcel. Can this wait? I'm a bit busy right now."

"Sorry to bother you, Bill, but it's important."

"Okay, what is it?"

"Bill, I'm not even sure I should be telling you this," he said cryptically.

I swiveled away from the C-SPAN feed. "Telling me what?"

"You have to promise not to share it with anyone—not even the guys in your office."

"Depends. What is it?"

"Alexander Perepilichnyy is dead."

39

Justice for Sergei

Marcel told me that Perepilichnyy had dropped dead in front of his house in Surrey during an afternoon jog, but that he had no other information.

It took several minutes for this news to sink in. Surrey was not more than twenty miles from where I sat. If this was foul play, which it appeared to be, then our enemies had brought their terror to us.

Marcel's request to keep this to myself was totally unreasonable, and I immediately pulled Vadim, Vladimir, and Ivan into my office. I told them the bad news, and they were utterly shocked—especially Vadim and Vladimir, both of whom had gotten to know Perepilichnyy well in the last year. As we spoke, Vladimir dropped into a chair and said something quietly to himself in Russian that I couldn't understand.

Just as we were talking, the Hermitage staff erupted in cheers and started high-fiving each other outside the glass walls of my office. I opened my door and asked what was going on. My secretary turned to me and said, "The Magnitsky Act just passed the House three hundred sixty-five to forty-three!"

This was huge news, but I wasn't in a state of mind to celebrate. Another person connected to this case had just died. I tried to bottle up my feelings about Perepilichnyy as best I could and joined the team to congratulate them on their hard work. I spent a few minutes talking about the vote and the next steps, but I didn't want to tell them about Perepilichnyy until I could digest the implications.

I returned to my office, put my head in my hands, and tried to make sense of what I'd just learned. Had Perepilichnyy been murdered? Were his killers still in the United Kingdom? Were they going to come after us? As much as I wanted to start making calls to people who could help me figure all these things out, I couldn't. I had to be at the New Diorama Theatre in forty-five minutes to host the play about Sergei that was taking place that night.

I went to the theater and attempted to push all my dark thoughts to the back of my mind. I made my way into the lobby, passing the brightest stars of London's human rights community—MPs, government officials, celebrities, artists, as well as close friends. We all took our seats and watched. The play was moving and powerful, and when it was over, three special guests and I carried folding seats onto the stage and began a panel discussion. The panel consisted of Tom Stoppard, the famous playwright; Vladimir Bukovsky, a former Russian political prisoner; and Bianca Jagger, Mick Jagger's ex-wife and a respected human rights activist.

Stoppard and Bukovsky shared their story about how Stoppard had written a play in the 1970s that helped free Bukovsky from a Soviet psychiatric prison. Using Sergei's story, they pointed out that after all this time almost nothing had changed in Russia.

Speaking last, I said to the audience, "Indeed, the situation in Russia is dire, but today there is one small ray of light. Just a few hours ago, the US House of Representatives voted on the Sergei Magnitsky Rule of Law Accountability Act to sanction the people who tortured and killed him. I'm proud to say that the bill passed with eighty-nine percent of the votes."

I'd planned to say more, but was cut off by an outburst of applause. One by one, people rose from their seats, and before I knew it, everyone was standing. They were applauding the campaign, but more than that, they were applauding this tiny bit of justice in the world. I couldn't help but be moved, and I stood and started clapping too, along with everyone else.

I shook hands and accepted congratulations as I made my way out of the theater, but all I could think of was getting home. I'd told Elena about Perepilchnyy on my way to the play, and more than anything I needed to talk to her.

When I got home, I found Elena sitting on the couch staring blankly at the living-room wall. It is never good to see terror in the face of one you love, but that was exactly what I witnessed in Elena that night. We were home, our children were asleep, and we were theoretically safe—but I was sure that Perepilchnyy had thought the same at his house in Surrey.

The next morning, I spoke to my London lawyer, Mary, and we agreed that we should alert the Surrey police as soon as possible. They had to understand that this case involved high-level Russian corruption and organized crime. Perepilchnyy wasn't someone who just dropped dead.

Mary drafted a letter, stressing that Perepilchnyy was a cooperating witness in a major Russian money-laundering case and might have been poisoned as Alexander Litvinenko had been in 2006. She urged the police to do a toxicology analysis as soon as possible.

Mary faxed the letter on Saturday, heard nothing on Sunday, and followed up on Monday with a call to the Weybridge police station. The duty officer confirmed that they'd received her letter, but strangely told her they had no record of any death involving someone named Perepilchnyy.

I thought that was absurd and asked Mary to get someone more senior who knew what was going on. She made more calls, and this time the police confirmed that Perepilchnyy had in fact died on November 11 on the private road near his house, but they were unwilling to discuss any other details. Mary pointed out that we had information that could be helpful to their investigation, but the police simply took her number and said that they would get back to us if they needed to.

By Wednesday, the police still hadn't contacted Mary. That day, I heard from Marcel that the initial postmortem results for Perepilchnyy had come back inconclusive. The coroner couldn't determine a cause of death. No heart attack, no stroke, no aneurysm. Perepilchnyy had just died.

This was worrying for one reason in particular: just before his death, Perepilichnyy had told us that he was on a Russian hit list and had been receiving death threats, making it reasonably likely that a Russian assassin was on the loose in the UK. If he'd gotten to Perepilichnyy, then he could just as easily get to us.

Mary hounded the police for the rest of the week but was continually rebuffed. I was so upset by the following Monday that I asked her what we could do to get them to act. Her advice was simple: "Go to the press." Normally lawyers advise you to stay away from the press in these situations, but it was such a matter of public interest, and the police were being so unresponsive, that in her opinion we didn't have any other choice.

That day, I got in touch with an investigative journalist at London's *Independent* newspaper and told him the whole story. I provided him with the documentation that Perepilichnyy had given us, and a list of phone numbers that he could use to verify different parts of the story.

Two days later, the *Independent* ran a story with the headline "Supergrass Who Held Key to Huge Russian Fraud Is Found Dead in Surrey."[1] Perepilichnyy's face covered the entire front page of the newspaper. Inside were a further five full pages describing every part of the story. The story ricocheted between every television station, radio show, and newspaper in the United Kingdom. Everyone was terrified that Russian organized criminals were settling scores on the streets of London.

Immediately after these stories came out, the Surrey police finally sent two homicide detectives to our office to interview us. Then, twenty-one days after Perepilichnyy died, the police announced they would do a full toxicology analysis on his corpse. In my mind this came way too late. If he'd been poisoned, by now it could be undetectable.

With a major homicide investigation under way and the press all

---

1 Supergrass is British slang for "informant."

over the case, whoever did this to Perepilichnyy would have been spooked and surely gone to ground. While the threat level was still high, I was no longer in a state of panic and felt comfortable enough to refocus on my responsibilities.

The Senate vote in Washington was now only days away. While I couldn't be there to witness it, I was going to be in the United States to give a speech at Harvard and to have some meetings in New York.

I flew to Boston on Sunday, December 2, and when I got off the plane, an urgent message from Kyle was on my BlackBerry. I called him as I walked toward immigration.

"Hey, Bill. What's up?" he said.

"I got your message. Is there something wrong?"

"Possibly. There are a number of senators who are insisting on keeping Magnitsky global instead of Russia-only."

"What does that mean for us?"

"Well, it's not just Cardin anymore. There's a growing group of senators led by [Jon] Kyl and [Carl] Levin who are also insisting on the global version."

"But I thought the whole Senate was behind it."

"There's no question that we have the votes, Bill. But if there's no consensus on which version to put up, Harry Reid won't schedule a vote," Kyle said, referring to the Senate majority leader. "And the clock's ticking."

"Is there anything I can do?"

"Yeah. Try to contact Kyl's and Levin's people and give them your arguments for why they should go with the Russia-only version. I'll try the same with Cardin."

"Okay. I'm stuck in Boston and New York for the next few days, but I'll do it."

I stopped in the hallway before reaching immigration and spoke with Juleanna. She wasn't as concerned as Kyle, but promised to get in touch with the senators' foreign policy staffs first thing Monday morning.

I cleared immigration and customs and went to my hotel. The

next morning I went to the Harvard Business School to present a case study that the school had written about my experiences in Russia. For the first half of the class, the students took turns telling the professor what they would have done if they had been in my shoes. I sat in the back row quietly watching as they came up with a few good ideas that I wished I'd thought of. The case study brought them to the point where our offices were raided in 2007, so they were only thinking about portfolio management and shareholder activism, not any of the criminal-justice issues. Unless they were following the news, they didn't have any idea what had happened after.

I took the podium for the second half of the class and told the whole story of the fraud, and Sergei's arrest, torture, and death. The mood in the room changed as I spoke. By the end, I noticed that some of the students were crying.

The professor, Aldo Musacchio, walked me out of the building afterward and told me that was the first time in his career at Harvard Business School that he'd ever seen students cry after a case study.

I finished my visit to Harvard and made my way to New York. By the end of the next day, and in spite of Juleanna's and Kyle's efforts, nothing in Washington had changed. Levin was immovable and Cardin wasn't showing his hand.

I went to sleep early on the night of the December 4, but woke up at 2:00 a.m. because of jet lag and all the eleventh-hour uncertainty surrounding the Senate. I knew I wouldn't be able to go back to sleep, so I took a shower, put on the hotel robe, then sat at my laptop and searched for *Magnitsky*.

The first thing to come up was a press release from Senator Cardin's office. It had been posted late the night before. I clicked on the link and read it. Cardin had compromised. He had dropped his demand for global. This meant the voting would go ahead.

I cleared my calendar for Thursday, December 6, and brought up C-SPAN on my computer. I sat in my hotel room alone, waiting, pacing, and ordering room service. Finally, around noon, the Senate voted on the Magnitsky Act. It all happened quickly. After half the votes were tallied, it was certain that the bill would pass. The final count was 92–4. Levin and three other senators were the only ones to vote against it.

It was almost anticlimactic. There were no fireworks, no marching band, just a roll call and then on to the next piece of business. But the implications were enormous. Since 2009, 13,195 bills had been proposed, and only 386 had made it out of committee and been voted in to law. We had completely defied the odds.

We had done so because of Sergei's bravery, Natalia's heart, Kyle's commitment, Cardin's leadership, McCain's integrity, McGovern's foresight, Vadim's brilliance, Vladimir's wisdom, Juleanna's savvy, and Elena's love. It had happened because of Ivan and Jonathan and Jamie and Eduard and Perepilichnyy and countless others, big and small. Somehow, our little idea of sanctioning those who'd killed Sergei had taken root and grown. There was something almost biblical about Sergei's story, and even though I am not a religious man, as I sat there watching history unfold, I couldn't help but feel that maybe God had intervened in this case. There is no shortage of suffering in this world, but somehow Sergei's tragedy resonated and cut through as few tragedies ever do.

More than anything I wished that none of this had ever happened. More than anything I wished that Sergei were still alive. But he wasn't, and nothing could bring him back. Nevertheless, his sacrifice was not in vain. It pricked the bubble of impunity that ensnares modern Russia, leaving a legacy that he and his family could be proud of.

40

Humiliator, Humiliatee

I was stunned when the act finally passed.

And another person was too: Vladimir Vladimirovich Putin.

For the previous few years, Putin had sat comfortably in the Kremlin, knowing that whatever happened in the US Congress, President Obama opposed the Magnitsky Act. In Putin's totalitarian mind, this was an ironclad guarantee that it would never become law. But what Putin overlooked was that the United States was not Russia.

In simple terms, the Russian response to the Magnitsky Act should have been a tit-for-tat retaliation reminiscent of a Cold War spy exchange. The Americans sanction a few Russian officials, and the Russians respond by doing the same. End of story.

But that is not how Putin decided to play it. Instead, immediately after the Magnitsky Act passed the Senate, he began a major quest to find ways to lash out and cause America real pain.

Putin's apparatchiks began floating ideas. The first was a proposed parliamentary resolution to seize $3.5 billion of Citigroup assets in Russia. This would certainly be vindictive, but it was a ridiculous idea. Somebody must have realized that if Russia seized Citigroup's assets, then the United States would seize Russian assets in America. Our opponents abandoned this and moved on.

The next idea they floated was a blockade of the Northern Distribution Network. This was the route the Americans used to move military equipment through Russia and into Afghanistan. The United States got supplies into Afghanistan in only two ways—through Pakistan or through Russia, and Putin understood perfectly how valuable this route was.

The problem with this idea was that if Russia followed through, officials at the Pentagon would look at a map and ask where they could put down their enormous foot to affect Russia's strategic interests in a similar way. The obvious place would have been Syria. Putin's government had invested a lot in propping up Syrian dictator Bashar al-Assad, and Putin wasn't going to do anything to jeopardize that investment. So this idea quickly died as well.

Putin needed to come up with something that didn't involve money or the military but that would still upset America.

That idea surfaced on December 11, 2012, when I was in Toronto to advocate for a Canadian version of the Magnitsky Act. That night I was giving a speech to a group of Canadian policy makers and journalists. During the question-and-answer session, a young female reporter stood and asked, "Today, members of the Russian Duma[1] announced that they are proposing a law that would permanently ban the adoption of Russian children by American families. What is your comment, Mr. Browder?"

It was the first I'd heard of this. I had a hard time processing the question, but after thinking about it for a moment, I responded, "If Putin is putting Russian orphans in the middle of this, it's one of the most unconscionable things he could possibly do."

This move complicated my psychology. Up until that moment, my fight with the Russians had been black-and-white. Picking sides was entirely straightforward: you were either on the side of truth and justice or you were on the side of Russian torturers and murderers. Now, by coming to the side of truth and justice, you might be causing harm to Russian orphans.

Putin's proposed ban was significant because over the last decade Americans had adopted over sixty thousand Russian orphans. In

---

1   The lower house of the Russian Parliament.

recent years Russia had restricted most American adoptions to sick children—those with HIV, Down syndrome, and spina bifida, among many other disorders. Some of these children wouldn't survive without the medical care they would receive from their new American families.

This meant that in addition to punishing American families who were waiting for Russian children to join them, Putin was also punishing, and potentially killing, defenseless orphans in his own country. To say that this was a heartless proposal doesn't even qualify as an understatement. It was evil, pure and simple.

Putin had hit his mark. He'd found something that Americans wanted and that he could take away without any threat of retaliation. More than that, he'd found a way to create a moral cost for supporting the Magnitsky campaign.

While Putin expected a bad reaction from the United States, he had no idea what kind of hornet's nest he'd stirred up in his own country. One can criticize Russians for many things, but their love of children isn't one of them. Russia is one of the only countries in the world where you can take a screaming child into a fancy restaurant and no one will give you a second look. Russians simply *adore* children.

This didn't stop Putin, though. The adoption ban law was given its first reading in the Russian Parliament on December 14, the same day that President Obama signed the Magnitsky Act into law.

The initial blowback inside Russia came from the most unexpected quarter. After the law was proposed, some of Putin's most senior confidants started to break ranks. The first was Olga Golodets, the deputy prime minister for social issues, who told *Forbes* that if this law was passed, "children with serious illnesses who require expensive operations will lose the opportunity to be adopted." Then Anton Siluyanov, Russia's finance minister, tweeted, "Logic of tit for tat is wrong because children will suffer." Even Sergei Lavrov, Russia's foreign minister, who carried out some of Putin's most odious policies around the world, said, "It is not right, and I am sure that eventually the Duma will make a balanced decision."

Because Putin ran such a tight ship, given this unprecedented display of dissent I started to assume that he must not be behind the adoption ban himself. I hoped and prayed that was true and that cooler heads would prevail. Defenseless children had to be taken out of this fight.

Putin rarely projects his intentions and is one of the most enigmatic leaders in the world. Unpredictability is his modus operandi. While he does this to keep his options open, he also never backs down from a fight or shows any weakness. Therefore, it was impossible to predict what he was going to do, but we were about to get a clearer view when Putin took the podium for his annual four-hour press conference on December 20, 2012.

This stage-managed production had animated backdrops and banks of lights, and many of the questions were softballs lobbed from either state-sponsored or self-censored journalists. Even though unexpected things rarely happened at these events, I knew that this would be the first time Putin would show his cards on the adoption ban.

I watched it on a live feed at the office. Vadim and Ivan joined me to see what Putin had to say and to translate. The first question came from Ksenia Sokolova, a journalist from a Russian glossy magazine named *Snob*: "In response to the American Magnitsky Act, the State Duma adopted restrictive measures against US citizens who want to adopt Russian orphans. . . . Does it not bother you to have the most destitute and helpless orphans becoming a tool in this political struggle?"

Putin shifted at his huge, angular desk and deflected as well as he could. He tried to look cool, but right off the bat the event had gone off script. "This is undoubtedly an unfriendly act towards the Russian Federation," he said. "Public opinion polls show that the overwhelming majority of Russians do not support the adoption of Russian children by foreign nationals." He then went into a long ramble about Guantánamo, Abu Ghraib, and secret CIA prisons, as if America's faults somehow made Russia's own abhorrent actions acceptable.

Three hours into the press conference, six of the fifty-odd questions asked of Putin had been about Sergei Magnitsky and the Russian orphans, and he was visibly angry.

Finally, toward the end of the event, Sergei Loiko of the *Los Angeles Times* stood up and said, "I'm going back to Sergei Magnitsky because you talked about it. Russia has had three years to give an answer"—he was referring to the investigation of Sergei's death—"what happened? What about the stolen two hundred and thirty million dollars that went to the police? That money could have been used to rebuild orphanages."

The hall erupted in applause. Putin was stunned. "Why are you all clapping?" he demanded. Putin had never experienced anything like this—the press was in open revolt. Everyone thought these things, but no one ever said them. Putin finally lost control. He lowered his voice, furrowed his brow, and said, "Magnitsky did not die of torture—he was not tortured. He died of a heart attack. In addition, as you know, he was not a human rights activist but a lawyer for Mr. Browder, who is suspected by our law enforcement agencies of economic crimes in Russia."

My heart skipped a beat. I knew that when my name passed Putin's thin lips, my life had changed forever. In the past, Putin had always steadfastly refused to mention my name. He'd been publicly confronted twice by reporters and always referred to me as "that man." He never dignified his enemies by mentioning them by name. But no longer. Hearing Putin say my name had a chilling effect, and I braced myself for whatever was going to come next.

The very next day, the adoption ban was voted on in the Duma, and in spite of Lavrov's wish that it make a "balanced decision," 420 members voted for it and only 7 voted against. A week later, on December 28, Putin signed the adoption ban into law. The Magnitsky Act had taken two and half years to become law in the United States; Russia's anti–Magnitsky Act took two and a half weeks.

The immediate fallout over this new law was heartbreaking. Three hundred Russian orphans who had already met their American families would never see the rooms that had been decorated for them on the other side of the world. Pictures of these children and their stories circulated throughout the international press. Their prospective parents descended on Capitol Hill, shouting, "We don't care about international politics, we just care about our babies!" I couldn't have agreed with them more.

As soon as the adoption ban went into effect, I started receiving calls from reporters, and all of them had the same question: "Do you feel responsible for what's happening to these orphans and their American families?"

I answered, "No, Putin is the one who is responsible. Only a coward would use defenseless children as human shields."

I wasn't the only one who felt this way. On January 14, Russian New Year's Day, people started to assemble on Moscow's Boulevard Ring carrying placards and homemade signs denouncing Putin. As the protesters made their way along the streets among a heavy police presence, their numbers grew and eventually hit roughly fifty thousand. This was not the usual crowd of politically active people, but instead included grandmothers, schoolteachers, children riding on their fathers' shoulders, and every other kind of Muscovite. Their signs said things like SHAME! and STOP LYING! and THE DUMA EATS CHILDREN! and HEROD! (The law quickly became known as Herod's Law, which referred to the brutal king of Judea who, to stay in power, had tried to kill the baby Jesus by ordering the massacre of all male infants in Bethlehem.)

Putin generally ignores protests, but he couldn't ignore this one, because it was big and it focused on saving children. The government couldn't repeal the law, but after the "March Against Scoundrels" it announced that Russia would invest millions in the state-run orphanage system. I was sure that the money would never find its way to its designated recipients, but it did show how rattled Putin was.

However, this whole affair cost Putin something much dearer than money: his aura of invincibility. Humiliation is his currency—he uses it to get what he wants and to put people in their place. In his mind, he hasn't succeeded until his opponent has failed, and he can't be happy until his opponent is miserable. In Putin's world, the humiliator cannot, under any circumstances, become the humiliatee. Yet this is precisely what happened in the wake of the adoption ban.

What does a man like Putin do when he is humiliated? As we'd seen so many times before, he lashes out against the person who humiliated him.

Ominously, that person was me.

41

Red Notice

At the end of January 2013 I found myself back in Davos at the World Economic Forum. On my second day there, as I was trudging through the snow outside the conference center, I heard a chirpy female voice call out, "Bill! Bill!"

I turned and saw a short woman with a big furry hat walking briskly toward me. As she got closer, I recognized her. It was Chrystia Freeland, the reporter who'd broken the Sidanco story so many years ago in Moscow. She was now an editor-at-large for Reuters.

She stopped in front of me, her cheeks flushed by the cold.

"Hey, Chrystia!"

"I'm glad I spotted you," she said urgently. Normally, she and I would have kissed on both cheeks and caught up, but she apparently had something important to tell me.

"What's going on?"

"Bill, I just came from an off-the-record briefing with Medvedev, and your name came up."

"That doesn't surprise me. I'm not too popular with the Russians these days."

"That's what I wanted to talk to you about. I need to tell you what he said—hold on." She dug a reporter's notepad out of her pocket, flipped through the pages, and stopped. "Here it is. Someone asked about the Magnitsky case, and Medvedev said, quote, Yes, it's a shame that Sergei Magnitsky died, and Bill Browder is running free and alive." She looked up at me. "That's what he said."

"Was that a threat?"

"That's how it seemed to me."

Panic pooled in my stomach. I thanked Chrystia for telling me and made my way into the conference center with this ominous information hanging over my head. I continued with my meetings, and throughout the day four other journalists who'd been at the same briefing pulled me aside and repeated Chrystia's story.

I'd been threatened many times by people from Russia, but never by the prime minister.[1] I knew my life was in danger, but this ratcheted the danger to a new level. As soon as I returned to London, I called Steven Beck, our security expert, and substantially increased my personal protection.

The threat also indicated the mind-set of Putin and his men. I took it as a signal that they didn't want to harm me just physically, but in any way they could.

The first bit of this nastiness came when the Russian authorities announced the date that they were going to begin my trial for tax evasion in absentia. They'd been using the threat of this fabricated case for years to try to intimidate me and get me to back down, but the passage of the Magnitsky Act had pushed them over the edge.

Putting me on trial when I wasn't in Russia was highly unusual. It would be only the second time in post-Soviet history that Russia would try a Westerner in absentia. But that wasn't the worst part. Their truly unbelievable move was to also try Sergei Magnitsky.

That's right. They were going to put the man they had killed on trial. Even Joseph Stalin, one of the most zealous mass murderers of all time, a man responsible for the deaths of at least 20 million Russians, never stooped to putting a dead man on trial.

But in March 2013, that is exactly what Vladimir Putin did.

Putin was creating legal history. The last time a dead person had been prosecuted in Europe was in 897 CE, when the Catholic Church

---

1   After serving as president, Medvedev returned to the office of prime minister in May 2012.

convicted Pope Formosus posthumously, cut off his papal fingers, and threw his body into the Tiber River.

The nastiness didn't stop there, though. Days before the trial was set to begin, NTV, the state-controlled television station, began aggressively advertising a one-hour, prime-time "documentary" about me called *The Browder List*.

I didn't even bother to watch it when it aired, but Vladimir called to give me a summary: "It is pure paranoid fantasy, Bill." He told me that by the time it was over, not only were Sergei and I accused of tax evasion, but I was also responsible for the devaluation of the ruble in 1998; I was guilty of stealing the $4.8 billion loan that the IMF had made to Russia; I had killed my business partner Edmond Safra; I was a British MI6 agent; and I had murdered Sergei Magnitsky myself.

I might have been upset by this, but their fabrications were so amateurish that no person watching this show could possibly believe a word of it. However, it wasn't clear that credibility even mattered to the Russian authorities. Everything they did came from a well-worn playbook. The same NTV crew made a similar "documentary" trying to tarnish the protest movement after Putin's reelection in 2012. They made another one about the famous anti-Putin punk band, Pussy Riot. After both films, their subjects were arrested and imprisoned.

Our trial began on March 11 at the Tverskoi District Court with Judge Igor Alisov presiding. Neither the Magnitsky family nor I would have anything to do with it, so the court appointed a pair of public defenders against our wishes. Both tried to withdraw when they realized they weren't wanted, but both were threatened with disbarment if they didn't carry on.

Every Western government, parliament, media outlet, and human rights organization viewed this as an appalling miscarriage of justice. We all stared in awe as the trial began and the prosecutor droned on for hours in front of an empty cage.

Everyone wondered why Putin was doing this. The cost to Russia's international reputation was enormous, and the upside to him seemed limited. There was practically no chance that I would end up in a Russian prison, and Sergei was already dead.

But this had a twisted logic. In Putin's mind, if he had a court judgment against Sergei and me, his officials could then visit all the European governments that were considering their own version of the Magnitsky Act and say, "How can you put a piece of legislation in place that is named after a criminal convicted in our court? And how can you listen to his advocate, who has been convicted of the same crime?" Pesky details such as the fact that Sergei had been dead for three years and killed in police custody after exposing a massive government corruption scheme never entered into Putin's equation.

Midway through, the trial ground to a halt because the two public defenders stopped showing up to court.

I wasn't sure what to make of this. Since the outcome of this trial was predetermined and controlled by Putin, I couldn't imagine that these defenders were acting of their own volition. I started to think that this was Putin's elegant way of getting out of this humiliating spectacle he'd created for himself.

But instead of folding, Putin doubled down. On April 22, the Russian authorities issued an arrest warrant for me as well as new criminal charges.

While this might sound dramatic, it didn't upset me the way the Russians intended. There was no chance I was going to be arrested in the United Kingdom. The British government had already recognized the process as "abusive" and had rejected all Russian requests to hand me over. I couldn't imagine any other civilized country handing me over either. So in spite of the aggressive noises from the Russian government, I carried on with my advocacy work.

In mid-May, I was invited to give a speech at the Oslo Freedom Forum, the Davos of the human rights world. On the day of the event, just before I was supposed to take the stage in front of three hundred people, I checked my BlackBerry and saw an urgent message from my secretary with "Interpol" in the subject line.

I opened it and read, "Bill, we've just been contacted by ███████ ██████████ who got a copy of an Interpol all-points bulletin in order to arrest you! The document is attached. Please call the office ASAP!"

I quickly opened the PDF, and sure enough the Russians had finally gone to Interpol.

Seconds after reading this, I was called to the stage to give my speech. I forced a smile, walked under the lights, and spent the next ten minutes telling the story I'd told so many times before about me, Russia, and Sergei. I managed to put the Interpol message out of my mind long enough so that I could get through my talk. After the applause, I hurried out to the lobby and immediately phoned my lawyer in London. She explained that the Interpol notice meant that any time I crossed an international border, I could be arrested. It was up to whatever country I was visiting to act on the warrant.

I was in Norway, and the situation there was potentially tricky. While the country had a stellar human rights record, it shared a border and a long history with Russia, and there was no telling what the Norwegians would do in this situation. I called Elena, told her what was going on, and asked her to prepare for the worst.

I booked an earlier flight home, grabbed my bags, and made my way to Oslo Airport. I arrived an hour and a half early and checked in at the Scandinavian Airlines desk. When I couldn't put off the inevitable any longer, I slowly made my way down the long corridor to Norwegian passport control.

Like Eduard and Vladimir before me, I was a bundle of nerves as I prepared to cross the border as a wanted man. I started to imagine the moment I presented my passport, and the look on the officer's face when he saw that I had an Interpol arrest warrant in my name. I imagined being put into a Norwegian detention center. I could see the months that I would spend in a spartan cell, and the drawn-out court proceedings as I fought my extradition. I could see the Norwegians buckling under Russian pressure and me losing this fight. I could see the Aeroflot plane that I would be thrown onto, bound for Moscow. I didn't even want to think about the horrors I would be subjected to after that.

No other passengers were at passport control. I had to choose between two equally bored-looking, young Nordic men in uniform. I decided to take the one on the left for no particular reason. I handed him my passport, interrupting a conversation he was having with the other officer.

He took it absently, opened it to my picture, and glanced at it. He then glanced at me, closed the passport, and handed it back. Thankfully, he didn't scan it through his machine, so the Interpol notice was never even flagged.

That was it. I grabbed my passport and made my way to the plane.

When I arrived in Britain, it was different. The Border Force scans every passport, and mine was no exception. But the British government had already decided not to act on any Russian requests in my case. It took the immigration officer a few extra minutes to process my entry, but when he was finished, he handed me my passport and let me go.

Even though I was safe in Britain, the Russians had me where they wanted me. By putting out a Red Notice, they could effectively prevent me from traveling, and by not traveling, they were betting that they could stop Magnitsky sanctions from spreading to Europe.

I had no choice: I had to deal with Interpol head-on. The day I got back from Norway, I issued a press release announcing the warrant, and it was picked up immediately. Journalists and politicians started calling Interpol to ask if they would side with the Russians or with me. Normally Interpol isn't accountable to anybody, but because of all the attention they were getting on my case, they decided to have a special meeting to determine my fate the following week.

I wasn't optimistic. Interpol has a reputation for cooperating with authoritarian regimes to chase down political enemies. In many cases Interpol had done the wrong thing. The most egregious example of this was in the lead-up to World War II, when Interpol helped the

Nazis pursue prominent Jews who'd fled the Reich. There have been many shocking examples since.

The day before Interpol's meeting, London's *Daily Telegraph* weighed in on my behalf with an article entitled "Is Interpol Fighting for Truth and Justice, or Helping the Villains?" The columnist, Peter Oborne, deftly used my case to illustrate that Interpol had a pattern of being abused by rogue nations such as Russia. "It is entirely likely that Interpol will find with the FSB and against Bill Browder," he wrote. "But in the court of international opinion it's not Mr. Browder who's on trial: it's Interpol itself, for its collaboration with some of the nastiest regimes in the world."

Two days later, on May 24, 2013, I was at my desk writing this book when I got a call from my lawyer. She had just received an email from Interpol rejecting the Russians' application for my Red Notice.

An hour later, Interpol published its rejection of Russia's request on its website. It announced, "The Interpol General Secretariat has deleted all information in relation to William Browder following a recommendation by the independent Commission for the Control of Interpol's Files." This was categorical and almost completely unprecedented. Interpol rarely rejected notices, and if they did, they never publicly announced them.

This repudiation must have made Putin even more furious. Once again, when it came to anything to do with me or Sergei Magnitsky, he was being publicly humiliated. If there was any chance that Putin was going to back out of the posthumous trial in the aftermath of the Interpol embarrassment, that possibility had vanished.

Judge Alisov resumed the case, and the trial finally concluded on July 11, 2013. That morning, the judge took his place in the small, hot courtroom and prepared to read his statement. The two court-appointed defense lawyers were there, along with two prosecutors. There were six guards in berets and black uniforms, but since they had no one to guard or cart away afterward they were an unnecessary formality.

Rarely speaking above a whisper, Judge Alisov read the decision. He hardly ever looked up from his papers. It took him well over an hour to describe all of Putin's fantasies about what Sergei and I had done wrong. When the judge was finished, Sergei and I had been found guilty of large-scale tax evasion, and I'd been sentenced to nine years in prison.

It was all a show, a Potemkin court. This is Russia today. A stuffy room presided over by a corrupt judge, policed by unthinking guards, with lawyers who are there just to give the appearance of a real trial, and with no defendant in the cage. A place where lies reign supreme. A place where two and two is still five, white is still black, and up is still down. A place where convictions are certain, and guilt a given. Where a foreigner can be convicted in absentia of crimes he did not commit.

A place where an innocent man who was murdered by the state, a man whose only crime was loving his country too much, can be made to suffer from beyond the grave.

This is Russia today.

42

Feelings

After reading this, you may wonder how it all made me feel.

The simple answer is that the pain caused by Sergei's death was so great that I couldn't allow myself to feel anything. For a long time after Sergei was killed I locked up my emotions so tightly that if there was any sign of their coming out, I would shut them down as quickly and as hard as I could. But, as any psychiatrist will tell you, avoiding grief doesn't make it go away. Eventually, the feelings will find their way to the surface, and the more you've bottled them up, the more dramatically they will burst out.

In my case, the dam burst in October 2010, almost a year after Sergei's death. I had been helping two Dutch documentary filmmakers access everyone involved in Sergei's story. They interviewed each of us and were making a movie that they planned to premiere before eight different parliaments around the world on November 16, the first anniversary of Sergei's murder. As we got closer to the release date, I became concerned that the movie wouldn't be good enough to show to these important decision makers. I assumed that because it was produced in such a hurry, it wasn't going to be high quality, and I was afraid it could do more harm than good.

Realizing how nervous I was and hoping to allay my fears, the producers invited me and Vadim to Holland to view the rough cut in October.

We flew to Holland and traveled to Oosterbeek, a small village an hour southeast of Amsterdam, to the home of Hans Hermans, one of the filmmakers. Before showing us the film, he served us a traditional

Dutch lunch of Edam cheese and salted herring in his small kitchen, then invited us into the living room. We sat on floor cushions as his coproducer, Martin Maat, started the movie.

The film, entitled *Justice for Sergei*, was not easy to watch. It didn't tell me anything I didn't already know, but it showed Sergei's story in a completely new light. In addition to the horror of his ordeal, there were the everyday facts of his life before he'd been taken into custody: his devotion to his sons, his love of literature, his enjoyment of Mozart and Beethoven. These details were harder for me to bear than any of those describing his detention. Achingly, the movie ends with his aunt, Tatyana, telling the story of a recent visit to Sergei's grave. After she left the cemetery, she walked by an old woman at the Metro station who was selling cornflowers. "She was so sad," Tatyana said. "I passed her, but returned to buy some flowers, knowing that's what Sergei would have done. Whenever he walked with his mother past a lady selling plastic bags, he would always buy one. When the lady would ask, 'Which one would you like?' Sergei would answer, 'The one no one else wants to buy.'"

These are among the last spoken words of the film, but not the final message. To drive it home—to really show what the film is about— the image fades and a simple track of guitar and clarinet music ramps up. Clips from old home movies appear showing Sergei: raising a glass to toast a summertime family gathering; inspecting a waterfall on vacation; standing in the doorway of his apartment, entertaining dinner guests; sharing an outdoor meal with his best friend, joking, laughing, pointing at the camera. There is Sergei, alive as he would never again be except in the hearts and minds of those who loved him—who *still* love him.

Up until that moment, I had held it all in, terrified of what would happen if I allowed myself to let go. Now, in that room in Oosterbeek, I let my guard down and the tears flowed as they've never flowed before or since. I cried, and I cried, and I kept on crying.

It felt terrible, but it also felt good to finally feel the pain. Hans,

Martin, and Vadim sat quietly, fighting back tears of their own, not knowing quite what to do.

Finally, I regained my composure and dried my eyes. "Can we watch it again?" I asked quietly.

"Sure," said Hans.

And we did, and I cried some more. That was when the healing finally began.

They say there are five stages of grief and that recognizing the pain is the most important one. That may be true, but recovering from a murder where the people who were responsible are walking free and blatantly enjoying the fruits of their crimes made recovery that much more difficult.

The main thing that has brought me some comfort has been the relentless pursuit of justice. Every parliamentary resolution, every news story, every asset freeze, every new criminal investigation, leaves me with a small feeling of relief.

The other thing that gives me some peace is seeing how Sergei's story has changed so many lives. In contrast to other atrocities in Russia, Sergei's murder has gotten under the cynical skins of Russians in ways that were previously unfathomable. Now prison guards across Russia worry about being too brutal in case they end up being held responsible for another Magnitsky. Now victims of human rights abuse in Russia feel that there is some recourse to justice as they gather their own "Magnitsky lists" to sanction the officials terrorizing them. Now Russia has been forced to focus on the horrible mistreatment of orphans who had previously disappeared from the national conscience. Now the concept of Magnitsky sanctions has been used as the main tool in fighting Russia over its illegal invasion of Ukraine. Perhaps most important of all, Sergei's story has given everyone in Russia, as well as millions of people around the world, a detailed picture of the true brutality of Vladimir Putin's regime.

This story has also changed matters outside Russia. The Russian authorities have been so brazen in pursuing me that they have ruined their standing with many international institutions. In a highly unusual step the Russian authorities applied again to Interpol to get a Red Notice issued for me, and for a second time they were rejected. Because of the abuses in my case, Red Notice requests from Russia are now no longer automatically accepted at Interpol.

The Russians also failed spectacularly on the libel front. The decision handed down by the British High Court in the libel case brought by Major Pavel Karpov was unprecedented. The judge decisively struck out Karpov's lawsuit and made legal history in England, creating a precedent that would prevent future libel tourists like Karpov from abusing the London courts in their efforts to silence critics of authoritarian regimes.

However, as important as these developments are, it is often difficult for my friends and colleagues to understand why I continue to fight.

In the summer of 2012, my old friend Jean Karoubi came to my house one Saturday for a family visit. We had a pleasant dinner where we caught up on business and family life, but as I was making tea in the kitchen, he came in and asked if we could speak privately. I took him to our living room and closed the door.

He sat down and said, "We've been friends for a long time, Bill, and I'm very concerned. You have a beautiful family, you're a successful businessman, and there's nothing you can do to bring Sergei back. Why don't you stop this campaign now before something else bad happens?"

This wasn't the first time I'd had this conversation, and obviously I'm aware of the possible consequences of what I am doing. Nothing upsets me more than the idea that my children could grow up without their father. That thought haunts me. Whenever I'm attending my children's school ballet or playing with them in the park, I wonder how many more times I will be able to do these things before it all comes tragically to an end.

But then I think of Sergei's children, and especially about how his young son, Nikita, will never see his father again. And I think of Sergei, who was in a far more precarious situation than me, but wasn't prepared to back down. What kind of man would I be if I *did* back down?

"I have to see this through, Jean. Otherwise, the poison of not doing anything would eat me up from the inside."

I certainly don't do this out of bravery, though; I'm no braver than anyone else and I feel fear as much as the next person. But what I've discovered about fear is that no matter how scared I am at any particular moment, the feeling doesn't last. After a time it subsides. As anyone who lives in a war zone or who has a dangerous job will tell you, your body doesn't have the capacity to feel fear for an extended period. The more incidents you encounter, the more inured you become to them.

I have to assume that there is a very real chance that Putin or members of his regime will have me killed someday. Like anyone else, I have no death wish and I have no intention of letting them kill me. I can't mention most of the countermeasures I take, but I will mention one: this book. If I'm killed, you will know who did it. When my enemies read this book, they will know that you know. So if you sympathize with this search for justice, or with Sergei's tragic fate, please share this story with as many people as you can. That simple act will keep the spirit of Sergei Magnitsky alive and go further than any army of bodyguards in keeping me safe.

The final question that everyone asks is how I feel about the losses I've incurred as a result of this quest for justice. I've lost the business I so painstakingly built; I've lost many "friends" who distanced themselves from me for fear of how my campaign might affect their economic interests; and I've lost the freedom to travel without the worry that I might be arrested and handed over to the Russians.

Have these losses weighed heavily on me? Strangely, the answer is no. For everything I've lost in certain areas, I've gained in others. For all the fair-weather friends who've abandoned me as a financial liability, I've met many inspired people who are changing the world.

If I hadn't done this, I would never have met Andrew Rettman, a political reporter in Brussels who has unrelentingly taken up Sergei's cause. Despite being disabled, for over five years he has hobbled to the most mundane meetings about the Magnitsky case at the European Commission and vigilantly reported on them to make sure that the bureaucrats there don't sweep this issue under the carpet.

Nor would I have met Valery Borschev, the seventy-year-old Russian prison rights advocate who, within two days of Sergei's death, had used his independent authority to enter the prisons where Sergei had been kept and compelled dozens of officials to answer his questions. In spite of the extreme risks to his safety, he exposed the glaringly inconsistent statements and the lies of the Russian authorities.

I would have never met Lyudmila Alexeyeva, the eighty-six-year-old Russian human rights activist who was the first person publicly to accuse Russian police officers of murdering Sergei Magnitsky. She stood by Sergei's mother and filed criminal complaints, and even when those complaints were ignored, she wouldn't let it go.

In this mission I've met literally hundreds more people who have given me a whole new perspective on humanity that I would never have gotten from my life on Wall Street.

If you asked me when I was at Stanford Business School what I would have thought about giving up a life as a hedge fund manager to become a human rights activist, I would have looked at you as if you were out of your mind.

But here I am twenty-five years later, and that's exactly what I've done. Yes, I could go back to my previous life. But now that I've seen this new world, I can't imagine doing anything else. While there is nothing wrong with pursuing a life in commerce, that world feels like watching TV in black and white. Now, all of a sudden, I've installed a wide-screen color TV, and everything about my life is richer, fuller, and more satisfying.

This doesn't mean that I don't have profound regrets, though. The obvious one is that Sergei is no longer with us. If I could do it all over again, I would never have gone to Russia in the first place. I would gladly trade all of my business success for Sergei's life. I now understand how completely naive I was to think that as a foreigner I was somehow immune to the barbarity of the Russian system. I'm not the one who's dead, but someone *is* dead because of me and my actions, and there is nothing I can do to bring him back. But I *can* carry on creating a legacy for Sergei and pursuing justice for his family.

In early April 2014 I took Sergei's widow, Natasha, and his son, Nikita, to the European Parliament to watch the vote on a resolution to impose sanctions on thirty-two Russians complicit in the Magnitsky case. This was the first time in the history of the European Parliament that a public sanctions list was ever to be voted on.

A year earlier, I had relocated the Magnitsky family to a quiet suburb of London where Nikita was able to attend a prestigious private school and where Natasha could stop looking over her shoulder every day. They felt safe for the first time since Sergei's murder, and I thought that it would help their healing to watch more than seven hundred European lawmakers from twenty-eight countries condemn the people who killed Sergei.

On the afternoon of April 1, 2014, we got on the Eurostar from London to Brussels. As we emerged from the Channel Tunnel in Calais, France, I received an urgent call from an assistant at the European Parliament. "Bill, the president of the Parliament has just received a letter from a major US law firm on behalf of some of the Russians on the sanctions list. They're threatening legal action if the vote is not canceled. They claim that the Parliament is violating the rights of these Russians."

"What? *These* guys are the rights violators! That's ridiculous."

"I agree. But we need a legal opinion to present to the president of the Parliament by ten tomorrow morning or the vote may not happen."

It was already six o'clock in the evening, and I couldn't imagine being able to find a top lawyer who would change his plans and stay up all night to write a convincing legal opinion.

I would have given up without even trying, but then I looked at Nikita, his face pressed against the train's window as he stared out at the fast-moving French countryside.

He looked exactly like a little Sergei Magnitsky.

"Okay, let me see what I can do," I said to the assistant.

I went to the space between the cars, the same place where I had sat with Ivan seven years before when we discovered that our Moscow offices had been raided. I started making calls and leaving messages, but after an hour and thirteen calls, I still hadn't been able to reach anyone. I made my way back to my seat agonizing about how I was going to explain all this to Sergei's widow and son.

But just before I reached my seat, my phone rang. It was Geoffrey Robertson, QC, a London-based lawyer who'd received one of my messages.

In the world of human rights, Geoffrey is a god. As a QC he was a member of a highly select group of English barristers known as the Queen's Counsel, who take on the most complex and difficult cases in the English courts. From the start, he had been one of Britain's most outspoken and ardent supporters of a global Magnitsky Act.

I explained the situation and prayed that we wouldn't get cut off by a poor mobile-phone connection. Thankfully we didn't, and at the end of our call he asked, "When do you need this by?"

I was sure he was expecting me to say two weeks or something similar. Instead, wincing, I replied, "Tomorrow morning at ten a.m."

"Oh." He sounded surprised. "How important is this, Bill?"

"Very. Sergei's widow and son are with me on the train to Brussels. We're heading there to watch the vote tomorrow. It would break their hearts if the Russians found another way to deny them justice."

There was a silence on the other end as he contemplated staying up well into the night to write this opinion. "Bill, you'll have it by ten a.m. tomorrow. We won't let the Russians take this away from the Magnitsky family."

The next morning, at exactly 10:00 a.m., Geoffrey Robertson sent in his legal opinion. It destroyed the Russians' arguments point by point.

I called the assistant and asked if the letter sufficed. He thought it was perfect, but he didn't know if it would convince the president of the Parliament to go ahead with the vote later in the afternoon. I'd done a lot to shelter Natasha and Nikita from all the political intrigue in the West, and I prayed that they wouldn't have to see it that day.

At 4:00 p.m. I met Natasha and Nikita at the entrance to the Parliament and took them up to the balcony of the plenary hall. Beneath us were the 751 seats of the parliamentarians, laid out in a broad semicircle. As we sat, we put on our headphones and clicked through the channels of the roughly twenty different simultaneous translations in which the Parliament conducts its business.

At 4:30 p.m., Kristiina Ojuland, the Estonian MEP[1] who sponsored the Magnitsky resolution, suddenly appeared on the balcony. Breathlessly, she told us that Geoffrey Robertson's opinion had indeed convinced everybody, and that the vote was going ahead as planned.

Kristiina then disappeared to introduce the resolution. We spotted her in her purple dress among the beehive of parliamentarians below. She stood and began her speech. Like many other speeches I'd heard before, she went through Sergei's story and the Russian government's cover-up, but then she did something unexpected. She pointed toward us and said, "Mr. President, we have with us in the visitors' gallery today the late Sergei Magnitsky's wife, together with his son and his former boss, Mr. Bill Browder. I am pleased to welcome our guests."

Then completely unexpectedly, the entire chamber of seven-hundred-odd parliamentarians stood, turned toward us, and erupted in applause. Not polite applause, but real, thunderous applause, which carried on for nearly a minute. I felt a lump in my throat and goose bumps on my arms as I watched tears welling up in Natasha's eyes.

The vote went through and there wasn't a single objection in the entire European Parliament. Not one.

Early in this book, I said that the feeling I got from buying a Polish stock that went up ten times was the best thing to ever happen to me in my career. But the feeling I had on that balcony in Brussels

---

1   Member of the European Parliament.

with Sergei's widow and son, as we watched the largest lawmaking body in Europe recognize and condemn the injustices suffered by Sergei and his family, felt orders of magnitude better than any financial success I've ever had. If finding a ten bagger in the stock market was a highlight of my life before, there is no feeling as satisfying as getting some measure of justice in a highly unjust world.

Acknowledgments

My opponents have engaged in a lot of crazy speculation regarding how I've managed to achieve some measure of justice for Sergei Magnitsky. The Russian government has alternately accused me of being a CIA agent, an MI6 spy, a billionaire who has bribed every member of Congress and the European Parliament, and part of a Zionist conspiracy to take over the world. Of course, the truth is much simpler. The reason why this campaign has worked is because anyone with a heart who has heard about Sergei's ordeal has wanted to help.

A number of people have done so publicly, and writing this book has given me the opportunity to acknowledge many of them. But for every person named in these pages, there are countless others who have gone unnamed but whose tireless work behind the scenes has been crucial to the success of this campaign. I was hoping to use this section as an opportunity to thank all of these people. However, I've decided that I do not want to risk exposing anyone else to the intimidation, harassment, and threats from Russia that follow those who publicly support the Magnitsky cause. The time to acknowledge all of those who have contributed will come, but only when the threat of retaliation from Russian organized crime and the Putin regime subsides.

So for now, to every one of you who has given their time and energy to the campaign, I hope you all know how grateful I am for your support. To all the politicians in the United States, Canada, and across Europe; to the men and women at the European Parliament, PACE, and OSCE; to all the lawyers who joined me in this fight for justice, often working pro bono; to the journalists who worked courageously and tirelessly to get the truth out; to the NGOs and individuals from around the world who pushed their governments to act; to the brave Russian activists who continue to risk their lives to fight for the betterment of their country; to my friends and colleagues, whose support has helped me over the years; and to anyone who has been moved by the Magnitsky story and expressed your care in any way you could, please know that I cannot express just how much I cherish the contributions you have made and the hard work you have done. All of it has mattered and has made a difference. None of what this campaign has been able to achieve would have been possible without you.

Finally, and most importantly, I need to thank the true heroes of this story—the Magnitsky family. It was tragedy that brought us together, and while I would give anything to undo what happened to Sergei, I am grateful for your friendship. Your bravery and determination in the face of unspeakable grief is awe-inspiring, and I know that Sergei would be proud of each one of you.

Index

Abdallah, Ken, 80, 81, 82
Abu Ghraib, 359
adoption ban law, 357–62
Aeroflot, 1, 56, 368
Afghanistan, 356
Air France, 152
al-Assad, Bashar, 357
Alexeyeva, Lyudmila, 376
Alisov, Igor, 365, 369–70
Alitalia, 243
American Chamber of Commerce,
    Moscow, 144, 145
American Communist Party, 12–14, 26
American Express, 59
Amnesty International, 292
Amsterdam, 371
Anichin, Alexei, 314
Animal House (film), 18
Anselmini, Jean-Pierre, 41
AP, 182
"The Armed Forces of Corporate
    Governance Abuse," 144–45
Armenia, 7, 260
Arthur Andersen, 51
Asea Brown Boveri, 92
Ashcroft, John, 306–7
Asian economic crisis (1997), 131–32
asset freezes and visa sanctions, 291,
    293–94, 297, 298, 299–309,
    327–29, 368, 373, 377
asset stripping, 144, 158–60, 165
Austria, 14, 312
Autosan, 30–39, 57
Azerbaijan, 7

Bahamas, 70
Bain & Company, 19–20, 24
Bangkok, 211
Bannister, Clive, 170
Barnevik, Percy, 92
Baucus, Max, 336
BBC, 50
Beck, Steven, 221, 274, 317, 364
beef importers, 334, 336
Beijing, 211
Belarus, 279
Belton, Catherine, 188, 203
Berezovsky, Boris, 91
Berlin Wall, fall of, 27, 29–30
billionaire psychology, 83
Blair, Tony, 186–89
Blokhin, Vasili Mikhailovich, 279–80
Bloomberg, 126, 187, 194
Boeing, 334, 336
bonds, 132
    1998 financial crisis and aftermath,
        131–38
    Russian market, 132–38
bonuses, 47–48
Borschev, Valery, 287, 376
Boston Consulting Group, 19, 24–25,
    41, 155
    Browder and, 26–41, 155
    Eastern European operations,
        26–41
    in London, 25, 26–27
"Bouncing Czech, The," 50
Bouzada, Ariel, 121
Bowers, Chris, 5–6, 7, 9

Bowring, Bill, 170, 173
Brandeis University, 14
Brazil, 191
Brenton, Tony, 172–73, 174, 176, 178
Brezhnev, Leonid, 117
British Airways, 56, 180, 270
British Petroleum, 112, 113, 116, 125,
    154
Brose, Chris, 307–9
Browder, Bill
  anti-corruption campaigns against
    oligarchs, 115–30, 144–48,
    154–69, 181, 192–93
  banned from Russia, 11–13, 169,
    170–89, 193
  begins Hermitage Fund, 76, 77–86,
    88, 95–103
  birth of, 15
  bodyguards of, 127
  at Boston Consulting Group, 26–41,
    155
  British citizenship of, 10
  Cardin List and, 298–309
  childhood of, 15–17
  communist background of, 12–14,
    26, 27
  congressional testimony on
    Magnitsky case, 302–5
  at Davos, 88–93
  death of Magnitsky and, 276–78,
    280–88, 327, 372–73, 376
  detained at Sheremetyevo Airport,
    2–11, 169–70
  Elena and, 3–11, 145–54, 161–64,
    170, 174–75, 187, 192–96, 209,
    225, 269–70, 276–77, 282, 299,
    341, 350–51, 355, 367
  as a father, 1, 3, 8, 114, 174–75,
    206–9, 272, 299, 316, 341–42,
    344, 374
  Gazprom theft and investigation,
    154–62, 192–93
  Hermitage lawyers as targets,
    237–53, 254–68, 360
  Interpol Red Notice for, 367–70, 374
  investigation into stolen companies,
    201–35, 252–53, 271–72
  Karpov's libel suit against, 344–45,
    374
  loses Russian visa, 170–89, 193–96
  Magnitsky Act and, 305–9, 327–39,
    340–50
  Magnitsky case, *see* Magnitsky case
  at Maxwell Communications
    Corporation, 41–51
  1998 financial crisis and aftermath,
    131–46
  in Poland, 27–39
  police raids on Hermitage offices,
    196–200, 203, 208–10, 216, 228,
    230
  Potanin vs., 115–30, 134–35
  Putin and, 166–69, 175–77, 183–89,
    236, 360–70, 375
  Russian criminal cases against,
    189, 190–200, 201–35, 236–53,
    270–72, 323, 343–45, 360, 364–70
  Russian raider attack, 213–27
  Sabrina and, 84–86, 94–95, 102, 114,
    117, 123, 134–37, 139–41, 174
  at Salomon Brothers, 52–76, 77
  Edmond Safra and, 72–76, 77–88,
    93, 94, 98, 100–102, 112, 119–32,
    138–39, 142
  Sidanco and, 104–30, 134–35
  tax-rebate fraud and, 231–37,
    252–53, 257, 264, 271–72, 288,
    301, 316–26, 328
  threats against, 273–74, 314,
    351–54, 363–70, 375
  trial on tax evasion in abstentia,
    364–70
  at University of Chicago, 19
  at Whiteman School, 15–17
Browder, David, 1, 3, 8, 114, 117,
    135–41, 174, 175, 208, 209, 272,
    273, 299, 316, 344
Browder, Earl, 12–13, 23–24
  as head of American Communist
    Party, 12–14, 26, 27

Browder, Elena, 3–11, 145–54, 161–
  64, 170, 174–75, 187, 192–96,
  206–9, 225, 269–70, 276–77, 282,
  299, 341, 350–51, 355, 367
Browder, Eva, 14–15, 16–17, 135
Browder, Felix, 12, 13–15
Browder, Jessica, 175, 176, 207, 208,
  209, 341–42
Browder, Raisa, 12, 13
Browder, Sabrina, 84–86, 94–95, 102,
  114, 117, 123, 134–37, 139–41,
  174
Browder, Thomas, 15
Browder, Veronica, 207, 209
Browder List, The (Russian TV
  special), 365
Bruder, Jason, 332–33
Brussels, 376–80
Bryanskih, Victor, 159
Budapest, 53, 88
Bukovsky, Vladimir, 350
Burkle, Ron, 80–81 and *n,* 82–84
BusinessWeek, 131, 160
Butyrka, 265–68, 276–78, 280

Canada, 340, 357
Cape Town, South Africa, 114–15,
  117
Capital Constellation Tower, 312
capitalism, 12, 27, 62, 269
  Russian transition to, 59–60, 87
Cardin, Ben, 263, 297, 335 and *n,* 338
  Magnitsky case and, 298–309,
    327–29, 341, 346, 353–55
Cardin List, 298–309
Caspian Sea, 226
Catholic Church, 364–65
cell phones, 48
Chaika, Yuri, 262
Chechnya, 288
Cheney, Dick, 306
Cherkasov, Ivan, 183–84, 196, 198,
  201–27, 230–35, 252–53, 298
  criminal case against, 201–27
Chicago, 9, 15, 17, 19, 24, 70

Chicago Tribune, 343
China, 2–3, 190
Chinese wall, 64
Chirikova, Evgenia, 329
Chubais, Anatoly, 91
Churchill, Winston, 228
CIA, 295, 359
Citibank, 209
Citigroup, 356
Clinton, Bill, 14
Clinton, Hillary, 297, 298, 333
  Magnitsky case, 298–301, 304
Cold War, 356
Colorado, 15–17, 18
Committee to Protect Journalists, 303
communism, 26, 92, 96, 97, 269
  American, 12–14, 26, 27
  fall of, 2–3, 27, 29–30, 40, 59, 158,
    291
Congress, US, 290, 302–9, 327–29
  Magnitsky Act, 305–9, 327–39,
    340–50
  Magnitsky case and, 302–5, 327–55
Council of Europe, 261–62
Creditanstalt-Grant, 99
Credit Suisse, 208, 209, 319–26
C-SPAN, 348
Cullison, Alan, 148–49
Cyprus, 312, 320
Czechoslovakia, 27, 40
  Velvet Revolution, 27

Daily Mirror, 42
Daily Telegraph, 44, 182, 369
databases, 158–59, 311–12
Davenport, Michael, 256–57
Davos, 88–93, 192–95
Delovoi Vtornik, 252
Department K, 203–5, 207, 227, 257,
  258, 322
Depression, 12
derivatives, 66
Detroit, 28
Deutsche Bank, 199
DHL, 237–38

dilutive shares, 115–30, 144–45
Domodedovo Airport, 247–48
Dow Jones, 182
Drexel Burnham Lambert, 21, 52
Dubai, 196, 312, 321, 324
Dudukina, Irina, 283, 327–28
Duncan, Terry, 197
Dvorkovich, Arkady, 177, 180, 195

Eastern Europe, 24, 26, 27, 41
  BCG operations in, 26–41
  fall of communism, 2–3, 27, 29–30,
    40
  MCC operations in, 45–46
  privatizations, 36–37, 41, 53–54
  Salomon operations in, 52–54
  See also specific countries
Echo Moscow, 236
Economist, 69
electricity, 69, 165
Elista, 226
Elle magazine, 307
embezzlement, 144
Ernst & Young, 59
Estemirova, Natalia, 303
European Commission, 376
European Parliament, 377–80
  Magnitsky resolution, 378–80
European Union (EU), 301
ExxonMobil, 154

fatalism, Russian, 298
Federal Border Service, 194, 195, 242
Federal Securities and Exchange
    Commission (FSEC), 127–29
Federation Council, 340–44
Financial Times, 2, 124–26, 129, 131,
    138, 160, 181, 182, 203
Finn, Peter, 180–81
Firestone, Jamison, 197–200, 201,
    213, 220, 222, 314, 315, 316–20
Firestone Duncan, 197–200, 202, 233,
    237, 254, 258
Fleming, Robert, 78
Flemings, 78–79

Forbes, 2, 6, 80, 182, 340, 358
Foreign Affairs, 147, 148
Formosus, Pope, 365
France, 73, 74, 131, 151–53, 187, 201,
    208, 209, 312, 377
Freeland, Chrystia, 124–26, 363–64
front-running, 183–84
FSB, 175, 178, 194, 195, 204–5, 223,
    260, 274, 279n, 317, 321–23, 341,
    369
  Department K, 203–5, 207, 227,
    257, 258, 322
Fulton, Philip, 274
Fyodorov, Boris, 90–91

Ganapolsky, Matvei, 236
Gasanov, Oktai, 248–49
Gazprom, 154–62, 165, 181, 192–93
  oligarch theft and investigation,
    154–62, 192–93
  stealing analysis, 155–60
G8 Summit (2006), 186, 187, 188,
    203
General Electric, 92
Geneva, 70, 83, 93, 218
Germany, 14
  fall of Berlin Wall, 27, 29–30
  Nazi, 14, 135, 280, 369
  World War II, 280, 369
Ghost Writer, The (movie), 299
Glover, Juleanna, 306–7, 332, 334–36,
    353, 354
Goldman Sachs, 19, 42
Golodets, Olga, 358
Great Britain, 1, 11, 52, 312, 314
  Border Force, 368
  Foreign and Commonwealth Office,
    171–72
  government, 170–73, 186–89, 261
  Magnitsky case and, 261
Greece, 139–40, 312
Greenacres, 80–82
Greene, Sylvia, 42
Gref, German, 175–78
Gregorian calendar, 117

Gremina, Elena, 347
Guantánamo, 359
GUM department store, 67 and *n*
Gusinsky, Vladimir, 91

Harvard Business School, 354
Harvard University, 20
  endowment, 122
Heathrow Airport, 1, 95, 126, 238,
  251, 252
hedge funds, 69, 70*n. See also*
  Hermitage Fund
Helsinki Commission, 263, 290, 295,
  300–301
Hermans, Hans, 371–373
Hermitage Fund, 1, 76, 363, 375
  anchor investors in, 77–88, 93, 94,
  100–102
  beginnings of, 76, 77–86, 88,
  95–103
  Browder banned from Russia and,
  11–13, 169, 170–89, 193
  Gazprom theft and investigation,
  154–62, 192–93
  investigation into stolen companies,
  201–35, 252–53, 271–72
  lawyers as targets, 237–53, 254–68,
  360
  MNPZ and, 98–100
  money removed from Russia,
  183–85, 196, 212, 215
  Moscow offices, 96–103, 121,
  196–200
  1998 financial crisis and aftermath,
  131–46
  operating procedures manual, 88,
  94
  police raids on, 196–200, 203,
  208–10, 216, 228, 230
  recovery, 166–67
  redemption orders, 185–86, 190
  run on the fund, 190
  Russian criminal cases against,
  189, 190–200, 201–35, 236–53,
  270–72, 323, 343–45, 360, 364–70

Russian raider attack, 213–27
  Sidanco and, 104–30, 134–35
  success of, 102–3, 131, 162, 166
  tax evasion charges, 201–4, 210,
  225–27
  tax-rebate fraud and, 231–37,
  252–53, 257, 264, 271–72, 288,
  301, 316–26, 328
  YouTube video, 264–65, 271–72
Hermitage Global, 191–92, 196,
  216
  launch of, 196, 216
"Hermitage Reveals Russian Police
  Fraud" (video), 271–72
Hersh, Ken, 22–23 and *n*
Hezbollah, 187
Holland, 371
Holtzman, Marc, 88–93, 95, 96, 192
Hong Kong, 211
House of Committee on Investigations,
  290
House of Representatives, US, 13, 290,
  302, 305, 346–50
House Un-American Activities
  Committee, 13
HSBC, 138, 170, 185, 187, 209
  Republic National Bank taken over
  by, 138–39, 142
human rights abuses, 261, 271,
  301, 303, 328, 350, 366–67, 373,
  376
  Cardin List and, 298–309
  documentation of, 286, 294, 301,
  331
  global legislation, 330, 346, 353,
  378–79
  Katyn massacre, 279–80
  Magnitsky Act and, 305–9, 313,
  327–29, 340–50
  Magnitsky case, *see* Magnitsky case
  sanctions used against, 291–94,
  299–309, 327–29, 368, 373, 377
  in Vietnam, 306
Human Rights Watch, 292, 303
Hungary, 53

Incheon Airport, 210
Independent, 182, 352
Indonesia, 131, 210
infrastructure, 111, 112
ING, 209
Intercommerz Bank, 233–34
Interior Ministry, 196–200, 220, 237,
    249, 250, 254, 262, 270, 271, 283,
    296, 327
  cases against Hermitage, 189, 190–
    200, 201–35, 236–553, 270–72,
    323, 343–45, 360, 364–70
  Hermitage lawyers as targets of,
    237–53, 254–68, 360
  Internal Affairs Department, 220,
    224, 314, 315
  Magnitsky arrest and imprisonment,
    254–78, 280–88
  raids on Hermitage Fund, 196–200,
    203, 208–10, 216, 228, 230
  wealth of officials in, 311–26, 343
International Bar Association, 262
International Monetary Fund (IMF),
    133, 365
  Russian bond market bailout,
    133–34
International Protection Centre, 303
Interpol Red Notices, 202, 270,
    367–70
  for Browder, 367–70, 374
Ireland, George, 44–51
Israel, 5, 71, 102, 187–88
Istanbul, 162, 242
Italy, 135, 240, 243, 245, 312
IVS1, 260

Jackson-Vanik amendment, 334–39
Jagger, Bianca, 350
Japan, 28–29, 55
Jews, 14, 135, 175
  Nazi persecution of, 14, 369
  Soviet, 334
Jordan, Boris, 117–19, 123–26, 128,
    219
Jordan, Nick, 117

JP Morgan, 21–23, 117, 183
Justice for Sergei (documentary),
    371–73

Kaban, Elif, 181–82
Kalmykia, 225–26, 228
Kameya, 198
  police raid on, 198–99, 203
  taxes, 202, 210
Karoubi, Jean, 77–78, 191, 192, 374,
    375
Karpov, Pavel, 203, 209, 216–19,
    224–27, 233, 296, 301, 310–15,
    319, 327
  libel suit against Browder, 344–45,
    374
  wealth of, 312–15, 343
  YouTube video on, 313, 314–15,
    322–23, 343
Kasparov, Garry, 329
Katyn massacre, 279–80
Katz, Eugene, 45
Kazakhstan, 7
Kazan, 214, 229, 230, 234, 238–43,
    248
Kerry, John, 331
  Magnitsky Act and, 331–39, 340
KGB, 106, 175, 279n
Khabarovsk, 247–50
Kharitonov, Dmitri, 256, 277, 281–82
Khayretdinov, Eduard, 209–27,
    229–35, 237–53, 255, 259, 282,
    367
  as a fugitive, 241–42, 246–48
  leaves Russia, 251–53
Khimki, 232, 233
Khlebnikov, Vyacheslav, 325
Khodorkovsky, Mikhail, 145, 167–69,
    183
  arrest and trial of, 167–69
Kiev, 258
Kirov, 311
Koifman, Sandy, 83–84, 88, 93, 142
Kommersant, 182
Korean Air, 213

Krasnoyarsk, 102
Krivoruchko, Aleksey, 267
Kuwait, 159, 191
Kuznetsov, Artem, 195–97, 209, 216,
    217, 224–27, 230, 232–33, 259,
    262, 296, 301, 310–15, 319
  wealth of, 311–15, 343
  YouTube video on, 313–15, 322–23,
    343
Kuznetsov, Vyacheslav, 159

Lake Como, 135–37
La Leopolda, 74, 78
Latvia, 119
Lavrov, Sergei, 358, 360
Lebanon, 187–88
Leutheusser-Schnarrenberger, Sabine,
    261–62, 264
Levada polling agency, 101 and *n*
Liar's Poker, 52
Lieberman, Joe, 327, 334–36
Lindquist, John, 25–30, 37, 40
literature, Russian, 96, 298
Litvinenko, Alexander, 317, 351
Logunov, Oleg, 313
Loiko, Sergei, 360
London, 1, 9, 10, 25–27, 33, 38, 41,
    78–79, 83–86, 95, 126, 170–82,
    183, 201, 206–7, 216, 225, 237,
    250, 251, 269, 322, 344, 364,
    369
  Boston Consulting Group in, 25,
    26–27
  courts, 374
  human rights community, 350
  Maxwell Communications
    Corporation in, 41–51
  Metropolitan Police, 237–38
  Russians in, 317, 347–53, 377
  Salomon Brothers in, 52–63, 64–70
  theater, 347, 350
Lopatinski, Yuri, 99, 104–5
Los Angeles, 28, 70, 80–82
Los Angeles Times, 360
LOT Airlines, 30

Ludwig, Bobby, 61–63, 66–71
Lukoil, 69, 105, 108, 111, 112
Lyne, Sir Roderic, 170, 186–87

Maat, Martin, 372, 373
Mafia, Russian, 150, 241, 289
Magnitsky, Natalia, 280–85, 331, 355,
    376
Magnitsky, Natasha, 254–55, 285, 377,
    378, 379
Magnitsky, Nikita, 254–55, 374, 377,
    378, 379
Magnitsky, Stanislav, 254–55
Magnitsky, Sergei, 202, 209–15,
    230–35, 252–53, 372
  arrest of, 254–68
  in court, 274–76
  death of, 276–78, 280–88, 327, 343,
    360, 366, 371–73, 376
  deteriorating health of, 265–68, 269,
    277
  funeral of, 285
  imprisonment and torture of,
    258–68, 269–78, 280–88, 296,
    304, 308, 331
  legacy of, 355, 371–80
  prison diary and documentation,
    278, 282, 286, 301, 331
  refusal to leave Russia, 252–53
  tax-rebate fraud and, 231–35, 237,
    252–53, 257, 272, 288, 314, 328
  trial on tax evasion in abstentia,
    364–70
  See also Magnitsky Act; Magnitsky
    case
Magnitsky Act, 305–9, 313, 327–29,
    340–50, 358, 366
  Congress and, 305–9, 327–29,
    340–55
  early drafts, 305–6, 308
  global, 330, 346, 353, 378–79
  Malkin delegation and, 340–44
  Putin's response to, 356–62
  vote and passage of, 343, 347–50,
    354–55, 364

Magnitsky case, 255–380
    arrest of Magnitsky, 254–68
    autopsy reports, 284, 331
    Cardin List and, 298–99
    Congress and, 305–9, 327–29,
        340–55
    death of Magnitsky, 276–78, 280–88,
        327, 343, 360, 366, 371–73, 376
    documented human rights abuses,
        286, 301, 331
    imprisonment and torture, 258–68,
        269–78, 280–88, 296, 304, 308,
        331
    legacy of, 371–80
    legislation, 305–9, 327–39, 340–50
    media on, 263–64, 270–72, 283,
        288, 301, 313–14, 330, 337, 343,
        352, 359–60, 369
    MPOC report on, 287
    Perepilichnyy and, 318–26, 347–53
    Putin and, 302, 328, 344, 356–62,
        363–70, 373–74
    state "investigation," 285–88
    state-sponsored cover-up and lying,
        286–88, 292
    Swiss bank accounts, 316–26
    visa sanctions and asset freezes,
        291, 293–94, 297, 298, 299–309,
        327–39, 368, 373, 377
    YouTube videos, 264–65, 271–72,
        310–15, 321–26, 327, 343
Mahaon, 234, 235
Malaysia, 131
Malev, 53–54
Malkin, Vitaly, 340–44
Malkin delegation, 340–44
Markelov, Viktor, 214, 248–49, 310
Marseille, 208
mathematics, 13, 14, 15
Matrosskaya Tishina, 260–61, 265,
    281, 285, 331
Maxwell, Kevin, 44, 51
Maxwell, Robert, 40–51, 52
    corporate fraud, 49–50
    death of, 46–47

Maxwell Central and East European
    Partnership, 42
Maxwell Communications Corporation
    (MCC), 41–51, 52
    bonuses, 47–48
    Browder at, 41–51
    Eastern European operations, 45–46
    share price, 46–47
Maxwell House, 41, 43
McCain, John, 306–9
    Magnitsky Act and, 306–9, 327, 332,
        335 and *n,* 341, 355
McCarthy, Joseph, 13
McGovern, Jim, 302–5, 308, 332, 341,
    355
McKinsey, 19
media, 91, 137, 165
    on Browder's banishment from
        Russia, 171–72, 180–82, 185, 187,
        194
    on Hermitage tax-rebate fraud, 236,
        252, 271–72
    on Magnitsky case, 263–64, 270–72,
        283, 288, 301, 313–14, 330, 337,
        343, 352, 359–60, 369
    on oligarch corruption, 124–30,
        160–61, 165
    on Perepilichnyy's death, 352
    persecuted journalists in Russia, 303
    Russian, 91, 182, 214, 236, 252,
        264, 288, 301, 359, 365
    on Russian adoption ban, 359–61
    on Sidanco's dilutive share issue,
        124–30
Medvedev, Dmitri, 193–95, 263, 364*n*
    Browder and, 193–95, 363–64
    Magnitsky case and, 262, 286–87
Mergers & Acquisitions Europe, 40,
    41
Mikheeva, Ekaterina, 310–11
Mikheeva, Fyodor, 310–11
Milan, 243, 245
Miller, Alexey, 162
MIT, 13, 15
MNPZ, 98–100

Molokova, Elena. *See* Browder, Elena
Morgan Stanley, 19
Moscow, 1–11, 12, 59, 66–70, 84,
  95–103, 104, 143, 163–65, 247,
  254, 311
  anti-Putin demonstrations, 361
  bureaucracy, 158
  Hermitage offices, 96–103, 121,
    196–200
  Interior Ministry, *see* Interior
    Ministry
  Kremlin, 107, 141, 165
  1998 financial crisis and aftermath,
    131–46
  Pushkin Square, 157–58
  real estate, 311–15, 321, 324–26
  Red Square, 59, 67
  taxis, 96
  voucher privatization, 67–70, 105
Moscow Detention Center No. 5, 258
Moscow Oil Refinery. *See* MNPZ
Moscow Public Oversight Commission
  (MPOC) report, 287
Moscow Registration Chamber, 158
Moscow State University, 147, 258
Moscow Times, 126, 188
Moscow Traffic Police, 4, 101, 312
Mossad, 5, 74
Murmansk, 55–59
Murmansk Trawler Fleet, 55–59
Musacchio, Aldo, 354

National Medal of Science, 14
National Security Council, 180, 182,
  341
natural gas. *See* oil and gas
Natural Gas Partners, 23*n*
Navalny, Alexei, 329
Nazism, 14, 135, 280, 369
Nekhoteevka, 242
nepotism, 45
New Diorama Theatre, London, 350
New Times magazine, 313–14
New Year's, 117, 175, 361
New York, 62, 70, 77–78, 129, 269

New York Times, The, 131, 160, 182,
  194, 236
Nice, 73, 74
Nizhny Novgorod, 247
NKVD, 279 and *n*
Norten, Richard, 237–38
Northern Distribution Network,
  blockade of, 356–57
Norway, 367–68
Novaya Gazeta, 288
Novocherkassk, 232
Novosibirsk, 287
NTV, 365
Nuremberg trials, 280
Nuskhinov, Dmitry, 226–27

Obama, Barack, 263, 293, 295, 301,
  329, 330, 334, 356, 358
Oborne, Peter, 369
Occidental Petroleum, 156
oil and gas, 60, 104, 144, 191
  barrels of oil (BOE), 156 and *n*
  Gazprom theft and investigation,
    154–62, 192–93
  MNPZ, 98–100
  oligarch corruption, 115–30,
    154–62, 167–79
  Russian, 60, 69, 98–101, 104–30,
    143–44, 167–69
  Sidanco, 104–30
  See also specific companies
Ojuland, Kristiina, 379
oligarchs, Russian, 3–5, 87, 91, 104,
  113–30, 134, 177, 221
  Browder's anti-corruption campaigns
    against, 115–30, 144–48, 154–69,
    181, 192–93
  corporate-governance abuse,
    144–48, 165–69
  corruption and theft, 115–30,
    144–48, 154–69, 181, 192–93
  1996 presidential elections and,
    91–94, 101–3
  1998 financial crisis and, 134–38,
    144–46

oligarchs, Russian *(cont.)*
  Potanin, 104, 113, 115–30, 134–35
  Putin and, 165–69, 183
  Wall Street and, 144
  See also specific oligarchs
Olswang, 344–45
One Hour Eighteen Minutes (play),
  347, 350
Oslo Airport, 367
Oslo Freedom Forum, 366–67
Ostrovsky, Arkady, 181
Oz (TV show), 256, 260

Pakistan, 356–57
Pan, Philip, 263–64
Parfenion, 229, 234, 235
Paris, 70, 151–53, 199
Park, Kevin, 211, 213
Parker, Kyle, 263, 295–97
  Magnitsky case and, 295–306,
    327–39, 341–46, 353, 355
Pastukhov, Vladimir, 179, 216, 237–
    40, 273–74, 282, 286, 320–21,
    349, 355, 367
  flees Russia, 242–45
Patrushev, Nikolai, 175
Pavel Karpov v. William Browder,
    344–45, 374
Pechegin, Andrei, 267
Perepilichnyy, Alexander, 318–26,
    347–50
  death of, 347–53
physics, 15
poisoning, 317–18, 351
Pluton, 214
poker, 47, 48, 50, 143
Poland, 27–39, 59, 60
  Autosan buses, 30–39
  BCG operations in, 27–39
  economy, 36
  fall of communism, 30, 36
  food, 32–33, 34–36
  Katyn massacre, 279–80
  privatizations, 36–39, 41, 54
Polanski, Roman, 299

Politkovskaya, Anna, 303
Potanin, Vladimir, 104, 113, 115–30,
    134–35
  Sidanco dilutive share issue, 115–30
preferred shares, 98–101
Preobrazhensky Cemetery, Moscow,
    285
press. *See* media; *specific publications*
PricewaterhouseCoopers, 161
Prikhodko, Sergei, 171, 178
Princeton University, 13
  Institute for Advanced Study, 13
privatizations, 36–37
  in Eastern Europe, 36–37, 41,
    53–54
  in Poland, 36–39, 41, 54
  in Russia, 54–63, 64–76, 87, 91–93,
    98–101
  voucher, 59–60, 67–70, 105
Proclamation 7750, 291, 293–94, 297,
    298, 299–309, 327–39
Prutkov, Yuri, 57–58
Pulkovo Airport, 56
Pussy Riot, 365
Putin, Vladimir, 162, 165–69, 175,
    183, 193, 280, 356–70
  adoption ban law, 357–62
  becomes president, 165
  Browder and, 166–69, 175–77,
    183–89, 236, 363–70, 375
  inner circle, 175–76
  leadership style, 359–62
  Magnitsky case and, 302, 328, 344,
    356–62, 363–70, 373–74
  oligarchs and, 165–69, 183
  response to Magnitsky Act, 356–62

radio, 236
Rassokhov, Rostislav, 224
Reagan, Ronald, 301
recessions, 131
  1998 Asian crisis, 131–32
Reid, Harry, 353
Renaissance Capital, 117–20, 219,
    220, 222

Republic National Bank, 72, 138
  HSBC takeover of, 138–39, 142
Rettman, Andrew, 375–76
Reuters, 46, 115, 116, 126, 128,
  181–82, 185
Rilend, 213, 214, 234, 235
Riyadh, 220
Robertson, Geoffrey, 378–79
Robertson, Julian, 70 and *n*
Romney, Mitt, 346
Roosevelt, Eleanor, 14
Roosevelt, Franklin D., 12, 14
Rostelecom, 69
Rozhetskin, Leonid, 118–20, 124
Russia (post-Soviet), 1–11, 156–57
  adoption ban law, 357–62
  Audit Chamber, 161
  bond market, 132–38
  Border Service, 194, 195, 242, 312
  Browder banned from, 11–13, 169,
    170–89, 193
  Browder's trial in abstentia, 364–70
  bureaucracy, 158, 232
  business culture, 125
  conspiracy theories, 166
  corporate-governance abuse,
    144–49, 165–69
  dachas, 104, 156, 249
  economy, 60, 87
  fall of communism, 2–3, 59–60, 112,
    158, 291
  fatalism, 298
  food, 67, 87
  Foreign Ministry, 172–73
  Gazprom theft and investigation,
    154–62, 192–93
  gulags, 96–97, 274
  human rights atrocities, 279–80,
    301, 328, 373, 376
  IMF bailout, 133–34
  independent thinkers penalized in, 6,
    96–97, 163–65
  Interior Ministry, *see* Interior
    Ministry
  literature, 96, 298

Mafia, 150, 241, 289
May holidays, 151
National Police Day, 327–28
1993 attempted coup, 197
1996 presidential elections, 87–93,
  94–103
1998 financial crisis and aftermath,
  131–46
oil and gas, 60, 69, 98–101, 104–30,
  143–44, 167–69
oligarchs, *see* oligarchs, Russian
orphans, 357–62
Parliament, 161, 340–44, 356, 357
  and *n,* 358–60
persecuted journalists in, 303
police raids on Hermitage offices,
  196–200, 203, 208–10, 216, 218,
  230
Politburo, 156
press, 91, 182, 214, 236, 252, 264,
  288, 301, 359, 365
privatizations in, 54–63, 64–76, 87,
  91–93, 98–101
raider attacks, 213–27
Red Notice for Browder, 367–70,
  374
response to Magnitsky Act, 356–62
roads, 243
Salomon operations in, 54–63, 64–76
shipping, 55–59
stocks, 3, 54–63, 64–76, 98–130,
  133–38, 144–45, 183–85, 198
tax law, 201–4
tax-rebate fraud, 231–37, 252–53,
  257, 264, 271–72, 288, 301,
  316–26, 328
theft of government money, 231–37,
  236–53, 257, 264, 271–72, 288,
  296, 301, 311, 316–26, 328
transition to capitalism, 59–60, 87
Ukraine invaded by, 373
visa sanctions and asset freezes on
  corrupt officials, 291, 293–94,
  297, 298, 299–309, 327–29, 368,
  373, 377

Russia (post-Soviet) *(cont.)*
 voucher privatization, 59–60, 67–70,
  105
 wealth gap, 156–57
 women, 147, 254
 as WTO member, 333–34
 Yeltsin's economic reforms, 87, 91
Russian Central Bank, 233, 234
Russian General Prosecutor's Office,
 262, 285, 287, 314
Russian raider attack, 213–27
Russian State Investigative Committee,
 220–26, 232–33, 252
russian-untouchables.com, 313
Russian Untouchables videos, 310–15,
 321–26, 343

Safra, Edmond, 72–76, 131, 138–39,
 365
 death of, 142
 Hermitage Fund and, 72–76, 77–88,
  93, 94, 98, 100–102, 112, 119–32,
  138–39, 142
Sagiryan, Igor, 219–23, 317
Saint Petersburg, 56, 186, 212, 213,
 217, 223, 229
Salomon Brothers, 52–76, 79, 106,
 225
 Browder at, 52–76, 77
 "five times" formula, 53, 54
 London trading floor, 64–70
 Treasury bond scandal, 52, 65
Samolov, Boris, 254
San Francisco, 70, 272
Sanok, 30–39
Saudi Arabia, 220
Sberbank, 165
Scandinavian Airlines, 367
Schmidt, Wolfgang, 27–31, 35, 38, 40
Scott, Kyle, 290–95, 329, 333
Securities and Exchange Commission
 (SEC), 52, 176
Senate, US, 302, 305, 307, 330–39,
 346, 354–55
 Finance Committee, 336, 340, 344

Foreign Relations Committee, 290,
 330–39
 Magnitsky Act and, 327–39, 340
Seoul, 210–13, 250, 251
Severov, Dmitry, 106–7
Shanghai, 2
Shao, Jude, 2, 3, 5, 6, 9
Sheremetyevo Airport, 2–10, 95, 169,
 243–44
Shuvalov, Igor, 174, 176, 178
Siberia, 69, 104
 oil, 69, 104, 110, 159
Sibneftegaz, 159
Sidanco, 104–30, 134–35, 219, 363
 dilutive share issue, 115–30
 FSEC investigation of, 127–29
Siemens, 92
Sikorsi, Leschek, 32–38
Silchenko, Oleg, 258–60, 265, 267,
 275–76, 277, 283, 327–28
Siluyanov, Anton, 358
Smith, Simon, 170–72, 181, 182,
 186–87, 256
Snob, 359
Sochi, 242
Sokolova, Ksenia, 359
Solent, David, 51
Soros, George, 70 and *n,* 92, 122
South Africa, 71, 114–15, 117
 apartheid, 114
South Korea, 131, 210–13
Soviet Union, 12, 24, 157, 253
 fall of, 2–3, 59, 112, 158, 280, 334
 Jews, 334
 Katyn massacre, 279–80
 World War II, 13, 228, 279–80
 See also Russia (post-Soviet)
Spain, 312
Stalin, Joseph, 6, 364
Stanford University, 2, 20–21, 106,
 272, 376
Stashina, Yelena, 267, 275–76
State Department, US, 289
 Magnitsky case and, 289–97, 302,
  304, 329, 341

Proclamation 7750, 291, 293–94, 297, 298, 299–309, 327–39
stealing analysis, 155–60
steel, 60
Steinmetz, Beny, 71–76, 83–84, 138
Stepanov, Vladlen, 316, 319, 321–26
  Swiss bank accounts, 316–26, 343
  YouTube video on, 321–23, 325–36, 343
Stepanova, Olga, 316, 319, 321–26
  Swiss bank accounts, 316–26, 343
  as Tax Princess, 326
  YouTube video on, 321–23, 325–26, 343
Stern, Carl, 24
stocks
  Chinese wall and, 64
  front-running, 183–84
  Gazprom theft and investigation, 154–62
  liquidity, 132
  MNPZ, 98–100
  1998 financial crisis and aftermath, 131–46
  preferred shares, 98–101
  Russian, 3, 54–63, 64–76, 98–130, 133–38, 144–45, 183–85, 198
  share dilution, 115–30, 144–45
  Sidanco, 104–30
  tourist, 99
Stoppard, Tom, 350
Summer Olympics (1980), 3
Summers, Larry, 133, 134
Sunday Express, 314
Sunday Observer, 187
Sunday Telegraph, 2
Surgutneftegaz, 69
surveillance, 221–23, 241–42, 317–18
Switzerland, 88, 89
  bank accounts and Magnitsky case, 316–26, 343
Syria, 357

Tarkosaleneftegaz, 156
Tatar Republic, 111

Tatarstan, 214, 229, 238
Tatneft, 111
Tatum, Paul, 126–27
tax-rebate fraud, 231–37, 252–53, 257, 264, 271–72, 288, 301, 316–26, 328
  Swiss bank accounts and, 316–26, 343
telephone, 69, 191
television, 91, 365
Templeton, Sir John, 70 and *n*
Templeton Asset Management, 70*n*
"ten bagger," 39
tennis, 163
Thailand, 131, 191, 210
Tiger Management Corp., 70*n*
Time magazine, 12, 131
Tokyo, 28, 55, 211
Tom Lantos Human Rights Commission, 302
Toronto, 70
Trammell Crow, 21
transfer pricing, 144
Truman, Harry, 13
Tuesdays with Morrie, 149–50
Turkey, 162, 191, 312
Turner, Fred, 338
Tverskoi District Court, 365

UK Law Society, 262
Ukraine, 30, 242
  Russian invasion of, 373
Unified Energy System (UES), 69, 165
United Arab Emirates, 191
United States, 256, 312
  beef, 334, 336
  communism in, 12–14, 26, 27
  Depression, 12
  IMF bailout of Russian bond market and, 133–34
  Magnitsky case and, 262–63, 269, 289–97, 298–309, 327–39, 340–55, 356
  Russian adoption ban and, 357–62
  Treasury bond market, 52, 65
Wall Street, 119, 144, 376
World War II, 13

United Steelworkers, 23
Universal Savings Bank, 233–34
University of Chicago, 14, 15, 19
University of Colorado, Boulder, 18
Ural Mountains, 274

Vasiliev, Dmitry, 127–29
Vedomosti, 182, 214, 236
Velvet Revolution, 27
Vienna, 14
Vietnam War, 2, 306
visa sanctions and asset freezes, 291,
    293–94, 297, 298, 299–309,
    327–39, 368, 373, 377
Vladivostok, 287
Volgograd, 225–26
von Pierer, Heinrich, 92
Voronezh, 246
Voronin, Victor, 257
voucher auctions, 68–69
voucher privatization, 59–60, 67–70,
    105
Vyakhirev, Andrey, 159
Vyakhirev, Gennady, 159
Vyakhirev, Rem, 159, 162
Vyugin, Oleg, 176, 178

Wall Street (film), 119
Wall Street Journal, 2, 48, 50, 126,
    148, 160, 182
Warsaw, 31, 35
Washington, D.C., 263, 269, 289–97,
    298–309, 327–39, 340–50
Washington Post, 160, 180, 263–64,
    330
Welch, Jack, 92
Weyerhaeuser pension fund, 122
Whiteman School, Steamboat Springs,
    Colorado, 15–17

Wicker, Roger, 327, 335 and *n,* 341
Winer, Jonathan, 289–91, 293, 295,
    297
Wolosky, Lee, 147
World Bank, 27–31, 38, 134
World Economic Forum, Davos
    in 1996, 88–93
    in 2007, 191–95
    in 2013, 363
World Trade Organization (WTO),
    333
World War II, 13, 228, 279–80, 369

Yale University, 14, 20
Year of Living Dangerously, The (film),
    24
Yeltsin, Boris, 87
    economic reforms, 87, 91
    1996 presidential elections, 87–94,
    97–98, 101–3
YouTube, 264, 310–15, 321–26, 327
    Hermitage video, 264–65, 271–72,
    310
    Karpov video, 313, 314–15, 322–23,
    343
    Kuznetsov video, 313–15, 322–23,
    343
    Russian Untouchables videos,
    310–15, 321–26, 343
    Stepanova video, 321–23, 325–26,
    343
Yucaipa, 81 and *n*
Yuganskneftegaz, 111
Yukos, 144, 145, 167, 183, 257
    oligarch corruption, 167–69

Zurich, 70, 89
Zyuganov, Gennady, 87, 89, 91–93,
    100, 102–3

About the Author

Bill Browder, founder and CEO of Hermitage Capital Management, was the largest foreign investor in Russia until 2005. Since 2009, when his lawyer Sergei Magnitsky was murdered in prison after uncovering a $230 million fraud committed by Russian government officials, Browder has been leading a campaign to expose Russia's endemic corruption and human rights abuses. Before founding Hermitage, Browder was a vice president at Salomon Brothers. He holds a BA in economics from the University of Chicago and an MBA from Stanford Business School.

About the Author

Get email updates on

BILL BROWDER,

exclusive offers,

and other great book recommendations

from Simon & Schuster.